Speaking the Nation

Speaking the Nation

The Oratorical Making of Secular, Neoliberal India

ANANDITA BAJPAI

OXFORD
UNIVERSITY PRESS

OXFORD
UNIVERSITY PRESS

Oxford University Press is a department of the University of Oxford.
It furthers the University's objective of excellence in research, scholarship,
and education by publishing worldwide. Oxford is a registered trademark of
Oxford University Press in the UK and in certain other countries.

Published in India by
Oxford University Press
2/11 Ground Floor, Ansari Road, Daryaganj, New Delhi 110 002, India

ISBN-13 (print edition): 978-0-19-948174-3
ISBN-10 (print edition): 0-19-948174-1

ISBN-13 (eBook): 978-0-19-909551-3
ISBN-10 (eBook): 0-19-909551-5

Typeset in Dante MT Std 10.5/13
by The Graphics Solution, New Delhi 110 092
Printed in India by Gopsons Papers Ltd., Noida 201301

Contents

To
'Our World'

Preface

Airports connote an autonomous space-time continuum that has a life of its own. Although dramatically in motion, this continuum is thoroughly disconnected from the temporalities of lives beyond its circumference. True to this tension inherent to the very nature of airports in general, during my trips between Germany and India while pursuing my doctoral studies (2010–14), I often found myself in the waiting halls of airports, where a nervousness of 'having to move' coalesced with a strandedness in time. The paradox was of walking in an in-between zone that was neither in the place one had left, nor in the one which one was leaving for. The impressive Buddha statues, the lavish carpets on the floors, and the boards with smiling Indian faces which had just been 'shopping'—all pointed to one particular mood. Inside the airports, an optimism prevailed and a 'New India' was being announced, one whose projections did not necessarily match with the realities of lives outside the airport, where the uniformed carpet cleaners and smiling perfume sellers return at the end of the day after work.

It is in this transit zone, between the continuities and discontinuities of Indian airports, that one is compelled to notice the giant banners, boards, and especially the books in the bookshops at the numerous terminals. All appear to be celebrating India as 'emerging', an 'economic powerhouse' steadily 'on the move' and more recently, since demonetization, its 'cashless' economy. In the 'new bestsellers' and 'non-fiction' sections, it is difficult to overlook the covers of magazines and books being sold, which carry a metaphor of speed in their title. Thus, the words 'rising', 'growing', 'transforming', 'shining', 'arriving', and 'emerging' are to be commonly found, attempting to make the entity of 'India' as glossy as the book covers themselves, and, perhaps, also as the people buying them.

Each visit confirmed that inside the airport building, every title, and indeed every book carrying it, seemed as timeless and spaceless an island as the airport itself. It was precisely in such moments that I, the international Indian student, myself 'on the move', stood looking at these books, wondering if I was also an adept of this heterotopic temple.[1] Did this relative disconnection from time and space at work in all these entities at once—the airport, the titles, the book covers, and my own migrant self—also not apply to the very idea of the 'New India'? It is here, in the waiting lounges of domestic and international airports in India, that the subject of this book was conceived.

Since 1991 and the formal institutionalization of the neo-liberal economic reforms, two evergreen topics seem to preoccupy scholarship on Indian politics and economy—the rise of the Hindu right and the challenges it poses to state secularism, and the transformations that have accompanied the 'opening up' of the Indian economy. The 'Emerging India' story is part of the latter transformation. Who constitutes this India and how are these dreams of an 'Emerging India' verbalized for the millions who live in the shadows cast by its realities?

*

India's Merchandized 'Emergence'

The following lines from a public awareness campaign run by *The Times of India*[2] flocked Indian television screens in 2007. Entitled 'India vs. India', it captures the essence of the imagery evoked by most discourses that discuss the 'India emerging' theme. In the video, Bollywood's demigod and 'living legend', Amitabh Bachchan, stands on a new bridge and addresses the Indian nation with his masculine voice, oozing with the seriousness and authority of a renowned and trustworthy teacher.

---

[1] In his essay 'On Other Spaces', Foucault develops the notion of the *heterotopia* to denote 'real places—places that do exist and that are formed in the very founding of society—which are something like counter-sites, a kind of effectively enacted utopia in which the real sites, all the other real sites that can be found within the culture, are simultaneously represented, contested, and inverted. Places of this kind are outside of all places, even though it may be possible to indicate their location in reality.' See M. Foucault, 'On Other Spaces', *Diacritics* 16, no. 1(1986): 22–7, here p. 24.

[2] *India Poised Anthem*, Times of India Initiative, 2007.

There is little doubt that he is articulating historic lines in a historic moment, which only he, the icon of Indian publicity, can announce:

There are two Indias in this country.

One India is straining at the leash, eager to spring forth and live up to all the adjectives that the world has been recently showering upon us.
The other India is the leash.

One India says 'Give me a chance, and I'll prove myself.'
The other India says 'Prove yourself first, and maybe then, you'll have a chance.'

One India lives in the optimism of our hearts.
The other India lurks in the skepticism of our minds.

One India wants.
The other India hopes.

One India leads.
The other India follows.

These conversions are on the rise.
With each passing day, more and more people from the other India are coming over to this side. And quietly, while the world is not looking, a pulsating, dynamic India is emerging.

An India whose faith in success is far greater than its fear of failure.

An India that no longer boycotts foreign-made goods, but buys out the companies that makes them instead.

History, they say, is a bad motorist. It rarely ever signals its intentions when it's taking a turn.

This is that rarely ever moment.
History is turning a page.

For over half a century, our nation has sprung, stumbled, run, fallen, rolled over, got up and dusted herself, and cantered, sometimes lurched on.
But now, in our sixtieth year as a free nation, the ride has brought us to the edge of time's great precipice.

And one India, a tiny little voice at the back of the head, is looking down at the bottom of the ravine, and hesitating.
The other India is looking up at the sky and saying, 'It's time to fly.'[3]

[3] *India Poised Anthem*, Times of India Initiative, 2007.

Amitabh Bachchan recites these lines, standing on a new, unfinished bridge in a high-tech port, probably of Mumbai, with deep waters running below. The bridge is a metaphor for continuity and transition across a void, a dangerous in-between resulting from the gap of two separated entities of land. Although spoken with an appeasing tone, the seriousness of the words produce a sense of urgency, a turning point with India standing at the 'edge of time', at the edge of an unfinished bridge with the future of abundance and development ahead. With a messianic allure, it is the 'messiah' of Indian cinema who invites Indians not to resist their 'conversion' to the 'other India', waiting ahead on the other side of the bridge where skyscrapers peep across the mist. The bridge allows for only two directions: either to stop the constructions and go back, or to push forward into bliss. The choice seems clear and preordained. The future lies ahead, but the crucial and irreversible moment is now. In the subtext, the lines announce a transition from the Nehruvian era of a 'mixed economy' to an assertive 'structurally readjusted' one. The message is thus to demarcate a shift, a rupture indeed, a break from a 'self-reliant' India of the period following the 1950s to a neo-liberal one since the early 1990s, by stressing the historic uniqueness of the present, the moment of change, and with each spectator watching the clip as being a crucial and inevitable participant of history in the making.

The recited lines, the campaign itself, are a part of a larger environment that celebrates India's foreseen emergence. In fact, the project of producing 'India on the move' or 'Rising India' has become the fascination of a multitude of descriptions whose designers are technocrats, former CEOs of large conglomerates, economists, journalists, former civil servants, ministers, foreign policy analysts, advertising gurus, and think-tank specialists, both Indians and internationals. Since 2000, the velocity of their production has intensified. One senses urgency, an aggression perhaps, in emphasizing the transition. Numerous discussions and models, situated especially within the disciplines of political science and international relations, now present accounts of how India's economic rise bears consequences for its simultaneous emergence as a crucial actor geopolitically. Related to the same are predictions of

---

[4] A.J. Tellis, *India's Emerging Nuclear Posture: Between Recessed Deterrent and Ready Arsenal* (New Delhi: Oxford University Press, 2001).

India's rise as a nuclear power,[4] its undeniable presence as the world's largest and youngest democracy,[5] its increasing role in the south-south east Asian security affairs, its rise as an IT super power,[6] etc.

How is this emergence publicly announced for the people of India by the authors of the reforms? How have its coordinates been 'sold' in their most official version despite and, in spite, of the very obvious shadows and crevices that they produce? Why is the unity of the nation embedded in state secularism such an important discursive stake for these new visions? These are some of the questions that informed the beginning of this book.

***

This book makes an argument for returning to sources which have long informed the nature of Indian politics—the speeches of its popularly elected heads—the prime ministers. What do the speeches tell us about the structurally adjusted, post-reform Indian economy? And how have the prime ministers utilized them to stabilize India's image as a secular, yet emerging democracy?

[5] According to the Population Council of India, '4 per cent of India's population is below the age of 25. Over seven out of 10 Indians are below the age of 35. It estimates that there are 315 million people between the ages of 10 and 24. It is estimated that there were 350 million Indians in the politically crucial age group of 15–34 in the year 2000. This number may rise to 485 million by 2030. By 2020, the average Indian will be 29 years old as compared to 37 in China, 45 in Western Europe and 49 in Japan.' For details, see http://www.popcouncil.org/projects/101_YouthInIndiaNeedsStudy.asp (accessed on 17 June 2013).

[6] E. Follath, 'India at Crossroads on Path to Superpower Status', in *Spiegel Online International* (6 September 2012); G.E. Mathew, *India's Innovation Blueprint: How the Largest Democracy Is Becoming an Innovation Super Power* (Oxford-Cambridge: Chandos Publishing, 2010).

Acknowledgements

Writing this page is in numerous ways bringing together the highly diverse, mosaic-like memories from the journey of writing the book into a singular bricolage. Many have encouraged, comforted, guided and stimulated me during this process. Though any mistakes and slippages are solely my own responsibility.

In New Delhi I am grateful to Sushila Ramaswamy from Delhi University for instigating an interest in topics related to Indian politics which seemed very distant to my 'natural sciences' schooling.

In Leipzig I am thankful to Matthias Middell and Ulf Engel who accepted me in the doctoral studies programme and were my supervisors. Ursula Rao has taken great interest in this project and her sharp observations shaped numerous aspects of the chapters. Her unending enthusiasm for new topics and her will to engage with all my endeavours have been a persistent source of support.

In Berlin, several bonds and institutional environments have been a crucial influence on how the dissertation became a book. I thank Michael Mann, who was the external supervisor of the dissertation and invited me as an affiliate to the Institute for Asian and African Studies at the Humboldt University in 2012. He continues to wholeheartedly support my passion for teaching, my myriad interests and shows unflinching trust in the research directions I continue to take as a faculty member at the department. I heartily thank the entire department for accepting me as part of the family. Nadja-Christina Schneider gave fruitful comments on one of the chapters that helped me tremendously.

In 2014 I joined the Leibniz-Zentrum Moderner Orient as a post-doctoral fellow, which initiated an important phase of academic discussions, presentations and the writing-up of the book. Ulrike Freitag, Katrin Bromber, and Dietrich Reetz have been very supportive figures. I especially thank the warm friendship I share with Nitin Sinha and

Abdoulaye Sounaye, which has also produced the necessary space of trust for sharing my chapters at different stages and my current research. I am highly grateful to Heike Liebau who has not just been the principal investigator of my project but a persistent source of strength. Her sincerity, humility, dedication and dexterity at managing social relationships continue to inspire me.

Margrit Pernau and all the friends and colleagues from the Colloquium at the Max Planck Institute, Center for the History of Emotions continue to add to the quality of my research and writing through their beneficial interventions. Deep gratitude also goes to the anonymous reviewers of Oxford University Press, whose inspiring comments and suggestions have helped improve the book.

There are certain 'places', which have been my temples of thought and my sites of ritualistic refuge. Where I have breathed life into many of the lines in this book. These are 'places' with a life of their own and peculiar as it may seem, have been crucial to this project. Könneritz str. 3, Josephstr. 15, Boddinstr. 6 and Elsenstrasse 81a are more than places—they have been my spaces of solace.

I have been fortunate to shape numerous precious bonds, which have dramatically catapulted my confidence while writing the chapters. I thank Joel Glasman for motivating me to continue writing during tough times, Marina Renault for her presence in trying times and David Frohnapfel, Maria Framke, Susan Baumgartl, Akshay Joshi and Stephan Beutner for their engagement with topics old and new.

Sadia Bajwa's sisterly presence for all these years has given me immense strength. Marett Klahn's friendship has brought vitality to life in Berlin. I feel highly fortunate for the academic and personal friendship I share with Franziska Roy. Our discussions continue to spark new ideas. Vandana Joshi has been, and is, a source of unconditional love and support both in Berlin and Delhi. I thank her for the soundness of the bond we share.

My family in Belgium and Germany has given me the feeling of being at 'home' away from many other homes. I thank the 'hood' from my childhood in India.

Stefan Binder has been an enthusiastic reader of all these chapters (several times!). With him I share an unconditional friendship that easily flows between the terrains of academic and personal life. I am deeply thankful to him for the innumerable occasions his re-assurance has rescued me from doubtful moments.

I am grateful for the unflinching support of my mother Sadhana Bajpai and my brother Abhinav Bajpai—they are the common thread of my personal life. My deep thank you to my father Anil Kumar Bajpai for the sun, rain, and dust that we lived together when seeking my admission in Delhi University—this book is my first attempt at reciprocation, if there ever can be one.

Peter Lambertz has been more than a source of support during these years. In him I have a friend, a critic, but most importantly, a listener. I thank him for the intellectual space we continue to share and for the many journeys we are yet to begin. He continues to rejuvenate my faith that there is always room for poetry in our prosaic lives.

Anandita Bajpai
Berlin, January 2018

Introduction

'Prolixity is not alien to us in India. We are able to talk at some length. Krishna Menon's record of the longest speech ever delivered at the United Nations (nine hours non-stop), established half a century ago (when Menon was leading the Indian delegation), has not been equaled by anyone anywhere. [...] We do like to speak.'

—opening lines, *The Argumentative Indian*[1]

The Spoken Nation

This is a book on 'speaking'. More precisely, it is about the elected heads of a state speaking. Its archive is material that may be regarded as exhaustingly unfashionable and jaded, the public addresses of the prime ministers of a postcolonial state. 'India', the ongoing discursive project, is like a phantasm, a specter of postcolonial multiplicity. As a relatively younger nation-state formed in 1947, it is often lauded for its achievements of democracy, pluralism, and more recently for its economic growth. At the same time, it is rebuked for nurturing exactly the opposite in its operation. Very often, for each lauded achievement that may describe India's being, exactly the opposite also quantifies its reality. However, what Achille Mbembe states in the African context also holds true for India, '[...] the postcolony is chaotically pluralistic, yet it has

---

[1] A. Sen, *The Argumentative Indian: Writings on Indian Culture, History and Identity* (New Delhi: Penguin Books, 2005), p. 3.

nonetheless an internal coherence'.[2] In spite of India's inherent contradictions, there is a consistency that ensures the durability of its existence.
India, the nation, is constantly performed through the spoken word.
There are speakers who invariably style, order, shape, and therein create
its being. This book is an attempt to trace how some of the prominent
authors of the nation, its elected political heads, who, at the same time,
are the protagonists and vanguards of the state, speak India into being.

It aims to analyse the re-profiling of India with *re*—as in repetition as
well as in reform—from the vantage point of its prime ministers. The
objective is to gauge how the Indian state has been recalibrating itself
since 1991 in periods of challenges from both perceived external and
internal actors, putting pressure on its leaders who wish to safeguard
their status as legitimate elites in power.

Since 1991 and the formal institutionalization of the neo-liberal economic reforms, a plethora of channels from both within and outside
India have profiled it as an 'emerging giant', 'the airplane that has taken
off', 'the next big thing!' bearing captions such as 'India Emerging',
'India Shining', 'India Rising', 'India on the move', 'a pulsating new
dynamic India!', 'Incredible India', 'Resilient India', and 'India Now'.
These discursive projections were initiated along with externally
produced economic speculations after the 'opening up' of the Indian
economy. In the last two decades, they have broadened in terms of
their scope and visibility in varied literature, extending to acronyms
and metaphors, describing India as the world's youngest, yet largest
functioning democracy, a nuclear power, a military power, coupled with
a fast-paced IT revolution, and a knowledge economy, to name some.
Such adulations have added a more recent, albeit prominent dimension
to the multiple imaginations of the project called 'India'.

Set against the backdrop of this literature projecting the 'New India',
which I provocatively call 'airport literature', due to its overwhelming
presence in the bestseller sections of bookstores located at the airports,
and which initially triggered my curiosity, this book proceeds with the
main question: how do the *Indian governments* actively profile 'India' vis-
à-vis this discourse of 'India Emerging'? More precisely, how have four
Indian governments, which have been in power at the centre since 1991,

---

[2] A. Mbembe, 'Provisional Notes on the Postcolony', *Africa: Journal of the
International African Institute* 62, no. 1 (1992): 3.

responded to, reinterpreted, and even reproduced such discourses in their own creative flavours, so much so that they become the vanguards of a shifting discourse of 'India, the democracy/economy in crisis' to 'India, the Emerging Power'? I approach this question by tracing how this staging of 'Emerging India' is linguistically operationalized in the spoken words of four Indian prime ministers after 1991, both for what they conceive as the outside world (referred to as 'external' audiences) as also for 'Indians' in and outside India (referred to as 'internal' audiences). The terms 'outside/external' and 'inside/internal' are emic categories, that is, they refer to the distinctions *as intended* and drawn in the addresses by the prime ministers.

The trope of emergence finds graphic manifestation in two cross-cutting and interrelated topics, which have been evergreen themes in scholarship on Indian politics and economy since 1991—secularism and the neo-liberal economic reforms. Since 1992, with the demolition of the Babri Masjid in the city of Ayodhya by supporters of the by then rampant Hindu right wing, state secularism in India has come to be severely challenged. How have the prime ministers attempted to rescue state secularism in such moments of crisis, and how do they attempt to ensure its durability as a necessary unifier of the nation through their spoken word? What does India's said emergence have to do with secularism? Since the reforms have implied a paradigm shift from the Nehruvian import-substitution economy to market liberalization, how have the prime ministers explained this shift to the population and the world and how are these transformations projected as the glossy embodiment of a new emerging India? These are some of the pertinent questions this book seeks to answer through the lens of prime ministerial oratory. In doing so, it will elucidate how the elected heads of India also consolidate their own presence, as well as that of the state as the legitimate 'voice' of the nation.

1991 in India

The year 1991 is often projected as a caesura in Indian history, primarily because it marks the 'opening up' of the Indian economy. Liberalization of the economy incorporated—deregulation of economic laws, initiation of privatization, a shrinking role of the then prevalent monopoly of the public sector, devaluation of the rupee, tax reforms, inflation controlling measures, opening up for international trade and foreign direct investment, and abolishment of the *license raj*.[3] Disagreements, however, abound within India on claims laid upon the ultimacy of the year. One of the contestations has been that the reforms had already started piecemeal during the prime ministership of Rajiv Gandhi in the 1980s. Such contentions, however, do not challenge the normative acceptance of the reforms per se, that is, they do not question whether market liberalization was and could be the only possible mantra for the Indian economy, as the balance of payments crisis occurred. At best, they have led to arguments on the *when* rather than the *why* of market liberalization. For a number of reasons listed below, I use 1991 as the starting point for the analysis.

Firstly, the year demarcates the beginning of the prime minister-ship of P.V. Narasimha Rao, who would be the first non-member of the Gandhi-Nehru family to serve a *complete* term in a Congress-led coalition government. In retrospect, this stands as a phase of enormous transitions in that before Rao, no other Congress (or non-Congress) politician, who did not belong to the Gandhi-Nehru family, had held the prime ministerial office for complete five years.

Secondly, though reforms did initiate already in the 1980s, they became *systematic* and were *institutionalized* in 1991 as a result of the balance of payments crisis (which led to gold reserves being airlifted as a condition for IMF loans repayments). More significantly, it is dur-ing Rao's term as prime minister that the *most graphic* explanations and elaborate narrations of market liberalization are laid out before the audiences, both those in India as well as the larger international public. Thus, even though the partial lifting of the license raj and the 'open-ing up' of Indian markets had commenced piecemeal during the 1980s, the *expression* of the drastic transitions occurs, starting 1991, when Rao made an appearance on the national television channel *Doordarshan*

---

[3] *License Raj* refers to the licensing controls on the private sector business activities. Literally, it stands for the *raj* or rule, the reign (Hindustani word taken from the terms *British Raj*, which stood for the colonial period of 1858–1947) of the licensing system. Private investors and enterprises in India (up to 1991) were obliged to acquire a state license from the government, which would per-mit the setting up and running of businesses. As the arrangement gave undue powers to government agencies that would grant licenses only to a selective few, it gave way to red tape.

to give a message to the nation, or later when he presented the union budget in July 1991. Because the narrative celebrating 'India Emerging' is intricately linked to and is a part of the transitions in the Indian economy, eventually traceable to the neo-liberal economic reforms, a glimpse and introspection into how the architects of the reforms (Rao as prime minister, and Singh, who would later become the prime minister in 2004, as the finance minister in his cabinet) translated these transformations to the audiences becomes imperative.

Thirdly, another significant transition after 1991 is the simultaneous liberalization of both print and mass media in India. The general shift after economic liberalization epitomized a move from political financing to advertising as a resource.[4] Whereas prior to the reforms, the press was fundamentally inspired by a developmentalist ideology and mainly relied on the political parties and the governments in general for its financing, after the reforms there has been a move towards rapid commercialization and drastic move to 'infotainment'. Besides, the almost aggressive influx of 24x7 news channels has inaugurated a general trend of the mass-mediatization of politics. This has borne consequences for not just a critical 'writing of the neo-liberal leader',[5] but also for how the addresses of the prime ministers themselves illustrate reflexivity on issues and criticisms that appear in media coverage at large. The liberalization of media thus does not simply imply that the words of the PMs acquire lesser weight, owing to the 'opening up' of a larger sphere of critique which was earlier formally more tied to governments, but that the speeches themselves underscore a greater awareness of and responses to such critique in defense of what is being communicated.

Fourthly, another development in India's political landscape, which also started gaining momentum in the 1980s, but witnessed a zenith-like moment after 1991, is the rise of Hindu nationalism. As mentioned already, in 1992, the demolition of the sixteenth-century Babri Masjid

---

[4] See U. Rao, *News as Culture: Journalistic Practices and the Remaking of Indian Leadership Traditions* (New York, Oxford: Berghahn Books, 2010); R. Jeffrey, *India's Newspaper Revolution: Capitalism, Politics and the Indian Language Press 1977–99* (London: C. Hurst and Co. Publishers Ltd., 2000); W. Mazarella, *Shovelling Smoke: Advertising and Globalization in Contemporary India* (Durham, NC: Duke University Press, 2003).

[5] See U. Rao, 'Neo-Liberalism and the Rewriting of the Indian Leader', *American Ethnologist* 37, no. 4 (2010): 713–25.

by Hindu fundamentalists in the city of Ayodhya, Uttar Pradesh (6 December), caused a religious uproar, leading to communal riots in the state and other parts of the country.[6] These events that severely damaged the secular image of the nation occurred one year after Rao would assume office, not too long after the liberalization of the economy.

In the context of these four developments, 1991, as the marker of a new government's term, stands as a year accompanied with some fundamental transitions. Though each of the aforementioned developments may or may not have reached a height through the culmination of a concrete event in 1991, they relate directly or indirectly to the story of market liberalization and state secularism. Thus, for the sake of tracing internal continuities and discontinuities within Rao's term, this work commences with the year 1991.

Scholarship from diverse disciplines has attempted to embed these transitions in India within a larger framework of changes taking place in an overarching global context after 1989.[7] These debates emphasize the emergence of new spatial orders that challenge the traditional authority of the nation-state. Externally, these challenges are deemed to be authored by forces generalized under the shorthand term 'globalization', and internally they are seen to be produced by forces of fragmentation, operating within the territorial ambit of nations. In the next section, I discuss these debates in light of the implications these transitions, visible across Asia, post-communist Europe and Africa, have for nation-states as actors. For the Indian case, my aim is to elucidate how exactly this transitional phase, underscored by a balance of payments crisis and communal tensions, was converted into a success story that culminated in the rhetoric of 'India Emerging'.

[6] The masjid had been built during the reign of the Moghul emperor, Babur, the founder of the dynasty. However, the spot where it stood is claimed (in Hindu mythology) to be the birthplace of the Hindu god, Ram. The demolition was staged with the purpose of eventually building a Ram mandir (temple) to demarcate the deity's birthplace.

[7] Though it must be emphasized that there are voices that also contest the overemphasis attached to a 'global 1989' when writing about sociopolitical and economic developments in India: See, for example, M. Mann, '1989 in India: Overcoming the Post-Colonial State', in U. Engel, F. Hadler, and M. Middell (eds) *1989 in a Global Perspective* (Leipzig: Leipziger Universitätsverlag, 2015), pp. 259–96.

The Nation State in a New World Order?

The year 1989 and its depictions as a 'global moment'[8] have triggered intense scholarly interest on the configuration of what has loosely been categorized as an emerging 'new world order'. The engagement within the disciplines of international relations and political science especially incorporates multifarious discussions on what constitutes the coordinates of this new global order. In this context, initial discussions have dealt with describing how the post-cold war world was no longer characterized by bipolarity, but led to a brief phase of USA's unquestioned geopolitical supremacy. The *new* global order within the international system of states, on the other hand, has been described as one where multiple poles of power can be seen as emerging, deflecting the axes of power to be concentrated not in one or two, but rather multiple sites.[9]

Starting from Bull's *The Anarchical Society: A Study of Order in World Politics*,[10] there have been numerous depictions of what the post-cold

---

[8] Engel, Hadler, and Middell, M. (eds), *1989 in a Global Perspective*.

[9] Discussions based on the emerging role of states such as India and China in a new world order include, for instance: A. Goldstein, N. Pinaud, and H. Reisen, *The Rise of China and India: What's in It for Africa* (OECD Development Centre Policy Insights, 19, Paris: OECD Publishing, 2006, pp. 1–150); H.G. Broadman, *Africa's Silk Road: China and India's New Economic Frontier* (Washington, DC: World Bank Publications, 2007). Parag Khanna, both these countries as part of the second world, see P. Khanna, *The Second World: Empires and Influence in the New Global Order* (New York: Random House, 2008). Journalist Fareed Zakaria discusses state-based balances of power on the global scale as the 'post-American world'. See F. Zakaria, *The Post-American World* (New York: Norton, 2008).

[10] Bull's focus is on defining *order*, approaching it from three different perspectives and timelines, 'The nature of order in world politics, an examination of order in the contemporary international system, and finally the alternative paths to world order.' Bull states that the current system of states is anarchical in that there is no higher level of authority over states, each state having ultimate sovereignty over its citizens within its borders, and the system forms a society in that there are certain 'common rules' which provides order to the international arena. H. Bull, *The Anarchical Society* (New York: Columbia University Press, 1977), as cited in R.W. Cox, 'Towards a Posthegemonic Conceptualization of World Order: Reflections on the Relevancy of Ibn Khaldun', reprinted in R.W. Cox and T. Sinclair, *Approaches to World Order* (Cambridge: Cambridge University Press, 1996), pp. 136–7.

war world order looks like. Some discuss the establishment of a 'post-modern international order'.[11] Sørensen describes world order as 'a governing arrangement among states, meeting the current demand for order in major areas of concern'.[12] There are four different aspects that acquire prominence in his own description, which he sums up in the following categorization:

> (a) The realist concern of the politico-military balance of war; (b) the liberal concern of the make-up of international institutions and the emergence of global governance; (c) the constructivist concern of the realm of ideas and ideology, with a focus on the existence or otherwise of common values on a global scale; and (d) the IPE (International Political Economy) concern of the economic realm of production, finance and distribution. On the basis of this analysis, I define the current order as an interregnum; a new, stable order has not been established but significant elements of the old order remain in place.[13]

Cox identifies 'three categories of interacting forces: material capabilities, ideas, and institutions'.[14] Derived from these, *a stable* world order is based on a fit between these three elements or a 'configuration of material power, the prevalent collective image of world order (including certain norms) and a set of institutions, which administer order with a certain semblance of universality (i.e. not just as the overt instruments of a particular state's dominance)'.[15]

These discussions have, however, not been limited to international relations' scholars and political scientists alone. Different disciplines have engaged with the subject, using varying vocabularies to quantify and describe the transitions in the post-cold war, Bretton Woods world. This has also been informed by the observation that in spite of speaking

[11] See G. Sørensen, 'What Kind of World Order? The International System in the New Millennium', *Cooperation and Conflict*, 41(4): 343–63; Sørensen, *Changes in Statehood:. The Transformation of International Relations* Houndmills: Palgrave Macmillan, 2001.

[12] Sørensen, 'What Kind of World Order?'. See also G.J. Ikenberry, 'America's Imperial Ambition', *Foreign Affairs*, 81(5), 2002: 49–60; G.J. Ikenberry, *After Victory: Institutions, Strategic Restraint, and the Rebuilding of Order After Major Wars* (Princeton: Princeton University Press, 2001).

[13] Sørensen, 'What Kind of World Order?', p. 343.

[14] Cox and Sinclair, *Approaches to World Order*, p. 98.

[15] Cox and Sinclair, *Approaches to World Order*, p. 103.

of 'New World Order(s)', political science in general, and international relations more specifically, have described the same as constituted solely within and through the category of nation-states.

Given that one of the main features of the transitions encountered by nations is the emergence of entities which are no longer restrained to or under the control of states, it has been argued that descriptions need to expand their horizons.[16] Callaghy, Latham, and Kassimir, for example, use the term 'transboundary formations' to speak of the different newer forms of order and authority, such as rebel militias, INGOs, transnational corporations, etc., which question the existence of the state as the sole form of authority and organization.[17]

The notion of sovereignty itself has come to be challenged by authors from new political geography, like John Agnew, who see it as 'neither inherently territorial', nor as 'exclusively organized on a state-by-state basis'.[18] Engel and Olsen describe in the context of African states how '(a)uthority in Africa is increasingly exercised beyond the state, the locus of sovereignty is shifting'.[19]

From the perspective of global history,[20] the same debate has been framed in terms of changing 'regimes of territoriality', which shifts

[16] For a comprehensive overview of the variety of voices in this discussion, and the different disciplinary approaches, see U. Engel and M. Middell (eds), 'Introduction: Global Cities, New Regionalisms, Decline and Re-Emergence of the Nation State, Empire, G 20 or Global Governance—Is There a Point of Convergence in the Debate on Changing World Orders?', in *World Orders Revisited* (Leipzig: Leipziger Universitätsverlag, 2010), pp. 7–16.

[17] T. Callaghy, R. Kassimir, and R. Latham, 'Introduction: Transboundary Formations, Intervention, Order, and Authority', in *Intervention and Transnationalism in Africa: Global-Local Networks of Power* (Cambridge: Cambridge University Press, 2001), pp. 1–20.

[18] J. Agnew, 'Sovereignty Regimes: Territoriality and State Authority in Contemporary World Politics', *Annals of the Association of American Geographers* 95, no. 2 (2005): 437.

[19] U. Engel and G.R. Olsen, *Authority, Sovereignty and Africa's Changing Regimes of Territorialization* (Leipzig: Leipziger Universitätsverlag, 2010), p. 3. Working paper series of the Graduate Centre Humanities and Social Sciences of the Research Academy Leipzig, 7, 2010, p. 3.

[20] S. Conrad, A. Eckert, and U. Freitag (eds), *Globalgeschichte. Theorien-Ansätze-Themen* (New York: Frankfurt am Main, 2008). For other references in the field of global history, see Engel and Middell (eds), 'Introduction'.

it away from positing fixed world orders.[21] Historian Charles Maier speaks of how, in any given historical period, there are dominant ways of aligning authority to territory. He terms the same as 'regimes of territoriality'.[22] Engel and Middell identify the transition from one such dominant regime of territoriality to another as a 'critical juncture of globalization', in particular when tensions and conflicts are involved.[23] In new political geography, this could be discussed in terms of 'regulatory landscapes'.[24] Engel and Middell sum up the position taken by new urban sociology and a particular tradition within political economy, both of which focus on the emergence of 'global assemblages'.[25] They state in the same direction:

---

[21] C. Maier, 'Consigning the Twentieth Century to History: Alternative Narratives for the Modern Era', *American Historical Review*, 105(3), 2000: 807–31; W.C. Opello and S.J. Rosow, *The Nation-State and Global Order: A Historical Introduction to Contemporary Politics*, 2nd ed. (Boulder: Lynne Rienner Publishers, 2004); see also M.D. Bordo, A.M. Taylor, and J.G. Williamson (eds), *Globalization in Historical Perspective* (Chicago: University of Chicago Press, 2003). For recent discussion on 'Empires', see M. Hardt A. and Negri, *Empire* (Cambridge: Harvard University Press, 2000); and, for a critique on their position, A.A. Boron, *Empire and Imperialism: A Critical Reading of Michael Hardt and Antonio Negri* (London: Zed Books, 2005); A. Colas, *Empire* (Cambridge: Polity, 2006); N. Ferguson, *Empire: The Rise and Demise of the British World Order and the Lessons for Global Power* (New York: Basic Books, 2003).

[22] Maier, 'Consigning the Twentieth Century to History'.

[23] See Engel and Middell, 'Bruchzonen der Globalisierung, Globale Krisen und Territorialitätsregimes—Kategorien einer Globalgeschichtsschreibung', *Comparativ* 15, no. 2 (2005): 5–38. For a discussion on the differences between 'regimes of territoriality' and 'regimes of territorialisation', see M. Middell and K. Naumann, 'Global History and the Spatial Turn: From the Impact of Area Studies to the Study of Critical Junctures of Globalization', *Journal of Global History* 5, no. 1(2010).

[24] See A. Hudson, 'Beyond the Borders: Globalisation, Sovereignty and Extra-Territoriality', in D. Newman (ed.), *Boundaries, Territory and Postmodernity* (London: Frank Cass, 1999), pp. 89–105.

[25] S. Sassen, *Territory, Authority, Rights: From Medieval to Global Assemblages* (Princeton: Princeton University Press, 2006); N. Brenner, *New State Spaces: Urban Governance and the Rescaling of Statehood* (Oxford: Oxford University Press, 2004).

The emergence of forms of transnational governance beyond the state has received attention in a number of disciplines, with empirical cases drawn from both the group of 'failing states' and globalising econo-mies.[26] While governance beyond the state usually is interpreted as a result of processes of globalization[27] or increasing deterritorialization,[28] the concept of global governance as one reterritorialization strategy exercised by nation states still enjoys substantial academic and practical support.[29]

Regardless of the agreements/disagreements, lexical differences and specificities of capturing or describing these transitions, one key ele-ment of most discussions, whether within political science at large or in other disciplinary fields, relates to the shifting role of nation-states as actors in this 'changing' new world order.

As a result, the paradigmatic role of nation-states as the prime units of analysis in understanding world order(s) has come to be questioned. In focus now is rather how nation-states have come under pressure to recalibrate their position vis-à-vis overarching meta-state or transna-tional non-state actors.

As anthropologists Hansen and Stepputat aptly summarize, '(T)he current rethinking of the state occurs at a juncture where the very notion of the state as a regulator of social life and a locus of ter-ritorial sovereignty and cultural legitimacy is facing unprecedented

---

[26] See D.J. Elkins, *Beyond Sovereignty: Territory and Political Economy in the Twenty-First Century* (London: University of Toronto Press, 1995). T.M. Callaghy, et al. (eds), *Intervention and Transnationalism in Africa: Global-Local Networks of Power* (Cambridge: Cambridge University Press, 2001); Engel and A. Mehler, '"Under Construction": Governance in Africa's New Violent Social Spaces', in Engel and Olsen (eds), *The African Exception* (London: Burlington VT: Ashgate, 2005), pp. 87–102 as cited in Engel, U. and Middell, M. (eds.), *World Orders Revisited*.

[27] For Africa, see J. Ferguson, *Global Shadows: Africa in the Neo-Liberal World Order* (Durham NC: Duke University Press, 2008) as cited in Engel and Middell (eds), *World Orders Revisited*.

[28] See Engel and Middell, 'Introduction'.

[29] See the programmatic article for the relaunch of the journal *Global Governance*. [T. Farer and T.D. Sisk, 'Enhancing International Cooperation: Between History and Necessity', *Global Governance* 16, no. 1–2 (2010): 1–12.]

challenges.'[30] Internally, these challenges become most graphic in the shape of separatist movements playing out along linguistic, ethnic, and religious lines, which tend to fundamentally disturb the notion of nation-states being the unifying and legitimate agents of spatial ordering (clubbed under the term 'fragmentation').[31] Externally, these challenges may be appropriately summed up under the umbrella theme of the perceived threat of what is amorphously termed as 'globalization'. As stated, these reflections have not been confined to the disciplines of comparative politics, international relations, and political science in general, but have also been a point of reflection for anthropologists and historians. Comaroff and Comaroff coherently sum up these perceived external threats levied by those who predict the collapse, even demise, of the nation-state:

> Nation-states, from this vantage, have been rendered irrelevant by world market forces (1) because capital has become uncontrollable and keeps moving, at its own velocity, to sites of optimum advantage; (2) because the global workforce has become ever more mobile as job seekers, increasingly managed by private agencies, migrate ever farther in pursuit of even the most menial of jobs, under even the most feudal of conditions; and (3) because these human flows seem, in varying proportions, to elude surveillance, despite the highly repressive mechanisms often put into place to monitor national frontiers. Under such conditions, state regulation of both capital and labor becomes obsolete, impossible; so, too, do fiscal designs that run counter to the mechanisms of global markets and/or the imperatives of global corporations. States, it is said, 'can no longer independently affect the levels of economic activity or employment within their territories [...].'[32]

Thus, forces within the nation-states, as also those without, are seen as causing a 'crisis' of the very category of 'the' nation-state and evoke contemplations on how to rethink them. Biswas, for instance, points out how speculations on the nature of this 'crisis' triggered special attention of journals such as *Political Studies*, which devoted an entire issue to

---

[30] T.B. Hansen and F. Stepputat (eds), *Sovereign Bodies: Citizens, Migrants and States in the Postcolonial World* (Princeton: Princeton University Press, 2005), p. 4.

[31] See S. Biswas, 'W(h)ither the Nation-State? National and State Identity in the Face of Fragmentation and Globalisation', *Global Society* 16, no. 2 (2002): 176.

[32] J. Comaroff and J.L. Comaroff (eds), *Millenial Capitalism and the Culture of Neoliberalism* (Durham, NC: Duke University Press, 2001), p. 28.

the title 'Contemporary Crisis of the Nation State?', later adapted to an edited volume by Dunn with the same title.[33]

Quantifying these transitions leads to debates which appear to be dividing authorship into two camps, on the one hand, those that proclaim the demise and irrelevance of the state, and, on the other, those who ardently speak for states still being the anchoring units that play a key role in the shaping of the global order. While the former argument may be seen in writings in favour of 'globalization',[34] such as those by Ross[35] or Lukacs,[36] the latter argument may be seen in the writings of authors such as Tölöyan who states, 'It is not yet time, to write [its] [...]

---

[33] See *Political Studies* 42(Issue Supplement s1), 1994: 1–233; and J. Dunn (ed.), *The Contemporary Crisis of the Nation State?* (Oxford: Blackwell, 1995).

[34] Other prominent voices which discuss the declining role of nation states are: S. Strange, 'The Westfailure System', *Review of International Studies*, 25(3), 1999: 345–54. See also Strange, *The Retreat of the State: The Diffusion of Power in the World Economy* (Cambridge: Cambridge University Press, 1996); V. Schmidt, 'The New World Order, Incorporated: The Rise of Business and the Decline of the Nation-State', *Daedalus* 124, no. 2 (1995): 75–106; J.M. Guehenno, *The End of the Nation-State* (Minneapolis: University of Minnesota Press, 1995); M. Horsman and A. Marshall, *After the Nation-State: Citizen, Tribalism and the New World Disorder* (London: Harper Collins, 1995). I. Clark, *Globalization and Fragmentation: International Relations in the 20th Century* (Oxford: Oxford University Press, 1997); as well as the best-selling *New York Times* columnist Thomas Friedman's celebratory account of globalization, T.L. Friedman, *The Lexus and the Olive Tree* (New York: Anchor Books, 1999).

[35] Ross asserts, '[...] until recently, that the regulatory role of national governments expanded progressively. Now, however, corporations are able to prevail on states 'to restrain regulations, cut taxes, and allocate more public funds toward subsidizing production costs', which puts 'global capital in a position to demand changes in state policy'. [R.J.S. Ross, 'The Relative Decline of Relative Autonomy: Global Capitalism and the Political Economy of State Change', in E.S. Greenberg and T.F. Mayer (eds), *Changes in the State: Causes and Consequences* (Newbury Park: Sage, 1990), as cited in Comaroff and Comaroff (eds), *Millenial Capitalism and the Culture of Neoliberalism*, p. 211.

[36] Lukacs explicitly states for example, 'In the long run, the power of the state, of centralized government, will weaken everywhere, an inevitability which will change profoundly the very texture of history'. [J. Lukacs, *The End of the Twentieth Century and the End of the Modern Age* (New York: Ticknor and Fields, 1993), p. 157].

obituary.'[37] Using Turner's argument, Comaroff and Comaroff, in a similar vein, state that the '"development of the global capitalist system" has "not led to any withering away of the state" at all.'[38] The argument here goes that the relevance of state boundaries has increased; especially because successful states still 'attempt to regulate, encourage or obstruct flows of workers, capital and commodities across their borders.'[39]

However, a third proposition is that instead of being preoccupied with the debate of whether or not nation-states are rendered irrelevant, the focus should flex to the question of locating how nation states, as active actors in this arrangement, respond and react to these transitions, which question their legitimacy both internally (that is, from within the strict territorial boundaries) as well as externally (by forces which cannot be categorized as being solely territorial in nature, but are rather transnational in both their operation and zones of impact.) Engel and Olsen aptly state in reference to states in Africa, 'In our view, processes of globalization are indeed characterized by forms of deterritorialization, including voluntary sovereignty transfers by states to supranational organizations, new regionalisms [...], emergence of "global cities", [...]'[40] As a result, questions that arise are: how do states react to these challenges of spatial reconfiguration of power and legitimacy? How do states attempt to reconfigure, reposit, and represent themselves so as to protect, retain, and safeguard their authority as the legitimate agents and voices of their populations?

In India, this reconfiguration and repositioning has duly informed the energies of its state and those who ritually speak for and on behalf

---

[37] K. Tölölyan, 'The Nation-State and Its Others: In Lieu of a Preface', *Diaspora: A Journal of Transnational Studies* 1, no. 1 (1991): 5, as cited in Comaroff and Comaroff (eds), *Millenial Capitalism and the Culture of Neoliberalism*, p. 30.

[38] Tölölyan, 'The Nation-State and Its Others'.

[39] T. Turner, *Globalization, the State, and Social Consciousness in the Late Twentieth Century*, n.d., unpublished manuscript as cited in Comaroff and Comaroff (eds), *Millenial Capitalism and the Culture of Neoliberalism*, p. 30. See also P. Hirst and G. Thompson, *Globalization in Question: The International Economy and the Possibilities of Governance* (Cambridge: Polity Press, 1996), p. 17.

[40] Engel and Olsen, *Authority, Sovereignty and Africa's Changing Regimes of Territorialization*, p. 7.

of the state. This has especially been the case in the face of moments dubbed as national 'crises', such as the balance of payments crisis of 1991 and the threat to state secularism after the demolition of the Babri Masjid in 1992. The attempt to rescue the case of state secularism and explain the drastic economic transitions after 1991 should thus been seen as a part of the state's attempts to reaffirm, recalibrate, and reconsolidate its position as the legitimate unifier, overarching problem solver, organizer, and voice of the nation. The aim of this book is to elucidate how exactly this transitional phase of perceived crises has been converted into a success story that culminates in the rhetoric of 'India Emerging'. This, however, also calls for a comprehensive understanding of the hyphenated nature of the nation-state and the inevitable role that the public speeches of elected political heads play, particularly in the Indian case, in fortifying and re-enforcing the coincidence of the nation and the state in the term 'nation-state'.

Nation-States and Ritualistic Public Oratory: Betwixt Persuasion and Pervasion

In her study of state-produced practices and rituals of nationalism in postcolonial India, Srirupa Roy poses the immanent question, 'What makes this manifestly produced entity (nation-state) stick? That is, what are the means by which the made world of nation-states comes to be seen as a found or a natural world?'[41] The question directs our attention away from the assumption that 'the nation is primarily an expression of the human need to "bond and cleave", interwoven with the equally basic and human propensity toward desire, fantasy and emotion',[42] as proposed by Anthony Smith. In turn, it invites us to take the *how* of manufacturing the nation, the concrete practices that produce it on a daily basis, seriously.

This is also a move away from the proposition made by one of the stalwarts of scholarship on nationalism, national identity, and the nation-state, Ernest Gellner, who states that,

---

[41] S. Roy, *Beyond Belief: India and the Politics of Postcolonial Nationalism* (Durham, NC: Duke University Press 2007), p. x.

[42] A.D. Smith, *The Ethnic Origins of Nations* (Oxford and Massachusetts: Blackwell Publishing Ltd., 1986), as cited in Roy, *Beyond Belief*, p. 9.

[...] the emergence of nationalism is best understood as a functional-
ist response to macrosociological changes set in motion in and through
the transformation of agrarian societies into industrial societies. In the
Parsonian terms of this classic transition narrative of *gemeinschaft* into
gesellschaft, the nation is a structural-functionalist byproduct of industrialization, encapsulating a distinctive set of modern 'pattern variables'.
Its emotive content and effective impact—the nation as a community of
feeling, or a 'crucible of emotion'—is of less interest than its formal or
structural features, as the means and also the outcome of the cultural
homogenization 'required' by an industrial polity.[43]

Roy proposes a fresh approach that does not take the hyphenated nature
of the nation-state as a given, but rather engages with the 'coincidence
of political authority and cultural essence' in the term. This implies '[...]
delineating the practices of "nationalizing the state" and "institutionalizing the nation" through which nation and state have been conjoined
[...].'[44] Practices of everyday routine through which a state makes itself
visible to the nation thus become the material means of consolidating
and solidifying its presence as the legitimate, answerable, and managing
authority of the nation.

Thus, understanding what guarantees the authority of the state as a
legitimate, institutionalized vanguard of the nation and also its durability as the same necessitates:

[...] a move beyond discussions of national identity as an internalized
belief, and of effective nationalising practices as those that engender
unisonant sentiments of love, loyalty, and belonging, to an exploration
of the political-cultural action context; that is, the ways in which discourses, practices, and visual-symbolic effects structure political action
to reaffirm the authoritative existence of the nation-state. It is through
repeatedly encountering rather than believing in the official imagination
of nationhood, through recognizing the sights and sounds of the state

---

[43] E. Gellner, *Nations and Nationalism* (Oxford: Blackwell Publishing Ltd.,
1983) and J. Adams, 'Culture in Rational—Choice Theories of State Formation',
in G. Steinmetz (ed.), *State/Culture: State Formation after the Cultural Turn*
(Ithaca, NY: Cornell University Press, 1999), pp. 98–122, as cited in Roy, *Beyond
Belief*, p. 109.

[44] Roy, *Beyond Belief*, p. x.

rather than 'buying into' its mythologies, that the nation-state is formed and reproduced.[45]

Roy categorizes this everyday encounter as *pervasion* by the state. Parades, state-produced documentary films, national anthems and flags, bureaucracies and paper work in state institutions, national television channels, centralized economic planning, visions of the future embedded in vocabularies of progress and development—all are aesthetic everyday practices that consolidate the legitimacy of the state as the unifier, problem-solver, organizer of the nation. It is in this sense that the speeches of the Indian prime ministers become the iconic forms that verbalize the visions of the state through its governments. They constitute the *repetitive* vocabulary of the state, the 'spectacular excessive signs of its own existence'.[46] They are therein, to borrow Mbembe's metaphorical vocabulary, part of a larger *ritual* that state power organizes '[...] for dramatizing its own magnificence [...] ceremonial displays through which it makes manifest its majesty',[47] in other words, displays that make 'state power highly visible'.[48] Uli Linke aptly sums up, 'Modern states are not just imagined or discursive cultural regimes but also embodied forms.'[49] [...] 'Nations are discursive phantoms with political bodies [...] the nation is habitually enacted [...].'[50] Understanding this cementing function of the words of the elected head of a state also enables an analysis that moves beyond the question of what spectators 'really' think or how it could be 'in their heads' when listening to a speech.

Roy, in reference to the enduring legitimacy of the state in postcolonial India, states that, 'Its success has less to do with the psychological processes of internalization and acceptance (the existence of people who buy into dominant nationalist ideologies) than with recognition and repeated exposure (the existence of spectators who "see" and

---

[45] Roy, *Beyond Belief*, p. 15.

[46] Hansen and Stepputat (eds), *Sovereign Bodies*, pp. 29–30.

[47] Mbembe, 'Provisional Notes on the Postcolony', p. 4.

[48] Hansen and Stepputat (eds), *Sovereign Bodies*, p. 29.

[49] U. Linke, 'Contact Zones: Re-Thinking the Sensual Life of the State', *Anthropological Theory* 6, no. 2 (2006): 205.

[50] Linke, 'Contact Zones', p. 210.

"know" the state).'[51] Further employing Timothy Mitchell's work, she asserts that the nation state is not a 'subjective belief',[52] but that '[...] it is through the habitual experiences of "encountering" the nation-state that the identification of the state and its idioms of nationhood takes place. The sights and sounds of the nation-state "clutter public space", and it is their familiarity or pervasiveness rather than their persuasiveness that engenders public recognition.'[53] This argument does call for close attention. Pervasion through everyday forms is then a key informer of how citizens relate to, experience, and recognize the state as a prime organizer of the nation.

The point this book will emphasize, however, is that pervasion and persuasion are not mutually exclusive in nature. One carries the potential of informing the other. In terms of the intentionality/ies of the speakers, one could start with the assumption that the more *pervasive* the state's presence, the higher the possibility that the more *persuasive* it can be, whereas the more persuasive it is, the higher the co-occurrence of pervasion in everyday worlds. Thus, on the one hand, the act of *speaking* the addresses may be viewed as a repetitive practice through which the state asserts its presence and through which its citizens encounter it on a regular basis. But, on the other hand, pervasion certainly aims at persuasion. To win over audiences, produce a sense of nationness, classical as these themes associated with political oratory appear to be, still remains an important stake for governments, particularly so in a country like India where the cohesiveness of 'the nation' is not a given but a constant process of work in progress. Hence, while

[51] Roy, *Beyond Belief*, p. 160.

[52] T. Mitchell, 'Society, Economy and the State Effect', in A. Sharma and A. Gupta (eds), *The Anthropology of the State* (Oxford: Blackwell Publishing Ltd., 2006), pp. 169–86; Mitchell, 'The Limits of the State: Beyond Statist Approaches and their Critics', *The American Political Science Review* 85, no. 1(1991): 93–5; and L. Wedeen, *Ambiguities of Domination: Politics, Rhetoric, and Symbols in Contemporary Syria* (Chicago: University of Chicago Press, 1999), pp. 33–5, as cited in Roy, *Beyond Belief*, p. 18.

[53] Mitchell, 'Society, Economy and the State Effect'; Mitchell, 'The Limits of the State: Beyond Statist Approaches and their Critics', *The American Political Science Review* 85, no. 1(1991): 93–5; and L. Wedeen, *Ambiguities of Domination: Politics, Rhetoric, and Symbols in Contemporary Syria* (Chicago: University of Chicago Press, 1999), pp. 33–5, as cited in Roy, *Beyond Belief*, p. 18.

my analysis agrees with Roy's assertions of moving 'beyond belief', it also takes *what* the respective governments envision and *how* it is presented to citizens with the aim of convincing listeners seriously. Besides, the two topical arenas, secularism and market liberalization, will show precisely that persuading is as important a stake as pervading through speaking.

My analysis of 1,202 speeches delivered before varied audiences grounds itself in a move beyond Chomskian formalism that has primarily focused on language as an isolated system with structures that are assumed to be organically given or pre-existing. The immense thrust laid in *linguistics proper* upon phonology (the sound systems of language), morphology (the grammatical structure of words), syntax (the grammatical structure of sentences), and semantics (formal aspects of meaning), though utilized by many other methodological investigations in the social sciences, has remained narrow in its conception of language.[54]

In sync with developments following the 'linguistic turn' (particularly known as such after Richard Rorty's *The Linguistic Turn*),[55] and the speech act theory in analytical philosophy, primarily associated with John Austin,[56] the aim has been to unravel how prime ministers *use* and *do* language within the social contours of their lives as icons of the state. It thus situates language use in its larger social environments that breed and feed discourses of the state. Language occupies a centrality in weaving the social matrices of discourses through both its internal structures as well as how these structures are put to usage for certain ends by politicians. In this sense, *parole* (speaking) and *langue* (language) should be viewed as mutually constitutive elements of language *use* or language in its *social practice*.

The terms political rhetoric and political oratory are often relegated to the ambit of ornamentation, suggesting language utilized for

---

[54] N. Fairclough, *Language and Power* (London: Longman, 1989), p. 6.

[55] R. Rorty, *The Linguistic Turn: Essays in Philosophical Method* (Chicago: University of Chicago Press, 1992).

[56] J.L. Austin, *How to Do Things with Words: The William James Lectures Delivered at Harvard University in 1955* (Oxford: Clarendon Press, 1962). See also J. Searle, *Expression and Meaning: Studies in the Theory of Speech Acts* (Cambridge: Cambridge University Press, 1979).

'impressive effect', but 'lacking in sincerity or meaningful content.'[57] A composite of two words, political rhetoric does not simply imply the usage of flowery, ornamental language, or poetic aestheticism, as it is often conjured to be. '*Rhetoric* denotes both the *ars bene dicendi et scribendi* (that is the practical art of speaking and writing well in public spheres through the use of various communicative genres) and the theory about eloquence.'[58] Jonathan Charteris-Black states,

> Classical rhetoric identified three main contexts within which speeches could occur. First is the *genus deliberativum*—a speech that needs to be persuasive because it deals with an important controversial topic within a public setting; next is the *genus iudicium* for making judicial decisions. Finally, there is the *genus demonstativum* or epideictic address that is undertaken for some form of display (as in eulogies).[59]

Many principles may be used in order to assess rhetoric, for example, clarity and comprehensiveness, grammatical correctness, evidence provided, and vividness, adequacy. Rhetoric incorporates three crucial elements of persuasion termed as logos, ethos, and pathos. Logos corresponds to rationally convincing the audience via the usage of '[...]

---

[57] The Oxford English Dictionary defines the two terms as follows,

'Rhetoric: the art of effective or persuasive speaking or writing, especially the exploitation of figures of speech and other compositional techniques. *He is using a common figure of rhetoric, hyperbole*; language designed to have a persuasive or impressive effect, but which is often regarded as lacking in sincerity or meaningful content: *All we have from the Opposition is empty rhetoric.*

Oratory: the art or practice of formal speaking in public. *The gift of persuasive oratory.*

Eloquent or rhetorical language: *learned discussions degenerated into pompous oratory.*' The Oxford English Dictionary (Oxford: Oxford University Press, 2012).

[58] Martin Reisigl, 'Analyzing Political Rhetoric', in Wodak Ruth and Michal Krzyzanowski (eds), *Qualitative Discourse Analysis in the Social Sciences* (New York: Palgrave Macmillan, 2008), p. 96.

[59] C. Sauer, 'Echoes from Abroad—Speeches for the Domestic Audience: Queen Beatrix' Address to the Israeli Parliament', in *Current Issues in Language and Society* 3, no. 3 (1996): 233–67; also in C. Schäffner (ed.), *Analysing Political Speeches* (Clevedon: Multilingual Matter, 1997); as cited in Jonathan Charteris-Black, *Politicians and Rhetoric, The Persuasive Power of Metaphor* (New York and Hampshire: Palgrave Macmillan, 2005), p. 9.

sound argumentation (*probare*), factual information (*docere*) and reasonable admonition or exhortation (*monere*).'[60] Ethos and pathos on the other hand, refer to the employment of non-argumentative forms of linguistic force, so as to reach persuasion or consent. The two differ in the sense that ethos refers to the usage of a more gentle and constant attitude creation, appealing to the emotion of an audience via 'advertising or through pleasure and entertainment.'[61] For example, emotionalization, suggestion, etc. Pathos refers to the arousal of '[...] momentarily violent, fierce, and intense emotions through rhetorical instigation (*movere*)',[62] for example, the usage of propaganda. Charteris-Black states that,

> The classical tradition of rhetoric went beyond the orator's act of communication to his qualities of character, or ethos. A model orator was necessarily morally virtuous (*vir bonus*) and could only persuade if his behaviour met with social approval. So successful rhetoric entailed both an effective heuristic or logos (the content of a speech), and a speaker who was ethically beyond criticism. There is, then, an inherent tension between evaluation of the linguistic choices that form a text and evaluation of the behaviour of the speaker. It is failure to understand this tension that has historically led to the emergence of a negative sense of rhetoric as over-decorative use of language; this sense assumes that rhetoric is style alone and not also the values and behaviour, or ethos, of the speaker.[63]

Rhetorical analysis in this context implies analysing 'the employment and effects of linguistics (including non-verbal) and other semiotic means of persuasion in rhetorical terms'.[64] Here, the term political (in political rhetoric) also expands over a multiplicity of definitions and areas—hinting at the debatable zone of public-private divides. In the context of this book, political rhetoric strictly refers to 'the use of rhetorical means of persuasion by politicians'.[65]

---

[60] Reisigl, 'Analyzing Political Rhetoric', p. 97.

[61] Reisigl, 'Analyzing Political Rhetoric', p. 97.

[62] Reisigl, 'Analyzing Political Rhetoric', p. 97.

[63] Charteris-Black, *Politicians and Rhetoric, The Persuasive Power of Metaphor*, p. 9.

[64] Reisigl, 'Analyzing Political Rhetoric'.

[65] Reisigl, 'Analyzing Political Rhetoric'.

My analysis thus calls for a move beyond the understanding of rhetoric as merely the ornamental usage of language that lacks sincerity. What remains outside the scope of this analysis, however, are questions of how serious the speakers are, if they *really* mean what they say, or the success or failure of their oratory in evoking conviction among audiences. It aims, nonetheless, to serve as an invitation for taking the usage of language, as embedded in its particular traditions of orality, seriously. Reducing political rhetoric to the now rampant understanding of decorative, stylized usage of language, hollowed out of content prevents giving due cognizance to how political rhetoric is an ever-popular modality of manufacturing discourses, of voicing statist visions, and of realizing political ambitions of pervasion and persuasion. Political oratory and its systematic analysis opens up an entire spectrum of novel possibilities, one that does not just give credence to technocratic truths and policy frameworks but that enables a consistent two-way traffic between the state and the nation.

Speeches serve two interrelated purposes. First, they become the tools to voice official state visions for the prime ministers, and second to nonetheless leave a space for the population to have a dialogic engagement with those visions. The latter foregrounds that when prime ministers speak, they do not just voice state visions, but that their words also take cognizance of the frictions they sometimes produce. Especially due to democratic voting that takes place every five years, as in India, they speak *to* but they also have to speak *with* the population. Thus, even the most new and novel visions often need to be cloaked in vocabularies that are familiar and therein appealing. In that sense, these speeches, in spite of having the texture of monologues are also intertextually linked to the 'pulse' and the 'mood' of the population, often pushing their authors to dialogue with criticisms and interventions. In this regard, speeches are more than parades and bureaucratic cultures; they lexically cement interactions. Though usually giving the impression of being unidirectional performances, they open a creative field of oratorical defeats and victories, they use pre-existing repertoires to convey messages that are new, they spring into existence an otherwise fragmented nation into a unified entity, and lastly, they reconfirm the authority of the state as a unifier of the fragmented nation. They can thus become the most graphic arena to see how national unity cannot be treated as a natural, organically existing order,[66] but how it is rather the consequence of a steady process of making and unmaking. Much as some speeches evoke awe and others sheer boredom, they ought to be taken seriously for '[...] eliciting recognition for and of the state as the authoritative representative of the nation: an effect that is achieved through iteration and ubiquity.'[67]

Secularism and Market Liberalization

The neo-liberalization of the Indian economy or discussions on the reforms per se and debates related to state secularism in the context of the rise of Hindu nationalism have been two themes that have evoked much scholarly attention. They inevitably appear directly or indirectly in research on postcolonial India, especially after the 1980s. This book brings forth a systematic and deliberate combination of these two themes, instead of reading their emergence as important merely owing to the occurrence of certain crucial events happening at the same time. It thus offers a framework for reading them together through the same analytical lens, as *one* topic. Differently put, it elucidates how the two themes can be looked at as being part of one and not two distinct stories from a specific perspective and analytical grid, that is, the vocabulary of springing the nation into existence.

In this section, I present a brief state of the art to delimit the varying perspectives and contexts within which the two evergreen themes of economic reforms and state secularism, as well as the overall subject of 'India Emerging' has been engaged with in scholarly investigations. I will then present how this book adds a new dimension to this ever-increasing literature and opens scope for a field of research, which has received little or no comprehensive and systematic attention so far, prime ministerial rhetoric as a building terrain for *selling* the statist visions of market liberalization and secularism, while weaving both in the same web of a 'New India'. It thus presents the anatomy of statist discourses through the lens of sources, which have not been engaged with seriously thus far, revisiting two themes, which have perhaps been

---

[66] Roy, *Beyond Belief*, p. 19.
[67] Roy, *Beyond Belief*, p. 19.

taken too seriously, though by weaving them through the same analytical lens.

In the context of the economic transitions following market liberalization, a vast body of scholarly literature has initiated discussions on the reforms per se.[68] However, this has been supplemented with literature on the subject of 'India Emerging', more so after 2000, whereby economic prognoses and discussions on India's speculated rise abound.[69] In a similar vein, extensive research has also been conducted on the opposition to the reforms[70] and their consequences for the organization of social and economic life of people in India. The rise of Hindu nationalism, *Hindutva*, the Hindu right wing[71] and its correlation

[68] Some of the research in this direction includes R. Nayar, 'When did the "Hindu" Rate of Growth End?', *Economic and Political Weekly* 41(19): 1885–90, 2006; M. McCartney, *India: The Political Economy of Growth and Liberalisation in India, 1991–2008* (London: Routledge, 2010); J.B. De Long, 'India since Independence: An Analytical Growth Narrative', in D. Rodrik (ed.), *Search of Prosperity: Analytic Narratives on Economic Growth* (Princeton: Princeton University Press, 2003); A. Kohli, *State-Directed Development, Political Power and Industrialization in the Global Periphery* (Cambridge: Cambridge University Press, 2004); J.N. Bhagwati and P. Desai, *India Planning for Industrialization* (Oxford: Oxford University Press, 1970); C.P. Chandrashekhar, 'Explaining Post-Reform Industrial Growth', *Economic and Political Weekly* 31, no. 35 (1996): 2537–45; B. Dasgupta, *Structural Adjustment, Global Trade and the New Political Economy of Development* (London: Zed Books, 1998).

This literature is indeed extensive and presents the narratives linked to the reforms through a plethora of lenses. It is, however, not my intention to discuss it in depth here, as it does not relate directly to the questions posed by this research.

[69] Among others, see A. Panagariya, *India: The Emerging Giant* (Oxford University Press, 2008); K. Basu (ed.), *India's Emerging Economy: Performance and Prospects in the 1990s and Beyond* (Cambridge, Massachusetts: MIT, 2004).

[70] P. Bardan, 'Nature of Opposition to Economic Reforms in India', *Economic and Political Weekly* 40, no. 48 (2005): 4995–98; C.P. Chandrasekhar and J. Ghosh, *The Market that Failed: Neoliberal Economic Reforms in India* (Delhi: Left Word Books/Naya Rasta Publishers, 2002); A. Ghosh, *Planning in India: The Challenge for the Nineties* (New Delhi: Sage, 1992); P. Patnaik, 'On the Concept of Efficiency', *Economic and Political Weekly* 32(43): 2807–13, 1997.

[71] For example, P. Van der Veer, *Religious Nationalism: Hindus and Muslims in India* (Berkeley: California University Press, 1994) and T.B. Hansen, *The Saffron*

to Indian secularism, and the changing configurations between politics and religion at large in India has been another thriving field of investigation for scholars working on India from varying disciplines. The topic of state secularism, especially in the advent of events such as Ayodhya (1992) and the Gujarat riots (2002), has led to vigorous academic debates on what defines its contours in its Indian avatar.

Another vast body of research explores the connection between Hindu nationalism and the changing media landscape in India.[72] Here, changing configurations of religion in the public sphere, politics, and media, and their emerging nexus in postcolonial India, has been an inevitable combination for numerous projects. Linked to this, the field of changing media landscapes, which inescapably bears references to the 'opening up' of the economy and the liberalization of media especially in the 1990s, has also attracted research from a variety of disciplines.[73]

In most literature, one is directly or indirectly introduced, and deservedly so, to the two topical themes of market liberalization and

---

Wave: Democracy and Hindu Nationalism in Modern India (Princeton: Princeton University Press, 1999); D. Ludden, 'Introduction. Ayodhya: A Window on the World', in D. Ludden (ed.) *Contesting the Nation: Religion, Community and the Politics of Democracy in India* (Philadelphia: University of Philadeiphia Press, 1996); C. Jaffrelot, *The Hindu Nationalist Movement and Indian Politics, 1925 to 1990: Strategies in Identity-Building, Implantation and Mobilisation* (with special reference to Central India) (New Delhi: Viking, 1993); and Z. Hasan, 'Communal Mobilization and Changing Majority in Uttar Pradesh', in *Making India Hindu: Religion, Community, and the Politics of Democracy in India*, ed. D. Ludden (New Delhi: Oxford University Press, 2007).

[72] For example see, A. Rajagopal, *Politics after Television: Hindu Nationalism and the Reshaping of the Public in India* (Cambridge et al.: Cambridge University Press, 2001); and S. Dasgupta, 'Gods in the Sacred Marketplace: Hindu Nationalism and the Return of the Aura in the Public Sphere', in B. Meyer and A. Moors (eds) *Religion, Media and the Public Sphere* (Bloomington: Indiana University Press, 2006).

[73] See U. Rao, *News as Culture Journalistic Practices and the Remaking of Indian Leadership Traditions* (New York–Oxford: Berghahn Books, 2010); R. Jeffrey, *India's Newspaper Revolution: Capitalism, Politics and the Indian Language Press 1977–99* (London: Hirst & Co., 2008); and W. Mazarella, *Shovelling Smoke: Advertising and Globalization in Contemporary India* (Durham, NC: Duke University Press, 2003).

religious nationalism. This is done in relation to changing landscapes of the urban city or the rural-urban relationships, the emergence of new social media and what liberalization has done to the 'traditional' media,[74] the transitions in state-corporation relations, the question of minority rights in a democratic setup, and what the perceived threat of right-wing *Hindutva* politics means for the secular image of the nation,[75] the rise of the new middle classes[76] and how market liberalization produces new faces of upward mobility beyond the texture of caste-driven class configurations or by engaging with the consequences of an open economy for the scattered, yet numerically large Indian diaspora.

Besides economic accounts, the theme of 'Emerging India' also finds expression in projections of India as a nuclear power,[77] its rise as an IT superpower,[78] and its relevance as a regional power in the security architecture of South/Southeast Asia.[79] Such accounts manifest themselves

[74] S. Udupa, 'News Media and Contention over "the Local" in Urban India', *American Ethnologist* 39(4): 819–34, 2012.

[75] R. Bajpai, *Debating Difference: Group Rights and Liberal Democracy in India* (New Delhi: Oxford University Press, 2011).

[76] See P. Van der Veer and C. Jaffrelot, *Patterns of Middle Class Consumption in India and China* (New Delhi: Sage, 2008); M. Säävälä, 'Entangled in the Imagination: New Middle Class Apprehensions in an Indian Theme Park', *Ethnos* 71, no. 3 (2006): 390–414.

[77] M. Hanson and R. Rajagopalan, 'Nuclear Weapons: Asian Case Studies and Global Ramifications', in T. William (ed.), *Security Politics in the Asia-Pacific: A Regional-global Nexus?* (Cambridge: Cambridge University Press), pp. 228–46; P. Malik, *India's Nuclear Debate. Exceptionalism and the Bomb* (London-New York-New Delhi: Routledge, 2010); B. Karnad, *Nuclear Weapons and Indian Security: The Realist Foundations of Strategy* (Delhi: Macmillan, 2002); G. Perkovich, *India's Nuclear Bomb: The Impact of Global Proliferation* (Berkeley: University of California Press, 1999).

[78] D. Sahoo, 'Economic Growth Efficiency of the Information and Technology Sector of India and Its Relevance to India', *Journal of Infrastructure Development* 4, no. 41 (2012): 41–58.

[79] To name a just few examples: W.L. Simon and V. Rai, *Think India—The Rise of the World's Next Superpower and What It Means for Every American* (New Delhi: Tantor Media, 2007); R. Meridyth, *The Elephant and the Dragon: The Rise of India and China and What That Means for All of Us* (New York: Norton, 2008); P.R. Chari, P.I. Cheema, and S.P. Cohen, *Perception, Politics and Security in South*

in a range of state- as well as non-state-led expressions. Nation branding campaigns and the campaigns of the tourism ministries of the past decades ('Incredible India') exemplify such endeavours.[80]

My own deeper probing into these state-supported 'Brand India' campaigns reconfirmed an absolute, unquestioned celebration of India as a rising economy and IT superpower in the making. However, the perceived audiences for most such campaigns were clearly more 'outside' of India, rather than those deemed to be the putative 'inside', an illustrative example being the campaigns of the India Brand Equity Foundation, which were, and still are, regularly staged at platforms like the World Economic Forum in Davos. The objectives of such campaigns were also lucidly homogenous—to incite for India a 'worldwide recognition among multinational corporations as well as the rich industrialized nations as an attractive destination for investments' and to project it as 'market-friendly'.[81] Though these campaigns were an intriguing subject in their own right, they were not sufficient for what I aimed to delve into, given I was rather interested in how the reforms have been marketed also for the Indian population. Campaigns like those of the India Brand Equity Foundation essentially appeared to exclude this dimension and sing songs to perceived external audiences, where no doubts could arise about the claims that India was changing.

This book makes a claim for the cause of material which has long been denied its due with regards to scholarship on India. It brings the two popular themes of market liberalization and secularism once again to the centre stage, albeit through the sole lens of the speeches of India's elected heads—the prime ministers.

Asia (London-New York: Routledge, 2003); A. Ayres and C.R. Mohan, *Power Realignments in Asia: China, India and the United States* (New York: Sage, 2009); M. Hanson et al., *Internal Conflict and Regional Security in South Asia: Approaches, Perspectives and Policies* (Geneva: United Nations Institute for Disarmament Research [UNIDIR], 2003); R.M. Basrur, *South Asia's Cold War Nuclear Weapons and Conflict in Comparative Perspective* (New York: Routledge, 2008).

[80] Here, Ravinder Kaur's research on the India Brand Equity Foundation's campaigns acquires prominence. See R. Kaur, 'Nation's Two Bodies: Rethinking the Idea of "New" India and its Other', *Third World Quarterly* 33, no. 4 (2012): 604.

[81] Kaur, 'Nation's Two Bodies'.

It is commonplace to find scholarship on a plethora of thematic foci dealing with India where excerpts from speeches/autobiographies of Nehru, or other prime figures in Indian politics, are utilized to formulate interesting opening vignettes of chapters. In historical accounts especially, the addresses of figures like Nehru and Gandhi have served as embellishments to support arguments forwarded by research that relies on other primary sources. Biographers of founding father figures and other political personalities do incorporate the public addresses of the same as an unavoidable source in presenting life trajectories. However, not many have treated the same as a source in itself. Though political rhetoric per se has been a fascination for many academic endeavours, this is a relatively understudied subject when it comes to India.

Some of the exceptions to this rule are Srirupa Roy's *Beyond Belief: India and the Politics of Postcolonial Nationalism*, Rochana Bajpai's *Debating Difference: Group Rights and Liberal Democracy in India*,[82] and Bernard Bate's *Tamil Oratory and the Dravidian Aesthetic: Democratic Practice in South India*.[83] Bate's work exclusively focuses on the transitions within Tamil oratory, as initiated by a relatively new generation of politicians since the 1940s who have innovatively adopted a style known as 'fine' or 'beautiful Tamil' (*centamil*) 'for its distinct literary virtuosity, poesy, and alluring evocation of a pure Tamil past.'[84] This 'Dravidian neoclassicism' or the 'centamil revolution', as Bate calls it, boasts of belonging to a longer tradition of utilizing an ancient mode of speech, in spite of being a fairly new convention. This research does share proximity with what I show in the case of the prime ministers in that it traces the continuities and discontinuities in oratorical styles and how newness is cloaked in what is presented as a homogenous 'past'. However, it has a strictly Tamil focus and Bate's energies are more invested in tracing how the elocutionary revolution or how 'the new, archaic, and distinctly literary mode of speech distinguished the new democrats who deployed it from a previous generation of relatively plain-spoken politicians'.[85] He thus

---

[82] Bajpai, *Debating Difference*.

[83] Bate, *Tamil Oratory and the Dravidian Aesthetic: Democratic Practice in South India* (Columbia: Columbia University Press, 2009).

[84] Bate, *Tamil Oratory and the Dravidian Aesthetic: Democratic Practice in South India*.

[85] Bate, *Tamil Oratory and the Dravidian Aesthetic: Democratic Practice in South India*, p. xv.

lucidly traces how this style of speech delivery simultaneously becomes a means to produce difference vis-à-vis 'ordinary' Tamil (*nadaimurai*) as well as the electorate at large. My analysis, though probing into similar questions of differences in vocabularies and styles of oratorical delivery, differs from Bate's insightful research, as it largely concerns itself with the overarching phenomenon of statist visions and the state's attempts to consolidate its authority through those visions, both nationally as well as internationally.

Rochana Bajpai's book deals with the question of group rights and democracy, but strictly through the lens of parliamentary debates in the Lok Sabha (or the Lower House of the Indian Parliament) and what the politicians have spoken in the house to make a cause for their statements and positions and which consequences this has borne for legislation at large. Though the chapters in this book also rely on such speeches delivered by the prime ministers in the parliament, they are not the only speeches used for the analysis. Roy's research focuses on the politics of nationalism as envisaged by the postcolonial state, especially in the eras of Jawaharlal Nehru and Indira Gandhi. Thus, here too, some chapters do utilize some of the addresses of the two prime ministers to present how postcolonial state formation was envisioned and performed in India after independence. However, this is in combination with a study of state-sponsored films and videos, school charts released by the state, a study of the Independence and Republic Day parades, etc. My assertion is that speeches of the prime ministers of India call for more academic attention as sources *in their own right*.

Rather than being viewed 'as a mirror of conclusions established elsewhere, by other means', speeches show the existence of 'an experimental zone where new possibilities and new identities are forged'.[86] Thus, they are not instruments that are made to fit into pre-grounded results relying on other sources, but rather become the sole modality for establishing what will be found out. What was said, to whom, where, and when—these seemingly banal questions thus emerge as imperative

---

[86] This is an argument made by Christopher Pinney for the cause of chromolithographs and calendar images in colonial and postcolonial India. However, it also applies aptly also to the addresses of the prime ministers, which have often been treated as 'banal' due to their overpowering, everyday pervasive presence. [See C. Pinney, *Photos of the Gods: The Printed Image and Political Struggle in India* (London: Reaktion Books, 2004).]

for treating the spoken text with the sensitivity that it demands rather than isolating it from its context.

For both the chosen topics of market liberalization and state secularism, debates on their pros and cons, the details they entail in terms of policy implications and technocratic truths, and their consequences have thrived in academic research. As stated, the neo-liberal economic reforms have been the subject of intensive research indeed from the perspective of what they entailed for the economy, strictly economic descriptions and speculations on their trajectory, debates on whether they should have been implemented, or if socialist developmentalism should have persisted, pros and cons of the reforms for different social strata of society, debates on whether 1991 is the landmark year that instrumentalized the reforms and if it deserves the label of being a caesura in Indian political and economic history, and finally the nature of opposition to the reforms in general. However, rarely has the *message* of the reforms, *as translated by their authors* to the audiences in and outside of India, been the subject of enquiry. This is all the more surprising given that a plethora of academic energies have been invested in understanding the working of Indian democracy and in qualifying its 'popular' nature. In the same context, it becomes all the more important to study how the technocratic truths of statist visions are translated for audiences so that transitions may become acceptable and familiar.

The same argument applies to the paradigm of secularism. An enormous body of work on the subject from a variety of disciplines, whose validity and utility I do not question in any way, has brought the subject to the forefront, especially after episodes such as Ayodhya and Gujarat. However, most of the literature on the subject largely bases its concerns on qualifying what Indian state secularism stands for in opposition to a homogenized 'Western' secularism. Here, producing difference appears to be the main priority in that secularism is presented either as a western imperialist project on Indian turf, an empty word hollowed of meaning, given it has no co-equivalent in any Indian languages, or, at best, a means to stage a distinction between Indian 'indigenous' understandings of religion as a 'way of life' from the 'insufficient', 'Western' understandings of the term.[87] Once again,

---

[87] See, for example, A. Nandy, 'The Politics of Secularism and the Recovery of Religious Tolerance', in R. Bhargava (ed.), *Secularism and its Critics* (New Delhi: Oxford University Press, 2005), pp. 321–43.

this book aims to address a fundamental question: especially in the face of events which attack the basis of a religiously pluralist nation, how do those who need to rescue the 'label' explain its necessity to audiences? And in order to achieve the same, how do they translate the notion for the nation?

The prime ministers, through their spoken word, may thus be viewed as the sensemaking and meaning-lending actors who translate the transforming politico-economic scenario to wider audiences. Their addresses provide a window to the repertoire of interpretative tools, the various tropes that are utilized to bridge the gap between economic transitions and the intuitive vocabulary of audiences. They show how attempts are made to recount sweeping economic changes so that they may be embraced by audiences as something familiar and 'Indian'. Thus, how the project of embedding this change in continuity is undertaken through the speeches is what this book seeks to uncover.

Srirupa Roy points out that these are times, '[...] when we know that if history is made from above, then it is undone from below; that for every dominating centre, there is a subversive margin. [...] If we want to breathe a new life into these tired clichés, then we cannot look away from the how and the why of the making and the centering.'[88] It is exactly with that 'above' and 'centre' that I engage, not to reinforce its validity, but rather to unravel the *how* and *why* of nation-state formation as envisioned by that 'above'. However, this is done here by focusing on certain very specific and recent developments in the Indian socio-economic and political landscape. What I address is not just an emerging representation of the nation, but more precisely the fundamental change(s) in that representation. This book thus contributes towards uncovering the subtleties of this process, and therein being the translator between a wider ongoing field that engages with debates on the reconfiguration of nation-states and how the same may be traced in the addresses of political heads. In doing so, I intend to channel the readers to the specific discursive historicity of the neo-liberal state in India and its synonymy to the narrative of 'India, the emerging economic power', as well as the statist vision of secularism and how that vision speaks to the trope of economic emergence.

[88] Roy, *Beyond Belief*, p. vii.

Interfacing the (E)merging Faces of India through Oratory

The Oxford English Dictionary defines an 'interface' as,

Noun
A point where two systems, subjects, organizations, etc. meet and interact;
A surface forming a common boundary between two portions of matter or space, for example between two immiscible liquids;
A device or program enabling a user to communicate with a computer;
A device or program for connecting two items of hardware or software so that they can be operated jointly or communicate with each other.

Verb
Interact with (another system, person, etc.)
Connect with (another computer or piece of equipment) by an interface.[89]

The book seeks to show how the oratory of Indian prime ministers constitutes an interface, 'a common boundary', a shared zone of contact, and a simultaneous modality of communication and translation *par excellence*. The spoken words of the prime ministers are the dual-faced lexical mirror that interfaces the perceived 'outside' and the 'inside', their addresses become the cement that enables interaction between these spatialities. This becomes lucidly graphic in their translation of state secularism to the putative outside and the putative inside (see Chapter 5). Each side of this two-way mirror reflects understandings of the paradigmatic notion that are derived from the particular context (internal and external). In internal settings, that is, when speaking to Indian audiences in and outside India, secularism acquires different ambivalent understandings that draw their resources from the Indian context of religious pluralism. In the external settings, the term is used as such to concretize the image of India, as being in ideological cohesion with the world as a 'secular' democracy. The ambivalences produced by the different understandings of the paradigm are never demarcated clearly in their contours within the addresses. Numerous Indian neologisms as well as vocabulary that draws upon a vibrantly pluralist context (both linguistic and religious) are used to re-evoke state secularism

---

[89] The Oxford English Dictionary.

as the founding principle of Indian democracy before Indian audiences. This repertoire may not necessarily conform to other understandings of the term in larger international scenarios embedded in nation-statist frameworks like the United Nations. Thus, while speaking to Indian audiences, an extensive range of neologisms which ground themselves in 'religious' tropes is employed, whereas in external scenarios, it suffices to state that 'India is secular', therein maintaining a silence on the chaos and ambivalences produced by explanations offered to internal audiences. The term 'secularism' thus becomes a terminological common ground on the basis of which the prime ministers produce parallel semantic zones, which allow for multiple comprehensions of the paradigm to coexist simultaneously.

A similar strategy and tactic is utilized to translate the neo-liberal reforms and the ensuing paradigmatic shifts in the Indian economy for the perceived external and internal audiences. Whereas the world is informed of how India is a nation in transition, a new emerging economy open to foreign investment, the putative inside is given a sense of cultural security by foregrounding that India's cultural core is unaffected, safe, and secure, in spite of market liberalization. Foreign investors are given the promise of a safe and secular democracy with an open economy, the glamour of seductive words and images that project the Indian economy as a glossy world to realize business success. Indians, on the other hand, are given the assurance that the reforms are a promise for a prosperous future, an enticing possibility to embrace growth, while simultaneously being rooted in the ontological security of a generalized 'civilizational past'.

Besides these spatially located demarcations, the words of the prime ministers also become a temporal interface between India's projected past and its projected future. They assist in constructing the image of India's new promising future, while also bridging with its past. Thus, words are used to generate a 'regime of historicity',[90] which François Hartog summarizes as 'methods of relating to time: forms of experiencing time, here and elsewhere, today and yesterday, ways of being in time'.[91] One of the construed regimes of historicity reflect the vantage

---

[90] F. Hartog, *Régimes d'Historicité: Présentisme et Expériences du Temps* (Paris: Seuil, 2003).

[91] Hartog, 'Time and Heritage', *Museum International* 57, no. 3 (2005): 7–18.

point of the present, which is 'the focal point of the representation of time; the past and the future are represented, thought of, and felt as departing from and returning to the present.'[92] Here, the emphasis flexes on the *here and now*. Within this discursive depiction of temporality, the past and the future are seen as departing from and arriving at the present moment of India's shining arrival in the world. This regime of historicity thus indicates how time is produced from the perspective of the present by instrumentalizing the categories of past and future in order 'to determine what the present is or is not'.[93] Each side of the dual-faced mirror, that is, the interface thus duly reflects back utopias and heterotopias of the past and the future.

Another form of temporality that finds expression and becomes the interface between the past and the present relates to how in varied contexts the prime ministers conjure the dreams of growth embedded in an idealized future. The shadows that lurk stubbornly around market liberalization and its ensuing economic inequalities are flattened and cloaked in the promise of a prosperous future for all. Trickle down is explained through such promises, in effect relegating those who are not the immediate winners of market liberalization to a 'waiting room of history',[94] to borrow Dipesh Chakrabarty's metaphor, with the promise of 'not yet, but for sure in the future'.

In his research on Dravidianist oratory in contemporary Tamil Nadu, 'a speech genre modeled on a written form that sounds old', Bernard Bate shows how politicians claim to evoke 'a pure Tamil past' by using fine or beautiful Tamil (*centamil*), a relatively new practice that began with the advent of mass democratic politics in the 1940s. He states,

> But modernity is perhaps even more often embodied in new things that appear very old, things that look both forward and backward, containing what Milton Singer called Janus-faced signs (1972: 400). Neoclassicism and the neogothic are the standard architectural examples of this trope,

---

[92] A. Hannoum, 'What Is an Order of Time? Review of Hartog, F., *Régimes d'Historicité: Présentisme et Expériences du Temps*, Paris: Seuil 2003', *History and Theory*, 47(3): 458, 2008.

[93] Hannoum, 'What Is an Order of Time?'.

[94] D. Chakrabarty, *Provincializing Europe: Post-colonial Thought and Historical Difference* (Princeton: Princeton University Press, 2000), p. 7.

styles that suggest not the now-and-henceforth, but a now that is intimately and organically connected to the past.[95]

In a similar vein, the chapters in this book will show how transformation in the form of the neo-liberal reforms is naturalized by borrowing heavily from a vocabulary that relies on a generalized, museified, and selective past. In this regime of temporality, the prime ministers evoke a repertoire of resources like figures of the national hero (Nehru and Gandhi), ideas and slogans that are seen as fundamentally indigenous to Indian political thought (for example Gandhi's *swadeshi*), and projections of a neo-liberalized economic present that paradoxically enough rely on vocabularies of a Nehruvian-socialist past.

As these internal tussles are interfaced by conjuring multiple temporalities within the ambit of Indian listeners, externally, the same production of temporality is utilized to indicate that India is now 'catching up' with the world, finally achieving coevalness with the world economy, to use Johannes Fabian's insightful words.[96] Speeches thus become the interface through which the categories of a flattened and homogenized, 'civilizational' past, as well as a generalizable shining future get to exist simultaneously.

The speeches also become an interface for topically cementing the two evergreen themes of state secularism and market liberalization. The chapters that follow will show how the prime ministers render the neo-liberal economic reforms inevitable and irrefutable by projecting them as the only valid modality for India to realize its economic destiny of growth and emergence. Fundamental to this discourse is that secularism is produced as a precondition for India's emergence. It is lexically conjured as the sole means, the fundamental basis for the existence and essence of a pluralist India. Thus, before Indian audiences, it is envisaged as a necessity to keep the road to emergence sanitized of internal strife, a unifier of the nation otherwise characterized by multiple subnational identifications. The two themes are also entangled through the oratory of the prime ministers when they use development as a healthy agenda that demands complete national attention, especially in the face

---

[95] Bate, *Tamil Oratory and the Dravidian Aesthetic*, p. 185.
[96] J. Fabian, *Time and the Other: How Anthropology Makes its Object* (New York: Columbia University Press, 1983).

of religious tensions, as a means to divert public attention to 'larger' causes of sustainable growth. This entanglement is, for instance, graphically visible in the following words of the current PM Modi, which were part of his election campaign speeches—'Secularism to me means India First'. The statement aimed at diverting the attention of audiences away from questions of religious difference and communal and caste politics to the overarching agenda of development for all (see Chapter 5). The slogan enabled Modi to use a new vocabulary to talk about a new India whereas simultaneously producing a necessary politics of difference with his opponents. For the putative inside it thus became a means to show that development was the priority of Modi's party, regardless of a citizen's religious background. For the putative outside, it became the necessary paradigm to project India a 'safe' democracy (utilizing the internationally revered vocabularies of liberalism, pluralism and democracy). State secularism was thus conjured as a pre-requisite to prove to the world that India is a safe democracy that offers the viable environment of religious tolerance and peace for investors to venture in its open markets. The illustration shows how secularism and market liberalization are woven and welded together rhetorically for both the external audiences as well as for the Indian population, whereby one is inextricably connected to and even an essential requisite for the other, both feeding into the discourse of an Emerging India.

Speeches do not just lexically spring the nation into existence; they are the material interfaces that produce the contact points, the common ground, the connection, and therein the necessary communication that resides in the hyphen of the nation-state. They are part of the everyday statist practices that manufacture the coincidence of the state and the nation. An ongoing discursive process, they produce the sanctity of the state as the authoritative consolidator, unifier, and governor of the nation—the legitimate 'voice' of the nation. Political oratory, especially of the elected head of the state, can thus become a vibrant arena to see how practices of 'nationalizing the state' and 'institutionalizing the nation',[97] as mentioned earlier, come to be conjoined.

The addresses of the prime ministers are thus an assemblage, whereby the themes of state secularism and market liberalization, the

---

[97] Roy, *Beyond Belief*, p. x.

putative external and the internal, the generalized past and the aspirational future are made to *merge* so that India can (*E*)*merge*.

A Note on the Public Speech of the Prime Ministers

This book argues for paying due scholarly attention to the immense weight that the spoken word, especially that of the politician, occupies in India. This requires an attentive evaluation of the longstanding history of orality and aurality in the Indian subcontinent (see Chapter 1). As in numerous other parts of the world, in India too, politicians speak in light of their particular tradition(s) of orality—a hitherto unexplored arena of shifting tropes, styles, strategies, and tactics.

The words of founding father figures in multiple postcolonial sites have been the interface that has actively translated their visions and nation-building schemes into popular lexical memory. This practice of speaking, and therein being heard and known, also diffuses in contemporary Indian politics in a plethora of ways. During election campaigns, it is a common sight to find large playgrounds, public parks, etc. reserved much in advance by political parties where speeches will be delivered and loudspeakers will intensely govern the soundscape. Candidates contesting for elections untiringly travel through their electoral constituencies to address audiences in such open spaces with strong microphones assisting their voices, sometimes even rendering them hard to ignore. While this can be observed in many parts of the world, an Indian specificity lies in the fact that during these periods elaborate and repetitively recited slogans are developed as part of the message of the parties. These slogans, though sometimes written on hoardings, posters, and party banners, mainly become popular in that they are repetitively *spoken* out for and repeated by audiences. Aural perception, a repetitive encounter with someone speaking, has been a popular modality to make people *learn* the message of the politician.

Addresses of the prime ministers formulate the most public and visible statements of an Indian politician both nationally as well as internationally. Their importance as one of the most popular modalities of communicating statist visions in India is confirmed by the fact that prime ministers are often judged in terms of *how often* they speak as well as through the prism of their rhetorical victories and oratorical talent, a point that I develop further in chapter 1.

Some of the ensuing issues related to addresses that I collected from various sources in India call for attention. First, the speeches delivered by politicians are often carefully designed, structured, and worded by an entire editorial team of experts. They represent an assemblage more than the expressions of an individual. In that sense, the Prime Minister's Office in India may be viewed as an assemblage in its own right. The question of ghostwriters then becomes immanent. This book lays its emphasis on the *office* of the prime minister per se. This does not imply that individual personalities disappear. There are many cues to trace the signature statements of the four personalities in their addresses. However, as the focal point in question is how these prime ministers manufacture, fabricate, re-shape, re-form the image of the nation through the cross-cutting themes of state secularism and market liberalization, and in doing so how they consolidate the authority of the state and their governments, their addresses are dealt with as words that are the official statements of the office of the Prime Minister. Readers are thus invited to deflect their attention to the office rather than solely the personality of the leader, though the two are not mutually exclusive.

The second problematic relates to the 'missing' addresses, those that could not be procured either as published volumes released by the Information and Broadcasting Ministry or from the collections of the different ministries. Especially with regards to the topic of state secularism, I was initially unable to trace the addresses delivered by Prime Minister A.B. Vajpayee in the immediate aftermath of the Godhra incident in Gujarat and the ensuing Hindu Muslim riots of 2002. Aware from my own memory of having 'watched' and read the same at the time of these events in India, I could not believe that there was no record of the same in any of the ministries which usually archive even the minutest details of parliamentary debates that usually last for hours. The 'missing speeches' soon became an obsession and led to what seemed to be a personal treasure hunt. In 2005, the government of India enacted the Right to Information Act[98] that marked a shift from the previous

---

[98] 'An Act to provide for setting out the practical regime of right to information for citizens to secure access to information under the control of public authorities, in order to promote transparency and accountability in the working of every public authority, the constitution of a Central Information Commission and State Information Commissions and for matters connected therewith or incidental thereto.' Right to Information Act, 2005, Act No. 22 of

Official Secrets Act, 1923, which put restrictions on information disclosure in India. The act enables any citizen of India to ask any 'public authority' (a government body or an instrumentality of the state) for information which would be provided within a period of thirty days (if not a concrete result, then an explanation of why the delay at the very least). This opened the possibility to retrieve the speeches. However, my attempts have led to an ongoing pursuance of the matter since January 2012 under the reference number (RTI/314/2012-pmr) with no consequences so far, leaving me with the option to either doubt the postal services in India or to conclude that a bureaucratic loophole is all that can explain why these speeches were never archived systematically. One of these crucial speeches, delivered by prime minister Vajpayee at a BJP party meeting in Goa shortly after the events in Gujarat, was however, rather recently released online, also a consequence of an RTI application, therein enabling that it could eventually be incorporated in the analysis.

The third issue relates to the language of the speeches. The excerpts cited throughout the chapters are exclusively in English. However, at least, with regards to the speeches that were delivered for the Indian audiences, the multilingual environment merits attention. Speeches are usually archived in Hindi and English for state records, even though it must be noted that three of the concerned prime ministers have been fluent in, and also delivered speeches in, more than just these two languages.[99] For the sake of consistency and readership, all excerpts are cited in English, numerous being official translations, as provided by the published volumes. The addresses were, however, collected both in English as well as Hindi, and often counter-referenced for the analysis.

This is an important caveat, especially in the context of chapter 5, which deals with state secularism. As the chapter will show, the interplay

---

2005, released by the Ministry of Law and Justice, Government of India, see online: http://rti.gov.in/, (accessed 16 June 2012).

[99] Manmohan Singh in Hindi, English, and Punjabi, whereas P.V. Narasimha Rao, being fluent in seventeen languages, including Spanish, French, German, Arabic, Telugu, Hindi, Urdu, Oriya, Marathi, Bengali, Gujarati, Tamil, etc., was known to have addressed audiences in numerous languages depending on the context. Similarly the current Prime Minister Narendra Modi has delivered speeches in Hindi, English, and Gujarati.

with Hindi and English has contributed to the development of a unique 'Indian' vocabulary to explain the paradigm of secularism. Thus, even though the 'official' India appears to be speaking English (here, I mean specifically when they speak in international contexts), concepts are not simply explained in a monolingual environment, rather what emerges is an eclectic mix of terminology that borrows heavily from other Indian languages like Sanskrit, Hindi, Punjabi, and Urdu. This makes multiple meanings and understandings to emerge; some of the terms used in English have different careers than those of Hindi terms. It is exactly for uncovering how this multilingualism becomes a consistently adopted strategy, an advantage that leaves room for semantic manoeuver that this book profited from cross-referencing the addresses delivered in Hindi and those in English (for details, see Chapter 5).

Besides, the poetry and prose written by A.B. Vajpayee (written and published only in Hindi) was also used to compensate for the temporal gap of certain missing speeches. Lastly, it ought to be mentioned that the advent of new social media has added an entirely new dimension to how speeches are accessed, provided, and reproduced on several platforms. This is especially true in the case of the current prime minister, Narendra Modi, who is highly popular for his usage of platforms like Twitter, Facebook, his own website, etc. Though a fascinating subject in its own right, this book limits its scope and does not delve into the new mediatization techniques employed by governments to reach audiences, hoping that this will evoke the interest of future scholarship on public oratory.

Four Prime Ministers

Pamulaparti Venkata Narasimha Rao (P.V. Narasimha Rao) (1921–2004) of the Indian National Congress party, a lawyer-turned-politician, served as the ninth prime minister of India from 1991–96. Given that the neo-liberal economic reforms were introduced during his term, he is often termed as the 'father of Indian economic reforms'. The government headed by Rao saw the Congress only as a minority party. Rao was the first non Gandhi-Nehru family prime minister who served a complete term of five years, and the first prime minister from South India (Andhra Pradesh, today's Telangana). A prolific writer, Rao is famous for knowing seventeen languages (among the Indian languages,

Telugu, Hindi, Urdu, Oriya, Marathi, Bengali, Gujarati, and Tamil, and foreign languages include English, French, Arabic, Spanish, German, Greek, Latin, and Persian).

Atal Bihari Vajpayee (A.B. Vajpayee) (1924*), a journalist who was one of the founding members of the erstwhile Bharatiya Jana Sangha party, and later a leading figure in the Bharatiya Janata Party (BJP), served as the tenth prime minister of India. He has, however, held the office thrice (non-consecutive terms): for thirteen days in 1996, thirteen months in 1998–99, and finally a full five-year term from 1999–2004. His term witnessed some crucial events such as the Kargil confrontation with non-uniformed Pakistani soldiers who had infiltrated the Kashmir valley border to occupy several border hilltops, the second round of nuclear tests (Pokhran II, also called *Operation Shakti*) which were conducted in 1998, the hijack of the Indian Airlines IC 814 from Kathmandu to Delhi which forced the release of five terrorists in Indian prisons, the attack on the parliament three months after the 9/11 attacks in the US, and the Gujarat riots of 2002, which followed the burning of the coach S6 of the *Sabarmati Express* in the town of Godhra. The second term of thirteen months saw Vajpayee lead a coalition government called the National Democratic Alliance (NDA), which could not sustain itself in power for five years due to the withdrawal of support from the All India Anna Dravida Munnetra Kazhagam (AIADMK) party under J. Jayalalitha. In the ensuing elections, the BJP was once again elected the single largest party, and formed the coalition National Democratic Alliance with Vajpayee as the prime minister. Vajpayee was known to be a prolific speaker and has been famous for his poetry in Hindi.

Manmohan Singh (1932*) from the Indian National Congress was the thirteenth prime minister of India. Singh completed his second term in 2014, being the only prime minister after Jawaharlal Nehru and Indira Gandhi to achieve the same. Before the office, Singh, an economist, held numerous positions during the 1970s and 80s, which include Chief Economic Advisor (1972–76), Governor of the Reserve Bank of India (1982–85), and Planning Commission head (1985–87). During Rao's term, Singh served as the Finance Minister of India and is largely credited to be the architect of the neo-liberal economic reforms. The active entry of Sonia Gandhi (wife of former prime minister Rajiv Gandhi) during the campaigning for the 2004 general assembly elections culminated in the Congress emerging as the single largest political party. However, in a surprise decision, Sonia Gandhi, as chairperson of the party, announced Singh as the prime ministerial candidate. The Congress led coalition United Progressive Alliance (UPA) served a complete five year term (2004-09) and Singh continued to serve as the PM after the Congress's next victory in the general assembly elections in 2009, which led to the coalition termed as United Progressive Alliance II (UPA II). His term witnessed some important legislations like the Right to Information Act (2005), the National Rural Employment Guarantee Act (2005), the National Rural Health Mission scheme whereas externally his government was known for the formulation of collectives such as the BRICs and the Indo-US Civil Nuclear Agreement with the United States (popularly called the Nuclear Deal), which made India an exception as a country to engage in civil nuclear energy exchange with the US in spite of not being a signing member of the Comprehensive Test Ban Treaty (CTBT).

Narendra Damodardas Modi (1950[*]) of the Bharatiya Janata Party, is the fourteenth and the current prime minister of India. He was the chief minister of the state of Gujarat from 2001–14. Infamous for the Gujarat riots of 2002 during his chief ministership of the state, Modi's election campaign for prime ministership witnessed a drastic transition in his public image supported by a new thrust in the mass-mediatization of Indian politics. This incorporated a hitherto unprecedented combination of relying upon both traditional media, especially vernacular print media, mass campaign rallies attended by millions, unending touring across the country, and untiring speaking, as well as rigorous new social media activity through Facebook, a personal website, blogs, and Twitter. He is the first prime minister since 1984, also the first in the list of prime ministers whose speeches this book analyses, to have won a simple absolute majority and who resides on a non-coalition government.

His election campaign focused enormously on what was dubbed as 'the Gujarat model', making development the primary agenda (by giving the example of the state's, now often challenged, progress). This became a means to divert public attention to 'growth', similar to but with a much more energized vigour, in comparison to his predecessors, from the communal politics of caste and religion based subnational identities. It also served to reform Modi's own image, as the man presiding over the Gujarat government at the time of the riots in 2002, to a prime minister for all. During his ongoing term, he has introduced several slogans and campaigns that call for systematic attention—'Make in India', 'My Government', 'Swachch Bharat' (Clean India), and 'Smart City' being some. Internally, Modi has returned to the evergreen topics of poverty eradication, women's equality, cleaning campaigns, and sustainable and inclusive growth, whereas externally he invites foreign investors. As aptly stated, 'In fact, he talks poverty at home, and business abroad.'[100]

As this volume proceeds for publication, Modi is persistently in news, both nationally and internationally, for the recent demonetization of the five hundred and one thousand rupees banknotes (announced on 8 November 2016), a step that was initially justified as a measure to curtail black money and terrorism sponsorship networks, and later as a move towards a cashless economy.[101] As recently as 2017, his party the BJP has emerged victorious in the state legislative assembly elections in Uttar Pradesh, Uttarakhand, Gujarat, Goa, Manipur, and Himachal Pradesh, with Modi personally seen as extensively investing his time in the party's campaigns. Much will need to be reviewed systematically in this direction, after this book has already made it to bookshelves. I have nonetheless incorporated the addresses of the current prime minister up to 15 August 2016 to open perspectives for new research and, at the same time, weave his rhetoric into a larger context of the oratorical traditions of the speaking prime ministers.

Preview of Chapters

Chapter 1 traces the distinct legacy of the prime ministerial office and the tradition of public speech in India to ground why this book utilizes speeches as sources and why only those of the prime ministers. The first section of the chapter traces how Jawaharlal Nehru, the first prime minister of independent India, negotiated the executive powers of the office to make it the most powerful one in the cabinet, hierarchically a higher

---

[100] R. Jagannathan, 'Who Is the Real Narendra Modi: A "Communal Czar" or an "Inclusive Icon"?', *Making Sense of Modi's India* (Noida: HarperCollins Publishers India, 2016), p. 84.

[101] N.D. Modi, *Mann ki Baat*, address to the nation on All India Radio, 25 December 2016, http://www.narendramodi.in/mann-ki-baat, accessed on 26 December 2016.

'First Among Equals'. It then extends into how his persona was used to give the office an irrefutable status. In that sense, his ideas were projected as the founding principles of Indian democracy, whereas his own public presence diffused into a number of state rituals. Nehru's legacy is also important because it laid the basis of what was defined as a 'New India'. Thus, in order to understand the underlying continuities and transitions between what Nehru called the 'New India' and what is envisioned as the 'New India' by prime ministers after 1991,[102] understanding Nehru's conceptions and outlooks becomes inevitable. The chapter traces how Nehru's visions (such as the Nehruvian consensus or the staging of the 'Unity in Diversity' master trope) and his pervasive public presence, textured the office as that of a teacher and caretaker, therein rendering it the face of the nation. As the following prime ministers have often been judged through the prism of oratorical styles and the aesthetics of public presence so well established by Nehru, this section also locates how the current prime minister, Narendra Modi, attempts to entangle and distance himself from Nehruvian styles of communicating with the Indian population. The chapter will show how, even if Modi appears to disentangle himself from Nehruvian aesthetics of style and speech as also his repertoire and vocabulary (for a detailed analysis see chapters 2, 3, and 4), *the grammar and protocols* of engagement with audiences appear to nonetheless be very similar. The second section of the chapter tracks the gravity of the spoken word in India by embedding it in its long-standing cultural history of orality and aurality. The aim of this section is to elucidate the cultural context in which the prime ministers' speeches come to acquire immense weight. A concluding part of this section brings the two themes of the Prime Minister's Office and public speech in India together and shows how the prime minister is also the tongue of the nation, therein grounding the importance of the prime ministers' speeches as material to be studied in its own right.

Chapters 2, 3, and 4 concretely ask how India's prime ministers have oratorically explained and defended the reforms of 1991 before both perceived 'internal' and 'external' audiences. The analysis has shown that in nearly all speeches explaining or justifying the reforms, both temporal (Chapters 2 and 3) as well as spatial (Chapter 4) references have

---

[102] These continuities and discontinuities are summed up and discussed in the general conclusion.

been rhetorically construed and instrumentalized to meet the aim of 'inevitablizing' their introduction. In line with De Certeau's[103] distinction between 'tactics' and 'strategy', with 'tactics' referring to opportunistic action within a temporal sequence of events, and 'strategy' being opportunistic action depending on a particular spatial arrangement, the prime ministers' oratorical moves related to the moment of the reforms have been described as 'temporalizing tactics' (Chapters 2 and 3) and 'spatializing strategies' (Chapter 4) respectively. The titles given to these chapters echo of Johannes Fabian's *Time and the Other*,[104] a theoretical framework which repetitively surfaces in Chapters 2, 3, and 4. In view of this, the analysis uncovers the discursive making of the reforms as propagated by those who have authored and had to justify them. The neo-liberal reforms were not accepted homogenously and produced skepticism at many ends—ranging from threatened public sector enterprises, discomfort on the increasing role to be played by foreign investors on Indian turf, right up to allegations of them being 'anti-people'. Rather than analysing any technocratic justifications of change, the intention of Chapter 2 is to screen how change itself, as a temporal momentum that challenges, if not threatens, an existing order of cultural security,[105] is explained and justified so that it may be inevitablized.

---

[103] De Certeau discusses the difference between tactics and strategy as follows, 'Strategies pin their hopes on the resistance that the establishment of a place offers to the erosion of time; tactics on a clever utilization of time, on the opportunities it presents and also of the play that it introduces into the foundations of power.' Thus, the word 'strategic' is used to highlight a more spatially informed technique of communication used by the prime ministers, whereas tactical on occasions where temporality becomes the analytical axis. See M. De Certeau, *The Practice of Everyday Life* (Berkeley: University of California Press, 1984), pp. 39–40.

[104] Fabian, *Time and the Other*. Chapters (2, 3, and 4) will elucidate how the prime ministers legitimize reforms by embedding them in *time* and, at the same time by using spatializing strategies to produce India's coevalness with the *other*, that is, to show how India is catching up with the 'developed' world. Hence, they emphasize how the reforms are rendered secure by producing 'Time and the Other'.

[105] For the concept of 'cultural security', J. Friedman and S. Randeria (eds), *Worlds on the Move: Globalization, Migration, and Cultural Security* (London: I.B. Tauris, 2004).

Chapter 2 thus shows how the present is thought of, narrated, and made real by producing the future. Here, the 'Details of Desire' and 'Making Growth Human' become the catchphrases for weaving the future into depictions of India's economic emergence. The last section illustrates how, paradoxically enough, imaginations of the future derive their legitimacy from the vocabulary of a socialist past. It is here that I seek to show how the newness of reforms is taken away by relying heavily on a repertoire of resources that embed that newness into something very old, familiar, and Indian. This section becomes the bridge to Chapter 3, which illustrates which specific resources from a selective past become the means to justify change and render it irrefutable. The chapter concludes with the temporalizing tactics of the current prime minister, Narendra Modi. Chapter 4 delves into spatializing strategies—how, for the putative outside, the rhetoric of prime ministers has pushed for announcing India as a changed nation that invites foreign investment in its open markets and showing how India is now gaining coevalness with the world. It shows how for the putative inside, the prime ministers produce the urgency of change in the form of reforms by projecting a transforming and fast globalizing world that necessitates that India also accepts change. At the same time, these audiences are given the assurance that even as India embraces transformations, its cultural and civilizational core remains secure and unshakeable.

In a similar vein as Chapters 2, 3, and 4, Chapter 5 traces how the modality of political oratory is operationalized for the sake of state secularism. Averting the focus from the sheer semantics-related discussions of the term in an often-generalized Indian context, this part turns our attention to what is actively done with the concept by the speakers. It investigates how the four prime ministers profile India as a 'secular' nation. It will be elucidated how the discursive production of Indian state secularism converges with the discursive staging of India's emergence, both for perceived 'internal' audiences as well as perceived 'external' audiences. The events of Ayodhya (1992) and Gujarat (2002) and the episodes of extreme religious strife intensified the urgency to reweave the idea of the 'national'. It is here that secularism became an important discursive stake. The prime ministers' public speeches have tried to rescue the unity of pluralist India through the ideal. Besides, after 1991 and the introduction of the reforms, this image of a socially and culturally unified and safe India has been crucial for the programme of 'opening up' the economy to foreign investment. Any destabilizing event prevents the same. Profiling India as secular has thus been a means to stage this stability, and therein materialize the future of India as emerging. The first section shows how numerous definitions, phrases, and terms, which borrow their vocabulary from the Indian context of religious pluralism, are used to make an argument for India's secularism before 'internal' audiences. The second, shorter part shows how the 'outside' is presented a secular and democratic India, which is in ideological cohesion with the world. A separate third part has been added to the chapter to present an analysis of the current prime minister, Narendra Modi's speeches. In the fourth section, the continuities and discontinuities in the oratory of the four prime ministers are presented systematically. In the concluding section, the two contexts of the outside and the inside are brought together and it will be illustrated how the prime ministers conjure temporal and spatial orders to forward the cause of Indian secularity. This implies how, depending on the context (therein the audience), and the references made in the name of a putative past and a putative future, the prime ministers profile India as secular. It will also be shown how the discursive staging of an 'Emerging India' intertwines with the projections of a secular India.

In the conclusion, I return to the findings of Chapters 2, 3, 4, and 5. Based on the same, I trace the noticeable consistencies and inconsistencies in the oratory of the prime ministers. Though Narendra Modi will be still in office as this book sees its release, and a more nuanced study of his speeches will be a welcome engagement at the end of his five-year term, strategies and tactics that have so far informed his oratory are nonetheless incorporated into this discussion. This precisely to not produce yet another tiring cliché of Modi's media magic since 2014, which conjures his uniqueness as a speaker, an outsider to Delhi, a media-active prime minister, but rather to show how his oratory in fact belongs to a longer tradition of the speaking, public presence of prime ministers. The more interesting facet to unravel then is not how what he stands for, does, or says what is new, but rather how he adds the perception of newness to a much older political practice. The conclusion then proceeds to a transversal discussion of how Nehru's 'New India' differs or conforms to the 'new New India'. How are the coordinates of the post-reform India different from the Nehruvian vocabulary of nation-building? And how can we trace this discursive difference through the oratory of the four prime ministers after 1991?

This section also reviews the results of the chapters in light of what is said and written about 'Emerging India', a discursive phenomenon embedded in the wider context of the new, market-driven media sphere, through sources I provocatively call 'airport literature'. Television, but also this literary genre, are part of this new media universe, which is itself a major result of the reforms it celebrates. The Indian nation, including the sign of its very name, has become a marketable commodity, a brand indeed, which promises people with dynamic perspectives of reliable growth and a visionary future. As can be seen from bookstores and their bestsellers' sections in airports and shopping malls, even in 2017, this wider discourse remains seemingly unmitigated. It presents 'Emerging India' as a tale of irresistible attire, of promising bliss, and miraculous stability, which also the prime ministers are to tell and sell. Finally, we return to how nation-states recalibrate and reconfigure their legitimacy in a world in persistent transition—what has been the nature of this reconfiguration in the Indian case, and what can we learn about how the prime ministers re-evoke and re-form resources to assert their authority as the voice of the nation through the speeches?

By analysing the rhetoric of four prominent prime ministers who 'speak' the nation, this book will show how they engage with the dual process of the simultaneous production of stateness and nationhood. In other words, how their rhetoric on the one hand produces *Indianness and India* itself, and, on the other hand, how their 'representations of nationhood' become the means of establishing themselves as the 'nation's authoritative representative'.[106] Thus, in narrating the nation, the heads of these governments not just produce notions of nationness, but also fabricate the legitimacy of their governments as a repository of truth, their own image as the agents of the nation.

---

[106] Roy, *Beyond Belief,* p. 14.

1

The Prime Minister's Legacy and Traditions of Public Speech in India

Introduction

> Words are tricky things always. In the final analysis the word is the biggest thing in the world. All the knowledge we have, everything we possess, is a collection of words which represent ideas.
>
> —Jawaharlal Nehru (excerpt from a speech delivered in October 1954)

The Office of the prime minister (PMO) and the tradition(s) of public speech/oratory have a distinct legacy in India, which cannot be overlooked in an analysis that aims to foreground the gravity of the *speaking* prime ministers. This legacy is directly linked to how Jawaharlal Nehru, the first prime minister of independent India, re-engineered the role and powers of the office in the newly constituted postcolonial state but also how his oratorical legacy continues to impact the expectations accorded to the speeches of the successive prime ministers.

The first section of the chapter traces how Nehru negotiated the executive powers of the office to make it the most powerful one in the cabinet, hierarchically, a higher 'First Among Equals'. It then extends into how his persona was used to give the office an irrefutable status. In that sense, his ideas were projected as the founding principles of Indian democracy, whereas his own public presence diffused into a number of state rituals. Nehru's legacy is also important because it laid the basis of what was defined as a 'New India'. Thus, in order to understand the underlying continuities and transitions between what Nehru called the 'New India' and what is envisioned as the 'New India' by the prime ministers after 1991,[1] understanding Nehru's conceptions and outlooks becomes inevitable. The second section of the chapter tracks the gravity of the spoken word in India by embedding it in its long-standing cultural history of orality and aurality. The aim of this section is to elucidate the cultural context in which the prime ministers' speeches come to acquire immense weight. A concluding part of this section brings the two themes of the PMO and public speech in India together and grounds the importance of the prime ministers' speeches as significant material to be studied in its own right.

The Nation's Face: Nehru and the Prime Ministerial Legacy

Strengthening the Executive

In the aftermath of independence, the political leadership of India, which had been at the apex of the nationalist movement for independence, opted for the Westminster system in congruence with that existing in Britain. This implied a constitutional heritage as per the British Parliamentary system of democracy, retained by a newly established state. Kumarasingham, in a comparative analysis of the political legacy of the British Empire in India and Sri Lanka, categorizes it as the Westminster model going east. 'The *Eastminsters* are countries in South Asia that retained the Westminster system but where it was transformed for local conditions [...] countries that, once independent, maintained core institutions and conventions of the Westminster system and former colonial power to remain part of the family while having different operational contexts and sometimes beliefs.'[2]

---

[1] These continuities and discontinuities are summed up and discussed in the general conclusion.

[2] H. Kumarasingham, *A Political Legacy of the British Empire: Power and the Parliamentary System in Post-Colonial India and Sri Lanka* (London, New York: I.B. Tauris, 2013), p. 5.

These subtle transformations of the model also offer a detailed insight into how the role of the Indian executive was re-engineered by the first prime minister, Jawaharlal Nehru, in ways that the office of the prime minister came to occupy ascendancy over those of other cabinet portfolios.

Though the topic of parliamentary democracy in India is an extensively researched subject[3] and does not require a lengthy introduction here, one aspect of the development of India's parliamentary system that deserves mention is the negotiation of its form during 1947–52. In 1950, India became a republic and adopted a lengthy written constitution. In 1952, the first nationwide elections based on the principle of universal adult franchise were held. It is during this interim phase that the PMO was defined in terms of its authority by Nehru.

In these nascent years of a heady post-independence era, Nehru would negotiate 'the ultimate power of the central executive, of which Prime Ministerial dominance was one of the central motifs'.[4] During the seventeen years of his term, Nehru not only held the position of India's top-ranking, popularly elected political head, but melded this with several other important ministry portfolios, which enabled him to enormously empower the PMO. The first move in this direction came when Nehru also became the president of his party, the Congress (the ruling political party), in 1950. In December, the same year, Sardar Vallabh Bhai Patel, the deputy prime minister, who had been in charge of the Home Ministry and the States Ministry, died. Patel was viewed as Nehru's fiercest competitor and perhaps the only political figure

---

[3] See B. Chandra and M. Mukherjee, *India after Independence, 1947–2000* (New Delhi: Penguin Books, 1988); A. Kohli, 'Introduction', in A. Kohli (ed.), *The Success of India's Democracy* (Cambridge: Cambridge University Press, 2001), p. 1–20; A. Kohli, *Democracy and Discontent: India's Growing Crisis of Governability* (Cambridge: Cambridge University Press, 1991); A. Kohli (ed.), *India's Democracy: An Analysis of Changing State-Society Relations* (Princeton: Princeton University Press, 1988); R. Kothari, *Politics in India* (New Delhi: Orient Longman, 1970); A. Varshney, *Democracy, Development, and the Countryside: Urban–Rural Struggles in India* (Cambridge: Cambridge University Press, 1995); S. Sarkar, 'Indian Democracy: The Historical Inheritance', in A. Kohli (ed.), *The Success of India's Democracy* (Cambridge: Cambridge University Press, 2001), pp. 23–46.

[4] Kumarasingham, *A Political Legacy of the British Empire*, p. 47.

who could match up to his nationwide popularity, particularly owing to his stronghold over the Congress Party. Zakaria writes, '(...) Patel died and with him the only serious challenge to Nehru's leadership in the Congress ended. Nothing could thereafter happen in the Congress without Nehru's approval; he was the lord and master of the party.'[5] In fact, no one was selected to succeed Patel as the deputy prime minister. This office was revived only in 1967 under Indira Gandhi's leadership.

In his capacity as the president of the Congress and the prime minister of India, Nehru founded the Indian Planning Commission in 1950, an advisory collective incharge of economic planning and development issues, best known for its Five Year Plans. These plans were envisioned to outline the programme of economic self-sufficiency, a prime agenda of the new postcolonial state. The commission, which Nehru chaired personally, was also termed as a 'super cabinet' in that it often made decisions related to the economy without any participation of the other cabinet ministers. On occasions, decisions were passed by the Planning Commission without any consultations with the finance minister. This implied that the deliberations of the Commission were an exclusive affair, outside the purview of control of the rest of the government ministries and single-handedly coordinated by Nehru himself. Besides the two, Nehru also held the portfolios of External Affairs, Commonwealth Relations, and Scientific Research.

During the interim years (1947–52), until the constitution was officially formalized (1950) and the first elections were held (1952), Nehru is known to have had several disagreements with influential Congress personalities who called for higher horizontal accountability both within and outside the cabinet. The biggest critics were the deputy prime minister, Patel, and the first president, Rajendra Prasad. On one such instance of conflict with Patel, Nehru is even seen as categorizing the prime minister as the 'first among equals' 'with the power to act when and how he chooses'.[6] The feud related to Nehru's interference

---

[5] R. Zakaria, 'Introduction', in R. Zakaria (ed.), *A Study of Nehru* (New Delhi: Times of India Publication, 1959), p. 56.

[6] In a letter addressed to Gandhi where Nehru elaborately describes the feud between Patel and himself, he writes, 'As I concieve it, the Prime Minister's role is, and should be, an important role. He is not only a figurehead but a person who should be more responsible than anyone else for the general trend of policy and and for the coordination of the work of various government

and claim for greater control in Patel's ministry. Patel's response was as follows.

> That conception, if accepted would raise the Prime Minister to the position of a virtual dictator, for he claims 'full freedom to act when and how he chooses. This in my opinion is wholly opposed to democratic and cabinet system of government. The Prime Minister's position, according to my conception, is certainly pre-eminent; he is first among equals. But he has no overriding powers over his colleagues; if he had any, a Cabinet and Cabinet responsibility would be superfluous.[7]

Another disagreement occurred between President Prasad and Nehru over the Hindu Code Bill. The Bill (1951) proposed to radically intervene in the Hindu religious code. Nehru had proposed to make marriage and property state affairs, attempting to remove them from the sole premise of Hindu law. Prasad as the president wished to use all available constitutional powers to halt the bill. However, a part of Nehru's emphatic thrust on having a 'secular polity' demanded the transformation of several Hindu religious laws.[8] In both the instances, Nehru managed to position the office of the prime minister as the one having precedence. It is important to note that this pre-eminence of the office was not a given of the new state's architecture, but rather negotiated as such by Nehru. Given that Nehru did not have any predecessor as a model and found himself cumulating several portfolios under his supervision, the prime ministerial office gained considerable authority during his first term.

Nehru's omnipresence with regards to the formal functioning of the government in particular and the Congress party in general is most

---

departments. The final authority necessarily is the Cabinet itself but in the type of domestic set-up we have adopted, the Prime Minister is supposed to play an outstanding role. This I think is important'. See J. Nehru, 'Letter to Gandhi, 6 January 1948', in L. Zackariah and U. Iyengar (eds), *Together They Fought: Gandhi–Nehru Correspondence 1921–1948* (New Delhi: Oxford University Press, 2011).

[7] Sardar Vallabh Bhai Patel, quoted in Kumarasingham, *A Political Legacy of the British Empire*, p. 47.

[8] For details on more conflicts of a similar nature and a detailed exchange of correspondence that Nehru had with the Minister concerned, see Kumarasingham, *A Political Legacy of the British Empire*.

aptly captured in the cartoons of the artist R.K. Laxman (1921–2015), most popular for creating the caricature of 'the common man' in his daily comic strip *You Said It!* for the newspaper *The Times of India*. In his cartoons, the 'common man' is usually presented as a mute spectator to what is happening in Indian politics. He never speaks but watches silently; on some occasions in irony, and on others in sheer helplessness and bewilderment.[9] In the cartoon titled 'Lightening the Burden', Nehru is seen crawling, carrying a pile of sacks on his back as ministers watch on. Each of the sacks bears a separate title—Planning, Defence, Congress, Foreign Affairs, etc. In the second half of the picture, one finds the ministers exclaiming, 'Poor Man—Let's carry his burden'.[10] They all take a sack to carry but one finds them sitting on Nehru's back along with the sacks. It thus graphically shows that the 'weight' of all ministries and, in effect also that of the ministers concerned, was carried by Nehru single-handedly.

In another illustration titled 'The Show Must Go On', we find 'the common man' watching a musical show where Nehru sits on a carpet with several instruments, each bearing a separate ministry portfolio (saxophone as Foreign Affairs; sitar as Domestic Affairs; the flute in Nehru's mouth as SRC Affairs; and the clash cymbals which Nehru plays with his feet as Congress Affairs). Nehru asks the audience, which mainly consists of politicians except the lone common man, 'Is there a Tabla Player in the Audience? No? (…) Very Well (…)'.[11] As a result, we see Nehru playing the tabla (titled Foreign Affairs) with his right hand as well. The final message of the cartoon is a dexterous Nehru playing

---

[9] Laxman describes the common man in his own words as follows: '[…] He has a permanent look of bewilderment on his face. And he is ubiquitous. […] He has been witness to every kind of political instability and economic setback the country has seen, and has survived all sorts of domestic crises for six decades now. Like the mute millions of our country he has not uttered a word in all these years he has been around. He is a silent, bemused and often bewildered spectator of events that in any case are beyond his control.' R.K. Laxman, 'Introduction', in *Brushing up the Years: A Cartoonist's History of India* (New Delhi: Penguin Books, 2008), pp. ix–x.

[10] R.K. Laxman, 'In Ink and Line', in R. Zakaria (ed.), *A Study of Nehru* (New Delhi: Times of India Publication, 1959).

[11] Laxman, 'In Ink and Line'.

the tunes of each ministry as also of his own party all by himself. A third impressive piece titled 'Welcome to India' shows a solo Nehru preparing single-handedly to welcome foreign guests. We find him 'Scrubbing the place clean (…) getting the flowers etc. ready (…) fixing the decorations (…) teaching them how to cheer spontaneously (…) preparing the darlings to sing (…) touching up culture (…) spreading the red carpet (…) and receiving them!'[12] The cartoonist himself described the piece in the following lines, which capture Nehru's overarching presence and command over the Congress and the cabinet alike

> […] a Prime Minister who, by force of circumstance as well as his own personality, has become the inevitable focus of all national activity. This concentration of power was quite evident in the day-to-day functioning of his Cabinet. Every Minister was supposed to function independently of the Prime Minister. But in reality the doctrine of collective Cabinet responsibility was carried to an extreme and it always happened that Nehru's was the deciding voice on every issue that came before the various Ministers. Furthermore, the shoulders of Nehru were never too small to carry any additional burden. When Chintaman Deshmukh resigned in a huff from the Cabinet, the public, […], was kept guessing who the next Finance Minister would be. After all, the show must go on. To the surprise of sooth-sayers, Nehru announced that he would assume that portfolio as well at a time when his hands were too full.[13]

Nehru's Institutionalized Presence

Nehru's omnipresence did not just confine itself to the formalized sphere of the ministries that he held under his control. The agenda of introducing a *repetitive* vocabulary of the state through parades, pedagogy, and presentations of the past ensured that Nehru himself permeated public memory in a multiplicity of ways as a public figure. A postcolonial state elaborately establishes rituals that become the 'spectacular excessive signs of its own existence'.[14] Usually, these signs

---

12 Laxman, 'In Ink and Line'.

13 Laxman, 'In Ink and Line'.

14 T.B. Hansen and F. Stepputat, 'Introduction', in T.B. Hansen and F. Stepputat (eds), *Sovereign Bodies: Citizens, Migrants and States in the Postcolonial World* (Princeton: Princeton University Press, 2005), pp. 29–30.

of excess intertwine with the visions, which the 'founding father'[15] enthuses into popular imagination. In the Indian case, the founding father himself could be viewed as lending *the face* to these visions. Nehru became the central designer, the mastermind behind what a 'New India' should look like. But his presence was not just restricted to his ideas. His pictures, symbols, and especially his words were the embodied forms,[16] which made 'state power highly visible'.[17] In that sense, he was the iconic face of the new independent India.

Not only did Nehru negotiate executive power in a way that the PMO would become the most prominent one, but during his term, laudations of Nehru became a common practice, a part of the state's means to establish its own legitimacy. To provide one illustration of the same, on Nehru's seventieth birthday, while he was still in office, *The Times of India* brought out a volume wherein numerous political personalities from across the globe wrote pieces on different assets of his personality. The editor of the volume, Zakaria, begins the introduction to the volume with the following lines that point out to the popularity of Nehru in Indian society at large:

> In 1929 [...] Gandhiji, whose word was law unto his people, spoke of him [Nehru] thus: 'He is as pure as crystal; he is truthful beyond suspicion. He is a knight *sans peur, sans reproche*. The nation is safe in his hands.' Since then Nehru has received—as he himself has admitted—in abundance and extravagance the love of his countrymen. They have idolized him; they have worshipped him. Even in the inaccessible tribal areas, his name is a household word; to the illiterate villagers he has become almost a god. To most Indians he has symbolized everything that is good and noble and beautiful in life. Even his faults are admirable; his weaknesses lovable. In a land of hero-worship he has become the hero of heroes. To criticize him is wrong; to condemn him is blasphemous. In the days of the struggle against the British, he was the arch-rebel who inspired the

---

[15] See P. Ahluwalia, 'Founding Father Presidencies and the Rise of Authoritarianism. Kenya: A Case Study', in *Africa Quarterly* 36, no. 4 (1996): 45–72.

[16] Uli Linke aptly sums, 'Modern states are not just imagined or discursive cultural regimes but also embodied forms'. See U. Linke, 'Contact Zones: Re-Thinking the Sensual Life of the State', *Anthropological Theory* 6, no. 2 (2006): 205.

[17] Hansen and Steppputat, 'Introduction', p. 29.

people; in his role now as Prime Minister he is the embodiment of their hopes and aspirations. They may be dissatisfied with his party; they may be unhappy under his Government, but such is their devotion to the man that he is not blamed for anything. He must remain above reproach. Like the Pope in the Middle Ages, Nehru has become infallible:

> O! he sits high in all the people's heart:
> And that which would appear offence in us,
> His countenance, like richest alchemy,
> Will change to virtue and to worthiness.[18]

Clearly, one may locate Nehru's *production* here by one of India's 'independent' newspapers, which currently enjoys the largest readership as an English language daily.[19] Eulogizing Prime Minister Nehru as the nation's face was thus an agenda that was not just appropriated by agents of the state per se, but also by the fourth estate.

In tracing how Nehru came to connote what India stood for, we also trace how the new state and, more importantly, the office of the prime minister authorized itself as the 'agent of transformation'. Already by the 1920s, the Indian National Congress had 'promised that its state would do everything that the British were doing, but do it better and do it more'.[20] Nehru, more than his Congress colleagues, was the figure who lent a voice to that transformation after independence. This is most visible in his addresses where we see the vocabulary of nation building being introduced for the first time. Paul Brass writes that for a large part of rural India (which constituted the majority of the Indian population), poverty continued being a lived reality and not much transformed economically in the decades following independence. Nonetheless, people continued 'venerating him as a deity-like figure'.[21] While 'the state' itself was

---

[18] R. Zakaria, 'A Many-Splendoured Life', in R. Zakaria (ed.), *A Study of Nehru* (New Delhi: Times of India Publication, 1959), p. 3.

[19] *The Times of India* was founded in 1838 and, according to the Indian Readership Survey (2012), is the most widely read English daily in India with a viewership of approximately 7.643 million. Available at http://mruc.net/irs2012q4_topline_findings.pdf, accessed on 13 October 2013.

[20] S. Roy, *Beyond Belief: India and the Politics of Postcolonial Nationalism* (Durham, NC: Duke University Press, 2007), p. 100.

[21] P. Brass, *The New Cambridge History of India* (Cambridge: Cambridge University Press, 1990), p. 22.

experienced as a distant presence in these vast stretches of the country, the prime minister's presence was nonetheless prominent and deeply felt.[22] For this majority of the Indian population, Nehru was not a mere representative of the state; he *was* the state, a personality who would lend a lasting inevitable authority to the PMO.

There are numerous machinations through which the project of citizen formation was forwarded by the state in post-independence India. From visual practices of chromolithographs,[23] posters, state-sponsored Films' Division's documentary films, short feature films, videos aired on the national television channel Doordarshan,[24] to school history textbooks, comic books, tourism ministry campaigns and regularly *performed* national events like Independence Day and Republic Day parades—all of these contributed to a ceremonial dramatization of events in the state's 'liturgical calendar' and 'furnish public proof of its prestige and glory by a sumptuous (yet burdensome) presentation of its symbols of status, displaying the heights of luxury in matters of dress and life style, thereby turning prodigal acts of generosity into grand theatre',[25] as has been shown by Achille Mbembe for postcolonial nations more generally.

Nehru was always prominently present in all such ritualized performances of the state. Thus, events like Independence Day and Republic Day came to be ceremonialized in a way that the prime minister would each year address the nation in a speech delivered from the historic Red Fort and hoist the national flag, a task Nehru personally performed for seventeen years. Comic strips, history textbooks, state-produced wallcharts for schools, statues, and chromolithographs—all produced Nehru for everyday visual consumption. Inaugural ceremonies of dams, reactor plants, and universities saw him cut the red string and deliver

[22] Christopher Pinney records this with the case of chromolithograph production, which extended to the remotest corners of India. Here, in many of the illustrations used, Nehru's images were as popular as photos of Hindu Gods. See C. Pinney, *Photos of the Gods: The Printed Image and Political Struggle in India* (London: Reaktion Books, 2004), p. 146.

[23] Pinney's *Photos of the Gods* is the most remarkable contribution in this direction.

[24] Among other voices, prominent is Srirupa Roy's *Beyond Belief*.

[25] See A. Mbembe, *Africa: Journal of the International African Institute* 62, no. 1 (1992): 9.

addresses. In 1954, the UN General Assembly appealed to all states to assign a day each year in the celebration of children and to promote child welfare. This Universal Children's Day falls on 20 November. Yet, in India, it is celebrated annually on 14 November, Nehru's birthday. From the rosebud which he wore on his coat to the collar of the coat, which is commonly called 'the Nehru collar' (or the famous close-necked jacket called the 'Nehru Jacket') by tailors until today, the symbolism around Nehru has diffused into public spaces in a diversified range of means. His book *The Discovery of India* was adapted in 1988 to a 53-episode television series in Hindi, *Bharat Ek Khoj*, aired on the national television channel. Actor Roshan Seth, who physically resembled Nehru,[26] was seen dressed in Nehru's trademark attire in each episode, narrating India's 5000-year long history as presented in the book. In other words, Nehru was penetrating the television screen weekly, even long after his death. The series thus made him the authoritative presence that would produce and narrate India's past for Indians and, in doing so, also reproduce his own iconic image as the voice of the nation, a legacy that has clung to the PMO until today.

Another befitting illustration of Nehru's pervasive presence are the documentaries produced by the Films' Division of India, a state-owned production house of the Ministry of Information and Broadcasting, established in 1948. One of these made in 1957, titled 'Our Prime Minister', shows Nehru as the omnipresent leader of postcolonial India. We also get a glimpse of Nehru's everyday life both at home and his office routines as the prime minister.[27] Such documentaries became a regular feature of the state-sponsored routinized familiarization to the *face of the nation* and have continued to be produced even in contemporary India, as newer ones were made on successive prime ministers such as Lal Bahadur Shastri, Indira Gandhi, Atal Bihari Vajpayee, Manmohan Singh, and Narendra Modi.[28] Another ambit where Nehru's deep-felt

---

[26] Also played Nehru's character in Richard Attenborough's film *Gandhi* (1982).

[27] *Our Prime Minister*—documentary film directed by E. Mir, produced by the Films' Division, Ministry of Information and Broadcasting, 1957.

[28] For example, another noteworthy documentary directed by S.N.S. Sastry, titled *Our Indira*, depicts the former prime minister, Indira Gandhi, in a similar vein in 1973.

impact becomes graphic is in academia (especially that emanating from India), whereby it is customary to term his prime ministerial span as the 'Nehruvian era' and the newly founded state as the 'Nehruvian State'. This metonymization, where a singular personality comes to stand for a time period and a nation-state reflects how Nehru came to be, and, to some extent, still is, anointed as the face of the nation.

More recent prime ministers (Rao, Vajpayee, and Singh) have also eulogized Nehru and credited him for building the stable footing of India's secular democracy and secure economic strength. This was in spite of whether they belonged to the Congress Party or not, and in spite of them *de facto* propagating stances that were drastically divergent from his (see also chapters 2, 3, and 4). In the 1202 speeches that this book uses as sources, there has not been a single direct reference in which a prime minister has questioned the *moral* authority and *correctness* of Nehru, even though what is promoted is completely in opposition to his visions and methods. This has something crucial to say about the inevitability of his presence in contemporary India. The following prime ministers, dyed under his influence, were and in many ways are the new Nehrus.

Prime Minister Narendra Modi (2014–present) has come under regular media scrutiny for his rhetoric of differentiation and distancing from Nehru.[29] Though it is indeed observable that Modi appears to disentangle himself from the Nehruvian aesthetics of style, speech as well as content, as also his repertoire and vocabulary (for a detailed analysis, see chapters 2 and 3), the *grammar* and *protocols* of engagement with the audiences nonetheless appear to be very similar. During the election campaign in 2014, Modi's pervasively unavoidable presence in urban and rural India alike reconfirmed the grammar of Nehruvian politics, that is, maximum exchange with audiences, repetitive stage presence, and powerful oratory.[30] In spite of belonging to the liberalized world

---

[29] To illustrate one of the numerous examples, M. Joseph, 'Why Do They Say That Modi Hates Nehru?' *Outlook*, 17 November 2014. Available at http://www.outlookindia.com/magazine/story/why-do-they-say-that-modi-hates-nehru/292512, accessed on 14 August 2016.

[30] S. Malik, 'From Narendra Modi's Team, Some Stats: 437 Rallies, 5827 Events, 3 Lakh Kilometres', Election News, *NDTV*, 9 May 2014. Available at http://www.ndtv.com/elections-news/from-narendra-modis-team-some-stats-437-rallies-5827-events-3-lakh-kilometres-560938, accessed on 26 August 2016.

of 'mediated populism',[31] as Roy and Chakravartty term it, Modi's ubiquitous national presence bore strong resemblances to Nehru's national omnipresence as the first prime minister. Relying heavily on new social media (personal website, Facebook, twitter, blogs, etc.),[32] yet very conscious of traditional media (vernacular print and visual media, speeches in open campaigning grounds), the prime ministerial campaign appeared to reiterate the Nehruvian protocol of presenting Modi as the new face of 'New India'. This was strategically and tactfully planned through a plethora of mechanisms, the most conspicuous being Modi's extensive touring of the country (just as Nehru did during and before his prime ministerial terms) with 437 large scale rallies, 5827 public interfacing events, and travelling over 300,000 kilometres across twenty-five states of India, the aim being 'to connect himself to the people everywhere',[33] as explained by the BJP president, Amit Shah.

In her essay analysing Modi's electoral victory, Kapila writes, 'The Modi mandate has declared a new form of "conservatism"—a political language that has ushered in the "individual" as the totem of change to direct India's future.'[34] As shown in the earlier section of this chapter, this language of emphasizing the individual leader's personality is as old as the first general elections in 1952. In 2014, paper masks of Modi's face profile were distributed all across the country, to be adorned by his supporters. Billboards and hoardings with his larger-than-life profile pictures (literally looking into or down upon the viewers) were an unavoidable sight in numerous cities. Slogans adapted to the typical campaign stylistics were echoed through loudspeakers and moving BJP party vehicles. The particularity of the campaign (though very similar to Nehru's own campaigns) was the almost US presidential election style promotion of a singular personality, its heavy reliance on the

[31] P. Chakravartty and S. Roy, 'Mr. Modi Goes to Delhi: Mediated Populism and the 2014 Indian Elections', *Television and New Media* (2015): 1–12.

[32] Modi's website: http://www.narendramodi.in, PMO website: http://www.pmindia.gov.in/en/, Twitter: @narendramodi and @PMOIndia, link to radio show *Mann ki Baat*: http://www.narendramodi.in/mann-ki-baat

[33] Malik, 'From Narendra Modi's Team, Some Stats'.

[34] S. Kapila, 'Conservatism and the Cult of the Individual in a Populist Age', in M. Desai et al. (eds), *Making Sense of Modi's India* (Noida: Harper Collins Publishers, India), p. 40.

charismatic persona of Modi rather than on the party manifesto of the BJP.[35] Thus, the slogans that became highly popular also *solely* utilized Modi as the iconic face of the BJP, or, more specifically, as the emerging face of the nation. Some examples of such buzzwords/slogans include '*NaMo*' (short for Narendra Modi); '*Har Har* Modi, *Ghar Ghar* Modi' ('Har Har' coming from slogans usually chanted by pilgrims hailing the Hindu deity Shiva—*Har Har Mahadev*. 'Har Har Modi, Ghar Ghar Modi' thus translates to Hail to Modi, Modi for every household); '*Abki Baar* Modi *Sarkar* ('This Time, Modi's Government');[36] 'ISN: I Support Narendra Modi'; '*Desh Ki Pukar Modi Sarkar*' ('The Nation's Call: Modi's Government'); '*Achche din aane wale hain*' ('Good times are arriving', which became the most iconic slogan of the campaign, repetitively used by Modi himself in his speeches), etc. The slogan 'Achche Din' was also adapted to a song and video format and became the official song of the BJP election campaign.[37] In September 2014, Modi launched the 'Make in India' campaign (for a detailed analysis of the same, see chapters 2 and 3). In 2016, a mobile phone brand called *Namotel* (inspired by the prime minister's name), sponsored under this campaign, launched the cheapest smartphone in the world that was sold at a meagre price of Rs 99 (less than 2 Euros) and tactfully called the 'Achche Din' model or set. As is lucidly clear from all these examples, Modi's face, his voice, and his words permeate the senses of his audiences in a plethora of ways, establishing the legitimacy of his iconic presence as the face of the nation through a repetitive pervasion of everyday Indian life.

One of the moments when speculations around Modi's politics of reviving Gandhi, while simultaneously discrediting, if not erasing, Nehru gained currency was when he embarked on the Swachch Bharat (Clean India) campaign, launched tactfully on Gandhi's birth anniversary 2 October 2014. This, however, should not be solely read

---

[35] Unconventionally enough, there was no party manifesto released by the BJP until very late, right before the elections.

[36] The slogan strongly resembles the one popularized for Prime Minister A.B. Vajpayee during his election campaign, '*Abki baari* Atal Behari' (translated as 'This Time Atal Behari').

[37] See videos on the theme of Achche Din, available at https://www.youtube.com/watch?v=WAhAD6YURtE and https://www.youtube.com/watch?v=O-KJzUlU0VI, accessed on 16 June 2014.

as a move to restage Gandhi on a national scale. The campaign was simultaneously used to *appropriate* Jawaharlal Nehru, a treasured figure whose iconography has been the sole possession of the Congress party. Modi merged this campaign successfully with the celebration of the birth anniversary of the first prime minister of India. The reconstituted National Committee for the Commemoration of the 125th birth anniversary of Jawaharlal Nehru (with Modi as its ex officio head) did not include anyone from the Nehru/Gandhi family as a member,[38] and commemoration celebrations were planned between 14 November 2014 (Nehru's birth anniversary) and 19 November 2014 (Indira Gandhi's birth anniversary), tactfully using the Bal Swachchta Mission (Children's Cleanliness Mission) as their central agenda (2014 was declared the *Year of Bal Swachchta* from then on). The celebrations were thus dyed in the colour of a campaign that had already been associated with Gandhi.

Just like Nehru's repetitive, celebrated presence, Modi seems to pervade television screens and newspapers, the World Wide Web through Facebook, twitter, and websites, and other social media platforms such as WhatsApp through forwarded messages. In fact, the popular 'Nehru Jacket' is now often renamed as the 'Modi Jacket'.[39] Merely two years

---

[38] The Committee was constituted during the UPA government, but witnessed a re-engineering after the BJP formed the government at the Centre. The Congress president resigned from the committee, whereas many others were dropped. See 'Modi Rejigs Nehru Panel', *The Telegraph*, 18 October 201. Available at http://www.telegraphindia.com/1141019/jsp/frontpage/story_18942143.jsp#.V6tnMhT3BXA, accessed on 15 January 2015. The Congress also organized a simultaneous celebration for which the prime minister was not invited. See 'Modi Govt. and Congress Hold Competing Events to Mark Nehru's 125th birthday', *Business Standard*, 15 November 2014. Available at http://www.business-standard.com/article/politics/modi-govt-and-congress-hold-competing-events-to-mark-nehru-s-125th-birthday-114111401265_1.html, accessed on 15 January 2015.

[39] See 'The Nehru jacket, now Modi style' The Times of India, 21 September 2014. Available at http://timesofindia.indiatimes.com/india/The-Nehru-jacket-now-Modi-style/articleshow/43043940.cms, accessed on 1 August 2016. See also P. Gahilote, 'Modifying Nehru', *Outlook*, 17 November 2014. Available at http://www.outlookindia.com/magazine/story/modifying-nehru/292518, accessed on 2 August 2016.

after his election as the prime minister, the high frequency of books written on his personality, his visions, his foreign policy, his past as a BJP politician, and, particularly, as a *chaiwala* or tea seller already match the voluminous book production on Nehru.[40] He is also the first of the four PMs since 1991, whose addresses this book analyses, who does not shy away from giving interviews, though on his own terms and for shows selected by him, even to private news channels (for example, Interview for 'India TV' on the show *Aap ki Adalat (Your/People's Court)* with Rajat Sharma and interview with Arnab Goswami for 'Times Now' on the show *Frankly Speaking*). Narendra Modi's trajectory thus clearly reflects highly locatable symptoms of the grammar of Nehruvian oratory and public presence, whereby, willingly or not, he only reconfirms Nehru's haunting presence in Indian politics even today.[41]

The Legacy of Nehru's Visions

The founding principles that were laid down as the cornerstones of the Indian nation-state by Nehru became another means of reasserting his authority and of therein rendering the office of the prime minister irrefutable. The transition from being a colony to becoming a newly decolonized nation entailed, among other agendas, the project of transforming the 'subject population' into a citizenry. In accomplishing the same, the state would therein become the true representative of the nation, a voice of its nationhood. It is in this context that Nehru's visions, as the first prime minister, diffused into public spaces in a plethora of ways.

[40] Some examples include A. Anand, *One vs. All: Narendra Modi: Pariah to Paragon* (Chennai: Notion Press, 2016); A. Marino, *Narendra Modi: A Political Biography* (India: HarperCollins, 2014); U. Mahurkar, *Centre Stage: Inside the Narendra Modi Model of Governance* (Gurgaon: Random House Publishers, 2014); N. Mukhopadhayay, *Narendra Modi: The Man, the Times* (Chennai: Tranquebar Press and Westland Books, 2013); and L. Prince, *The Modi Effect: Inside Narendra Modi's Campaign to Transform India* (London: Hodder and Stoughton, 2015). The list is almost inexhaustible and cannot be summarized here in its entirety.

[41] S. Gupta, 'Modi Is Our Most Nehruvian Prime Minister since Nehru', *Business Standard*, 27 May 2016. Available at http://www.business-standard.com/article/opinion/shekhar-gupta-modi-is-our-most-nehruvian-pm-since-nehru-116052701152_1.html, accessed on 2 August 2016.

A closer view into Nehru's addresses indicates that even the vocabulary of a 'New India', so commonly flaunted and projected by the more recent political heads, is not so new. Thus, in order to grasp the contours of what defines the *new* in the contemporary project of the 'New Emerging India', as fabricated by its more recent political heads, the nuances of Nehru's *sayings and doings* cannot be overlooked (The author has developed the differences and underlying continuities in the conclusion). What defined Nehru's understanding of 'New India'? In pointing out some of the core defining characteristics of the vocabulary of nation building that Nehru adopted, it will become clear how his presence has come to occupy immense authority. It will also explain how the PMO came to occupy such a central significance in Indian politics.

Nehru stressed the importance of what he termed as the 'Temples of Modern India'—new dam projects, new industries, and new universities (all termed collectively with the adjective 'Big' attached to them in his speeches). Universities, dams, and industrial plants/public sector units were seen as the stepping stones to a much-desired 'self-sufficiency'[42] for India. They were projected as a natural pathway that would materialize the dreams to 'step out from the old to the new, when an age ends, and when the soul of a nation, long suppressed, finds utterance'.[43] Thus, manufacturing engineers, atomic energy reactors, research institutes, dams, or steel itself was seen as a part of manufacturing the New India (Nehru states in an address, 'We must start with the machine which makes the machine'[44]). This legacy lingers on and makes Nehru's influence highly ubiquitous. The Indian Institutes of Technology, which were founded under Nehru's supervision during the 1950s, have acquired prominence worldwide in producing engineers and scientists of reputation. Nehru is therein hailed as the architect of that 'scientific

[42] This phrase acquires a figurative quality in contemporary India, symbolic of the socialist habitus and phraseology much associated with Nehru's visions and policies.

[43] J. Nehru, 'A Tryst With Destiny', speech delivered on the eve of India's independence, 00:00 hrs, 14 August 1947.

[44] J. Nehru, cited in R. Inden, 'Embodying God: From Imperial Progresses to National Progress in India', *Economy and Society* 24, no. 2 (1995): 245–78, at p. 265.

progress', the benefits of which are reaped by Indians today. It is commonplace to find politicians speak about Nehru's legacy that has led India to be termed as the 'Software, IT power'.

Two other frameworks merit mention here in terms of the continuing legacy of Nehru that made the PMO the strongest representative of the state, and the state itself the connecting glue for the nation. First is the category of the 'unity in diversity' trope for the nation and, second is the discursive playing out of Indian distinctiveness, especially on the international scene. Both these themes have percolated time and also find continuity in political rhetoric that belongs to the period after 1991. They stubbornly stick back in definitions of Indian nationhood even today. However, these defining 'master codes' cannot be assumed as a given. They are products of a cautiously sketched programme that aimed at defining the *Indianness* of India in that it repetitively fabricated the diversity of India as its very unifying and unique force.

Given that Nehru was the designer of these two variables, as highly visible in his repetitive addresses, his own presence lingers on and has endured the changing nature of Indian democracy.

In her study of state practices in postcolonial India, Roy refers to the same as follows:

> (t)he repeated encounters with the unity-in-diversity master code took place in a variety of ways, such as the regional cultural performances during the pageantry of commemorative rituals and the images of spear-bearing Naga tribals, fez-wearing Muslims, and masked Kathakali dancers that invariably graced the People of India wall charts in school classrooms, as well as the allocation of state resources and political recognition to groups that could successfully demonstrate their possession of a territorialized and materially distinctive cultural heritage or ethno-linguistic identity.[45]

This 'logic of newness as bricolage',[46] a theme played out in many theatres so that citizens encountered it in their everyday lives, shares a familial resemblance also to how the four prime ministers, after 1991, profile India, particularly so in correlation to secularism debates (see Chapter 5). This does not imply that the idea of Indian diversity, as its unifying glue, did not exist in colonial times and was solely a Nehruvian

---

[45] Roy, *Beyond Belief*, pp. 19–20.

[46] Roy, *Beyond Belief*, p. 142.

coinage. However, what I wish to emphasize is that Nehru made the idea an *institutional* reality. One illustration of the same is that for the cultural tableaus for Independence Day and Republic Day parades, Nehru stressed that individual federal states should pick one unique cultural aspect (dress, dance, or landscape) that would be presented at the parade. Thus, for example, even though Uttar Pradesh and Bihar had much in continuity linguistically, as also in terms of dances, folklore, music, and landscape, the emphasis was on the production of difference rather than similarities. This was done so that in the end the entire parade with over 26 cultural tableaus would look like a constellation of variety, a syncretic mix with each individual unit being unique. It is this that also re-enforced the abstraction of the state as the agent of unification.[47] Nehru as the author of this institutionalization of diversity became the face of that state, therein also making the PMO the official bearer and agent of the state.

The second theme to sanctify the PMO by producing the nation was in emphasizing India's uniqueness. The theme enacted itself out not just with reference to the 'inside', that is, those belonging to India, but also for how India was produced before the world. This claim for distinctiveness acquired its most graphic shape in the Non-Aligned Movement, which stood for a new way, a possibility for countries to avoid becoming satellites to either of the two power blocks in a Cold-War-torn world. Another emblematic articulation of this claim was the idea of having a 'mixed economy', 'a middle path' entailing 'combined principles of socialist and laissez faire economics'. This register of making claims to Indian distinctiveness has percolated right up to the rhetoric of the current prime minister, Narendra Modi.

Nehru's planning (as may be captured in the five year plans), his elocution of breathing a new vitality into India in terms of making it an economically 'self-reliant' nation, and his vision of an era where India 'discovers herself again'[48] encompassed the simultaneous project of producing the state as the 'caretaker' of its citizens. This imagination conjured the new postcolonial state as the umbrella abstraction that was collectively accountable to the citizens, oversaw the common

[47] For a detailed discussion, see Roy's chapter 'Marching in Time' in *Beyond Belief*.

[48] Nehru, 'A Tryst With Destiny'.

good for all and provided the roadmap of how it could be realized. It was fabricated through the voice of its enacting agents as a materially enacted space, which was devoid of the banal profanities of everyday corruption, communalism, and self-motivated agendas. In that sense, 'the' state was something 'beyond' being just a governing body and 'above' the impurities of 'politics'. This projection of the state as the ultimate benefactor, however, also implied the simultaneous fabrication of what Srirupa Roy calls the 'infantile citizen'.[49] This was a shorthand term for the homogenized category of the Indian citizens who needed protection, but above everything else, 'education'. '[...] the ideal citizen of postcolonial India was defined in terms of his dependence upon, and intimate relationship with, the lineaments of state authority, with individual freedom seen to derive from rather than precede and make possible the sovereignty of the nation-state.'[50] In producing the state as something beyond the corruptness of everyday politics, Nehru was also making a statement for himself, rather for the PMO, as an office that was above others. The aim was twofold—first to project the office as neutral, free of biases, and therein above the politics of separatism; and second to make the figure of the prime ministers the true 'teacher' and 'caretaker' of the nation.

This depiction of 'New India', with Nehru as its prime engineer, is well captured in Inden's account of a cartoon dated 25 January 1959. 'Shankar (cartoonist) comments on the birth of a "New India" that Nehru as midwife, would bring about through the use of his co-ordinative rationality in an adaptation of Sandro Boticelli's "The Birth of Venus" (1485–06) where he replaces Venus with India and the Nymph with Nehru, receiving India as she comes ashore with a cloth having the word "Planning" across it.'[51]

It cannot be denied that the prime ministers to follow Nehru have in more ways than one also contributed to recalibrate the position of the prime minister in Indian politics. During Indira Gandhi's term, when a state of emergency was announced as per Article 352 of the Constitution (nineteen months in total from 26 June 1975 to 21 March 1977), and elections and civil liberties were curtailed, much was also

---

[49] Roy, *Beyond Belief*, p. 20.

[50] Roy, *Beyond Belief*, p. 20.

[51] Inden, 'Embodying God', p. 268.

stated against the assumed moral infallibility of the prime minister. To announce the emergency was Indira Gandhi's personal decision, which was undertaken in the wake of her being accused of winning the elections through electoral fraud. However, the executive powers of the prime minister had already been so calibrated by that time that it only required her to 'recommend' the president that a state of political turmoil existed in the country and that an emergency ought to be announced. Though her own image suffered immense loss after this, the very fact that a dictatorship-like situation (allowing her to rule by decree) could come into existence, single-handedly executed by the prime minister, shows the immense power that the office of the prime minister had come to occupy.

My purpose in outlining how Nehru redefined the PMO is not to eulogize his legacy or his individual personality. This section thus ought not to be read as another account celebrating Nehru in a biographic account. The aim has been to point out that through a negotiation of his plans, powers, and persona, he *did* something that raised the PMO in its status, making it truly higher than the 'First Among Equals'.

To sum up, this section has shown how, by strengthening the position of the prime minister in the executive through an institutionalized and pervasive everyday presence and through the legacy of his visions based on the Nehruvian consensus, exceptionalism, and the 'Unity in Diversity' master code, the first prime minister crafted himself, and, more importantly, the PMO as the face of the nation. His successors have all, directly or indirectly, contributed to the same grammar, and the current Prime Minister Modi's electoral politics and pervasive popular presence since his election only reaffirms an even more aggressive return to the same.

The Nation's Tongue: Public Speech and the Prime Minister's Office

Oral/Aural India

On a cursory glance, ritualistic annual addresses such as the ones delivered by the prime ministers on the commemoration celebrations of Independence Days and Republic Days may appear to be the result of Nehru's single-handed attempts to render the new postcolonial state visible through its routinized pervasive presence. Though true for these specific speeches of the prime ministers in contemporary India, the immense weight that is commonly attached to the spoken word in general can only be evaluated if one takes into account the long-standing history of orality and aurality in the Indian subcontinent. As in numerous other parts of the world, in India, too, politicians speak in light of their particular tradition(s) of orality. It is therein imperative to cast the focal gaze onto the gravity that is accorded to public speeches by their receiving populations. This particularly relates to the impact of the 'sound' of the speaking prime ministers.

In their study of Hinduism as 'A Culture of Sound', Wilke and Moebus aptly observe that:

> In Hinduistic India [...]. Since earliest times, sound has enjoyed great cultural importance. 'Reading' out a religious text in Sanskrit means 'reciting' it in a musically pleasing way and with the utmost care regarding correct pronunciation. In turn, simply listening to the sound of a religious text is already held to be auspicious and purifying. In the scholarly traditions, as well as in everyday life, we find a great focus on the sonic dimension.[52]

They assert, 'There is some justification in calling Hinduism a highly sound-based culture. The audible and recited word is of major importance.'[53] The listening and simultaneous recitation of texts is an important method of learning in general. 'When texts are read out, they are aesthetic events. Language as expressive sound has its own independent validity of meaning, its own ability to communicate, and its own aura.'[54] Jack Goody, known for his extensive writing on themes of orality and literacy in Africa, Europe, and Asia,[55] questions the *oral* dimension of learning the Vedas, Hinduism's oldest texts, within the context of the

---

[52] A. Wilke and Oliver Moebus, *Sound and Communication: An Aesthetic Cultural History of Sanskrit Hinduism* (Berlin: De Gruyter, 2011), Foreword, p. v.

[53] Wilke and Moebus, *Sound and Communication*, p. 2.

[54] Wilke and Moebus, *Sound and Communication*, p. 5.

[55] Among others, his works on the same include J. Goody (ed.), *Literacy in Traditional Societies* (Cambridge: Cambridge University Press, 1968); J. Goody, *The Logic of Writing and the Organization of Society* (Cambridge: Cambridge University Press, 1986); J. Goody, *The Power of the Written Tradition* (Washington: Smithsonian Institution Press, 2007).

Brahmanical education system in India.[56] He disputes the notion that these texts have been transferred through generations 'purely by oral means'. Though there is currency to the fact that India also has a strong literate culture,[57] Goody has been challenged on many fronts for reducing the learning tradition(s) in India to 'mere oral residues in a literate culture',[58] and therein undermining the importance of orality and aurality in Hinduistic learning at large. Fuller contests Goody's claims when stressing that 'the verbatim memorization of texts which exist in a written and usually printed form, and the memorization of those texts as heard from the guru'[59] has been an essential ingredient of Hinduistic learning at large.

This is, however, not just true for religious instruction offered in Brahmanical *Gurukuls* alone. *Shlokas* and *mantras*, derived from numerous 'ancient texts', and usually in Sanskrit, are often also learnt verbatim by people in their everyday lives. The same holds true for Buddhism and its Pali texts, as well as for Islam where the Quranic verses (usually in Arabic) are often studied and memorized by aurally learning and speaking rather than by reading.[60] Kirmani, in his study of the aesthetic dimension of the Quran, states '[...] There is no true understanding of the Quran without an appreciation of its aesthetic dimensions, i.e. its

---

[56] Though India does not acquire preeminence in Goody's work, this point is dealt with in *The Interface between the Written and the Oral* (Cambridge: Cambridge University Press, 1987), pp. 110–22.

[57] As is evident from the fact that the Vedas are *written* manuscripts.

[58] Goody, *Literacy in Traditional Societies*, p. 14, cited in C.J. Fuller, 'Orality, Literacy and Memorization: Priestly Education in Contemporary South India', *Modern South Asian Studies* 35, no. 1 (2001): 1–31, p. 1.

[59] Fuller, 'Orality, Literacy and Memorization', p. 3.

[60] The very distinction between orality/aurality and literacy may be seen as an artificial one (resulting from the ideal of ocular focus of European modernity; see R. Bauman and C.L. Briggs, *Voices of Modernity: Language Ideologies and the Politics of Inequality* (Cambridge: Cambridge University Press, 2003). Reading, one may contest, appears to be only a visual act because it is inaccessible to the social ear. The reader's silence, however, is not solely silence, but rather inaudibility. This because her inner voice, inaudible to others, resonates consistently inside the fleshy corpus of her inner ear, whether with full or partial pronunciation of the words. The author is grateful to Peter Lambertz for this insightful comment.

literal quality and sonic realization.'[61] Interestingly, all three of the languages are usually not known to most people who often simply aurally memorize texts, mantras, and verses, and therein bodily internalize them in order to know them.[62] This is not to state that meaning does not hold relevance in these contexts (usually instruction also incorporates translation of meaning to vernacular languages), but to emphasize that the 'sound' of what is said carries an immediate emotive and sensory power that is given high importance. In his analysis of the historical role of rumours, spread by word of mouth, in the spread of the sepoy and peasant rebellions of 1857–58 in colonial India, Guha summarizes the functional immediacy of speech when stating, '[...] Speaking, as linguists say, differs from writing not merely in material, that is, by the fact of its acoustic rather than graphic realization, but in function. [...] Speech, responds to any given stimulus more urgently, emotionally, and dynamically than written utterance.'[63]

To reduce the written and oral to a simplistic dichotomy is, however, to ignore the complexly ambiguous ways in which the two are interwoven in practice. Sudipto Kaviraj aptly points out that the distinction between literate and oral in India is not identical or analogous to that between the educated and illiterate.[64] He contends that in the subcontinent, 'even the educated have their own traditions of oral performance'.[65] (Kaviraj refers here not just to the Vedic education, but to the instruction in colonial and postcolonial India in general.) Thus, though writing has been known, atleast to the few, its utilization has been sparse, precisely because of the varied nature of social interactions between the literate few and the illiterate majority, as well as because

[61] N. Kirmani, *Gottist Schön: Das ästhetische Erleben des Koran* (*God is Beautiful: The Aesthetic Experience of the Koran*) (München: Beck, 1999), as cited in Wilke and Moebus, *Sound and Communication*, p. ix.

[62] Hearing here is musical (related to rhythm and sound), rather than a sequence of linguistically signified intellectual argumentation.

[63] J. Vachek, cited in R. Guha, 'Transmission', in A. Rajagopal (ed.), *The Indian Public Sphere: Readings in Media History* (New Delhi: Oxford University Press, 2009).

[64] S. Kaviraj, 'Writing, Speaking, Being: Language and the Historical Formation of Identities in India', in A. Sarangi (ed.), *Language and Politics in India* (New Delhi: Oxford University Press, 2009), p. 315.

[65] Kaviraj, 'Writing, Speaking, Being'.

of the internal 'distribution of functions between speaking and writing'.[66] Kaviraj may be criticized for clubbing the multiplicity of experiences of orality and literacy under the homogenous and essentializing category of 'the Indian culture'. However, he does make a powerful argument in favour of a need to sensitize how literacy and orality are dexterously interwoven in the everyday lives of people. It is here that the importance of orality ought to be given due recognition, in spite of the writtenness of texts, mythologies, and religious instruction. In this regard, he reminds us that 'enormous and essential structures of social exchange and communication are entrusted to oral continuity rather than written codification'.[67] Clearly speaking carries historical weight.

My point in stressing the orality of learning in India has a two-pronged objective—first to highlight the culture of *listening* and repeating, and second to the unquestionable authority of the teacher figure who *instructs*. This irrefutable role of the teacher is well-documented in the case of traditional Sanskrit learning, even in contemporary India. Michaels lucidly sums up:

> The future of the Pandit is perhaps linked with some constituents of knowledge that cannot be obtained through Western methods which focus on abstraction, impersonal teaching, writing and reading. There is for instance the unparalleled focus on orality in traditional Sanskrit scholarship *which implies a long history of personal contact with the teacher.* To be sure, pandits do not object to the use of written and printed books but they also do not believe in books as the ultimate source of knowledge. They favor oral communication and presentation with its technical consequences for style and the forms of texts, i.e. sutra style, use of meters, repetitions etc. (Emphasis added)[68]

This complex of aural learning (and therein knowing) from a verbal source of speech is a process that has also translated into present-day classroom scenarios and academic instruction in India more generally. The methods of instruction practised in the academic system at large become a revelatory arena for how aurality/orality percolates through the veins of the country as a legitimate learning and knowing technique.

---

[66] Kaviraj, 'Writing, Speaking, Being', p. 316.

[67] Kaviraj, 'Writing, Speaking, Being'.

[68] A. Michaels (ed.), *The Pandit: Traditional Scholarship in India* (New Delhi: Manohar, 2001), p. 11.

They point to the importance of listening and, therein, the significance of speaking itself.

Contemporary academic training in India often emphasizes *memorizing* the lecture of the professor word by word.[69] The phrase for 'learning by heart or rote' in colloquial Hindustani is *'muh-zabani yaad karna'*, which translates as learning by mouth and tongue, whereas the more Sanskritized Hindi word for the same is *'kanthastha'*, where *'kantha'* stands for throat. Personal studying itself is often generally done on the basis of core books, which can guarantee good examination results and grades. Here, learning implies replication through memorizing—the better the lessons are learnt and reproduced, the better the grade. The idea of plagiarism is therefore, very often, an absent rule that opposes the supremacy of the 'teacher' teaching and the sincere student recapitulating each utterance as a marker of vocal self-perfection.[70] Fuller aptly summarizes this in the context of his own research:

> [...] the nature of Indian instruction, in which students spend so much time learning by rote, not only in elementary schools when first learning grammar or arithmetic tables, but even in degree-level colleges, where they commonly write down material delivered in lectures so that they can memorize it for examinations. This practice is prevalent, for instance, in the quite prestigious English-medium colleges in Madurai favoured by Brahman families. Thus for the majority of Indians, education remains highly dependent on the oral transmission of and memorization of knowledge [...][71]

One question that arises is whether this is a marker of the 'postcolonial' ambivalence, most graphically visible in the classroom, whereby

---

[69] All who have studied in India or are studying India and been to India will not refuse noticing this at some point or the other, especially if in contact with Western European academic training. The visual scene of the classroom where the teacher speaks and the students repeat after her (sometimes, multiple times with kinaesthetic movements) is one that strikes most observers in schools based in remote villages and cities alike.

[70] The author certainly does not refer to all scenarios, but wishes to emphasize the importance which is paid by students to the lectures of professors at universities. The examination format whereby students often produce these lectures as answers to the questions asked in a defined period of time very often also ensures absence of footnoting in the answer scripts.

[71] Fuller, 'Orality, Literacy and Memorization', pp. 29–30.

the penetration of decontextualized learning leaves behind traces of uncertainty, an unease that renders reflexivity and critical questioning difficult. Chakrabarty, in an account of the 'infiltration' of 'Western' intellectual tradition in colonial and postcolonial India, argues that it is hard to encounter Indian social scientists or those who research 'Indian' topics utilizing arguments forwarded by Indian logicians, grammarians, or aestheticians. 'Sad though it is, one result of European colonial rule in South Asia is that the intellectual traditions once unbroken and alive in Sanskrit or Persian or Arabic are now only matters of historical research for most—perhaps all—modern social scientists in the region. They treat these traditions as truly dead, as history.'[72] The same however does not hold true for frameworks that borrow from Marx or Weber, whose works are treated as more 'authentic' or at least 'scientific'. In that sense, their works continue living in the academic tradition in India at large.

Chakrabarty's observations are full on to the point. Marxist and liberal thought permeate Indian terrain in dealing with what may be categorized as 'local issues'. The enlightenment inspired liberal vocabulary of human rights, and justice is a sign of this influence. However, whereas Chakrabarty discusses that Marx and Weber are read in contemporary Indian academia, he does not deal with the question of *how they are read and taught* in classrooms.

An interesting arena that calls for further research in this direction is the second-hand transfer of these 'classical Western' texts. This often does not happen through a reading of the texts per se, but rather by word of mouth, translated in the lectures of teachers that are then written down to be learnt by students or through 'guidebooks',[73] which

---

[72] D. Chakrabarty, *Provincializing Europe: Post-Colonial Thought and Historical Difference* (Princeton: Princeton University Press, 2000), p. 5. It should be noted that Chakrabarty acknowledges the nineteenth-century Renaissance in India, where many intellectuals, such as Raja Ram Mohan Roy, did propose a resort to sources that were Indian. However, this category, he argues, is by far a minuscule minority.

[73] In the Hindi-speaking belt in India, these guidebooks are popularly called *Kunjis*. 'Kunji' literally means key. These short abridged books are seen as providing quick answers to all questions, and it is commonplace that students often do not buy original versions but rather these books to learn classical texts. These books themselves mostly do not observe any rules of plagiarism.

often reproduce professors' spoken explanations of the written texts. This aural and oral mode of learning is not merely a recent invention emerging from the colonial trauma that left the subcontinent bereft of any confidence in its own 'knowledge systems', and which thus calls for a 'decolonization of imagination',[74] but its roots go deeper in the precolonial modes of learning. As discussed earlier, the culture of orality / aurality in learning is most graphically visible in the ancient Vedic tradition which, according to Graham, 'represents the paradigmatic instance of scripture as spoken, recited word.'[75] Fuller states 'A corollary of the spoken word's primacy is that in teaching the Vedas and other texts, although 'written texts have been used', 'a text without a teacher to teach it directly and orally to a pupil is only so many useless leaves or pages.'[76]

Thus, largely even in contemporary India, the one imperative mode of contact between the listener/student and the teacher is the oral transmission of instruction, which may or may not employ written texts. It is no surprise that these 'habits' of learning have permeated the public spaces in more intrinsic ways than imaginable. Public opinion in India is spread by 'listening' to political speeches and debating on their contents. Listening is thus also a means of 'learning' the message communicated by the politician. In fact, for most of India, it still is *the most effective* and essential instrument and contact zone with the governments and their political heads.

Importantly, also during the colonial period, the nationalist movement itself relied heavily and primarily on the spoken word of figures like Gandhi and Nehru. This is not to undermine the important role played by the print media in mobilizing the movement. Similarly, the

---

[74] J.N. Pieterse and B. Parekh (eds), *The Decolonization of Imagination: Culture, Knowledge and Power* (London: Zed Books, 1995).

[75] W.A. Graham, *Beyond the Written Word: Oral Aspects of Scripture in the History of Religion* (Cambridge: Cambridge University Press, 1987), p. 68.

[76] Fuller, 'Orality, Literacy and Memorization', p. 1. Similarly, in his discussion of the fate of Sanskrit education in modern India, Gerow emphasizes the disruptive effect of secular educational influence, but he also vividly points out that there is an equally notable continuity between what is commonly dubbed as 'traditional and modern education'. See E. Gerow, 'Some Thoughts on Indian Government Policy as it Affects Sanskrit Education', in E. Gerow and M.D. Lang (eds), *Studies in the Language and Culture of South Asia* (Seattle: University of Washington Press, 1973).

development of public reason, 'public culture', and urban space through discussion *outside* the ambit of congress circles can also not be denied. As Chakrabarty rightfully points out in the context of eighteenth- and nineteenth-century Bengal, the 'adda' or '*majlish*' or '*baithak*'[77] have been key contributors in the development of 'democratic speech'. But even if literary addas did and still do exist, addas as spaces of discussion have relied primarily on listening and speaking rather than on 'reading'.

Bernard Bate, in his study of oratory in Tamil Nadu in colonial India, traces the shift from English oratory to vernacular oratory, captured in the significant shift from 'hall meetings' limited to groups of educated elite circles to mass meetings (such as the satyagraha of 6 April 1919 in Madras Presidency) attended by larger audiences. He writes, 'Much has been written of how this politics [Tamil Nadu] was mediated by newspapers, handbills, and chapbooks, and the dominant narrative of such events privileges the circulation of print and print culture of vernacular language [...].'[78] The crucial role of vernacular oratory has, however, remained eclipsed by this academic overemphasis on print culture. His work thus:

> Explores the relatively lesser-known story of the role and impact of vernacular oratory on the development of the mass political in Tamil Nadu from the Swadeshi movement (1905–08) to the formation of labor unions (1917–19), and the explicit attempt to persuade non-elites into speech, action and ultimately politics. [...] Tamil oratory was an infrastructural element in the production of the political, at least the political as we understand it in twentieth-century Tamil Nadu where oratory becomes the defining activity of political practice. When elites made the conscious move to begin addressing the common man, when Everyman was called to join into the political, a new agency was formed along with a new definition of what politics would look like.[79]

In a country where a majority of the population was, has been, and even today is essentially non-literate (that is, the incapability to read or write

---

[77] All refer to a dwelling place, fixed or permanent, a haunt, a meeting place, a club, a company or meeting place of idle talkers, their meeting place to talk. See Chakrabarty, *Provincializing Europe*, pp. 180–230.

[78] B. Bate, '"To Persuade them into Speech and Action": Oratory and the Tamil Political, Madras, 1905–19', *Comparative Studies in Society and History* 55, no. 1 (2013): 66.

[79] Bate, '"To Persuade them into Speech and Action"', p. 166.

in a language used and spoken), it was the *speeches* of the national heroes, and local heroes in particular, that were the prime movers of staging grand protest staging like the Civil Disobedience Movement, the Quit India Movement, or the Dandi Salt March. In no accounts do we find that Gandhi managed to mobilize millions of followers for these protests through his well-documented, written works, such as the renowned books *Hind Swaraj* (1909), which reflects much of his political thought, or *My Experiments with Truth* (1921), his autobiography. These written works have been more the affair of academia and a relative minority of literate Indians at large. Instead, in all instances, one finds Gandhi 'speaking'. His words were heard by large audiences and then repeated rather than read. In fact, this direct engagement with people was one of the main reasons why his popularity increased as he moved through rural India. Most of the prior nationalists ('English in training and taste')—like Gandhi himself in his younger years—had no such stronghold over the bulk of the Indian population. This was largely owing to the fact that numerous leaders had not 'reached' rural India, which therein often also meant that they had not 'spoken' enough publically. It thus follows that 'speaking' did not just establish *the most available* contact between the activist/nationalist/leader and the listeners, but that it was in fact *essential* for the contact to work in the first place.

The Speaking Prime Ministers

> It is a voice we have often heard. A voice that captures the thoughts and moods of a whole people. The voice of Jawaharlal Nehru. It is the voice of a man that has found an echo in the hearts of the Indian people. A voice ever guiding and inspiring them to newer and greater heights of progress and enlightenment. Towards a New India that is now in the making.[80]

These lines from the 1957 Films' Division produced documentary *Our Prime Minister*, (mentioned in the previous section), narrated in the opening scene, lucidly reiterate the irrefutable significance accorded to Nehru speaking. In the first scene, we see a radio set within the camera's focus and all we hear is the sound of the prime minister. This scene rapidly changes into the next shot, depicting a household to show

[80] Mir, *Our Prime Minister*.

how Nehru's voice permeates the everyday lives of common Indians. Lastly, as the commentator narrates the earlier lines, the camera zooms into a loudspeaker, transmitting Nehru's familiar voice addressing the nation. While his visions were graphically made available, for example, through the cultural tableaus for parades or via the specter of the large dams, his speeches became the necessary interface that actively translated these visions into popular lexical memory. The deep felt impact of these words can be gauged from the fact that terms/phrases like 'New India', 'Unity in Diversity', 'Temples of Modern India', 'at the stroke of midnight hour [...]', etc.,[81] have permeated through and sedimented in people's vocabularies over the last decades.

In 1952 (merely five years after independence), India had its first nationwide general elections. While most European democracies had initially only allowed the most literate and educated strata to vote, universal adult franchise was introduced from the very outset in India. This explains the necessity for oral/aural mass communication through speech. There is indeed a long tradition of speaking leaders using the power of their words to address people.

This practice of speaking and therein being known also diffuses in contemporary Indian politics in a plethora of ways. During election campaigns, it is a common sight to find large playgrounds, public parks, etc., reserved much in advance by political parties. Candidates contesting for elections travel intensely through their electoral constituencies to address audiences in open spaces with strong microphones assisting their voices, sometimes even rendering them hard to ignore. While this can be observed in many parts of the world, an Indian specificity might lie in the fact that during these periods, elaborate spoken slogans are developed as part of the message of the party. These slogans, though sometimes written on hoardings, posters, and party banners, mainly become popular in that they are repetitively spoken out for and repeated by audiences. Autorickshaws with party banners usually have loudspeakers attached to them where a constant commentary runs, inviting people to vote for the party. The slogans are constantly spoken out aloud on these moving party vehicles. Thus, even though an individual may not necessarily attend an election campaign speech, slogans permeate the general aural atmosphere in which one carries

---

[81] Nehru, 'A Tryst with Destiny'.

out everyday movement and work. It is this aural perception, a repetitive encounter with someone speaking, which makes people learn the message of the politician.[82] No surprise then that during the election campaign period, most people are able to recount the slogans of the politicians (and therein associate them with their respective parties) on the tip of their fingers. In that sense, slogans, which are persistently spoken and are hard to erase from immediate public memory, are

[82] Examples of such slogans, which became popular during election campaigns in the period after 1991, include *'Lathi utthavan, tel pilaavan, Bhaajpa bhaghaavan'* ('Take your sticks, oil them well and chase the BJP out'), used by President of the Rashtriya Janata Dal Party, L.P. Yadav; *'Congress ka haath aam nagrik ke saath'* ('Congress's hand with the common man', [also its party symbol]), slogan used by Congress Party, *'Desh ki aandhi, Sonia Gandhi'* ('Wind of the nation, Sonia Gandhi'), slogan used by the Congress Party, *'Tilak, Tarazu Aur Talwar Inko Maro Jute Char'* (implies that the three upper casts—Brahmins, represented by the 'Tilak'; Baniyas, represented by the 'Tarazu'; and Thakurs,—should be kicked), used by Mayawati President of Bahujan Samaj Party; *'Vote Atal, vote kamal'* ('Vote for Atal Behari Vajpayee, vote for the lotus' [lotus is BJP's symbol]), slogan used by the BJP; 'India is Shining', slogan used by BJP; *'Bahubali ko crore, dal badloo ko lakh, janata ko mila khaak, yehi hai sukhad ahsas'* ('Crore to the muscle-man, lakh to political defector, nothing for the people, this is the feel good factor'), slogan of the Rashtriya Janata Dal in Bihar, ridiculing the BJP's 'feel-good' factor campaign, 2004. A slogan popularized when Atal Bihari Vajpayee was campaigning for prime ministership was *'Abki baari Atal Bihari'* ('This time Atal Bihari'). The most recent slogan which acquired immense popularity was the electoral slogan for Prime Minister Narendra Modi, *'Abki baar Modi sarkaar'* ('This time Modi government'), BJP's election campaign slogan, 2014.

The tradition of slogan chanting is, however, much older and a technique that dates back to the nationalist movement itself. During the long course of the movement slogans such as *'Angrezon Bharat Chodo!'* ('British, Quit India!'), used during the Quit India Movement; *'Swaraj Mera Janamsiddha adhikar hai, aur main ise laker rahoonga'* ('Freedom is my birthright and I shall have it'), Bal Gangadhar Tilak of Indian National Congress; *'Tum mujhe khoon do, main tumhe aazadi doonga'* ('Give me your blood and I shall give you freedom'), Subhash Chandra Bose while mobilizing volunteers for the Indian National Army. The same may be associated with prime ministers. Lal Bahadur Shastri coined the popular slogan *'Jai Jawan, Jai Kisan'* ('Victory to the Soldier, Victory to the Farmer'), whereas Indira Gandhi is well known for *'Garibi Hatao'* ('Remove Poverty').

'compressed performances', to borrow Pinney's vocabulary.[83] They produce the immediacy of the message that the politicians wish to communicate in a condensed, precise form that relies on brevity, rhyme, wit/humour, and memorization for its repetitive presence and impact.

It is not surprising that slogans are usually composed as rhythmic and rhyming couplets, catchy to hear, and adapted to musical tunes that can be sung as recourse to efficacy. Slogans are an intrinsic part of campaigning in most countries, but their rhyming composition and adaptation to the tunes of popular Bollywood songs is a particularity in India, which once again points to the aurality of their perception.

My intention in emphasizing these habits of aural reception and oral repetition of politicians' or teachers' messages is not to present a culturalizing account that produces 'Indians' as unreflexive repeaters of what is taught or told. There is indeed a vibrant environment of questioning, arguing, or debating, as Amartya Sen aptly demonstrates in *The Argumentative Indian*. He sums this up in saying that 'the tradition of argument has helped to make heterodoxy the natural state of affairs in India'.[84] Sen tracks evidence of the same from a variety of illustrations, ranging from the rule of king Ashoka to the Moghul emperor, Akbar, in the sixteenth century, both vociferous in encouraging public dialogue. My thrust is rather on the *mode of transfer* used to convey messages at large, that is, the *spokenness* of these messages, debates, and dialogues. Listening and speaking are the two important acts in perceiving and retaining messages. Sen aptly sums up this cruciality at the end of his book's introduction by quoting the eighteenth-century reformist Ram

---

[83] Pinney develops this by relying on the works of Roy Wagner and Marilyn Strathern, who have researched how certain cultural practices treat images as compressed performances. Marilyn Strathern suggests that 'for Melanesians, images are not representations in the sense of a screen onto which meaning is projected. Rather, the experience [of an image's] effects is at once its meaning and its power' (R. Wagner, *Asiwinarong: Ethos, Image, and Social Power among the Usen Barok of New Ireland* (Princeton N.J., 1986), p. 216; M. Strathern, 'Artefacts of History: Events and the Interpretation of Images', in J. Siikala (ed.), *Culture and History in the Pacific*, Finnish Anthropological Society Transactions, No. 27 (Helsinki: Finnish Anthropological Society, 1990), pp. 125–38, at, p. 136, both cited in Pinney, *Photos of the Gods*, p. 8.

[84] A. Sen, *The Argumentative Indian: Writings on Indian Culture, History and Identity* (New Delhi: Penguin Books, 2005), p. 12.

Mohan Roy: 'Just consider how terrible the day of your death will be. Others will go on speaking, and you will not be able to argue back.'[85] The ultimate helplessness of death lies not in any other loss, but in the inability to speak.

In a vibrant atmosphere where much speaking, listening, and repetitive exposure to the *sound* of the state pervade the everyday lives of citizens, it becomes clear that the prime minister is not just the face of the nation, but also its very tongue. The public addresses of the prime ministers formulate the most consistent communication, a contact zone between the audiences and the state, a non-changing format through which the message of the government is presented to the largest audiences possible.

The addresses of the prime minister also formulate the most public material in that its access is not an affair for a limited few, but rather has a wide appeal for large audiences. This is essentially embedded also in how the nature of voting, and democracy at large, have developed in India, particularly after Nehru's prime ministership. A view into the voting patterns and turnouts indicates that unlike the United States of America, voting in India has been more the affair of the poor than the elite. The messages of the prime ministers reach audiences not just through their physical presence at the *site* of the delivery, but are mediated through a range of channels. The radio and the television have been particularly prominent in this direction.

Another reason why this book utilizes the addresses of the prime ministers is because they are the most visible statements of an Indian politician, both nationally and internationally. This does not imply that other ministers have not been speaking or are any less relevant, but it is rather a reflection on the format of whose speaking holds weight in international forums also.

In case of commemorations and national emergencies, it is the word of the PMs that address the nation, not of other ministers (no other ministers' addresses are as consistent and as frequent as those of the prime minister). The speeches of the prime ministers acquire currency also because of the immediacy of transmission between the 'official' government versions of events and the people at large.

Another point that merits attention here is how prime ministers are often judged through the prism of oratory talent. It explains why

---

[85] Sen, *The Argumentative Indian*, p. 33.

figures like Atal Bihari Vajpayee (who is also known to be a prolific Hindi poet) are termed as 'successful' and 'good' politicians because of being eloquent speakers. On the other hand, those like P.V. Narasimha Rao and Manmohan Singh, who were not viewed as eloquent and impressive public speakers, are presented in compensatory, justification-laden language. For example, a commonplace remark for Singh and Rao was that even though they were not good speakers/orators, they possessed 'other' skills that justified their occupancy of the office. The same speculations are made for Narendra Modi, who has become popular as the 'talking prime minister' in distinction to Manmohan Singh, who was often criticized for his silences and ridiculed as *Maun*mohan Singh ('*Maun*' meaning silence in Hindi, which translates into the 'quiet' Singh) by BJP politicians.

On 12 February 2014, Modi launched a public platform termed *Chai pe Charcha* (Conversations over Tea) during his campaign, ahead of the elections in May 2014. This platform, a 'mega outreach programme', saw large screens installed at 1000 tea stalls over 300 cities in the country with Modi conversing with numerous citizens (through satellite, internet, DTH, and mobile networks) who had posted their questions to him on the platform's website. At the launch, while sipping a cup of chai, Modi called tea stalls in India the 'footpath parliaments' of India, its hubs of discussion and debate. The platform was dubbed as 'Modi's Nationwide Tea Party'.[86] Tea thus became a metaphor for the famous American Tea Party Movement, a reference to the 'Indian' tradition of debate and discussion over tea (see adda, as mentioned earlier), but most importantly an iconic sign of Modi himself, who had, almost aggressively, been emphasizing his very humble background as a chaiwala (tea seller) throughout the campaign.[87]

[86] R. Bhan, 'Narendra Modi to Launch "Chai pe Charcha" Campaign Today', *NDTV*, 12 February 2014. Available at http://www.ndtv.com/cheat-sheet/narendra-modi-to-launch-chai-pe-charcha-campaign-today-550542, accessed on 15 August 2016. For a recorded telecast of the show, see https://www.youtube.com/watch?v=-aZtmizf7CU, accessed on 15 August 2016.

[87] I was taken aback by the proportions of Modi's outreach during my stay in New Delhi at the peak of the election campaign (15 January–31 May 2014). On the festival of Holi (17 March 2014), three days before the submission of my doctoral thesis, which, at the time, did not incorporate Modi's speeches in its analysis, I received an automated phone call on my Indian mobile phone. In

In a similar vein, since 3 October 2014, Modi, in line with the Nehruvian tradition of 'speaking to the people', initiated a show on national radio (All India Radio), DD News, and DD National (national TV Channel, Doordarshan), titled 'Mann ki Baat', whereby he speaks once a month directly to the Indian population.[88] Clearly, the prime minister is judged by how often he speaks and how well he can speak. This has something to say about the weight given to speaking, but more precisely to the prime ministers speaking.

This section has thus illustrated how, in order to duly comprehend the significance of public speaking, it is inevitable to plunge in the larger cultural context of orality and aurality (especially in the spheres of education and political mobilization) in which the tradition of oratory and public speaking are embedded. It has traced the specific trajectory of how speaking has become the most important and effective instrument for politicians and leaders to communicate their message(s), and for audiences to receive them. Finally, it focused on how addresses of the prime ministers are the most public, most audiovisual, and the most frequent and consistent (both nationally and internationally) transmitters of state messages, rendering the prime minister the tongue of the nation.

---

a clear crisp voice, the pre-recorded voice of Modi wished me on the festival of Holi, ending with an anything but subtle plea to vote for him and the BJP. What was remarkable about the call was that despite being aware that it was not a live phone call, it successfully produced a sense of immediacy, whereby the listener felt as if Modi was directly speaking to him/her. It is no surprise that the campaign itself was being produced as having created the 'Modi Wave' (*Lehar*).

[88] The recorded version of the show and the text of what is said by the PM can also be accessed online on Modi's website. See *Mann Ki Baat*, http://www.narendramodi.in/mann-ki-baat, first accessed on 6 January 2015, last accessed on 25 December 2016.

2

Time and Temporalizing Tactics I

Of Futures to Come and Futures Past

During my visit to the Publications Division of the Ministry of Information and Broadcasting, New Delhi in January 2012, I had the opportunity to interact with several state employees working at the division. I was trying to locate certain public speeches of the prime minister, which were unavailable, even untraceable, at the parliament library's archive, the Ministry of External Affairs, or the collections of the Prime Minister's Office. To add to my curiosity, the missing addresses delivered by prime minister Vajpayee were from 2002, the year of the Gujarat riots, which would be a crucial source for my chapter on state secularism (see Chapter 5). In search for answers as to why only the addresses belonging to this time frame were missing, I spoke to numerous *sarkari karamcharis* (government officials) employed at these departments ranging from the man selling books at the Ministry's Publications Division, a cameraman who had accompanied several prime ministers to record their addresses in and outside India, the *bade babus*—as higher-up officials are often called—directors of the Film Division and the Audio-Visual Division, to the editorial team responsible for publishing the addresses of the prime ministers. It is in this context that the following conversation with the gentleman at the cashier desk of the Publications Division's bookshop occurred. When asked about the missing speeches, he retorted back with the following question:

But why are you still obsessed with Hindu–Muslim riots when Ayodhya and Gujarat are long over? We are secular, and the world today is talking about how India will be a superpower soon. Madam, you are in Germany, why don't you write about that? You should write about that.

A.B.: Yes, I am writing about that, in a way.

Then you must concentrate more on your topic.[1]

Though my initial attention was riveted more to how there seemed to be an obvious disinterest (or perhaps a jaded fatigue) in discussing anything related to the Gujarat riots, his words later led me to another equally engaging question. How has the discourse of an 'Emerging India', 'India, the Superpower of the Future', penetrated the lexical archive of this employee? He later added:

You people, like to make mountains out of mole hills. *Bhai*, if they couldn't publish the speeches of that year, they couldn't. Finish. These things keep happening. We have a lot of work to do here. Now you come and make the connection to Gujarat and Godhra and the riots. You people (journalists—he did not remember that I am a researcher) always look for problems. You don't want to write about India as an economic superpower. You will never write about anything positive. This is India's problem. Everywhere in the world, like in BBC they are talking about us becoming superpower, our *netas* (politicians) talk about it, but our own people want to go outside and only talk about negative things.[2]

This conversation prompted me to the following question: How is the 'neo-liberal' dream[3] marketed successfully by India's political discourse-makers to the extent that an otherwise distanced government official has acquired this optimistic nationalizing vocabulary?

The 'opening up of India', a phrase popularly used for market liberalization, implied drastic transformations for the economy, this meant a reduced role to be played by the formerly pervasive public sector enterprises, abandoning of the *license raj*, therein granting more liberty to the private sector (deregulation), removal of barriers to encourage greater foreign direct investment, and the devaluation of the rupee. But these

[1] Conversation at the Publications' Division, Ministry of Information and Broadcasting, New Delhi, India, 21 January 2012.

[2] Diary notes, A. Bajpai, Noida, India, 21 January 2012.

[3] Why I use this word here will become evident in the analysis.

transitions also meant a paradigmatic shift in the ideological leanings of the leadership, a move away from the quasi-socialist model inspired by the Nehruvian vocabulary of political non-alignment and economic self-reliance. How have these transformations, both economic and also ideological, been explained to people?

Studies of these phenomena have mainly focused on quantifying the results of the reforms, the recalibration and realignment of the different political camps they have provoked, debates that discuss their pros and cons of, and finally those that argue whether 1991 is a caesura in Indian history or primarily a state-produced narrative.[4] However, it is rarely the technocratic truths that stick back in the common man's[5] head and lexical memories. In view of this, my analysis takes a different stance by approaching the discursive versions of the reforms as propagated by those who have authored them and have had to justify them. The neo-liberal reforms were not accepted homogenously and produced scepticism at many ends, ranging from the threatened public sector enterprises, discomfort on the increasing role to be played by foreign investors on Indian turf, right up to the allegations of them being 'anti-people'. In general, these oppositions have also contributed to the conjuring of what is loosely termed as 'globalization' as a cultural threat to Indian self-understandings. Rather than analysing any technocratic justifications of change, the intention of this chapter is to screen how change itself, as a temporal momentum that challenges, if not threatens, an existing order of cultural security,[6] is explained and justified so that it may be made inevitable.

The study of the prime ministers' speeches revealed the utilization of remarkably numerous temporal justifications to frame and justify

---

[4] For example, some of the voices celebrating the reforms and their impact are G. Das, *India Unbound: From Independence to the Global Information Age* (New Delhi: Viking and Penguin Books, 2000); S. Tharoor, *India: From Midnight to Millenium and Beyond* (New York: Arcade Publishing, 1997); and K. Nath, *India's Century: The Age of Entrepreneurship in the World's Biggest Democracy* (New York: McGraw-Hill, 2008).

[5] I discuss this term common man or *Aam Admi*, as it is popularly termed, later in the chapter.

[6] For the concept of 'cultural security', see J. Friedman and S. Randeria (eds), *Worlds on the Move: Globalization, Migration, and Cultural Securit* (London: I.B. Tauris, 2004).

the reforms as an event embedded in time. This insight has encouraged the decision to orient this chapter (and Chapter 3) towards analysing the PMs' reform-related speeches mainly through the specific lens of temporality, that is, to uncover how change is embedded in a temporal order or sequence, which is equally discursively produced in speeches for audiences both outside and inside of India. Thus, the intention is, to follow Johannes Fabian's formulation, to shift our attention 'from the semiotics of time to the pragmatics of temporality (that is, from what time "means" to what people "do" with time)'.[7] Fabian's insights on the production of the anthropological object, which always implies a co-production of time frames in which the object is placed, is directly relevant to what the PMs do with the nation. When PMs 'write, [...] narrate, (and) tell a story, [...] a narration is never a "natural" way of expressing experience and insights into prose, narration is a construction with time.'[8] The prime ministers' narratives of the *new* nation are always produced *in* and *with* time.[9]

François Hartog proposes a helpful conceptual tool to study temporality, that is, the relationship between a putative present and a putative other time, be it past or future.[10] Coining the notion of *regimes of historicity*, Hartog conceptualizes 'the way in which a society considers its past and deals with it. In a broader sense it designates the method of self-awareness in a human community. [...] (T)he concept highlights methods of relating to time: forms of experiencing time, here and elsewhere, today and yesterday, ways of being in time.'[11] One such

---

[7] J. Fabian, 'Of Dogs Alive, Birds Dead and Time to Tell a Story', in J. Bende and D.E. Wellbery (eds), *Chronotypes: The Construction of Time* (Stanford: Stanford University Press, 1991), p. 188.

[8] Fabian, 'Of Dogs Alive, Birds Dead and Time to Tell a Story', p. 196.

[9] Fabian explains, 'The most literary story still involves action on the part of its author. Action requires timing, telling a story, above all involves choices between what is said, discursively and explicitly, and what is unsaid but nevertheless 'stated' by the narrative structure. That narration is also a matter of timing.' (Fabian, 'Of Dogs Alive, Birds Dead and Time to Tell a Story', p. 196.) Fabian has canonized this point in his important monograph on *Time and the Other: How Anthropology Makes Its Object* (New York: Columbia University Press, 1983).

[10] F. Hartog, *Régimes d'Historicité: Présentisme et Expériences du Temps* (Paris: Seuil, 2003); Hartog, 'Time and Heritage', *Museum International* 57, no. 3 (2005): 7–18.

[11] Hartog, 'Time and Heritage', p. 8.

regime of historicity, for instance, that becomes graphic in the oratory of the PMs is when the speakers produce and utilize India's generalized past and future synchronously to evoke a present which projects an 'Emerging India'. Reviewing Hartog's framework, Hannoum argues that in such a projection the 'present is the focal point of the representation of time; the past and the future are represented, thought of, and felt as departing from and returning to the present. In other words, in this order of time, the categories of past and future are instrumentalized to determine what the present is or is not.'[12]

Chapters 2 and 3 aim to uncover the multiple temporal orders which can be traced in the oratory of the prime ministers. This chapter is chiefly structured along the overarching category of a projected future. Each of the following sections presents one of the particular tactics used by the PMs to, consciously or not, produce a temporal order in which the economic reforms appear as indisputable.

Linguistic Tropes of a Changing India

India is like an elephant. It has to remain standing on its own feet. We will be crushed to death if it falls on us. Therefore the elephant has to stand on its own legs. The elephant has to walk on its own legs. If it does not walk, if it collapses, even if you bring another elephant, it won't be able to lift this elephant. So please understand, I want you to appreciate this point that India should always be standing on its own feet, on its own legs. Any activity which really incapacitates this country, makes it difficult for this country to go ahead with the economic agenda, is an act of treason. It is a great disservice to this country. Please understand this. Please remember this.[13]

This excerpt from a speech delivered by prime minister Rao, two years after the formal institutionalization of the neo-liberal economic reforms, aptly captures the mood of change in which the opening up of the economy was embedded. India is likened here to an elephant that becomes ungovernable once it collapses. The reforms are

[12] A. Hannoum, 'What Is an Order of Time? Review of Hartog, F., *Régimes d'Historicité: Présentisme et Expériences du Temps*, Paris: Seuil 2003', *History and Theory* 47, no. 3 (2008): 458.

[13] P.V.N. Rao, 'Let Us Concentrate on Development', address at a public meeting, Mangalore, 20 March 1993.

made inevitable by producing the urgency of ensuring that the elephant stands on its own feet. An allegorical link is thus established between the economy and the elephant with a warning that once the unmanageable animal falls down, no other economies of the world can come to its rescue. Thus, Rao's message is to save the animal (metonymic of India itself) from falling, and the reforms are produced here as the unavoidable means of doing the same.

This tactic of conjuring a temporal order where change becomes incontestable may be located in the numerous metaphors of speed used in the addresses of all the three prime ministers. A temporal continuity between the present and an ideal future is established, and India is projected as moving steadily towards that future through an innovative lexicon of motion. Thus, illustrations of India as 'rising', 'shining', 'growing', 'on the move', and 'emerging', are utilized to establish how (i) India is changing and (ii) market liberalization has been the unarguable means of attaining that change. The following excerpts provide befitting examples of how such optimistic metaphors forward the cause of an economically emerging India.

India is on the move. An India full of self-confidence is marching forward on the path to progress.[14]

The rise of India as an economic power, particularly as an IT power figures today in the discourse of all seminars, conferences and writings all over the world.[15]

India has emerged as a modern economy, an important industrial economy and a knowledge power.[16]

India's international standing has risen. Our voice is being heard attentively in the capitals of the world.[17]

India today is a nation on the move. The momentum for progress has started gathering speed.[18]

[14] A.B. Vajpayee, 'Together Let Us Build a Stronger Nation', address to the nation on Indian Independence Day, New Delhi, 15 August 2000.

[15] M. Singh, 'Creating an Environment for Growth and Development', inaugural address at the Infosys Leadership Institute, Mysore, 12 February 2005.

[16] Singh, 'Creating an Environment for Growth and Development'.

[17] Vajpayee, 'Together Let Us Build a Stronger Nation'.

[18] Vajpayee, 'A Vision of Cooperative Endeavour', address at the Asia Society, New York, 7 September 2000.

I can sum up the brief narration of the government's multi-faceted initiatives in the economic sphere in just five words—"India is on the move." [...] The world will soon see the emergence of a strong and prosperous India. [...] As economically resurgent, India will be a source of stability and long-term growth for the world economy.[19]

Today the Indian economy is poised to emerge as a formidable force.[20]

[...] India, a forward moving and a forward looking nation [...][21]

Change is thus, expectedly, seen as being celebrated by the prime ministers. In the following lines delivered by Singh years later while addressing an Indian audience, once again the unavoidability of the economic emergence of India is projected. However, temporality persists to be the major referral hinge around which this rise is linguistically materialized.

It is our ambition to do better than we have done. People talk about the Asian century. I am not an astrologer and I am not the one who is good at forecasting. Anyway, I am told of those who forecast that when their forecasts come true, in the words of Dante, they are condemned to go to hell. But I have a dream. That is what I stated when I first presented the budget in 1991. Victor Hugo has said that "No power on Earth can stop an idea whose time has come." [...] The emergence of India as a major powerhouse of the global economy is one such idea whose time has come.[22]

Here, the terms 'whose time has come' beautifully reflect how a temporal order is construed to render the reforms irrefutable. Transformation itself becomes the key marker of this order within which the reforms are first framed and then justified. The underlying aim is to show how 'no power on earth' can stop India's emergence. This rise is produced as a predestined, fated, inconvertible, and normative reality. The imagined future, no longer elusive, is to be realized *here and now*. All such linguistic tropes formulate the first strategy to

[19] Vajpayee, 'India is on the Move', address at the India Economic Summit, New Delhi, 5 December 1999.

[20] Vajpayee, 'Resolve Conflict between Globalization and Local Values', address at the University of Mauritius, Port Louis, 11 March 2000.

[21] Vajpayee, 'Resolve Conflict between Globalization and Local Values'.

[22] Singh, 'Economic Reforms: Taking the Momentum Further', address at the New York Stock Exchange, 22 September 2004.

build an environment within which India's economic rise is discursively staged and becomes manifest.

During the initial phase following the introduction of the reforms, as transformations were still being grasped in their contours,[23] most of Rao's addresses construe a temporal order where the future is produced as one 'full of hope and optimism'. This pattern may be traced even in Rao's last year in office when concrete results in terms of rising GDP growth rates and decreasing inflation rates were available as expected evidence of growth.[24] However, during Vajpayee's and Singh's terms, the projections of India, the economic superpower of the future, acquire vigour, becoming more emphatic, confident, and consistently accelerating in their velocity and occurrence. To mention some examples, Vajpayee states:

> [...] But we know that this achievement is only a stepping stone. It is not the attainment of the final goal which is to see the rise of India as an economic superpower; [...] India—a forward moving and a forward looking nation; [...] Dear Countrymen, a bright future is knocking at India's door.[25]

[23] This period may be categorized as an establishment phase when the reforms were newly institutionalized, and when, for the first time, the prime minister is seen as addressing the nation directly to explain what the reforms entail, how the economy will be transformed in the near future and how its liberalization will bring benefits that will reach one and all.

[24] For example, Rao states: 'The optimistic prospect of the future is already visible. [...]' (Rao, 'Towards Accelerating the Pace of Economic Growth', excerpts from reply to the Debate on the President's Address in Lok Sabha, New Delhi, 8 March 1994).

'I will only say that in this long journey of the nation, we have come to a point where we can look to the future with a certain amount of confidence and optimism'. (Rao, 'Thrust on Social Sector Development', excerpts from Reply to the Debate on the President's Address in Lok Sabha, 28 April 1995).

'I take a balanced view and on a balance I say, the future for India is bright but the way for India will never be smooth'. (Rao, 'India's Resilience to Come Out of Storms', address to the Indian Community, Guild Hall, London, 14 March 1994).

[25] Vajpayee is the first prime minister who attaches the metaphor of speed to India. The first occasion when this occurs in an address is when Vajpayee states 'Friends India is on the Move!'. Vajpayee, 'Have Faith and Confidence in the Future of India', address at the Inauguration of the Annual Session of the Confederation of Indian Industries, 28 April 1999.

In Singh's statements, this celebration becomes even more repetitive and vehement—for example, statements like the following:

The going has never been as good for India in the past as it is now. Our economy has been growing at an impressive pace of over 8%. Such rapid growth over three successive years is unprecedented in Indian history. Wherever I go, I see our nation on the move [...] India is certainly on the march. [...] There is a visible progress all around. [...] India is witnessing one of the most far reaching transformations of this century. Over a billion people are seeking salvation within the framework of an open economy and an open society. [...] India is experiencing an explosion of creativity and entrepreneurial spirit that has unleashed an economic boom.[26]

All of these illustrations reflect the embrace of change. They are charged with an optimism of achievement, and rejoice the transitions induced by the reforms. But an obvious question that demands attention is if such a change has been or can be homogenously celebrated in a country like India? The transformative power of new economic orders and their ensuing ideological shifts are almost never unaccompanied by simultaneous frictions. As stated earlier, the institutionalization of the reforms produced uncertainties for a spectrum of factions in the country, ranging from the employees of the now-shrinking public sector right up to the vanguards of national sovereignty, who perceived them as reopening India for 'foreign' invasions. Thus, though the previous illustrations highlight an important aspect of staging India's rise as embedded within the logic of open markets, they are in no way reflective of *all* the multifarious strategies that the authors of the reforms have used over the years to naturalize change for *larger* audiences. The following sections will show how the same has been attempted in the

---

Another example where Vajpayee projects India's emergence emphatically, 'You make me confident of India's destiny. As I speak these words to you, standing on the soil of a nation, which has dominated this century, I clearly see a great future beckoning India in the 21st century. For ours is a nation in the ascendant. We have the economic potential and the civilizational resources to emerge as a strong, prosperous and benign Global Power'. (Vajpayee, A.B., 'NRIs: India's True Ambassadors', address at the gathering of Members of Indian Community, New York, 26 September 1998).

[26] Singh, 'India Marching Steadily towards New Frontiers'.

public addresses of the prime ministers, so that the sanguineness of lines mentioned earlier gets transformed into the intuitively accepted lexical memories of people.

Producing the Future

As evident, the usage of metaphors indicating the momentum of India's transition is the initial tactic of generating 'India—the emerging economy of the future' by making *direct* references (in the beginning and end of most addresses) to the category of the future. In doing so, the prime ministers utilize it as an instrument to validate the unavoidability of the present in the form of the neo-liberal economic reforms. The following may be viewed as some befitting examples of such direct references:

We are pledged to the emergence of a new India in the new century.[27]

Today on this day, we move towards a Future that is full of hope. [...] The Future appears to be full of hope and I call upon and invite you to march ahead towards that Future.[28]

Have faith and confidence in the future of India. The clouds of uncertainty and instability will pass. Together we shall take India into the 21st century as a strong, self-confident and prosperous nation.[29]

Greatness is our Past—and also our Future.[30]

Beyond the strategy of making direct references to an abstract future, the prime ministers also produce the *vision* behind that future. A prominent strategy to make audiences 'buy' the reforms is by embedding them as the prime mover of the idealized future. This entails linking the future with the promise of growth. Growth is produced as a human necessity, and the reforms are rendered unavoidable by presenting

---

[27] Vajpayee, 'Get Down to the Task of Nation Building', first address to the nation after Lok Sabha Elections, New Delhi, 16 October 1999.

[28] Rao, 'Towards Hopeful Future', address to the nation on Indian Independence Day, 15 August 1992.

[29] Vajpayee, 'Have Faith and Confidence in the Future of India'.

[30] Vajpayee, 'Greatness Is Our Past—Also Our Future', address to the nation on Indian Independence Day, New Delhi, 15 August 1999.

them as the means to achieve growth. Since 1991, the different prime ministers have built an inexhaustible list of ingredients to make people associate with the vision behind the ideal future and accept the reforms as the means to realize that future.

However, this is a future which is no longer elusive or distant, but approachable and invested in the *here*.[31] Here, the idea of development itself is made generational. A linear thinking is produced and the present becomes imminent because it is connected through a generational relationship to the future. Development, as this linear production, a promise of the *near* future, is retrieved, brought 'back' paradoxically to the present in the here and now. Temporality thus emerges as a strong, playable instrument that helps realize the rhetoric ambition of teleporting development to the present from the future.

The visions of the idealized future entail three specific co-ordinates (structured into three sections): 1. The promise of growth, 2. The promise of growth for *all*, and 3. The promise of growth which is made *Indian*.

Details of Desire: Promising Growth

Among others, the constituents of this future include—the promise of an employed and educated youth, an emphatic embracement of science and technology, a vision where 'small people' are 'thrown up into big chairs'[32] (implying upward mobility to all, regardless of their

---

[31] J. and J.L. Comaroff mention this resort to the *here and now* as a constituent of the future in the context of rising occult economies and new religious movements which they view as one of the three most conspicuously identifiable products of 'neo-liberalism in its millennial manifestations.' They state, 'We seek […] to draw attention to, to interrogate, the distinctly pragmatic qualities of the messianic, millennial capitalism of the moment: a capitalism that presents itself as a gospel of salvation; a capitalism that, if rightly harnessed, is invested with the capacity wholly to transform the universe of the marginalized and disempowered.' This investment in the 'here and now' may also be viewed as a feature of discourses on market liberalization in India [J. Comaroff and J.L. Comaroff (eds), *Millenial Capitalism and The Culture of Neoliberalism* (Durham, NC: Duke University Press, 2001).]

[32] Singh, 'Heralding an Era of Change at the Grassroots', address at the Collectors' Conference, New Delhi, 20 May 2005.

class or caste background), an economy that has successfully integrated itself into the global economy, an India which is the future harbour of multinational corporations, a 'modern' India, a thriving knowledge economy, a major trading nation, 'a modern, globally competitive and humane industrial economy',[33] and finally what Vajpayee summarizes as 'growth, more growth and still more growth'.[34]

The aforementioned ingredients of an emerging India are presented differently in the various speeches. One befitting example of the same may be located in the following lines delivered by Prime Minister Rao:

> The vision is one of a strong vibrant economy, completely open as a part of the global economy, interacting with economies of other countries the world over and at the same time having transparency as a result of the democratic process.[35]

On another occasion, Rao states:

> We are working now on an exciting national agenda for building a new India which is economically strong, technologically advanced and socially a cohesive and integrated society.[36]

The projections of a successful future also incorporate presentations of a desired 'modern' society. However, what this amorphous term (modern) entails is never concretely defined by Rao. On one occasion, Rao states '[w]e want to modernize—we want to be a modern society. I am talking of an India which wants to be equal to other nations. India does not want to be backward all the time.'[37] True to its postcolonial

---

[33] Singh, 'Creating an Enabling Atmosphere for Growth', address at the ASSOCHAM's JRD Tata birth centenary celebration, New Delhi, 24 August 2004.

[34] Vajpayee, 'Harmonizing Economic Liberalization and Social Liberalization', inaugural address at the Annual Session and National Conference of the Confederation of Indian Industries, New Delhi, 28 April 1998.

[35] Rao, 'Economic Reforms: An Irreversible Course', interview to the Wall Street Journal, 30 January 1995.

[36] Rao, 'Indian Industry to Re-Define Its Goal', Address at the Inauguration of the India International Trade Fair, New Delhi, 14 November 1993.

[37] Rao, 'The New Industrial Policy', intervention in Lok Sabha during the Debate on the Demands of the Industries Ministry, 26 August 1991.

flavour, Rao's address illuminates the urge and desire to *become* modern, to not be 'backward', reminiscent of the headiness of the era of
a newly independent sovereign nation state in 1947. It also echoes of
the Nehruvian vocabulary of a new India (I deal with the subject of
how the more recent visions of a New India are different from those of
Nehru's in the conclusion). This postcolonial habitus and vocabulary
that speaks of a 'modern' India is a continually persistent trend that may
be located in all addresses.[38]

Another constituent of the ideal future is projecting India as an
IT superpower. However, one notices in certain addresses that this
imagination is loaded with, or finds co-occurrence to, new moralities
of consumption, a consciousness whereby 'science and technology'[39]
are seen as stairways to a still ambivalent, loosely defined, yet promising
'modernization'. Through shorthand terms for new media, with terms
like 'modernization' and 'technology', the PMs expand the constituents
of an economically emerging India. It is an India that is not 'consigned
to mediocrity',[40] but one where 'modern science and technology' will
'make it possible as never before in human history that chronic poverty
does not have to be the inevitable lot of a majority of human kind'.[41]
Thus, imagination itself, as aptly stated by Appadurai, is produced as 'a
collective, social fact. Ordinary people, more than ritual specialists or
charismatic leaders'[42] (in this case, also more than the elite), are given
the possibility to engage in the new social project called 'India'. The

---

[38] As predictable, such claims are thus not new, and may be traced very
well also in Nehru's rhetoric. Pinney states, 'Prime minister from independence
until his death in 1964, his approach to India was, as he had himself written,
similar to that of a "friendly westerner". He was "anxious to change her outlook and appearance and give her the garb of modernity. High-profile heavy
engineering projects and a centralized administration were marks of his success, [...]"' [Pinney, *Photos of the Gods*, p. 146].

[39] These are terms used loosely in the addresses for all developments made
in mass media, medicine, space research, software industry, and information
technologies.

[40] Vajpayee, 'Let Us Look Ahead', address to the nation on being elected the
prime minister of India, New Delhi, 22 March 1998.

[41] Singh, 'Heralding an Era of Change at the Grassroots'.

[42] A. Appadurai, *Modernity at Large: Cultural Dimensions of Globalization*
(Minneapolis: University of Minnesota Press, 1996), pp. 5–6.

elimination of poverty, predictably so, is thus the essential index of an ideal future.

Yet another repetitive ingredient of the future is how the city is perceived within the purview of the addresses. Apart from numerous references to the imagined future of the global cities, icons of 'India Shining', a new denomination of the futuristic city is that of the 'hi-tech city'. To support this imagination, software hubs like Bangalore are repetitively evoked as prototypes that are creatively enmeshed in the process of producing an emerging India. The following befitting address by Vajpayee elucidates the same,

> Coming to Infosys city is also like coming to a temple—but a temple of a different kind. Pandit Nehru [...] had called factories and dams 'Temples of Modern India' thereby underscoring their importance in nation-building. In today's New Economy, I think that the new temples of modern India are our Information Technology parks and the campuses of software companies like Infosys. I see here a happy confluence of Saraswati, Laxmi and Shakti. The New Economy is driven by knowledge. It is a producer of wealth and prosperity. So much so, that Laxmi seems to have a soft corner for software companies. However, beyond being a miracle of the mind and the market, information technology is also a great source of strength for our nation... after March 1998, our government took two major initiatives to make India a strong and self-confident nation. One was 'Operation Shakti' at Pokhran. The other was 'Operation IT' piloted by a national task force. [...] Both these initiatives have succeeded beyond our expectations. Nobody can deny that these have significantly bolstered India's prowess- one has given us military Shakti and the other has given us economic Shakti.[43]

In the excerpt, Hindu 'religious' resources are utilized in projecting the phenomenon of Indian emergence. Three Hindu goddesses associated with wealth, knowledge, and power (Laxmi, Saraswati, and Shakti) are equated to India's information technology boom, which is presented here as one of the essential ingredients of India's economic rise. When one enters the Infosys city,[44] one is exposed to the divine energies

---

[43] Vajpayee, 'Bolstering India's Prowess in Information Technology', address at the Infosys City, Bangalore, 19 January 2001.

[44] One of the most successful initial software companies in India founded by Nandan Nilekani who has also authored the book *Imagining India: The Idea of a Renewed Nation* (New York: Penguin, 2009).

of a Hindu temple—'a temple of a different kind', says Vajpayee, but one where one is bound to be touched by the blessings of the three goddesses in the form of wealth, knowledge, prosperity, and strength. Information technology thus becomes the pathway, the desired, almost divine, promise to a confident and strong India, a medium that has not just generated new possibilities for millions, but, more importantly, has magnified India's 'prowess', boosting its economic might but also its perception as a nation by the world community, whereas such hi-tech cities become icons of information technology. It is befitting at this point to mention a consistent strategy that the prime ministers use to render the reforms inevitable. Though Vajpayee is essentially referring to a change here, he does so not by exposing its newness, as a 'break-away', but rather normalizes it, camouflages it with continuity with a 'religious past'. The temple—a divine physical space, is an irrefutable place—holy and unquestioned—the allegory of the temple may be read here as rendering that vision of the hi-tech city irrefutable as well.

Important to add here is the fact that such a statement is also reflective of the speaker, prime minister Atal Bihari Vajpayee. It could perhaps not immediately be associated with Prime Ministers Rao and Singh, but is symbolic of a particular style of 'BJP talk'. By this I specifically refer to the party's history that may be traced back to the Hindu right wing, the rhetoric of its members which is informed by a vocabulary that derives its resources from Hinduism and is embedded in the Hindi language and its staunch opposition to the 'intrusion' of all that may be categorized as 'foreign'– from 'foreign goods' to 'foreign technology' right up to 'foreign traditions' like Valentines' Day. Vajpayee's words here do fit this style well in the kind of resources (reference to Hindu Goddesses) they rely on. However, the contents of the message stand in sharp contrast to BJP talk. What Vajpayee idealizes here is the Infosys city, beaming with its youth, its urban language, technology, and aspirations that aim at nothing below the Silicon Valley. This is not to state that Vajpayee purposely invents these religious references here to induce a sense of Hinduness among his listeners, but rather a reflection on the personality of the politician himself—his public self which is loaded with a certain vocabulary. This also helps one draw the subtleties of differences within the addresses. The question to ask here is how a party that has severely criticized the economic reforms until 1995 justifies its own adaptability and thorough insistence on the reforms when in power, both to its audiences as well as to itself. More than a justification through religious/philosophical/civilizational means for his audiences, I quote this statement here to see how the new 'neo-liberal' politician reflexively justifies it to himself, and also to chalk out the manifestations of the architecture of the ideal future that does not shy away from new technologies and open economies but embraces them.

Future with a 'Human Face': Growth as Human Necessity

Through their words, the prime ministers attempt to make growth an accessible, believable, and visible entity to *all*. This equation of 'growth for all' was first translated in Rao's public addresses as 'Growth with a Human Face',[45] implying that the benefits generated by the new economic transitions in India would be experienced by and available to all Indians. Thus, it is emphasized that they do not merely offer possibilities only for those who already inhabit the upper economic strata

---

[45] One observation worthy of mention here is that out of an initial sample of seventy-eight speeches delivered by Rao (which are directly categorized in the collected volumes under the section 'Economic Affairs') from 1991–95, the phrase 'Growth with a Human Face' appears sixty-eight times.

Though, during his term, Vajpayee refers to the same idea, a conscious attempt is made by him not to repeat a phrase coined by Rao. A substitute in his addresses for 'Growth with a Human Face' is 'social liberalization'. For example, 'Together create a mindset, a revolution to harmonize the objectives of economic liberalization and social liberalization'. Vajpayee, 'Government—Industry Partnership for Growth', address at the first meeting of the Trade and Industry Council, New Delhi, 18 September 1998.

However, Singh, who also belongs to the Indian National Congress and a coalition government, led by the same, is seen as repeating most of Rao's vocabulary. Thus, in the following lines, as in many other examples, 'the Human Face' reappears. 'Structural reforms in a democracy, to be durable, must involve consultation with all stake holders particularly the workers and trade unions. Our government is committed to reforms with a Human Face. The working classes of our country have my assurance that we shall never pursue a path which affects adversely the interests of the workers of the toiling masses of our country.' [Singh, 'Towards Promoting Employment Led Growth', address at the Shram Awards Function, New Delhi, 4 October 2004.]

of society. With the underlying comprehension that a vast majority of India lives in deprivation, in abject poverty, and in extreme conditions, but simultaneously also aware that it is the same majority that comprises the invaluable vote bank in India, an emphatic thrust of *producing* the 'Emerging India' thus incorporates a discourse that will make the same majority *believe*, at the very least, in *some* elements of this emerging India.

The following lines, derived from Rao's address, are an illustration of this 'Growth with a Human Face'.

During the last two years we have embarked on a radical restructuring of our economy [...] addressing the complex and inescapable social needs of our large population. The time has now come to step out in the larger world, as it were and we have done so in a well-considered systematic way, neither fighting shy of certain positive steps in liberalization nor going overboard and pulling all stops at the risk of widespread human distress. Ours is, in a word, reform with a Human Face. And our deregulation and liberalization programme has already started yielding notable results and is also gathering momentum towards an integration of the Indian economy with the global economy.[46]

In the aforementioned lines, Rao makes the attempt of balancing the neo-liberal agenda and 'addressing the complex and inescapable social needs' of the Indian population. This idea of reforms with a human face is furthered in the following lines:

Over the last two years especially, we have embarked on a restructuring of our economy on the basis of deregulation, liberalization and modern management and marketing techniques. We have tried to build on the foundations laid during previous decades of economic development. The objective of the new reforms is to plan the economic future of India in a manner where the pressures of inflation and recession are resisted and where fiscal discipline and emphasis on increased productivity become practical norms. I must also point out that the processes of economic modernization and reforms are being fashioned, taking into account all aspects of human existence and all ingredients which constitute the quality of life; the ingredients of literacy, health, shelter, required minimum

---

[46] Rao, 'Indo-Singapore Friendship and Co-operation', address at the banquet hosted in honour of the prime minister of Singapore, New Delhi, 24 January 1991.

incomes and environmental safety. That is what we call reform with a human face. And this is no idle expression.[47]

The objective is to assure audiences that what appears to be transition is in fact a measured, informed, controlled, and calibrated conquest of the future, so as to render it predictable and henceforth familiar and desirable. So often is this phrase repeated by Rao that towards the end of his term, one finds that its constitutive elements are no longer explained explicitly, but that it reflects lexical repertoire that is employed as an established normative truth, a fact.

> I have been making it clear right from the beginning, right from 1991 itself, about the philosophy which we have accepted. The philosophy of economic reforms with a Human Face. I am not talking about the human face for the first time this year or last year. [...] I have been saying that we have to be always looking at the human face, thinking of the human face and being careful about orienting our programmes in the best interest of the country and the poorest of the poor in the country.[48]

This category of the 'poor' emerges forcefully on numerous occasions in almost all addresses of all four prime ministers, which deal either specifically with the reforms or are placed in a category titled 'General Economic Affairs' in the collected volumes of public speeches. Some examples include:

> 'We will keep the common man, the poor, particularly those who live in the villages at the centre of our development vision'.[49]

> 'The thrust of whatever new reform has been taken has been only to lift the downtrodden in this country, those who have nowhere to go'.[50]

> 'Government concessions must be for the poor and the really needy.'[51]

---

[47] Rao, 'Common Indo–China Approach for Asian Resurgence', address at the Beijing University, China, 9 September 1993.

[48] Rao, 'Thrust on Social Sector Development'.

[49] Vajpayee, 'Human Development and Public Governance', address at the 78th General Meeting of ASSOCHAM, New Delhi, 11 December 1998.

[50] Rao, 'Thrust on Social Sector Development'.

[51] Rao,'Towards Accelarating the Pace of Economic Growth', excerpts from reply to the debate on the President's Address in Lok Sabha, New Delhi, 8 March 1994.

'The economic reforms we have initiated have no other aim than to create employment for all and bring the fruits of prosperity for all—especially to those who have so far been deprived of it'.[52]

'We have to make determined efforts to meet the economic challenges before the nation. We have to accelerate and broaden our developmental process, so that no child of Mother India remains hungry, homeless, unemployed or is without access to medical care'.[53]

In the following lines one finds Rao establishing that the transformations induced by market liberalization are embraced not because of external pressures or due to helplessness, but rather because they are a necessary, desirable change that will ensure the realization of the envisioned future. This implies economic growth, but one that is attained within the contours of social justice, one that promises 'the greatest good of the greatest numbers'.[54] An important constituent of this is the assurance of rural development,[55] rural employment, and a rejuvenation of the agricultural sector.[56]

---

[52] Vajpayee, 'Strengthening Transpareny in Governance', statement on the completion of one year of the National Democratic Alliance Government, Mumbai, 13 October 2000.

[53] Vajpayee, 'Together Let us build a Stronger Nation'.

[54] For example, 'What we are seeking to establish is the greatest good of the greatest numbers. Consumer satisfaction undoubtedly gives pleasure and pleasure is an essential ingredient of "good" but pleasure and good cannot be taken as identical. There must surely be a social, psychological and perhaps spiritual content of good which is not purely market determined and I believe there is.' (Rao, 'New Challenges of Unipolarity', Jodidi Memorial Lecture, Harvard University, Boston USA, 17 May 1994).

[55] For example, Vajpayee states: 'Reach out to the rural sector not merely because it is large, but because the needs of rural India cannot be bypassed. The rural sector needs high quality products to derive the advantages of globalization.' (Vajpayee, 'Maximize the Benefits of Economic Liberalization', address at the India Economic Summit, New Delhi, 26 November 2000).

[56] Some illustrations include: 'I want to assure our farmer brothers who are the backbones of the Nation that they will never suffer under this government.' (Vajpayee, 'Harbinger of Progress', address to the nation on Indian Independence Day, New Delhi, 15 August 1998); 'Ours is a government that represents and cares for every section of the Indian society. Even so, I have no hesitation in saying that it represents, first and foremost, the farmers and

I am merely saying that I have no right to throw millions of people out of their jobs overnight because I want a particular change. If someone asks me to do so, I would say in all humility that either he does not know my country or what I am really trying to do. We have to find solutions which involve reforms, certainly but which are also humane. In India we call it reform with a Human Face. The schemes of change must therefore take full note of local contingencies and make allowance for them. [...] Each society has to find its Middle way [...] and this should be the approach of countries that accept change. They accept change because they think that change is necessary not because they are helpless, not because there is no other way ... we have to evolve our own thinking, our own way of mending our shoe.[57]

It is apt to mention here that one of the harshest critics of the opening up of the economy has been the salaried class—the public sector employees, a class which, according to Pranab Bardan, is 'determined to preserve (and enhance) its salaries and prerequisites, job security (irrespective of efficiency or merit), promotion on the basis of seniority and a general lackadaisical work culture. To the extent that reforms bring in more competition and threaten the pre-existing job culture and practices, this class is adamantly opposed to them.'[58] Its grievances are voiced primarily by the losely-termed collective, 'the Left'. Bardan ironically mentions, 'The Left in India, in aiming at "the dictatorship of the proletariat" has given us instead the dictatorship of the salariat.'[59] Whereas, in most addresses, the expansion of the private enterprise is justified under the garb of giving impetus to the 'creative energies' of private entrepreneurs, even small-scale businesses and an increased thrust on efficiency,[60] here, Rao lends a voice on behalf of the 'small man', albeit before an external audience. One may thus acknowledge a sense of self-reflexivity,

---

the rural community of India' (Vajpayee, 'Value Addition in the Agriculatural Sector', address at the 'Agro-Advantage' Maharashtra Conference, Mumbai, 6 November 1998).

[57] Vajpayee, 'Value Addition in the Agriculatural Sector'.

[58] P. Bardan, 'Nature of Opposition to Economic Reforms in India', *Economic and Political Weekly*, 40(48), 2005: 4995–8.

[59] Bardan, 'Nature of Opposition to Economic Reforms in India'.

[60] On one occasion, Rao is seen as justifying the loss of employment in the public sector as follows: 'Employment will be generated inspite of exit policy but not bloated employment.' (Rao, 'Secularism, Non-Alignment and Removal of Poverty', interview with 'The Gentlemam', Mumbai, February 1992).

an awareness of allegations on the reforms, which explains the explicit thrust on speaking for the salaried class, and also perhaps those who belong to informally unorganized labour. Strategically enough though, this eclectic mix of different class strata are confused thoroughly and reduced to the shorthand term 'poor'[61] in the addresses.

No 'Total Capitalism' for India: Making Growth 'Indian'

A noticeable observation is the linguistic apparatus utilized to sell this growth with a human face. While terms like 'opening up', 'liberalization', 'deregulation', coupled with 'democracy', find repetitive co-occurrence in the same line frequently, there is a shying away from the term capitalism. Out of the approximate 1,202 addresses that my analysis covers, the term is almost never used in any of the speeches except on two occasions. Hilgers states that in any given social environment, the term neo-liberalism ought to be researched in its specific contexts in order to trace a comprehensive historicity of the term.[62] The almost visible absence of the term 'capitalism' is another finding of this analysis, which helps comprehend the discursive career of neo-liberalism in the Indian context.

It is the relative newness of the lexical repertoire that renders it usable and sellable from the early 1990s unto contemporary oratory. By using it, the speakers introduce a new space for defining and therein fixing the coordinates of 'neo-liberalism'.[63] The term 'capitalism', however,

---

[61] Other usages which appear in the speeches include 'the masses' and 'the common man' or *aam admi*. For example, Vajpayee uses the term 'masses' here, 'We have accorded priority to social sector development, particularly health, primary education, drinking water and rural road construction. Policies and programmes are being re-shaped so that the benefits of growth percolate to the masses' (Vajpayee, 'Maximize the Benefits of Economic Liberalization', address at the India Economic Summit, New Delhi, 26 November 2000).

[62] Hilgers states lucidly: 'Studies of neoliberalism seem to sometimes consider the Western neoliberal trajectory as the neoliberal trajectory per se [...] I argue that the development of an analytical perspective that considers the production of neoliberalism "at a global scale" [...] must take into account the trajectories of a variety of states.' [M. Hilgers, 'The Historicity of the Neoliberal State', *Social Anthropology*, 20(1): 80–94, here p. 80, 2012.]

[63] Pranab Bardan, however, has also pointed out the same for neo-liberalism. In his work on the nature of opposition to market liberalization, Bardan

has had its own career in the Indian context. It has unpopularly been associated with the ambiguous category of the 'West', and therein utilized to establish a difference with an abstract generalized 'other', thus, usually being evoked in a specific culturalist context. It also carries the historical weight of being associated with economic exploitation during colonial rule and as being essentially 'anti-poor' in postcolonial India. This is very lucid in Nehru's own words from *The Discovery of India*, where he mentions:

> The world market that the new capitalism was building up would have, in any event, affected India's economic system. The self-sufficient village community, with its traditional division of labour, could not have continued in its old form. But the change that took place was not a normal development and it disintegrated the whole economic and structural basis of Indian society. A system which had social sanctions and controls behind it and was a part of the people's cultural heritage was suddenly and forcibly changed and another system, administered from outside the group, was imposed. India did not come into a world market but became a colonial and agricultural appendage of the British structure.[64]

As evident, capitalism occurs in the context of imperialism and is held responsible for the disruption of indigenous economic self-sufficiency. This stance would find continuity in Nehru's oratory in postcolonial India, whereby capitalism and imperialism were persistently projected as symbiotic forces.[65] Besides this indexical negative connotation, the

---

beautifully sketches the linguistic apparatus and titles used by both pro-reformers as well as reform opposers in India. 'The pro-reformers identify the opposition as belonging to the "looney left" caught in a time warp, oblivious of global changes and elementary economics. The other side paints the reform mongers as "neo-liberal" (a widely used term of abuse in certain circles) and lackeys of global capitalism oblivious of the poor and the dispossessed.' [Bardan, 'Nature of Opposition to Economic Reforms in India', p. 1995.]

[64] Nehru, *The Discovery of India* (New Delhi: Oxford University Press, 1985 [1946]), p. 303.

[65] This is evident in his works in as early as during the 1930s when Nehru wrote *Glimpses of World History* in the form of letters addressed to his daughter from prison. For a comprehensive overview of the correlation, Nehru drew between imperialism and capitalism and how he combined nationalism and internationalism in his writings and speeches. See M.L. Louro, 'India

absence of the term in the speeches also reveals that it is not used because there is nothing 'Indian' about it. Producing allegories, which help in rendering market liberalization immediately familiar to internal audiences, requires that the vocabulary used for doing the same is *creatively* 'Indian'. Capitalism, both as a term as also an abstract ideological signifier, could not have filled the postcolonial vacuum that constantly struggles and yearns for its own stamp of distinctive uniqueness. This also explains the repetitive emphasis on phrases, like 'Mixed Economy as the Indian Way', and 'We Had Our Own Middle Path', through which the prime ministers try to distance themselves from the idea of *total* capitalism, rescuing the reforms from being judged as anti-poor, while, in effect, speaking about 'opening up' of the economy. In the following lines, one finds Rao making a reference to capitalism and placing the 'poor' at the centre of his agenda.

> I do not think that the world situation as I see it today, really points towards unlimited capitalism. I would not agree with that. And I would not agree to have that as a programme in this country. We will have to think of the pro-poor programmes. We will have to think of the massive poverty that is ailing the nation. [...] The advent of total capitalism will not be able to solve our problems. We are convinced of that. That is why we have to have a third way. That third way is that while we open up, while we become part of the world economy, we will have to have our programmes absolutely intact because we consider them absolutely necessary for our people [...] there will be no dilution on that. We have deliberately included all the programmes for the poor in the budget.[66]

Another illustration where capitalism is produced as undesirable and 'the poor' are made to believe in the inevitability of the reforms as a project that will realize their dreams of growth is in the following lines:

> We need not accept the proposition of unlimited capitalism and leave the poor out. Our position was stated very clearly and in 1993 I had stated

---

and the League against Imperialism: A Special "Blend" of Nationalism and Internationalism' in A. Raza, F. Roy, and B. Zachariah (eds), *The Internationalist Moment: South Asia, Worlds and Worldviews, 1917–39* (New Delhi: Sage, 2015), pp. 22–55.

[66] Rao, 'Economic Reforms Help. Economic Sovereignty', excerpts from reply to the debate on the President's Address in Lok Sabha, 9 March 1992.

that the Budget of 1993–94 intended to give a major push to our policy of reducing poverty and increasing employment. This is what we called 'Human Face.' From day one upliftment of the poor is an article of faith with us.[67]

This section has shown how the reforms are rendered legitimate and indisputable by generating the promise of growth. Growth is produced as a necessity that is projected in the future. Reforms are thus presented as materializing the desire for growth, rendering these aspirations believable and attainable. The first part has highlighted some of the ingredients of that desired growth—ranging from educated youth, to open markets, to India being an IT power, to advancement through science and technology, among others. Here, theme parks, IT hubs like Bangalore, and India's emergence as a knowledge economy, all become the iconic markers of India's growth. The second part showed how the reforms are crafted before the audiences to produce this promised growth as inclusive, encompassing one, and all in India. They are thus rendered 'human', equitable, and just under the lexicon of 'Growth with a Human Face'. The last section has shown how the project of emergence and development is given a particularly Indian stamp by dissociating it from the term capitalism, which is loosely viewed as a 'western' achievement.

Growth in a 'Waiting Room': The Other within Will Also Win

In spite of the claimed promises of growth with a 'human face', which is guaranteed for all Indians, a vast majority of the Indian population, which lies at the fringes of the receiving end of these new economic developments and will not see the materialization of their benefits in the near future, is 'assigned a place elsewhere', a 'waiting room condition'.[68] This, to borrow Johannes Fabian's framework, refers to a denial of coevalness, 'a temporal distancing' through which the prime ministers generate the promise of growth, but relegate it to

---

[67] Rao, 'Thrust on Social Sector Development'.

[68] D. Chakrabarty, *Provincializing Europe: Post-colonial Thought and Historical Difference* (Princeton: Princeton University Press, 2000), p. 7.

the future with the underlying message of 'not yet, but for sure!'[69] This implies that the prime ministers inform the *aam admi*, the common man, a shorthand term used here for the vast majority of Indian population, that they are partaking in the formation of this new India and that, *eventually*, they too shall be incorporated. Trickle down is thus sold to most audiences, and hope is generated for a putative, prosperous future.

The existence of allochronic (occurring in different genealogical times) discourse has been the key subject of inquiry in Johannes Fabian's work (*Time and the Other—How Anthropology Makes its Object*),[70] which delves into temporal distancing between the subject and the object of anthropology, showing how a researcher often relegates his/her object of inquiry to a 'different time zone' when writing about it. Dipesh Chakrabarty's *Provincializing Europe* engages with the same problematic ('waiting room of history'), though in the context of the question of independence and the colonial condition.[71] This framework can also be used in illustrating how, even within the category of what is

---

[69] This does not imply that contemporary India, post the introduction of the neo-liberal reforms, has not witnessed noteworthy economic transformations for some sections. For reflections on the emergence of new middle classes, see Säävääla, 'Entangled in the Imagination: New middle Class Apprehensions in an Indian Theme Park', Ethnos 71, no. 3 (2006): 390–414 and Säävääla, 'Auspicious Hindu Houses: The New Middle Class in India', *Social Anthropology* 11, no. 2 (2003): 231–47.

[70] J. Fabian, *Time and the Other: How Anthropology Makes its Object* (New York: Columbia University Press, 1983).

[71] Chakrabarty elucidates through the example of John Stuart Mill's *On Liberty* and *On Representative Government*, how in the essays, although self-rule was proclaimed as the highest form of government, 'According to Mill, Indians and Africans were not yet civilized enough to rule themselves. Some historical time of development and civilization (colonial rule and education to be precise) had to elapse before they could be considered prepared for such a task. Mill's historicist argument thus consigned Indians and Africans, and other "rude" nations to an imaginary waiting room of history. [...] We are all headed for the same destination, Mill averred, but some people were to arrive earlier than others.' The same underlying idea may be applied to 'trickling down' of the rewards of neo-liberal economic reforms and an open economy to the *aam admi*, the common man, who is promised growth but is required to wait for it to reach him. [Chakrabarty, *Provincializing Europe*, p. 7.]

loosely called 'the rest', 'the East', 'the postcolonial', the 'Other' within is forcefully produced as a category and temporality lends the toolkit with which this category is projected and maintained. On one side of the spectrum is the politics of time that construes the 'Emerging India', a new India of the future, which is now 'catching up' with the world. Here, India is one, a homogenous entity that experiences market liberalization uniformly. Whereas, on the flip side is the category of the 'Other' *within* that India which is relegated to an imaginary waiting room, being denied coevalness. The underlying message is that they too *will* be incorporated in receiving the benefits of market liberalization, but *only eventually*.

A more direct or relatively speedy success for some is thus justified in the camouflage of a promissory note, a waiting phase for most. A very illustrative example of this is when Rao, during the motion of confidence in the Lok Sabha, while presenting the reforms for the very first time in parliament, said:

> What have I done? What had the government done? We know that there are no alternatives to what we have done. We have only salvaged the prestige of this country. *Sarvanaashe samutpanne ardham tyajati panditah.* This is precisely what we have done. I do not say that the economy has been booming or is going to boom immediately. What I am saying is sarvanaashe samputpanne.[72]

In the excerpt, Rao clearly presents the reforms in the parliament as the last option to save 'the prestige of this country'. The Sanskrit *shloka* (meaning, when everything is at stake, the wise give up half of it to save the other half) may be seen as a response Rao gives to the opponents of the reforms during the debate. The harshest critique came from the BJP (as mentioned earlier, later an ardent supporter of the reforms when in government) and the Janata Dal Alliance, whereby the former voted for 'no' (but was outnumbered) and the latter walked out of the parliament. The basis of the critique was that the reforms were elitist and anti-poor. In the given excerpt, though Rao camouflages his answer to this criticism in the statement that there was no other alternative, at the same time, the shloka indicates that Rao is aware that 'a half'

[72] Rao, 'Reply to the Debate on Motion of Confidence in Lok Sabha', 15 July 1991.

needs to be given up to save the other half though he is not explicit in describing what comprises 'that half'. An important caveat to add here is that unlike in many of Rao's speeches that use the Sanskrit language from the Upanishads, the Sanskrit shloka here is neither explained nor translated within the text of the speech. It could, in fact, be considered a phrase that was not meant to be understood by numerous members in the house.[73]

Later, in the same speech, Rao states: 'I do not say that our economy has been booming or is going to boom immediately [...] The journey, the *Mahaprasthana* starts today [...] this is not the final solution, this is only the beginning.'[74]

On another occasion, he states: 'We are fully aware that there are no shortcuts along the path we have chosen. The process will be long and sometimes painful. Our people are ready for it [...]'[75]

In the first message to the nation about the reforms, Rao explicitly states: 'Friends, it will be dishonest for me to pretend that the job of repairing our economy will be easy, quick or smooth. Each one of us will be called upon to make sacrifices.'[76]

A pertinent question to be posed is what are the details of these 'sacrifices' and who would need to make them? As will be shown in the following section, the same logic underpins the introduction of foreign

---

[73] This episode is attested by Jairam Ramesh, a Congress MP at the time, who, in his detailed book on the episodic months of July–August 1991, states how he '[...] could see that most people did not understand what the prime minister was saying. I recall A.N. Verma looking at me with a puzzled expression, then whispering, *Kaho, Pandit, kuch samjhe?* (Tell me, wise one, do you comprehend this?) Later, I told Verma that the Sanskrit saying in the prime minister's speech means that the wise man, in the event of total ruin, wriggles out by giving up half his possessions; this is done in the hope that he will save himself from total destruction by using what is left properly.' J. Ramesh, 'Chapter 13: The Sanskritist Prime Minister', in J. Ramesh (ed.), *To the Brink and Back: India's 1991 Story* (New Delhi: Rupa Publications, 2015).

[74] Rao, 'Reply to the Debate on Motion of Confidence in Lok Sabha'.

[75] Rao, 'Globalization Should Lead to a More Caring Society', address at the India Forum meet of the World Economic Forum, New Delhi, 18 November 1991.

[76] Rao, 'Re-Structuring the Economy', broadcast to the nation post inception of the Economic Reforms Plan, 9 July 1991.

investments and privatization as well as greater exports from the agricultural sector or rapid industrialization.[77]

In specific addresses, where the prime minister speaks directly for the
amorphous category of the 'common person', new dreams are generated. They are new because they introduce a new world of consumption patterns to the people, and yet they are dreams because it is in the
nature of these new consumption patterns, in the near future at the
very least, to not become available to all. An economy of producing
new demands and rendering them culturally valuable, even essential,
is at work which at best caters to produce only a fantastic dream of
the supply, and, in so doing, leaves new crevices that slowly crack the
already weak economic structures of division. The following lines
provide a remarkable example of these expanding 'dreams'. Newly
generated desires of consumption coupled with equally new promises
of their availability are intertwined in the logic of market liberalization
and increasing industrialization.

> But what is the involvement of the people in the industrialization of the
> country. Are we really able to realize their full involvement? [...] You will
> never prosper unless you give that stake to the common people in what
> you are doing. There was a time when people said 'if you build a road,
> I don't have a car, so, why do I need a road? We have heard these things
> from our own villagers. Now nobody says we don't want a road. They
> are clamouring for roads. They are clamouring for schools. They are
> clamouring for everything—TVs, Radios, you name it. Why? Because
> the people have understood the advantage of it. In some cases they
> have become status symbols also. If you have a TV there is something
> respectable about it. If you don't have a TV you go to the next house to

---

[77] For example, Rao states:

A large industry will have to enlist the support of hundreds and thousands of
people in order to exist. This is what is happening in large industries wherever we
have them. It is not throwing people out of employment; it is getting people in.
Then, what about services? It is not just the manufacturing sector. What about
the services sector? If there is an industry, how many people get employment in
services, in serving that industry? Now this is an expanding activity, circle after
circle, each larger than the previous one. This is how it will expand. We do not
have a ready made map, as I said. But I can see that the result of this industrial policy is going to be good for the whole country. [Rao, 'The New Economic Policy
for the Good of the People', address at Nippon Denro Ispat Ltd. (Foundation
Ceremony), Maharashtra, 7 March 1992.]

watch TV, then you are somehow inferior. Even if it has become a status symbol there is something which is happening by way of change in the thinking of the people. That should be welcomed, that should be fully channelized for industrialization.[78]

Rao is speaking here to a very particular audience, a conference organized for the chief executives of public sector enterprises. No surprise then that the category of 'the villager' appears forcefully as one that is temporally distanced, as if inhabiting another temporal zone or a 'different genealogical time'.

Some points that emerge from these lines are: First, Rao indicates a shift, a change in operation in the choices desired by the 'villager' who is slowly learning the advantages of not just roads but also radios. Second, a connection is established between the 'people' and industrialization in India. As per this link, 'common people' are allowed to participate in India's economic success, and through this shift they are becoming stakeholders in the process. Third, new items of consumption, so far unfamiliar, and certainly not available to all, get embedded in the vocabulary of growing dreams. Fourth, because there is a sea change in how people think and their new dreams (wish for new 'things'), industrialization should increase to provide those 'things' to people. However, this change in people's 'thinking' appears to emerge out of thin air, with no discussion on *how* these demands are generated and *who* produces these demands. Lastly, the role of 'the villagers' here is relegated to no more than being the passive receivers of a new inexhaustible list, first of a demand that is generated, and then of the promise of a supply to that demand. The purpose is to establish that the change being introduced is not a result of ideas emanating from the leadership or external/international pressure, but, rather, true to its democratic style, a demand which initiates in the Indian village itself.

[...] There is a perception that the present reform strategy is elitist-driven. And that it is designed to help industry and the corporate sector without its benefits trickling down to the poorest sections of the society and leaving the rural economy untouched. The fact that *in the long run* (my emphasis) a strategy which leads to high rates of economic growth

---

[78] Rao, 'Challenges Before the Public Sector Enterprises', address at the Inauguration of a Conference of Chief Executives of Public Sector Enterprises, New Delhi, 30 July 1994.

has overall benefits for the average man whether by way of improved rural connectivity at lower tariffs, assured supply of water, better roads and improved infrastructure is forgotten. A concerted approach in this area needs to be evolved if we are to sustain the momentum of economic changes, indeed we must, if India is to achieve the rates of growth necessary to eliminate poverty.[79]

In the aforementioned lines, a discursive loop seems to be in operation. The logic runs—industry and the corporate sector need to be assisted, for only in doing so can the benefits reach the common man *in the long run*. The promise of neo-liberalization is improved rural connectivity, water supply, better roads, and infrastructure. It is these *long-term* benefits that are thus produced here as the justification for the reforms not being elitist-driven. This is not to state that the prime ministers do not speak of making growth inclusive, reducing poverty, or improving the 'lives of millions', or the 'Daridranarayan—our poor brethren'[80] (as Rao calls them); in fact, it is quite the contrary. However, what I wish to emphasize is that these millions are asked to be patient and invited to wait, so that growth may reach them. Reforms therein become inevitable, even though some stand to benefit from them *earlier* than others (who happen to be the majority).

This is also not to state that the addresses do not reflect an awareness of the allegations staged against market liberalization (in that they are elitist). These allegations have often been eloquently staged by the opposition in India. Ironically, each party that supports and furthers the

---

[79] Vajpayee, 'A National Approach to Economic Policies', address at the Reconstituted Economic Advisory Council, New Delhi, 30 August 2000. It is interesting to note that during the process of categorizing the material, it appeared that the category of the poor, the villager, the farmer is almost always referred to in the addresses, but never directly, that is, a majority of the published speeches do not directly address farmers or villagers in rural settings. It is only in the Independence Day commemoration speeches that one finds all prime ministers talking directly to an imagined 'poor' population. This also says something about the category of 'the poor', who are always spoken *about* in all contexts. But who they specifically are is not elaborated. Thus, the category appears more as a discursive one with no specific margins, always represented as either being on the fringes or as one that is promised a future, but rarely addressed directly.

[80] Rao, 'Our Commitment: Unity and Uplifting the Poor', address to the nation on Indian Independence Day, New Delhi, 15 August 1994.

cause of neo-liberal economic reforms, when in power, has a record of being their severest critic when in the opposition (see Pranab Bardan). The idea of 'selling growth' and making it a realizable dream for people, through political oratory, is a dynamically reflexive process, and the addresses are thoroughly informed with an intertextual vocabulary that can respond to allegations made against the reforms. This reflexivity may be noticed in Vajpayee's following address. Interestingly enough, the lines were delivered in the US at an India–US Business Summit, thus also before audiences percieved as 'external'. We find Vajpayee highly aware of the criticism of trickle-down effect, and making the reforms appear inclusive through the promise of equitable development.

> We want to alter the focal point of change. As a result of our efforts, reforms are being perceived less and less as being elitist driven. We are taking concrete measures to cushion the impact of change on the weaker sections of the society. The trickle-down effect of growth is often slow. Which is why we are consciously trying to harmonize faster economic growth with equitable development. We are determined to ensure that the benefits of reforms do not bypass the common man.[81]

Neo-Liberalism as a Socialist Project

I started this chapter with the statement that my study of the prime ministers' speeches has revealed the use of innumerable temporal jus- tifications in order to frame and justify the reforms as an event embed- ded in time. The main objective of the analysis is thus to show how change produced through the reforms is inserted in a temporal order or sequence in the speeches so that they become something which is indisputable. This section will illustrate how transformation in the form of reforms is naturalized by borrowing heavily from a vocabulary that relies on India's socialist past. 'Let us look to the future. We have to create a prosperous, self-reliant and self-confident India. Indeed we have already embarked on this path. We will march further in this direction. We are being counted among the ranks of successful nations. We must not stop. Rather, we must step up the speed of our journey.'[82]

---

[81] Vajpayee, 'USA: India's Largest Trading Partner', address at the US–India Business Summit, New York, September 2000.

[82] Vajpayee, 'Together Let Us Build a Stronger Nation'.

In the excerpt, Vajpayee makes reference to India's putative future. However, a closer attention points towards the socialist overtones used to describe that future. It categorically reflects the Nehruvian-socialist style of oratory. Phrases like 'self-reliant' and 'self-confident' call out for due attention.

A key particularity of the political rhetoric of the socialist era (which may be associated with Nehru as well as the successive Shastri and Indira Gandhi governments) is a lexicon constituted of terms like 'scientific temper', 'secular nationalism', but, above all, 'developmentalism'.[83] It is here that terms like 'self-reliant', 'self-sufficient', and 'self-confident' came to be popularized by Nehru with the claim for 'Big Industries, Big Dams, and Big Universities' being the 'Temples of a "modern" India'.[84]

In fact, in the previous excerpt, Vajpayee speaks very much on the lines of that Nehruvian socialism when talking about the future. In his book *The Discovery of India*, Nehru writes: 'The objective for the country as a whole was the attainment, as far as possible, of national *self-sufficiency*. International trade was certainly not excluded, but we were anxious to avoid being drawn into the whirlpool of economic imperialism. We wanted neither to be victims of an imperialist power nor to develop such tendencies ourselves [...]'[85] (author's emphasis).

Thus, adulations like 'self-sufficient India' or 'self-reliant India', already used in Nehru's canonized book, but repetitively emphasized during his term later on, stand as iconic signs of Nehru's words, in

---

[83] Manu Goswami sums up the prevailing mood, as also the ongoing legacy of the Nehruvian era by aptly describing it as follows:

Nehru, who would become the first prime minister of postcolonial India and a chief architect of the left and liberal anti-imperial national developmentalist models elaborated by third world states at the Bandung Conference in 1955, has long been regarded as the incarnation par excellence of the modernizing, rationalist, and secular imperatives of institutional nationalism. Nehru held up the universalistic project of national development as embodied in "a heavy engineering and machine-making sector, scientific research institutes, and electric power as the "temples" of India's future. [M. Goswami, *Producing India: From Colonial Economy to National Space* (Chicago, University of Chicago Press, 2004), p. 3.]

[84] For a detailed account of the Nehruvian vision of 'Temples of Modern India', see S. Khilnani, *The Idea of India* (London: Penguin, 1997).

[85] Nehru, *The Discovery of India*, p. 398.

fact of Nehru himself, which have not left public lexical memory, and have produced a sense of national security. In the previous excerpts, Vajpayee, though propagating a sweeping shift from the quasi-socialist model, uses the same vocabulary that stands as figurative of the security of the past to produce the security of the future. In the following lines, Rao is seen as establishing the link at the very onset of the institutionalization of the reforms in 1991 in an address to the nation: 'My objective is to make India truly self-reliant. Self-reliance is not a mere slogan for me. It means the ability to pay for our imports through exports. My motto is: Trade, not aid. Aid is a crutch. Trade builds pride. And India has been trading for thousands of years.'[86]

In this excerpt, socialist nostalgia reminiscent in the usage of a vocabulary constituted by terms like 'self-reliant' and 'self-sufficient' is accommodated and made to share the same semantic space with the neo-liberal logic of an open economy. It is this rhetorical *merging* that constitutes the texture of an *(E)merging India* narrative. The attempts to establish the same were at their pivotal best during Rao's term. The themes of open markets and self-reliance are thus clubbed and merged together, whereas external aid is established as undesired. The underpinning idea of producing change without revealing its uncontrollability is beautifully summed up in the following excerpt, also by Vajpayee, whose addresses, with their inherent distinctions from those delivered by Singh and Rao, nonetheless provide a consistency to the story.

> We have not embraced [...] globalization in a blind manner. We are sequencing the pace of change to suit our own needs, particularly in sensitivity to its social, cultural and human consequences so that transitional adjustments are orderly. This is particularly so in the area of privatization and disinvestment. [...] The transition from a socialist model of growth which we practiced for many decades, to an economy governed primarily by market forces, has to be calibrated with care and caution.[87]

Vajpayee informs an 'internal' audience in a highly ritualistic address delivered to the nation on Independence Day that India's move towards privatization and disinvestment is, in fact, a calibrated one, undertaken with 'care and caution'. Here, the term globalization, though celebrated in most addresses that are delivered before the external audiences, IT

---

[86] Rao, 'Re-Structuring the Economy'.
[87] Vajpayee, 'Together Let Us Build a Stronger Nation'.

professionals, and private sector enterprises, becomes an indexical sign for an abstraction that calls for caution and a measured approach. The above is the only occasion when any of the three prime ministers openly addresses the shift from the 'socialist model of growth' to 'an economy governed primarily by market forces'. This blatant admission is essentially missing in the speeches delivered by both Rao and Manmohan Singh. In that sense, the earlier lines may be treated as demarcating a paradigmatic shift in the strategies adopted in addressing the transition itself. However, a careful reading of the *entire* address confirms the same insecurity in Vajpayee's tone that demands that the new transformations be presented in the garb of the old. Thus, once again, the address is replete with notions of self-sufficiency, sovereignty, and 'sensitivity' to the social, cultural, and human consequences.

In the following excerpt from Rao's address, economic sovereignty resurfaces in the advent of an attack made on the reforms. Change is once again produced by taking away its unpredictability and uncontrollability.

> One very serious objection has been raised about the Government policies to the effect that the country's economic sovereignty has been jeopardized. This is a serious allegation by any standards and this cannot be taken lightly either by the Government or by this House or by the country. But before making an allegation like this, it is also necessary that to realize how serious it is. […] There is absolutely no question of any Congress Party Government in India at any time—past, present or future, jeopardizing the sovereignty of India, whether political or economic. […] There can be no question of playing with the economic sovereignty of India.[88]

These lines indicate that the cause of economic sovereignty here is defended in the name of a political party. The Indian National Congress becomes the legitimizing hinge around which the door of transition is made to turn. But that door opens a new passage, a new space, by not shutting away entirely the one room from the other. Like nationalist historiography itself, it stands midway, half open and half shut, to both the spaces of the socialist past and the neo-liberal present, leaving it to the prime minister in a given context what he chooses to do and not

---

[88] Rao, excerpts from reply to the debate on the President's Address in Rajya Sabha, 10 March 1992.

do with it. The past is *made* safe and revoked selectively and is used to celebrate the future. Two other examples where Rao defends the claims for economic sovereignty, in spite of structural adjustment and 'foreign' intrusion in domestic economy respectively, while using the Indian National Congress as a legitimizing hinge, are as follows:

> The World Bank belongs to India as much as the United Nations belongs to us. The World Bank and the IMF have been approached for assistance not for the first time now. We have done it several times before. There is hardly any country which does not knock at the doors of the World Bank. Countries which are not members of the World Bank are now knocking at the doors of World Bank to gain entry. I would like to say that this prejudice or bias or opinion sought to be created against an international financial body is not in the interests of this country. Yes, we do not fully endorse the structure, the working of the Brettonwoods institutions. We have been constantly trying for the reform of these institutions, both in the Non-Aligned Movement and at the United Nations, and we will continue to do so. But to say that taking a loan from the World Bank or the IMF amounts to selling the country is something which is totally unacceptable. And I have to protest against this language being used against any Government, particularly the Government belonging to the Indian National Congress, which brought us our Independence.[89]

Another illustration, in the same direction, in defence of multinational corporations may be found in the following example:

> Imports and exports are normal things in the economic life of a country. It is not that you have to manufacture everything in this country. This is not done. Take a car. You will find that the crankshaft is made by one country and the engine by another country. They all combine because they specialize in these things. They don't think that national sovereignty is lost if they don't manufacture everything. That kind of a national sovereignty is a false notion. That has been given up long ago. If you and some other country can come together and manufacture something good, something cheap here, they will come and do it. Between the two they become a multinational. In the multinational scene, India is already there. So, all that rhetoric about multinationals we will have to forget. When two countries some, two governments come, two industrialists from different countries come, they will have to have a common multiple so that all the countries profit. There is no

---

[89] Rao, 'Economic Reforms Help Economic Sovereignty'.

question of one country being allowed to exploit the other. That is what really is the idea. I don't think anyone can exploit India any more. That era has gone. When it is cooperation, it is not a clash of sovereignties. It is a matter of cooperating with countries. When they can cooperate among themselves, why not we? We can cooperate amongst ourselves and also with them.[90]

As already mentioned, the phrases 'self-reliant' and 'sovereign' echo the prevalent mood of the socialist model, most visible in Nehru's addresses, but also heavily employed in Indira Gandhi's rhetoric. Rao is once again seen as defending the government against the allegation that 'national sovereignty is lost' by increasing multinational presence on Indian turf. Here, the words that rescue national sovereignty are 'a common multiple' and 'cooperation'. A point worthy of mention is that though Nehru stands as symbolic of a spaceless, unbounded, time-less, national figure, used as a referral point, almost 'religiously', by all prime ministers in their speeches, regardless of their own political party backgrounds, Indira Gandhi, whose era may be summed up with more vigorous socialist hues, dubbed in slogans like *Garibi Hatao* ('remove poverty'), is a figure used more *cautiously* and never out of the context of the Indian National Congress.[91]

---

[90] Rao, 'New Direction to Agriculture', address at a conference of chief ministers on Agricultural Policy, New Delhi, 5 March 1993.

[91] This may more generally tell us something about personna and aura generated around a founding father figure like Nehru who, through his involvement in the staging of the nationalist movement, and his writings as well, has come to become the face of the nation. Though the socialist vocabulary is more prominent in Indira Gandhi's speeches (also its link to praxis if one sees the history of bank nationalisation for example), the real attribute of the travelling lexical memory is given to Nehru. The postcolonial habitus and nostalgia of museification and deification of the first leader(s) and their almost pious presence in history is highly visible here. In that sense, they become the stalwarts, the carriers of the national self. Indira Gandhi may not enjoy the same space here as Nehru also because of the period of the national *emergency*, seen as a blemish for Indian democracy. However, on one occasion, Indira Gandhi is specifically evoked as a figure in the context of claims for self-sufficiency and economic independence in Rao's words when he speaks of the Green Revolution.

We are no longer begging for food grains from abroad. Some 20–25 years ago we were facing a drought in the country. At that time when we tried to buy food

What the earlier illustrations make abundantly clear is that all three prime ministers (as will also be shown for Modi's temporal politics in Chapter 3), regardless of their individual party affiliations, have attempted to normalize the transformations induced by the neo-liberal reforms by rendering them not so new. As the future embedded within change (in the shape of the reforms) entailed something new, the vocabulary of a recent economic past has been used by the prime ministers to describe that new in order to take away the anxiety, the unpredictability, and the contingency attached to it. The presence of terms and phrases which one may locate in Indira Gandhi and Nehru's rhetoric indicates that the aim is to ensure that change may be embraced, but, at the same time, a sense of security prevails. The message is thus not so much to inform internal audiences that a drastic transition is in operation, but rather to naturalize it in continuity, giving people an assurance of it being calculated, contained, measured, and inevitably a part of the sacred history of the nation. Thus, neo-liberal reforms paradoxically, at least lexically, become a socialist project.

***

This chapter has attempted to circumscribe how the three Indian prime ministers—Rao, Vajpayee and Singh—have profiled India as an 'Economic Powerhouse of the 21st Century', an adulation used for the first time by Prime Minister Vajpayee. It has pursued the specific question of how the prime ministers 'sell' neo-liberal reforms to different audiences, particularly those perceived as 'Indian', in their public addresses. In other words, how are reforms predetermined as being the foundation of India's (achieved and desired) economic success?

This question has been approached through the very specific lens of temporality. The main aim of the prime ministers is to render market liberalization indisputable. The analysis has uncovered how, in order to do this, the speakers generate an attitude towards time or

---

grains from other countries, they taunted us, whether they sold the grains or not. They asked us why we didn't think about our increasing population and why we are not doing enough to step up food production. We had to suffer such taunts. Indira Gandhi was angered and she felt strongly about the self-respect of the nation. In 3 or 4 years after that our farmers brought us the Green Revolution.

'ways of relating to and being in time' in their audiences. This implies that changes introduced by neo-liberal reforms are justified by embedding them in a temporal order for audiences both outside and inside of India.

The first section has highlighted the various linguistic tropes, that is, different metaphors of speed (motion), which set the stage for profiling India as an emerging economy. The second section deals with the overarching category of the future. It started with the initial strategy of making direct references to the future of the nation. The next part of this section has highlighted the coordinates of that ideal future—'The Details of Desire'—as envisioned by the respective governments. Part of this architecture incorporates conjuring India as the ideal democracy, as having an ideal, vibrant economy that engages with the world economy, ideal GDP rates of growth, and an efficient private sector. It is also here that visions of an idealized modernity are presented before internal audiences. The section has shown how the prime ministers speak of a future with a 'Human Face'. Growth here is presented as a human necessity, and the reforms are produced as the inevitable means of achieving the same. This section also shows how, in the face of criticisms levied against the reforms, the prime ministers have tried to address these attacks through the generation of an ideal future for *all*, that is, by promising growth that is inclusive and equitable. Lastly, the section shows how growth is made Indian by denying the embracement of 'unlimited capitalism'.

The third section has illustrated how, in spite of these promises, an internal 'Other' is temporally constituted. This refers to the vast majority of the population that lives on the fringes of the economy, but is given the hope of being *eventually* included in the dream of growth, being assigned a 'waiting room' of time. The fourth section has demonstrated how market liberalization is presented before Indian audiences by borrowing thoroughly from socialist vocabulary. Terms and phrases which are indicators of the quasi-socialist model associated with Nehru and Indira Gandhi's eras are used abundantly to advance the neo-liberal reforms, which, in reality, exemplified a paradigmatic shift. Thus, neo-liberalism is presented as a socialist project to produce a sense of security and take away the contingency attached to a completely new future. As this concluding section graphically shows, the categories of the future and the generalized past are not mutually exclusive. Visions of the future intertwine with, or rather, are *made to entangle* with lexical memories. Like a remixed song that offers a new composition with new beats, but always reminds the listener of the old melody, the future is never wholly free of remembrance.

3

Time and Temporalizing Tactics II

Of Iconic Past(s) and Good Times

The previous chapter has shown how the present is thought of, narrated, and made real by producing the future. As the last section in the chapter illustrated, paradoxically enough, imaginations of the future derive their legitimacy from the vocabulary of a socialist past. In that sense, the future of 'Emerging India' is one that is *remembered*. We now 're-turn' to how 'the past' is produced, being called *the past*, to feed into, and supplant the present making of 'Emerging India' in the first section. In this ordering of time, the simultaneity of breaking and bridging with a heritag*ized* selective past is kept alive. The second section of the chapter traces how the reforms are embedded in a temporal order, which is presented as something preordained, even destined for India. This shorter section elucidates how the speakers naturalize a particular sequence of events, which legitimize the change that the reforms embody as something predetermined, an act of providence. The third section focuses on the temporalizing tactics of the current prime minister, Narendra Modi, starting with the suggestive slogan *Achche Din aane wale hain* (good times / days are about to arrive), which hallmarked his electoral campaign of 2014. The slogan not only aptly captures the temporalizing mood of the campaign for the cause of electoral victory, but its popularity also indicates how through it Modi himself became a popular brand, the prime mover and sole guarantor of good times.

Breaching with the Past

A break emerges in the addresses in the form of how the need for the new is presented before the audiences. Here, descriptions of a flawed inherited economy are overplayed, and the need to break away from the *immediate economic* past is produced with a sense of urgency. During his entire term, Rao is seen as making innumerable references to the economic condition by referring to the economy with adjectives like 'broken', 'sick', 'paralyzed', 'in shambles', 'disrupted', 'turbulent', 'dark',[1] and even 'dangerous'.[2]

Here, more than the change itself, the need for the change and the unavoidability of that change acquires prime importance. To cite two such examples, 'The country had come to a grinding halt. The economic situation was really ghastly and if we had not taken the steps which we actually took, I shudder to think where the government and the country would have been today.'[3] '[...] Our Gold had to be pledged'.[4]

Rao clearly builds up the urgency of the moment in the aforementioned lines by using phrases/words like 'grinding halt', 'shudder', 'ghastly', and finally the highly iconic, yet symbolic, 'our gold had to be pledged'. These confirm the sense of emergency that is lexically built up within the addresses. The emergency and its immediacy are then presented as being rescued by the solace of the reforms.

One year after the institutionalization of the reforms, however, Rao was already referring to the optimism of the transitions. Here too, one nonetheless finds references made to the turbulence of the past. The emergency of the moment is, however, produced as a thing of the

[1] M. Singh, 'Economic Reforms—Taking the Momentum Further', address at the New York Stock Exchange, New York, 22 September 2004.

[2] P.V.N. Rao, 'Let us Concentrate on Development', address at a public meeting, Mangalore, 20 March 1993.

[3] Rao, 'Thrust on Social Sector Development', excerpts from reply to the debate on the President's Address in Lok Sabha, 28 April 1995.

[4] Rao, 'Towards Hopeful Future', address to the nation on Indian Independence Day, 15 August 1992.

immediate past. Thus, while a slight optimism is projected into the future, the period before 1991 is still remembered as turbulent. Hence, a break from the *immediate* past is produced. This may be gauged in the following examples:

'The country has been saved from the claws, the jaws of bankruptcy, we have brought it back.'[5]

'We have come a long way since 1991 and the conditions of 1991. [...] from 1991 to 1992 we were of course only fire-fighting.'[6]

'For the last 47 years all of us have been investing money into these big projects, power projects, steel factories and other factories which would swallow thousands of crores. [...] In 1991 that is 3 years ago, they have emptied out the treasury. When it passed into my hands India was penniless. When my government came to power our condition had been miserable.'[7]

'Let us admit old mistakes. Let us admit the distortions. Only then we will make any progress. It is not possible to close our eyes to what has happened; close our eyes to what should have happened, but not happened; let us not be dogmatic-this is not the way of progress. We will have to be pragmatic; we will have to see where we have gone wrong and we will have to correct those things.'[8]

'Desperate maladies call for drastic remedies.'

' [...] bold measures to restore our sick economy to health.'

'For the last 18 months there had been paralysis on the economic front. The last two governments postponed taking vital decisions. The fiscal position was allowed to deteriorate. The balance of payments crisis became unmanageable. Non-resident Indians and foreign lenders became more and more reluctant to lend money to India. Consequently, India's external reserves declined steeply and we had no foreign exchange rate to import even such essential commodities as diesel, kerosene, edible oil

[5] Rao, 'Thrust on Social Sector Development'.

[6] Rao, 'Thrust on Social Sector Development'.

[7] Rao, 'Private Investment in Power Sector', address while laying the foundation stone of a 1000 MW Thermal Power Station at Palavalsa, Vishakhapatnam, 29 August 1994.

[8] Rao, 'The New Industrial Policy', intervention in Lok Sabha during the debate on the demands of the Industries Ministry, 26 August 26, 1991.

and fertilizer. The net result was that when we came to power we found the financial position of the country in a terrible mess.'[9]

In the given excerpts, we find Rao tactically distancing himself from the Nehruvian import-substitution model, though importantly, never from the figure of Nehru himself. The urgency of the economic situation is lexically built up by using the terms/phrases like 'claws', 'jaws', 'fire-fighting', 'emptied treasury', 'penniless', 'miserable', 'mistakes', 'distortions', 'dogmatic', 'maladies', 'sick', 'paralysis', 'unmanageable', and 'terrible mess'. But the same addresses do not end at this negative vocabulary, and also bear words of optimism and hope for the future. This is indicated by the use of 'brought it back', 'progress', 'pragmatic', 'remedies', and 'health' (in their order of appearance in the above excerpts)—terms that are made to share the semantic space with a vocabulary that breaks with the past.

This tone of producing a moment of crisis or emergency, and therein a hope attached to the reforms, does not emerge similarly in Vajpayee's addresses. An immediate caesura with the pre-Rao economy could symbolize an implicit eulogy of the Rao government's achievements. There is an absence, rather a silence, in Vajpayee's speeches that ought to be read through the prism of the workings of coalition politics and individual party trajectories. To continue with the reform agenda, which in reality had been floated by the Rao government, and yet to promise something *new* to the vote banks is no easy task, guided as it may be by the logic of short-term vision in democracies in general.

The only instance in his speeches when Vajpayee also makes references to 'overcoming the past', similar to Rao's oratory (the tone is so similar that in the absence of knowing it one could have guessed that Rao was the speaker) is the following excerpt: 'What is required is a change in the mindset, in the fixed inherited notions about subsidized public services. We should not be prisoners of the past. Subsidized services should be restricted to only those who cannot afford to pay.'[10]

It is here that a brief insight into Vajpayee's individual rhetoric acquires importance. How to forward the agenda of the reforms and

[9] Rao, 'Re-Structuring the Economy', broadcast to the nation post inception of Economic Reforms Plan, 9 July 1991.

[10] A.B. Vajpayee, 'Accelerate Economic Growth', opening address at the National Development Council, Meeting, New Delhi, 19 February 1999.

yet creatively make them his own? This may be located as beautifully put in action in the following excerpt:

> The first phase of economic reforms was launched in 1991. Some of the reforms brought about positive changes. Unfortunately the measures taken to free the economy were not matched by checks and balances and we have paid a price for those lapses. [...] In our view reasons lie in the failure of the government to affectively address the core concerns of the Indian industry. They lie in the failure of the industry to appreciate the concerns of the government. They also lie in the failure of both the government and the industry to convince the common man that he too has a stake, a vital stake in the reform process.[11]

Here, by virtue of addressing the 'failure of the government', Vajpayee first locates an 'other', selects the 'flaws' of the previous government, and connects this to the lack of common man as an important actor in the reform process. True to the oratory style of Indian vote bank politics, *the common man*, an amorphous category for producing recognition among the audiences, is revoked here to simultaneously: (i) point to the failure of the prior government, and (ii) to gain the confidence of those who identify with the category. The second stage of creatively appropriating the reforms is to regularize them. This may be seen in the following excerpts:

> 'The reform process has become irreversible. In fact my government has depoliticized the economic agenda.'[12]

> 'India's commitment to reforms is something that does not change with the change of government. It is irreversible. My government is determined to broaden, deepen and further strengthen the reform process.'[13]

However, the 'originality' of his own government is produced in the following line which occurs repetitively throughout his term, 'India urgently needs a reform of the reform process'.[14]

---

[11] Vajpayee, 'Harbinger of Progress', address to the nation on Indian Independence Day, New Delhi, 15 August 1998.

[12] Vajpayee, 'NRIs: India's True Ambassadors', address at a gathering of members of the Indian Community, New York, 28 September 1998.

[13] Vajpayee, 'NRIs'.

[14] Vajpayee, 'Harmonizing Economic Liberalization and Social Liberalization', inaugural address at the Annual Session and National Conference of the Confederation of Indian Industries, New Delhi, 28 April 1998.

As stated in the last section of Chapter 2, in Manmohan Singh's addresses, references to 1991 do not utilize the socialist vocabulary of self-reliance or economic sovereignty, even when hinting at the transformations. Singh's rhetoric does have a parallel to Rao's in that both breach with the Nehruvian economy though without questioning the authority of Nehru's figure. However, Singh's oratory on change is enthused with more positive descriptions than Rao's. The year 1991 in this context becomes a historical fact. The following is one of the numerous illustrations of the same. (In fact, Singh makes numerous cross references to Rao, the obvious link being his own portfolio in the Rao government and the establishment of continuity with the Congress legacy.) 'In 1991 we took a momentous decision to reverse that process, to enlarge the scope of competition, both internal and external in our economic life. We took the decision that India's future lies in integrating itself with the evolving global economy. That it is only then that the vast latent developing potential can be fully realized.'[15]

The only exceptional instance where Singh does use Nehruvian repertoire to explain change is the following excerpt. This exceptional example, which stands out against Singh's general oratory, may be explained by the context to the address. Here, Singh is in fact addressing an audience perceived as 'external' at the New York Stock Exchange in 2004. The talk was titled 'Economic Reforms—Taking the Momentum Further'.

> Changes have been made in the economic policies in every living society. These changes have to be made. Panditji himself used to say that we are living in a dynamic world and we cannot be slaves all the time of the past. So we have made changes, but the basic thrust of our economic policies remains what was conceived at the time of independence- to promote a self-reliant, progressive, humane and egalitarian society.[16]

Singh speaks in favour of breaching with India's socialist, import-substitution inspired, protectionist economic past, all of which stand symbolic of the Nehruvian era, but he uses the very figure of Nehru to establish transition. Thus, though loaded with the socialist style of speech with its emphatic thrust on self-reliance and a 'progressive, humane

---

[15] Singh, 'Economic Reforms—Taking the Momentum Further'.

[16] Singh, 'Towards a New Era of Growth and Development', address in reply to the debate on the Motion of Thanks to the President's Address in the Lok Sabha, 10 March 2005.

and egalitarian society', what Singh's lines actually do is to introduce a conspicuous shift. But that shift is authenticated, lent legitimacy, and justified by using words of the 'national hero' himself. Once again, the last line in the excerpt outlines the consistent underpinning message. We have made changes in the favour of an ideal future, but the core, the essence of Indian economy, rather of India itself, is still the same.

Reconnecting with the Past: Nehru and Civilization Speak

The second, more prominently present, mechanism of employing the past is done by bridging with it, deifying it, and retrieving it to make sense of the present, rather, to *lend* sense *to* the present. This occurs in two specific ways within the purview of the addresses. First, through the figure of the national hero, the memory of the independence movement; and second through what I term as 'civilization speak'.

The category of the national hero is most commonly re-evoked with regards to Jawaharlal Nehru who is projected as the iconic epitome of the postcolonial setting within which the Indian economy finds its trajectory, but also thrives. In this regard, references to Nehru echo not only with a deification of the politician, but also to a continuity established with his economic vision for an independent India. The following is an apt illustration of the same:

> The idea of a mixed economy did not come from any book. It came from that great man, Jawaharlal Nehru. So, such ideas are not necessarily wedded to any particular philosophy. It is good that under Jawaharlal Nehru we made agriculture the occupation of millions and millions of people rather than put it under a single proprietor, government. If we had done that it would have been disastrous. In fact it had become disastrous in countries where this was done. Now, looking back we can say that we were right, but when they were doing it they always said we were wrong. We had our own way of finding out what is good for the country and this is the strong point of India. We have the power to think, to innovate, to implement, and also correct our mistakes as we go along.[17]

These lines open a window to many messages at work: first, the emphatic thrust on a 'mixed economy' and Nehru himself emphasize the necessity

[17] Rao, 'New Direction to Agriculture', address at a conference of chief ministers on Agricultural Policy, New Delhi, 5 March 1993.

felt to establish continuity with the past. The story Rao wishes to communicate to his audiences is that there is no break. India continues, unabashed, on its trajectory. As it does so, it adapts. However, its essence remains the same—not out of sight—but remembered and celebrated. Second, the category of the 'they' is used to firmly establish the 'us'. Finally, by stating 'we had our own way [...]. We have the power to think, to innovate [...]', he, yet again, emphasizes Indian uniqueness, its exceptionalism. In fact, here 'India' itself is produced by Rao. The underlying message is that India is different, it can change; but that change is not new, it lies embedded in 'our' past and, so, in accommodating the change, 'we' do not change the spirit of India—we only make it reshine. A reference to 'mixed economy' becomes the legitimizing hinge for change. Although Rao cloaks economic change in the garb of historical continuity, it is nonetheless important to ask which features of the economy after 1991 reflect that India follows the logic of the same 'mixed' model? Another very befitting example of celebrating Nehru as well as Nehruvian mixed economy and, therein, exceptionalizing India is the following:

> Nehru was able to see the negative points of both the systems and thought of a system which avoided these negative points. Although it was slow, although people laughed at it in the beginning. 'Oh! It is neither this nor that, you cannot have only this or only that.' Now the same countries are telling us what is mixed economy? How did you do it? How is it that you have got such flourishing private industries? How is it? Because 50 years ago, 40 years ago we consciously took a decision.[18]

As evident, the category of *'the other'* (evident in the usage of terms like 'other countries' and 'people') once again silently permeates the discourse, strongly informing how *the self* is perceived, but also narrated in establishing 'difference'.[19] Though one finds Rao pointing out

[18] Rao, 'Challenges Before the Public Sector Enterprises', address at the inauguration of a conference of chief executives of public sector enterprises, New Delhi, 30 July 1994.

[19] Singh is seen as establishing the same bridge with Nehru and his developmentalism in the following way: 'A lot of things have happened in our country in the last 50 years. It is my sincere conviction that but for the solid foundation of our economic—the scientific infrastructure that Panditji created, the temples of learning—universities, institutes of management and technology [...]

concretely how the Nehruvian model was 'neither-nor' and how the Indian economy was uniquely designed for a 'middle path' or a 'mixed model', what is not clarified and left for the audiences to interpret is how exactly the neo-liberal reforms ensure continuity to that mixed model. In other words, how will India liberalize its market on its own terms, given that the very act of 'opening up' the economy implies succumbing to the precedents of the Bretton Woods system? These clarifications, however, are omitted, and the speeches remain ambivalent on how India adapts to structural adjustment on its own terms, even if the address is meant for an audience that would grasp the details of market liberalization and its workings.

A final example that explicitly establishes this link to Nehru and the mixed economy model is the following:

> Mixed Economy-Nehru's gift to India [...] not a mechanical part a mixture of the other two systems but a system by itself [...] it is not a hotchpotch. [...] This again is symbolically true to the Indian liberal tradition. India has never looked at progress in a single uni-directional straight and narrow path [...] it is much more a holistic attitude, a holistic philosophy [...] that view has come back in our modern times.[20]

Once again, the Indian economy, presented here as a legacy of Nehru (therein, the transformation to market liberalization is underplayed, even camouflaged), is stamped and coloured with an Indian flavour. The intention is to communicate that the Indian way is not a simple hybrid form of capitalism or communism—it is a uniquely 'Indian' invention, not a 'hotchpotch'. Change is normalized and made *Indian* here by stating that India, in fact, has a 'liberal tradition' that has not been stagnant or stationary. Hence the new is not so new, it is a return to the *older* tradition of accepting variety. The 'Indian view' in 'modern times' is not a drastic, foreign, unfamiliar view; it is an essence which has returned or 'come back'.[21] On one occasion, Rao even states before

---

the public sector investments that were made to promote self-reliance—we would not be where we are today' (Singh, 'Towards a New Era of Growth and Development').

[20] Rao, 'Stability—A Prerequisite for Economic Reforms', inaugural address at the 67th annual session of FICCI, New Delhi, 9 December 1994.

[21] Singh, on another occasion, is seen as stating, 'We have always been by and large a free enterprise economy' (Singh, 'Economic Reforms—Taking the Momentum Further'). Another example of celebrating Nehru in Rao's words,

a perceived external audience (in Japan) how India has embraced *Advaitism*, 'Welcoming the new without losing the old.'[22]

This excerpt tellingly links to how a generalized, museified, selective past is produced for the cause of market liberalization, so that the reforms may acquire legitimacy and currency among audiences. In an account of the opposition to the neo-liberal economic reforms in the face of their immediate formal institutionalization in 1991, Shashi Tharoor states:

> Arrayed against them (supporters of reforms) are the impressive forces of reaction, grouped largely under the banner of economic nationalism. During the years of the Rao government, the right-wing, pro-trader BJP party joined forces with the Communists and Socialists to attack the economic reforms on a nativist platform. The slogans of *Swadeshi* self-reliance suited both the right and the left parties.[23]

Zooming out of Tharoor's rather generalized dealing and pro-reform presentation of the transitions in Indian economy, this excerpt does sum up the lines along which contestation to the reforms was politically organized. The query that then arises is that how does a BJP-led government justify its pro-reforms shift when in power after 1999? In the following lines, Vajpayee does that on the very same lines as have been utilized in staging protest to market liberalization during Rao's term. This claim for swadeshi[24] in fact becomes a legitimizing ground

---

'Nehru told them that we would grow bankrupt if we did not have our own factories. He was a great man. He had sown this seed' (Rao, 'Private Investment in Power Sector').

[22] Rao, 'India and Japan', address at the Japan Institute of International Affairs on the occasion of the 40th anniversary of the establishment of diplomatic relations between Japan and India Tokyo, 23 June 1992.

[23] S. Tharoor, *India: From Midnight to the Millenium and Beyond*, 3rd ed. (New Delhi: Penguin Books, 2007), p. 181.

[24] The word 'Swadeshi' derives from Sanskrit, and is a sandhi or a conjunction of two Sanskrit words. '*Swa*' meaning 'self' or 'own', and '*desh*' meaning country, *Swadesh* would be 'own country', and *Swadeshi*, the adjectival form, would mean 'of one's own country'. The opposite of Swadeshi in Sanskrit is videshi or 'not of one's country'. Historically, it refers to the movement set in colonial India that called for a boycott of foreign goods and a simultaneous encouragement of domestic production (source: http://www.thefreediction-ary.com/Swadeshi, accessed on 3 December 2013).

for the reforms. Vajpayee was seen during his term as not only embracing market liberalization, but also vouching upon furthering them.

> I am reminded of what Ramkrishna Paramhansa[25] told an aspirant. Life is like a boat. The natural place for it to be is on water. But one cannot let the water enter the boat and drown it. This is what my colleagues and I mean by Swadeshi. The natural place for the country to be in is in the world. But we are not to let the powerful currents now rocking world markets drown us. Instead we are to put those very currents to our favour. Let us therefore make the boat of our national economy stronger and sturdier. Let us do it in the shortest possible time frame by unleashing the productive energies of Indian people. And let us accomplish this challenge by eradicating poverty and unemployment at the earliest. In a word, step over the Past and grasp the Future![26]

We return to the category of temporality here. Once again, a move to an ideal future is presented here—a *new* future awaiting India, where the 'productive energies of Indian people' shall be unleashed. But this promise of the future is presented in the clothing of the past. The future is fabricated yet again by employing a resourceful figure from the past, Ramkrishna Paramhansa. Swadeshi, a word with its own unique career during the nationalist movement for independence, celebrated as the symbol of Gandhi, of 'India' itself, and also the reference point around which the BJP had formerly attacked the reforms, is twisted and turned around here in its meaning, which shares the same semantic space in the earlier lines with foreign investment. The objective, however, is to use a specifically Indian term with a specifically 'Indian' history to inculcate a sense of cultural security. The boat of India shall sail on world waters, but in a measured, calculated, contained, and controllable pace and fashion. Two objectives are thus at work through one argument here—first, a term that is very alive in public memory is re-evoked to make people identify with the new. Its meaning, however, itself is flexed to suit the purpose of favouring 'foreign' investment. Second,

[25] Ramkrishna Paramhansa is a nineteenth-century Bengali mystic, who was also the inspiration behind the Ramkrishna Mission founded by his chief disciple, Vivekananda. Both Ramkrishna and Vivekananda are important figures in the Bengali and Hindu Renaissance of the nineteenth and twentieth centuries respectively.

[26] Vajpayee, 'Let Us Look Ahead', address to the nation on election as the prime minister of India, 22 March 1998.

the *new* is once again presented in such a way that its *newness*, and the anxiety attached to that newness, is taken away. Besides, it also becomes a response to Vajpayee's own prior political grounding within the BJP rhetoric.

Abstract, yet specifically selected, resources from mythologies and scriptures, which are presented as iconic signs of 'Indian civilization' (this is presented as a homogenous unified entity) in their vagueness, are a recurrent category in the addresses of all four prime ministers. One illustration of the same are the following lines:

> In developed countries the income of an unemployed is protected to some extent through social welfare. Yet social problems still constantly arise. This has compelled the realization of the role of work in the human psyche. The basic role of action in the human psyche is stated in the Indian tradition when Shri Krishna says in the Bhagwad Gita 'There is nothing for the Supreme Being to attain and yet I engage in action' This is what Lord Krishna says. This is the real thing. What is *Karma*? The definition of the philosophy of *Karma* is not to work for wages but *Karma is Dharma*. That is the kind of thinking which is perhaps engrained in all our thinking [...] compensated unemployment cannot substitute for employment.[27]

Rao aims at achieving multiple objectives here: first, the logic behind the absence of social welfare is provided by embedding it within the rhetoric of the philosophy of work. This is done by using an ancient, revered Hindu scriptural text that lends legitimacy to the claim made. Second, further in the address, one locates the link made to foreign investment in Indian industries when Rao claims that the partnership with 'foreign' investors will ensure the dual purpose of the government, using the saved money for social welfare programmes and simultaneously producing employment. The inherent ethic of 'work' is thus linked implicitly to the generation of employment. Thus, the past (a particular kind of past) looms like an ever-present shadow that materializes the future, whereby the *Gita* and the intricacies of neo-liberal markets are made to share the same discursive space.

In the following lines, Vajpayee aims at the same objective of establishing the 'Indianness' of India by celebrating 'Indian philosophy'.

[27] Rao, 'Stability, a Pre-requisite for Economic Reforms', inaugural address at the 67th annual session of FICCI, New Delhi, 9 December 1994.

'History itself is teaching both business and political leaders in the world what Indian philosophy has explained ages ago viz. there is no single exclusive path to reach the Truth. Similarly there can be no single model or solution to the problems of economic development.'[28]

The illustrations cited in the category of the past ('Civilization Speak and the National Hero') as well as those cited in the category of the future ('Neo-Liberalism as a Socialist Project', Chapter 2) indicate that temporality is conjured and fabricated in the addresses of the different prime ministers so as to make the reform process inconvertible and inevitable. This implies that the present is produced in relation to a putative other time (past or future) to lend it authority. In other words, transformations which entail the new, which in turn entails unpredictability, a potent unexplainable insecurity, even a danger, are rendered 'normal' and 'Indian'.

Naturalizing the Inevitable: A Messianic Moment in a Sacred Sequence of Events?

Another tactic in the addresses of both Vajpayee and Rao is to embed the reforms in a temporal order, which is presented as something preordained and destined for India. By this, I specifically mean that both the speakers naturalize a particular sequence of events, which legitimize the change that the reforms embody as something predetermined, an act of providence. Here, the reforms are inscribed in a bigger cosmic scheme whose occurrence cannot be refuted, which, in turn, renders them as something unstoppable and inevitable. The following example illustrates this technique:

> Within the last decade the world has undergone climatic changes [...] an existing order suddenly collapsed. [...]. We, in India are also in the process of readjustment. The task is somewhat easier for us because we have always been a liberal democratic society with a 'Mixed Economy'. The mix may have to change from time to time, but we never needed convincing that a mix was needed. And so was change. Indian philosophy has always taken change to be basic to the universe. The only point

---

[28] Vajpayee, A.B., 'Government Asserts its Commitment to Economic Reforms', inaugural address at the 71st session of FICCI (Federation of Indian Chambers of Commerce and Industry), New Delhi, 24 October 1998.

of discussion has been whether there is a reality that changes or whether change is the only reality. For us time was not the measure of change, change itself denoted time, with no two moments being the same. We never had problems conceiving the eternal, as without beginning and end. We did not assume the phenomenon of time stopping, either at the 'Big Bang' or at the 'Second Coming'.[29]

In these lines delivered by Rao, the category of 'change' itself is lent continuity by camouflaging it in a cyclical temporal order. 'Time' does not stop, but rather is measurable only through the transitions that it stages. Thus, even though the speaker is referring to change, its transformational capacity is normalized as continuity, an episode, which occurs as a part of a larger sequence of events or a predetermined order. The reforms are therein cloaked in temporal continuity, which is produced as the basis of the universe. Here, continuity is not just produced by quoting from the generalizable category of 'the past' (as reflected through the use of terms like mixed economy or Indian philosophy), but rather by emphasizing that change itself is in tune with Indian philosophy. In other words, acceptance of change as preordained is the very marker of historical continuity.

We never thought of today as the be-all and end-all of all things. We have always thought of tomorrow, always thought of the Future. The kind of prudence you find in Indian society is something to be proud of. [...] This country has to have its own distinctive stamp on the future. Future not only of this country but the future of mankind. [...] I think we have a mission. Starting from Buddha and Gandhi this country has never looked only in words. It has a mission; it has had a mission. [...] I am saying that there is something from this part of the world which has emanated, which has not really looked inwards alone [...] which has shed light everywhere outside and in this context of liberalization, new industry, new society, the new industrial society that we are envisaging, is absolutely different. [...] I think it is going to be very different from the industrial society.[30]

Once again, in the given excerpt, Rao emphasizes the category of the future and its fundamental importance for a 'prudent' Indian society.

[29] P.V.N. Rao, 'Perspectives on Indo-British Relations', address to the indologists, Nehru Centre, London, 15 March 1994.

[30] Rao, 'Stability—A Prerequisite for Economic Reforms', inaugural address at the 67th annual session of FICCI, New Delhi, 9 December 1994.

On a first glance, they seem to suggest that the present is projected through a breach (in that it is not the 'be-all and end-all of all things'). But what appears to be a temporal breach is in fact cloaked in continuity. India is projected as having a 'mission' to fulfil for itself and the world. Once again, there is a performance of a 'larger' scheme, which demands being enacted. Thus, that which is new in the form of the reforms (liberalization and a 'new' industrial society) becomes indisputable as part of a natural, predetermined temporal design. However, this does not imply that the past disappears as the ground is prepared for the future. The figures of Buddha and Gandhi, both of whom are made to share a deified space in the speech, become the legitimizing hinges to naturalize the temporal order being introduced. The message thus runs: the changes introduced by the reforms are part of a preordained order whose occurrence is unstoppable. This order is in sync with India's destined role of 'having a mission', and, finally, the 'past' authenticates this cyclical ordering through the figures of Gandhi and Buddha.

Both the preceding excerpts echo of traditions of what has been termed as 'sacred time', which embeds events in a larger scheme and naturalizes or legitimizes them by producing them as inevitable and irreversible in that they were conceived as part of a sequence of events that has already been decided or written.[31]

---

[31] Schwartz sums up sacred time as follows: 'There has to be an appreciable gravity to sacred time that makes it worthy, comprehensible, and memorable. Sacred time must be that time during which people individually and collectively bear the weight and fate of the cosmos. Neither that weight nor that fate can be long sustained by any one person; it must therefore be presented within a sacred theatre of sacrifice and renewal, atonement and attunement, that is undeniably momentous. So Hindi men and women throughout northern India at the end of the rainy season move back and forth between participation and spectatorship in the epic play cycle of the *Ramlila*, lasting some places as long as thirty days, reenacting the life of the god *Rama*, his victory over the demon king *Ravan*: a and his shattering of the great cosmic bow of *Shiva*, the god of devouring time; so the Mayan ball games with their deadly ritual replay of the motions of the heavens, and so the human sacrifices on the Mexica (Aztec) pyramids, where the years were bound together in spirals of death and rebirth that encompassed people, plants, cities, kings, and the gods themselves, eaten up by time.' [H. Schwartz, 'Sacred Time', in L. Jones (ed.), *Encyclopedia of Religion*, 2nd ed. (Detroit et al.: Thompson-Gale, 2005), pp. 7986–997.]

This preordained temporal order is then juxtaposed to a cultural order, whose givenness and certainty can also not be questioned. The following lines belong to the very same excerpts, which have been quoted earlier.

> [...] What I would like to emphasize is that India is undergoing another massive change, an extensive change this time. We, of this generation, are fortunate to be the humble mid-wives of the emergence of change at this juncture. In the process of this change and adjustment that we have undertaken, we recognize and incorporate the following three postulates as essential ingredients: (i) that the economies of all nations need to be globalized; (ii) that the market is the best available instrument for achieving the most efficient allocation of resources and that market forces should be relied upon to impart dynamism to the economy and; (iii) the role of the state needs to be reconsidered.[32]

> India is too large a country, too complicated to think of today alone. (...) We are not perfect but we have to see that the Future is brighter. I have been telling this to ordinary people. You don't have to tell the mother that she has to think of her daughter's marriage. She starts doing it the moment a daughter is born. So this society is like that. We never thought of today as the be-all and end-all of all things. We have always thought of tomorrow, always thought of the Future. [...]

These excerpts produce the acceptance of change itself as an event embedded in time. Change is presented as something cyclical and repetitive, whose occurrence cannot be altered. In both the excerpts earlier, the prime minister juxtaposes this temporal order to a cultural one. Thus, the figure of the 'humble midwives' and the 'mother' become the agents of the temporal order, whose 'mission' is to be the caretakers of the transitions introduced by a higher cosmic scheme. The same agency is attached to India in the following excerpt, where Vajpayee repeats a vision of an Indian nationalist and socio-religious reformer, Sri Aurobindo.

> We enter the 21st century with a civilizational history that stretches back to more than 5000 years. From time immemorial we have nourished traditions and values. They are our real strength. They are the gift India has

---

[32] Rao, 'Perspectives on Indo–British Relations', address to the indologists, Nehru Centre, London, 15 March 1994.

preserved for the world through ages. They are the truths to which the world has now begun to turn to- for direction, for solace, for wisdom. As Sri Aurobindo said, 'The sun of India's destiny would rise to fill India with its light, and overflow India and overflow Asia and overflow the world. Let us make that vision come true. Let us make the new century an Indian century.'[33]

Just as an Indian mother who cannot and must not but start preparing for the wedding of her daughter the day she is born, and just as a midwife whose job necessitates the role of the agent responsible for realizing childbirth, there is an ultimacy attached to the role of those who are the agents of economic transitions in India. In turn, India's role itself is that of an agent which spreads the message to the world.

The immediacy of the very moment, or the temporal order, however, is then introduced by giving it a millennialist twist. Here, the idea of the prosperous future is made possible by situating it in the *here and now*. The idealized future becomes possible, even thinkable, only through the present. This implies that only if the act destined for the mother or the midwife is executed in this looming present, can the destiny of the future be realized or actualized.

Achche Din (Good Times) and the Temporalizing Tactics of Modi's Oratory

In 2014, BJP's prime ministerial candidate, Narendra Modi, entered the electoral campaign with the suggestive slogan *Achche din aane wale hain* (good times/days are about to arrive). The slogan not only aptly captures the temporalizing mood of the campaign, but also that of Modi's oratory in general. It became viral both in and through traditional (rallies, print, and visual press) as well as new social media channels (Facebook, Twitter, Instagram, Youtube, blogs, etc.). As an entry point, the slogan is highly indicative of the means to conjure a blissful future by generating promises, hope, optimism, and collective desires.[34] It simultaneously

---

[33] Vajpayee, 'Make the New Century India's Century', address to the nation on the eve of New Year, New Delhi, 31 December 1999.

[34] After the victory, Modi tweeted, 'India has won, Bharat ki vijay, acche din aane wale hai' (India has won, good times are about to arrive) @narendramodi (16 May 2014).

aimed at (i) employing a politics of time for electoral victory, one that situated itself in the near 'future', generating the collective aspiration of good days which were promised to arrive if people elected Modi, and (ii) making Modi a popular brand, the prime mover and sole guarantor of these good times. It is in the same context that the 'Gujarat Model of Development', projected as an economic miracle tailored by the Modi government in the federal state, became the buzz phrase to forward the cause of *Achhe Din*. In fact, *Achhe Din* became the lexical site for sealing market liberalization as the sole, inevitable means to achieve the promise of growth. In a recent analysis of the campaign and, particularly, the slogan in new social media, Ravinder Kaur succinctly sums up that it 'discloses the historical moment when capitalism was reified as the sole vehicle of people's aspirations—that is, unchallenged by any other political alternative'.[35]

Like his predecessors, Modi skilfully utilizes temporality as a modality to conjure the inevitability of the current economic environment. The noteworthy difference though is that the former prime ministers (Rao and Vajpayee) needed to establish a relation of co-equivalence between a promising future and the reforms per se, whereas with Singh and Modi as prime ministers, almost thirteen and twenty-four years later respectively, that relationship emerges as a pre-established oratorical truth. It is thus no surprise that there are rarely any moments when Modi is seen as directly referring to the reforms of 1991, barring limited exceptions when he purposely utilizes them as a means to validate the difference and uniqueness of his government's economic vision in comparison to those of his predecessors. Thus, reforms are mentioned to prove that the Modi government will do what previous governments started—only more substantially and better. Two such exceptional instances may be seen in the following excerpts:

> We are trying to complete the cycle of economic reforms speedily. We are also keen to see that our policies are predictable. We are clear that our tax regime should be stable. In the last few months, we have taken several steps in this direction.[36]

[35] R. Kaur, 'Good Times brought to you by Modi', *Television and New Media* 16, no. 4 (2015): 324.

[36] N.D. Modi, address at the Vibrant Gujarat Summit, Gandhinagar, 11 January 2015.

[...] true reforms are those which result in transformation in the lives of citizens. As I have said before, my goal is 'reform to transform.[37]

Hence, the challenge is not levelled against the reforms per se, but rather on how their execution has remained an incomplete process to be duly finished by the Modi government. This difference of not having to validate the reforms in each utterance, however, does not imply that the prime minister does not require to persuade and pervade his audiences, nor does it reduce the resort to temporality as a means to situate the vocabulary of economic transitions. For India to grow, 'arrive', and even 'emerge' in the words of the prime minister, change is consistently produced as a positive momentum in the *right* direction. The following section presents Modi's temporalizing oratory in the light of the consistencies and inconsistencies that can be read vis-à-vis his predecessors' rhetoric. How is the present government presented as the legitimate vanguard of a promising future of emergence, and which temporal tactics become the means to substantiate that claim?

Tropes of Emergence—Changing India in the Times of Modi

Linguistic tropes abound the oratory of the current prime minister, who has often been projected as a successful speaker in comparison to his immediate forerunner, Manmohan Singh. In one of the numerous regimes of temporality, metaphors and allegories are utilized persistently to announce that India has arrived. On such occasions, India's economic trajectory is celebrated and 'Emerging India' (a process in the present-continuous tense) is made to shine. Some prominent illustrations are as follows:

India is changing fast;
India is growing fast;
India is moving faster than expected;
India is learning even faster;
India is ready than ever before.[38]

---

[37] Modi, address at Economic Times Global Business Summit, New Delhi, 29 January 2016.

[38] Modi, address at the Vibrant Gujarat Summit, Gandhinagar, 11 January 2015.

We are dreaming big;
And our dreams are numerous;
Our dreams can become the seeds of your growth;
Our aspirations can propel your ambitions.[39]

I am happy to tell you that today India is poised to contribute as a new engine of global growth: PM @narendramodi[40]

In all the three examples, a metaphor of speed is put to use to show that India is in motion. The economy becomes symptomatic of the velocity of change with which it advances. Thus words like 'changing', 'growing', 'propel', and 'poised' show the propensity towards motion, whereas descriptions like 'new engine of growth' and 'seeds of growth' become the metaphoric links to enunciate the effect. The phrase 'ready than ever before' shows the confidence with which Modi projects the certainty of preparedness. The first two excerpts, delivered to a mixed audience of Indians and investors from the putative outside, show how 'dreams' and 'aspirations' are the keywords in Modi's repertoire that become axiomatic of the essential good of market liberalization. In the following excerpt from an address delivered on the inauguration of the 'Make in India' campaign, Modi announces India's arrival in the world markets, a telling illustration of how India has not just become coeval with the world, but is one of the best places to invest.

I have been saying that this century is Asia's century. My advice to you is to Make India your center; if you want this century to be your century. I invite everyone sitting here and also those not here, to be a part of India's unfolding story.

This is the best time ever to be in India;

And it is even better to Make in India.[41]

Here, the words 'best time ever' and 'if you want this century to be your century' suggest how the present is conjured as a significant historical moment that announces India's arrival. The audiences of the speech are

[39] Modi, address at the Vibrant Gujarat Summit, Gandhinagar, 11 January 2015.

[40] Modi, tweet after keynote speech at 41st AGM of US–India Business Council (USIBC), Washington D.C., 7 June 2016.

[41] Modi, address at inauguration of Make in India Week, Mumbai, 13 February 2016.

primarily foreign investors who are assured that this is the best time to invest in India. Such celebrations of a present can also be gauged in the following excerpts, 'Friends! Today India is a land of opportunities'[42] and 'Experts are unanimous that India is one of the world economy's brightest spots.'[43]

Once again, the aim is to proclaim that Indian economy has 'taken off'. The words 'opportunities' and 'brightest spots' emphasize the positive environment within which open markets are eulogized. Whereas Rao was seen as comparing the Indian economy to an elephant in the previous chapter, Modi redefined it through the symbolism of a lion. In the following excerpt from a speech delivered in Germany for the 'Make in India' campaign, Modi states:

> The symbol of lion for Make in India has been chosen very carefully. We know that our biggest need today is to create jobs for our 65% population which is young. Hence, Make In India is the need. Hence the lion because the lion cannot be stopped. We are confident that our journey to make India a global manufacturing hub cannot be stopped that too by our own rules and regulations. We must and we will make corrections wherever it is required.[44]

Thus, from being an uncontrollable elephant to being an unstoppable lion, the prime minister has attempted to transform the image of the Indian economy, emphasizing its arrival in the world. Whereas he is careful in selecting a vocabulary that speaks of making 'corrections', he nonetheless draws the imagery of the lion that is uncontrollable. This announces that the Indian economy has changed (even as it looks ahead onto more transitions).

Intertwining the Future in the Present: India's 'Work in Progress'

These celebrations of the generalized present are, however, not the only means of conjuring temporality. The glossy present of a structurally

[42] Modi, address at the Vibrant Gujarat Summit, Gandhinagar, 11 January 2015.

[43] Modi, address at Bloomberg India Economic Forum, New Delhi, 28 March 2016.

[44] Modi, address at the joint inauguration of the Indo–German Business Summit, Hannover, 13 April 2015.

adjusted economy is not surgically removed from the conjecture of an even shinier future. In this regime of historicity, the future and the present are intricately intertwined and synchronously produced, that is, the present is projected through the lens of an even brighter putative future. Change itself becomes the referential hinge that directs the present, whereas a generalizable future attaches all necessary positive vocabulary of prosperity to it.

> Ladies and Gentlemen, we have begun our journey towards a transformed India. A transformed India, with one sixth of humanity will mean a transformed world. The journey will be long. But the progress we have achieved so far, convinces me that we will reach our destination. I invite you to join us on that journey. It is a journey which offers the exciting possibility of not only building a better balance sheet for your company but of building a better India, building a better America, and building a better world.[45]

The given address delivered at the US–India Business Council illustrates how, once again, a metaphor of motion is utilized to speak of a changing India. The 'journey' is packaged as departing from a transformed past ('progress we have achieved so far') and leading to an even more transformed India of the future. 'India' is not just produced as catching up with the world, but also as a prime mover of building a better world, therein underlining its global significance. It is clear that Modi's announced 'destination' here are open markets in India which will realize their full potential if businessmen attending this meeting participate in investing in those markets. The direct audiences of these lines cannot be put into the sanitized containers of a putative 'inside' or 'outside', but are rather a very particular clique of entrepreneurs from both ends of the world.

These instances of producing a prosperous transition to the future indicate a similar tactic as employed by Modi's predecessor, Manmohan Singh.

> [...] our relationship is primed for our momentous future. The constraints of the past are behind us, and foundations of the future are firmly in place. In the lines of Walt-Whitman, 'The Orchestra have sufficiently tuned their instruments, the baton has given the signal.' And to that, if I might add, there is a new symphony in play.[46]

[45] Modi, keynote speech at 41st AGM of US–India Business Council (USIBC), Washington D.C., 7 June 2016.

[46] Modi, address at the joint session of the US Congress, Washington D.C., 8 June 2016.

The aforementioned excerpt, from a speech delivered to an audience consisting of US congressmen (at the joint session of the US Congress), shows how Modi employs metaphorical language to present an emerging India. Whereas the allegory of a journey leading to an optimistic 'destination' could be traced in the previous example, here the momentum of transition is presented through the allegory of a 'new symphony' that tunes and flavours India's economic future. In other words, the promise of a future and present is presented here as a moment in time that is unstoppable and invested in the now (as indicated by 'The Orchestra have sufficiently tuned their instruments, the baton has given the signal'). In the lines below, delivered to a mixed audience of entrepreneurs at the Vibrant Gujarat Summit, Modi captures the sheer speed of transition by stating, '[...] there are immense possibilities for global investors in India. The process of development we are taking up is not incremental. We are planning to take a quantum leap.'[47]

It is important to note that temporalizing tactics are never surgically separable from spatializing strategies. Though the following chapter (see chapter 4) will enunciate how spatial contexts particularly demarcate a specific kind of rhetoric, the spatial environment also often governs how Modi temporalizes his oratory. Thus, before a putative outside, the optimism of India's emergence is more rampant, whereas before a putative inside, Modi presents it more through the prism of emergence as a continuous work in progress. Growth here is a temporally generational achievement—like one of the many roads and underpasses to be seen in multiple sites of the new India—consistently 'under construction'. In a tweet that the prime minister posted, derived from his speech in New Delhi on the completion of two years of the government, Modi stated, 'Government's belief is in "Vikasvad". Politics of development will transform the nation.'[48]

Not only does he refer to transformation and development, the title of the speech, *Ek Nayi Subah* (A New Dawn), is also very telling in this case. Most addresses where it is clear that the perceived audiences are

---

[47] Modi, address at the Vibrant Gujarat Summit, Gandhinagar, 11 January 2015.

[48] Modi, tweet: @PMO India.7:23 hrs, 30 May 2016, derived from address 'EK Nayi Subah', event on the completion of two years of the government, New Delhi, 28 May 2016.

Indians, but more specifically ritualistic speeches which address diverse groups and not just entrepreneurs, Modi speaks of transformation as a catalysing force, though with a vocabulary that carefully projects it as a constant work in progress. Change and emergence are thus cloaked in concrete steps that are announced for the near future. An example of the same can be seen in the following excerpts from the speech delivered to the nation on the anniversary of Indian independence.

> Friends! We are on the path of transformation. To start this process, we are making efforts to change the work culture. We have to strengthen our institutions and systems of delivery. To drive this change forcefully, we have recently re-constituted our Planning Commision. Now it is known as NITI Aayog.[49]

> [...] The World Economic Forum has said that India has reached above 19 ranks as compared to earlier positions and India is moving up and marching ahead rapidly. [...] the way we are marching ahead with a dynamic and predictable economy in our country and also in global reference- the recently passed GST law, is also an empowering step towards it. [...][50]

> Then, a time came when people asked for the plan unless the drawing of the plan came, there was a time when people asked for the budget. Today the mood of the country has changed in 70 years. It does not get satisfied with the announcement, it is not satisfied by seeing the plan, if a budget provision is made, it is not ready to accept this. It is accepted when things get implemented on ground and we cannot bring things on ground with the old pace. We have to speed up our work, increase the pace and then we can say we have done something.[51]

Thus, as the last example demonstrates, even as Modi speaks of change and 'pace', he carefully embeds it in the necessity to 'implement' that change through concerted action. Similarly, as he speaks of an India that 'marches ahead rapidly', he does so by carefully situating that transition and motion in words that suggest effort and empowering steps. This is a tactic that is governed by the spatial context in which

[49] Modi, address at the Vibrant Gujarat Summit, Gandhinagar, 11 January 2015.

[50] Modi, address to the nation on Indian Independence Day, New Delhi, 15 August 2016.

[51] Modi, address to the nation on Indian Independence Day, New Delhi, 15 August 2016.

the prime minister speaks, a very ritualistic moment of Independence Day celebrations, indicating the awareness that the audiences are not restrained to those in the private sector, but to all citizens of the country. Thus, the prime minister does not boldly and only celebrate India's emergence, but he rather presents change through the lens of a balanced vocabulary that can be abstract enough to flatten differences among audiences; at the same time, offering a generalizable mood of optimism. In the same speech, Modi states, 'Let us proceed forward with a new determination, new energy, new enthusiasm by getting inspiration from these great persons who sacrificed their lives for our freedom. We did not get an opportunity to die for our country but we have the opportunity to live for the country. We should dedicate our life to the nation.'[52]

As indicated, Modi emphasizes the *newness* of enthusiasm, energy, and determination, but he does so carefully, using the illustration of the nationalist movement as an example of serving the nation. Thus, as the change that speaks of the new is embraced, the nation and its economy are synchronously produced as a laboratory requiring constant dedication. Here, contrary to what was shown previously, India is not a country that has arrived, but rather one that requires persistent investment by its citizens in order to realize its potential of economically arriving in the world. Srirupa Roy presents the discourse of nationalism in Nehruvian India as a time when the nation was defined in terms of its needs discourse.[53] In a similar tone, Modi carefully describes the new India as demanding the enthusiasm and enterprise of its governments and citizens. The notable difference though is the unavoidable relationship between the nation and corporation. The vocabulary to show growth is incremental in nature. The liberalized economy demands that citizens participate in the venture of building a new India, but the movement towards that neo-liberal future is never challenged. It is assumed as a necessary good. Change itself in this context implies a move towards something (an ever more open economy) that is necessarily positive and fundamentally better.

[52] Modi, address to the nation on Indian Independence Day, New Delhi, 15 August 2016.

[53] Roy, *Beyond Belief.*

Proving Growth, Promising Growth: Common Man Replaces the 'Other Within'

In continuation with his predecessors, Modi also employs the tactics of producing the 'Details of Desire' (see chapter 2), especially to assure Indian audiences that the future is one that is promising. Here, part of the vocabulary to produce a putative future is to (i) show and prove that growth has happened and continues to happen, and (ii) promise further growth and prosperity embedded in a neo-liberalized economic present. These details of desire are not so distinctive from what has been shown or promised by Rao, Vajpayee, or Singh, and are in strict continuity with their rhetoric. Thus, in order to prove growth, the GDP rate of growth is cited and comparisons are drawn with those of the previous years. Two such befitting examples are as follows:

> India is one of the brightest economic opportunities in the world today. Our macroeconomic fundamentals are robust, and at 7% plus, we are one of the fastest growing economies of the world.[54]

> Many of you are aware of the contribution India can make to the global economy at a time of economic stagnation in many parts. For the last four quarters, India has been the fastest growing large economy in the world. In 2014-15, India contributed 7.4% of global GDP in purchasing power terms. But it contributed 12.5% of global growth. Thus its contribution to growth is 68% higher than its share of the global economy. FDI in India has increased by 39% in the last 18 months, at a time when global FDI has fallen.[55]

The audiences for such mechanisms showing growth are mixed—most of such speeches are delivered both in and outside India. The noteworthy phenomenon, however, is that Modi attempts to prove that there has been a transition, a move towards something more promising and optimistic. What Prime Minister Rao had termed as 'Growth with a Human Face' is now re-emphasized under the slogan 'growth for all'; the message is hardly different in its contents. The style, vocabulary, and grammar of

---

[54] Modi, press statement by prime minister during his visit to Belgium, Brussels, 30 March 2016.

[55] Modi, address at Economic Times Global Business Summit, New Delhi, 29 January 2016.

communicating the same, however, are cloaked in a politics that gives more weight to the amorphous category of the 'common man'.

> I have always said that development process should benefit the common man as well as the business sector.[56]

> More than 70 thousand villages are now free from the practice of open defecation. We are working towards bringing change in the lives of the common man.[57]

> Make in India is a drive to fulfill unmet demands of the common man.[58]

> We have to increase the quality of life of the common citizen.[59]

In fact, this emerges as a common tactic utilized by the prime minister. The contents of his speeches when compared to those of Rao, Vajpayee, or Singh show exactly the same coordinates of promising a prosperous future, the assurance that as India advances with open markets and embraces foreign investment, it also embarks on the project of development that is sustainable and equitable. However, Modi's oratory seems to especially and repetitively emphasize the benefit of the 'common man'. As stated in the introduction, this is part of a habitus of speaking 'poverty at home' (that is, addressing the evergreen issue of benefitting *all* citizens, especially the poor) and speaking 'business abroad'. The common man, the generalizable category that evokes recognition across numerous class, caste, and religious scales is particularly emphasized when Modi addresses Indians. The larger and repetitive aim is to promise a future to this category that will make the economic present an irrefutable good, that is, solidify market liberalization as the only viable means towards growth.

Interestingly, this category can easily be subsumed under what I refer to as the 'other within' in chapter 2, that is, those who were the audiences of Rao's temporalizing discourse, but not the immediate winners

---

[56] Modi, address at the Vibrant Gujarat Summit, Gandhinagar, 11 January 2015.

[57] Modi, address to the nation on Indian Independence Day, New Delhi, 15 August 2016.

[58] Modi, address at inauguration of Make in India week, Mumbai, 13 February 2016.

[59] Modi, address at Economic Times Global Business Summit, New Delhi, 29 January 2016.

of market liberalization. This large faction of the Indian population has, over the decades, been given assurances of 'not yet, but eventually', that is, explaining trickle down becomes the means to produce the certainty of a secure future. The logic of *eventual* coevalness thus pervades the oratory of all the prime ministers. In Modi's oratory, one sees that the categories of the villager, the poor, the non-elite, the farmer, and the small-scale businessman are merged together under the amorphous entity of 'the common man', who is then defined in terms of unmet dreams and desires.

> Till only 25–30 years back, if not more, there were many people in the world who thought that India was a country of snake charmers, it was a country which practiced in black magic. The real identity of India had not reached the world, but my dear brothers and sisters, our youngsters, 20-22-23 years old youngsters have mesmerized the whole world with their skills in computers. Our young IT professions have given a new path of making a new identity of India. If our country has this strength, can we think something about the country? Our dream is, therefore, of 'Digital India'. When I talk of 'Digital India' I do not speak of the elite, it is for the poor people. You can imagine what a quality education the children in villages will get, if all the villages of India are connected with Broadband Connectivity and if we are able to give long distance education to the schools in every remote corner of the villages.[60]

In the aforementioned lines, delivered on the occasion of the Independence Day, Modi once again evokes the category of 'poor people'. A prominent distinction with previous prime ministers like Vajpayee and Singh is that whereas it is very clear that all refer to sustainable and equitable growth for all, the divide that is drawn between the extreme poor and the more obvious takers, consumers, and producers of the new economy (or those who are inserted in it) is a prominent one. These two categories are lexically kept apart, even if mentioned in the same speech. In the given excerpt, Modi lexically bridges these by bringing the project of 'Digital India' together with the 'poor', the non-elite, and the 'every remote corner of the villages'. This in fact may be seen as one of the most successful tropes and formulae of the Modi government even during the election campaign. Regardless of

---

[60] N.D. Modi, address to the nation on Indian Independence Day, New Delhi, 15 August 2014.

the real-time impact of campaigns such as Digital India and Make in India, it is for the first time that one sees that promises like Digital India, Smart India, Start-Up India are made the bridge between open markets, a language immersed in India's rise as an 'IT superpower' or a 'global manufacturing hub' and the category of the 'poor'.

Breaching and Bridging Pasts

Just as in the case of his three predecessors, three prominent tactics are used by Modi to conjure a relationship with a generalized past, whereby specific resources are presented as metonymic for the entire nation's past. These include: (i) breaching with the past, especially dissociating from the rhetoric of the previous governments; (ii) bridging with the past by evoking a referential vocabulary that relies on national heroes and a generalizing civilizational ethos, and (iii) producing the present and the future where market liberalization is a reified truth by simultaneously bridging and breaching with a generalized past.

However, Modi's oratory is replete with attempts to produce newness in his own argumentation skills and rhetoric in general in comparison to what has been said previously. As reforms become a reified truth of the neo-liberal present and future, he produces lexical breaches with the immediate past of the UPA government to revalidate the legitimacy of his own government. This breach with the past can be located in the following excerpt:

> Sometimes it costs more to repair the old house but it gives us no satisfaction. Thereafter, we have a feeling that it would be better to construct a new house altogether and therefore within a short period, we will replace the planning commission with a new institution having a new design and structure, a new body, a new soul, a new thinking, a new direction, a new faith towards forging a new direction to lead the country based on creative thinking, public-private partnership, optimum utilization of resources, utilization of youth power of the nation, to promote the aspirations of state governments seeking development, to empower the state governments and to empower the federal structure. Very shortly, we are about to move in a direction when this institute would be functioning in place of Planning Commission.[61]

[61] Modi, address to the nation on Indian Independence Day, New Delhi, 15 August 2014.

In these lines, a discontinuity is produced with the country's economic past, which is epitomized here by the Planning Commission, a body constituted and in existence since the first Nehruvian government and compared here to the 'old house'. The emphasis on the new (through words like 'a new design, a new structure, a new body, a new soul, a new thinking, a new direction, a new faith towards forging a new direction to lead the country') is produced by breaching with the Nehruvian past.[62]

Another telling example is how Modi produces a positive vocabulary for urbanization, a word which evokes a long history of social movements against internal displacement, internal migration, and the plight of shifts from agrarian production to migration in the construction sector.

> There was once a time in our nation when, if you dig out old newspapers and read many articles and the analysis, when urbanization was considered a big threat. On each occasion—urbanization is happening, what will happen, how will it be—these were the conversations. My thinking is different. Let us not consider urbanization to be a problem, let us see it as an opportunity. It is an opportunity that urbanization is taking place. Let us not consider it a threat but rather an opportunity. If we will consider it to be a threat then our way of dealing will be something like: 'O God! Look someone people have settled there, what should we do now? How should we get water supply there, how should we organize electricity supply there- what should we do to organize a school for their children there? What a headache!' Instead, if we consider urbanization an opportunity and think of it as 'this is how our Pune looks like right now—this is how it could look like in 2025. These are the avenues—this is the direction in which we can proceed, this is the way in which we can move forward, this is how we can rise in the sky, this is how we can speed up, that much work can be done for water drainage, this arrangement [...]' if we start thinking like this from now on, then urbanization will change into an opportunity. This is why we want to transform urbanization into an opportunity.[63]

---

[62] Another illustrative example where a break with the past is produced can be found in Modi's tweet: 'Younger generation in India is thinking and aspiring so differently, that government can no longer afford to remain rooted in the past.' [@PMO India, 26 August 2016, 7:40 a.m.].

[63] Modi, address on the launch of the Smart Cities Mission projects in Pune, 25 June 2016.

> That is why I said that this is not a game of high buildings. A changed
> life demands speed.[64]

As lucidly visible in this excerpt, urbanization is produced as an opportunity and people are called upon to participate in converting it from a
threat to something that opens new avenues. It, however, also becomes
clear that Modi's addressees are not people who are directly affected by
these new spatial configurations, but rather those who are called upon
to facilitate rapid urbanization. Thus, a repertoire of words replete with
optimism and promise, such as 'we can move forward, this is how we
can rise in the sky, this is how we can speed up', and 'a changed life
demands speed' provides the necessary twist through which urbanization is fabricated as essentially good, a great chance. What remain
absent are the shadows that rapid urbanization casts upon old social and
economic configurations and the adverse story of displacement. The
lines do not address the receivers of urbanization projects for 'Smart
Cities', but ironically the hardships of those who must design them.
The first three lines on the other hand produce a complete breach with
the past culminating in the line, 'My thinking is different'.

In line with his predecessors, Modi also evokes references from the
past to produce continuity with the present. Thus, national heroes
and a generalized and homogenous civilizational legacy become the
legitimizing hinges to produce the discourse of change. A noteworthy difference to all his predecessors though is that references to the
words of Jawaharlal Nehru are noticeably absent from Modi's oratory.
Modi's predecessors (even Vajpayee from the BJP) have sold the reforms
and the opening up of the economy by utilizing a lexical oratory that
nonetheless derives heavily from Nehruvian repertoire (also that of
his successors, Lal Bahadur Shastri and Indira Gandhi). Whereas direct
references to the names of Shastri and Indira Gandhi are scanty, Nehru
is prominently present both as an iconic name that lends legitimacy to
claims that are made as well as through the repetition of his oratory—
his words.

As mentioned in chapter 1, Modi speaks of the logic of market liberalization in a vocabulary that does not rely upon a Nehruvian socialist
past to legitimize the neo-liberalized present. Nor does he make Nehru

[64] Modi, address on the launch of the Smart Cities Mission projects in Pune,
25 June 2016.

the authoritative voice to lend legitimacy to his claims. However, *the grammar and protocols* of engagement with Indian audiences are strikingly similar (see chapter 1). Within the addresses, Nehru is replaced by other national heroes, most prominently, Gandhi and Sardar Vallabh Bhai Patel.

One noteworthy moment is when Modi re-evokes the words of Prime Minister Lal Bhadur Shastri, as none of his predecessors have done:

> Brothers and sisters, I want to call upon the youth of the country, particularly the small people engaged in the industrial sector. I want to call upon the youth working in the field of technical education in the country. As I say to the world 'Come, make in India', I say to the youth of the country—it should be our dream that this message reaches every corner of the world—'Made in India'. This should be our dream. Whether, to serve the country, is it necessary for the youth to be hanged like Bhagat Singh? Brothers and sisters, Lal Bhadur Shastri had given the slogan 'Jai Jawan, Jai Kisan'. A soldier sacrifices himself at the border and protects Mother India. Similarly, a farmer serves Mother India by filling the godowns with grains. This is also nation's service. Filling the granary is the biggest nation's service that a farmer provides. That is why Lal Bahadur Shastri had given the slogan of 'Jai Jawan, Jai Kisan'.[65]

In this speech, delivered to a large national audience on Independence Day celebrations, Modi makes a call to the youth of the country—a relationship to the future is conjured in order to speak of the present—as emphasized in the word 'dream'. Another national hero of the past whose imagery has existed in the rhetoric of all prime ministers (but who is more emphatically and repetitively evoked in Modi's addresses) is Bhagat Singh, known as the young nationalist who was hanged to death during colonial rule. In the lines, Modi makes a call to the youth of the country. Just as Shastri's slogan of 'Victory to the soldier! Victory to the Farmer!' is reiterated to emphasize the importance of the farmer who serves the nation by growing crops for the nation's granaries and the soldier who protects the motherland, the youth of the present is called upon to assist in the project of 'Make in India'. This does sound as being

---

[65] Modi, address to the nation on Indian Independence Day, New Delhi, 15 August 2014.

in line with the socialist import-substitution economy, emphasizing production at home for self-reliance. What is different is that the youth is called upon to 'Make in India' *with* the foreign investor. Open markets here not only imply the export of goods 'Made in India', but also foreign direct investment to help 'Make in India'. However, in a lexical twist, the farmer and the soldier of the socialist period, the most iconic signs of the nation, come to share the same semantic space within the speech as the youth who are called upon today to assist the world as it is invited to 'Come Make in India'. A putative future ('dream'), imagery from the socialist past (*'Jai Jawan, Jai Kisan'*), and a structurally adjusted present ('As I say to the world 'Come, make in India', I say to the youth of the country—it should be our dream that this message reaches every corner of the world') are thus synchronously evoked for the cause of an open economy.[66]

Not only are national figures evoked, but like the previous prime ministers, the rhetoric of producing a 'civilizational ethos' for the cause of market liberalization is a commonly used tactic also for Modi. For example:

> India has to be seen from a different angle. It is not just a country of today. It is also an old civilization. It is not just a country of a few cities. It is a country of thousands of towns and several hundred thousand villages. It is a country of diverse communities. Therefore India has its own solutions for many pressing problems.
>
> Our philosophy is a philosophy of conservation.
> Our culture teaches us nurturing of nature
> Our way of life is that of harnessing

[66] In another speech, Modi evokes the words of Swami Vivekananda on the occasion of the Independence Day and uses a resource from the past to speak of India's future: 'I am reminded of the words of Swami Vivekananda. He had said, "I can see before my eyes Mother India awakening once again. My Mother India would be seated as the World Guru. Every Indian would render service towards welfare of humanity. This legacy of India would be useful for the welfare of the world." These words were spoken by Swami Vivekananda ji, his dream of seeing India ensconced as World Guru, his vision, it is incumbent upon us to realize that dream. This capable country, blessed with natural bounty, this country of youth can do much for the world in the coming days.' (Modi, address to the Nation on Indian Independence Day, New Delhi, 15 August 2014).

Such thoughts and practices have existed in India for centuries. Thus, whatever we will do, it will be aligned with our culture, ethos and beliefs. Because we know this is what will work in India.[67]

Whereas this excerpt may suggest that there is no link drawn between market liberalization and a generalized civilizational ethos, it is interesting to see that these lines occur in a speech whereby entrepreneurs from India, but also from abroad are being addressed to invest in India's open markets. Attended by a highly diverse range of international dignitaries (prime ministers of Bhutan and Macedonia, Secretary of State John Kerry, UN Secretary General Ban Ki Moon, World Bank President Jim Yong Kim, dignitaries from Australia, Canada, Denmark, Fiji, Iran, Israel, Japan, Mauritius, the Netherlands, Poland, Romania, Russia, Singapore, UAE, and the United Kingdom), the speech starts on a note of optimism celebrating India's open economy. The excerpt is placed between this mood of optimism and a latter half where the prime minister only speaks of 'Digital India', 'Make in India', 'I-ways', and finally 'the Ease of Doing Business' (Modi adds in the end, 'And I am sure, you will not find all of them together at any other destination. India offers you the potential of low cost manufacturing. India has low cost and high quality manpower'). Thus, what appears to be an excerpt, speaking of an 'Indian' civilization, is tactfully timed into the architecture of the speech. At the same time, the line, 'Such thoughts and practices have existed in India for centuries. Thus, whatever we will do, it will be aligned with our culture, ethos, and beliefs' serves the purpose of producing a sense of cultural security, whereas in reality, the prime minister addresses a transition.

---

[67] Modi, address at the Vibrant Gujarat Summit, Gandhinagar, 11 January 2015. Another befitting example, 'This country has been built on such foundation of ancient cultural heritage, where we were told of only one mantra during Vedic period, which is indicative of our work culture, which we have learnt, we have memorized—"Sanachchhdhvam Samvadadham sam wo manasi jaanataam". We walk together, we move together, we think together, we resolve together and together we take this country forward. Having imbibed this basic mantra, 1.25 crore of countrymen have taken this nation forward.' (Modi, address to the nation on Indian Independence Day, New Delhi, 15 August 2014).

In fact, this tactic of dressing up the new in the old is in continuity with that of Modi's predecessors. Like Singh and Rao, who were seen as quoting Gandhi when speaking about embracing change, Modi is also seen as presenting transitions and embracing the putative outside, but by dressing them in attire that appears to be old and familiar. This is achieved by rendering the idea of change itself as something very Indian. To illustrate, 'These efforts have been to tap ideas from inside. The next step is to bring in ideas from outside. Culturally, Indians have always been receptive to ideas from elsewhere. It is said in the Rigveda: Aano bhadra krtavo yantu vishwatah, which means let us welcome noble thoughts flowing in from all directions.'[68]

Thus, as Rao and Singh utilize Gandhi's idea of 'allowing winds to blow into the house from all directions', Modi also speaks of welcoming noble ideas from all directions by referring to the Rigveda. Change introduced through the 'ideas' from the putative outside is thus skilfully converted into an Indian achievement to produce a sense of security.

Some addresses also illustrate the tactic of synchronously utilizing resources from the past (bridging with the past), whereas, in reality, suggesting something new within the same speech (breaching with the past).

> [...] India offers you a solid platform to test and launch your making and designing capabilities. In addition, our maritime location makes it easy to market products in several other continents. We are trying to further enable and harness this vast potential with path-breaking initiatives. Campaigns like Digital India and Skill India have been designed to prepare people to take part in this process. We have launched financing schemes which are dedicated to promote entrepreneurship. We are giving loans through MUDRA Bank without any collateral. I have also impressed upon the banks to particularly finance young entrepreneurs belonging to the Scheduled Castes and Tribes as well as women entrepreneurs.
>
> Only this will realize the dreams of Mahatma Gandhi who wanted industries to be run in villages and cottages.
>
> Only this will realize the dreams of Dr. Bhimrao Ambedkar who advocated the need to move surplus labour from agriculture to other occupations.[69]

---

[68] Modi, address at the Transforming India Lecture, New Delhi, 26 August 2016.

[69] Modi, address at inauguration of Make in India week, Mumbai, 13 February 2016.

The aforementioned lines can be gauged to have a highly encouraging tone of optimism, whereby Modi announces how the benefits of the open markets are meant to supplant the entrepreneurial energies of the young and those at the fringes of caste and gender hierarchies. The examples of Gandhi and Ambedkar are utilized as referential, legitimizing hinges for the cause of running industries in villages and cottages and the need to shift labour from agriculture to other occupations. At the same time, what is not mentioned is Gandhian insistence on self-sufficient and autonomous village economies and their decentralized existence, which would be in sharp contrast to the idea of opening up the village economy to external forces. It is also not mentioned that the shadows cast by adverse conditions that forcefully push farmers to move to contract labour jobs after losing their lands. Thus, what is in reality a breach with the past is produced by bridging with it through iconic figures and their visions. The language of transition is however not a hidden one; change is projected at the same time as continuity.

Empowering Epithets: The Proverbial Prime Minister

The Hindustani word '*Jumla*' is used to connote an idiomatic expression, a phrase, or an epithet that describes something or a given state of affairs. Prime Minister Modi has often been described as a *Jumla* prime minister, especially in reference to the innovative vocabulary and catchy slogans used by him in his oratory. Modi's oratory, though essentially similar in its tenets and contents to that of Manmohan Singh, uses new lexical resources embedded in varying regimes of temporality to bring the point home. What has thus emerged over the last two years of prime ministership is an array of epithets that style economic visions and the nation into being. Some of the slogans and phrases that thus occur repetitively in Modi's speeches include: 'Make in India',[70] '*Sabka*

[70] To give an example: 'We will continue to strengthen the "Make in India" initiative. It is not intended for only manufacturing for the domestic market or import substitution. It is as much about making world-class products and services for the whole globe. That is why, for us, improvements towards free trade are important' (Modi, keynote speech at 41st AGM of US–India Business Council [USIBC], Washington D.C., 7 June 2016).

Saath, Sabka Vikas',[71] 'Smart City Mission',[72] 'MyGov platform',[73] 'smart economic hubs',[74] 'Digital India',[75] 'Clean India' or 'Swachh Bharat',[76] 'M-Governance or mobile governance',[77] 'mantra of total

[71] For example, 'We should create new opportunities for citizens to progress and also give them a choice of opportunities. Opportunity is like oxygen to the aspirational citizen and we are keen that this is never in short supply. In simple terms, it means Sabka Saath, Sabka Vikas' (Modi, address at Economic Times Global Business Summit, New Delhi, 29 January 2016).

[72] For example, 'Creating opportunities for cities and towns to grow is very crucial. Urban areas are an engine of growth. A key initiative for urban transformation is the Smart City Mission. The Mission has several "firsts". It is the first time that certain areas in cities will be comprehensively developed in a systematic and qualitative way. These areas will act as "light houses" which will eventually influence the rest of the city. It is the first time that there has been such extensive citizen consultation. Nearly 2.5 million people participated through contests, discussions, polls, blogs and talks on the MyGov platform. This is a major break from the top-down approach to urban planning. It is the first time that allocation of funds in a government scheme is done not by decisions of Ministers or officers but on the basis of competition. This is a good example of competitive and cooperative federalism' (Modi, address at Economic Times Global Business Summit, New Delhi, 29 January 2016).

[73] Modi, address at Economic Times Global Business Summit, New Delhi, 29 January 2016

[74] For example, 'And, we want to turn our villages into smart economic hubs and connect our farmers better to markets and makes (sic.) them less vulnerable to the whims of weather' (Modi, address at the Digital India Dinner, San Jose California, 26 September 2015).

[75] For example, 'When you think of the exponential speed and scale of expansion of social media or a service, you have to believe that it is equally possible to rapidly transform the lives of those who have long stood on the margins of hope. So, friends out of this conviction was born the vision of Digital India' (Modi, address at the Digital India Dinner, San Jose California, 26 September 2015).

[76] For example, 'Yesterday, on 2 October on the eve Mahatma Gandhi's birth anniversary, more than 1.25 crore countrymen have started the "Swachh Bharat" movement' (Modi, address to the nation through show on All India Radio, *Mann ki Baat*, New Delhi, 3 October 2014).

[77] For example, 'I now speak of M-Governance or mobile governance. That is the way to go in a country with one billion cell phones and use of smart phone growing at high double-digit rates. It has the potential to make development a truly inclusive and comprehensive mass movement' (Modi, address at the Digital India Dinner, San Jose California, 26 September 2015).

transformation', transformation with transparency, reform, perform, and transform',[78] 'Start-Up India', and 'Stand-Up India'.[79] Some of these epithets emphasize exactly the same visions laid down by Manmohan Singh in his speeches. Thus, while Singh was seen as utilizing phrases like 'Made in India' or 'Brand India' in favour of opening markets in India to FDI, but simultaneously emphasizing the strengthening of the manufacturing sector, Modi campaigns for 'Make in India'.

Two further examples of continuity include the following:

> India is blessed with three Ds. These are: Democracy, Demography and Demand. To this, we have added the fourth D that is Deregulation. Today's India is this four dimensional India.[80]

> E-Governance as a foundation of better governance—efficient, economical and effective.[81]

The usage of these empowering epithets should not be confused here as sheer ornamental and decorative vocabulary that lacks serious content. It is not the intention of this volume to challenge the sincerity of such idiomatic and epithetic expressions. A thorough analysis in comparing these visions to their implementation is much needed. The important message that emerges is that the contents of the discourse(s) utilized to legitimize the logic of market liberalization and reify it as the only inevitable means for economic prosperity has remained unchanged. The linguistic repertoire utilized to do the same, however, has witnessed a new styling. Modi's proverbial epithets, which also play on onomato-poetic expressions and rhyming phraseology, in fact forward the same cause as that of the previous prime ministers. What has changed is the lexical apparatus that presents these contents to the audiences.

[78] For example, '[...] I have tried to do several things in every range with the mantra of Total transformation, Transformation with transparency, Reform, Perform and Transform' (Modi, address to the nation on Indian Independence Day, New Delhi, 15 August 2014).

[79] 'While talking about "Stand-Up India", we are also often talking about 'Start-Up India'. We are laying the emphasis on Substance than on Symbolism.' (Modi, address to the nation on Indian Independence Day, New Delhi, 15 August 2014).

[80] Modi, address at inauguration of Make in India Week, Mumbai, 13 February 2016.

[81] Modi, address at the Digital India Dinner, San Jose California, 26 September 2015).

The election campaign focused enormously on what was dubbed as the 'Gujarat model', making development the primary agenda (with the illustrious example purported through the example of the state's progress, now often challenged). This became a means to divert public attention to 'growth', though with a much more energized vigour in comparison to his predecessors, from the communal politics of caste- and religion-based sub-national identities.

★★★

This chapter has shown how the overarching category of 'the past' is used to make the reforms inevitable. The first section has shown how a temporal breach is introduced with the nation's recent past by categorizing the economy as 'sick' and the era as 'dark'. This is done to justify change for Indian audiences, especially during Rao's term, in the immediate aftermath of institutionalizing the reforms. However, a confusing pattern emerges when a simultaneous bridge is made through a selective commemoration of what is dubbed as 'the past'. Section two of this part shows how the prime ministers refer to a homogenized 'civilizational' heritage in order to establish an exaggerated composite continuity with the present. Here, illustrations of Indian (which, in effect, refers to primarily Hindu) scriptural references abound. The next part of section two has illustrated how the figure of the national hero also becomes a legitimizing basis for the reforms. Personalities like Gandhi and Nehru, even if in stark contradiction to the logic of neo-liberal economics, are cited as spaceless, timeless icons, and become the justificatory hinge for the staging of the reforms.

Besides the discursive production of a homogenized past and an aspirational future, the first three prime ministers also conjure another unchallengeable order of time that necessitates that the reforms be accepted. Here, the vocabulary of 'destiny', embedded in how acceptance of change itself is an Indian characteristic, becomes the legitimizing means to render transformation as something very natural.

In the last section, the chapter has introduced the temporal tactics that emerge in the rhetoric of the current prime minister, Narendra Modi, as read through the lens of continuities and discontinuities with his predecessors. In line with the three prime ministers, Modi's oratory is also heavily embedded in the politics of time. The pasts and the futures of the Indian economy are conjured in order to make a case for the present neo-liberalized economic order. An important difference however is that unlike Rao, who needed to establish a relation of co-equivalence between a promising future and the reforms, and Vajpayee who needed to justify the shift in the stance of his own political party which was a staunch opponent of the reforms when in opposition, Modi was required to do none. He neither builds the relation of coequality between an open economy and a prosperous future, nor does he justify his government's agenda of favouring and furthering the reforms. Both emerge as a pre-established oratorical truth in his speeches.

The challenges facing the project of 'Emerging India' are no longer levied on ideological terrains, that is, questioning the economic order that reifies market liberalization, but rather on how their execution has remained an incomplete process. Modi speaks of transformation as a catalysing force, though with a vocabulary that carefully projects it as constant work in progress. Whereas in one particular regime of historicity employing the present, the Indian economy is produced as having 'arrived', in another simultaneously used one, it is rather projected as one that requires persistent investment by its citizens in order to realize its full potential. Whereas in the rhetoric of the previous prime ministers, even if sustainable and equitable development for the poor and the logic behind evermore open markets to foreign investment existed in different kinds of speeches delivered before varying audiences, in Modi's addresses, one sees that the categories of the villager, the poor, the non-elite, the farmer, and the small-scale businessman are merged together under the amorphous entity of 'the common man', who is then defined in terms of unmet dreams and desires. The proverbial epithets like Digital India, Start-Up India, Stand Up India, E-governance and M-Governance, Connected India, Design in India, etc., thus, address all citizens at the same time within the purview of the same speech and are not surgically removed for addresses meant for special entrepreneurial or external audiences only. Modi has thus brought the flashiness of the vocabulary embracing market liberalization, at least at the discursive level to all strata of Indian audiences, whereby he can speak as comfortably about irrigation and seeds to farmers as Digital India and Make in India.

A prominent difference between Modi's oratory and that of others is whereas his predecessors (even Vajpayee from the BJP) have sold the

reforms and the opening up of the economy by utilizing lexical repertoire that derives heavily from Nehruvian socialist vocabulary of self-
reliance and self-sufficiency, Modi abstains to use Nehru's words as a
legitimizing hinge for his own authority. He also refrains from evoking
the figure of Nehru as an iconic sign to produce the legitimacy of his
economic vision. However, the *grammar* and *protocols* of engagement
with Indian audiences are strikingly similar (see chapter 1).

Finally, his utilization of epithets that continue to make him highly
popular shows that the contents of the discourse(s) used to legitimize
the logic of market liberalization and reify it as the only inevitable
means for economic prosperity has remained unchanged over the past
twenty-five years. What has in fact changed with Modi is the linguistic
repertoire used to do the same, whereby a new style and reservoir of
idiomatic expressions are used to sell the same contents.

The analysis of the speeches of the first three prime ministers especially has led to one core finding. The prime ministers have attempted
to normalize the transformations induced by the neo-liberal reforms
by rendering them not so new. As the future embedded within change
(in the shape of the reforms) entailed something new, the past has
been used by the prime ministers to describe that new in order to take
away the anxiety, the unpredictability and the contingency attached to
it. More concretely, this reflects in how the prime ministers speak of
the reforms by using different resources from the past, ranging from
a generalized civilizational heritage to a vocabulary bearing socialist
overtones. This is done so that change may be embraced, but, at the
same time, a sense of security prevails. The message is thus not so much
to inform internal audiences that a *drastic* transition is in operation, but
rather to naturalize it in continuity, giving people an assurance of it
being calculated, contained, measured, and anyway an inevitable part
of the sacred history of the nation.

Christopher Pinney, in his detailed study of chromolithographs from
colonial and postcolonial India, ranging over a time span of over 120
years, states in reference to the Indian nationalist movement and its
usage of imagery to mobilize people that:

> [...] It is clear that the nation is invoked primarily through allegory. This
> is an allegory open to 'linguistic' decoding and was highly susceptible
> to colonial control. Within a few decades, however, it was superseded
> by what we might term 'figure' or the affective. In part, this history

was determined by a dialectical constraint: figural affective intensities required the semiotic infrastructure of allegory and other political significations, which of necessity had recourse to substitution. Once allegory had done its laborious work, figure could transform these associations into immediate identifications.[82]

In the context of this chapter, I have shown how allegory appears in innumerable lexical forms and shapes, indicating how economic transition(s) were enacted, but, more importantly, how, in their initial phase, they were explained and communicated. However, the transformation of the allegorical into a figurative reference is done through the referential hinge of temporality. The main objective is to ascertain that once the figurative vocabulary of 'India Emerging' is used, it makes the economic reforms inevitable and gets transformed immediately into something with which the audiences can relate. Thus, the goal is not so much to debate on whether India will rise or not. Behind these narrations, which are loaded with optimism, is the desired aim to render the reforms as something preordained and indisputable. The past appears and disappears in the words of the prime ministers to establish the irrefutability of the transition. This implies that it is produced and used with such routinization that it comes to stand as a sign for the future and the present alike.

One of Pinney's image producers says, 'images should be new, but not too new'.[83] The same could be stated for numerous slogans, terms, and phrases that come to be repetitively used by all prime ministers in consistency or by each one individually. What is being produced is new, but the attire of the transformations is not too new. 'Growth with a Human Face', 'self-sufficiency', 'self-reliance', 'sovereignty', 'just, humane society', 'religious' mythological references, the national hero, etc. are all constituents of that figurative vocabulary where allegory has done its work and a reference to the same immediately enables a sense of familiarity, participation, and identification for the audiences.

---

[82] C. Pinney, *Photos of the Gods: The Printed Image and Political Struggle in India* (London: Reaktion Books, 2004), pp. 112–14.

[83] Pinney writes, 'The repetitive volatilization of popular texts ensures that we never experience them for the first time: it is always (like the new hit song) already half-heard, half-seen as we encounter it in its ubiquity in our daily lives.' (Pinney, *Photos of the Gods*, p. 178).

The new thus emerges in the garb of the old. Therein lies a unique Indianness to the political rhetoric in that that which stands as a change (in the shape of market liberalization) is presented as normal, controllable, measured, contained, and secure. Just as Pinney's commercial artists maintain 'archives of early images',[84] the prime ministers maintain an archive of resources from the past—terms with a particular 'Indian' career. The objective at hand is that they come to denote something specific to the listeners—tropes that are revoked subtly to take away the unpredictability and newness of what is being introduced and stamp it with an Indian flavour.

This leads to another important collateral finding. In order to achieve the same goal of naturalizing change, each of the individual prime ministers refers to different resources from 'the' past. While Congress-affiliated Manmohan Singh and P.V. Narasimha Rao employed a higher degree of socialist rhetoric (particularly Rao, because he is the initiator of the transition—the sense of caution is thus most noteworthy in his addresses), A.B. Vajpayee's rhetoric is more reminiscent of an amalgamation of Nehruvian developmentalism, a socialist vocabulary borrowing heavily from Indira Gandhi's era (though Indira Gandhi herself is never revoked as a figure). His vocabulary also reflects the BJP-laden Hindu and Hindi language rhetoric.

In spite of these differences in the cosmetics of composition and the resources borrowed, the overarching narration of 'India, the emerging economic power' has had a coherent, traceable consistency. The reforms are intricately enmeshed within the emergence and the continuation of the 'Emerging India' story. It has been normalized and popularized as part of the agenda of *each* government, because each of the political parties in power has furthered the cause of the reforms. Hence, there are not four stories being narrated by four individuals, but rather a consistent one, which may have been *moulded* and *adapted* in the texture of the lexicon of the individual leader, but its intentionality and inherent mechanisms have stuck, stayed, and spilled over.[85]

---

[84] Pinney, *Photos of the Gods*, p. 206.

[85] In fact, Singh even makes a reference to this briefly in one of his addresses: 'It must be recognized that there has been an element of continuity mirroring an evolving consensus, on many aspects of our foreign and external economic policy. I draw your attention to the fact that initial response of our government

The narrative of 'India, the economic powerhouse of the 21st century' is one which has its limited 'takers' and, though it stands as being consistently challenged on many fronts, it has in fact penetrated the intuitive vocabulary of some (who do not accept it without its inherent loopholes), but do carry a wish, an aspiration that is eager to acquire the *form* of the discourse.

In conclusion, it may be said that what perhaps makes the government official working in the bookshop, whom I mentioned at the beginning of Chapter 2 (who has in fact been in the same job regardless of the changing governments and through the terms of all four prime ministers), acquire, 'buy' the rhetoric, even insist on it and produce it before me, is the very texture of *how* the neo-liberal state is narrated and therein materialized in India. The *new* in the 'New India' can exist, because it is seen through the lens of the *old*, a lens with a coloured glass, which opens the possibility of seeing the future in the present, but projects it in a colour that dyes the future with shades of the past. The *neo* in the neo-liberal thus comes in the form of that which is new indeed, but a *familiar* new, an 'Indian' new.

---

in the early 1990s to the new post Cold War world has since evolved under successive governments, in a direction set by us at the time.' This may also be viewed as part of popularizing the reforms first by claiming that a consensus exists around them and second by establishing the Congress as a trendsetter, an initiator (Singh, 'India and the World—A Blueprint for Partnership and Growth', address at the Hindustan Times Leadership Initiative Conference, New Delhi, 5 November 2004).

4

'The World Is Changing (…)'

Othering and Spatializing Strategies

We have seen how the narration of India as an economically rising nation (and therein the process of rendering the neo-liberal reforms inevitable) is attained through the temporalizing tactics of producing a temporal frame of reference (blissful past and future) in which the reforms appear as an irrefutable, messianic key moment. The categories of an idealized future and a homogenized past are synchronously conjured in the addresses to entrench the reforms as an event necessitated in and by time. Thus, depictions of an ideal future and a museified, selectively extracted, past help justify and frame the reforms as inconvertible and intertwined with the profiling of 'Emerging India'.

In this chapter, we flex the lens to another important category, which also constitutes a strategy of construing the transitions as unavoidable. What the prime ministers speak and how they speak is highly dependent on the spatial context, that is, the audience for which the speech is intended. The classifications of 'internal' and 'external' audiences become graphic here. This implies calculated rhetorical strategies, depending on whether the *perceived* audiences are 'internal' (that is, Indians in and outside India) or 'external'. This chapter will illustrate which lexical tools are utilized by the prime ministers in which specific context in order to naturalize the reforms and, therein, authenticate claims to India's economic emergence to both the audiences.

For the Putative Inside

The World Is Changing, So Must India

The first spatially informed technique of legitimizing the transitions in Indian economy and situating them as an unquestionable means to achieve an ideal future is to convince perceived internal audiences of an *outside world in transition* that necessitates change in India as well. This includes presenting in depth before audiences a narrative of a post-1989 world. The New World Order, which is linguistically produced in the speeches, is described as one whereby the globe is no longer fixated upon one or two poles of power but invested in multiple geographical sites. This order is described as one making change a global reality, even a necessity. Within India, the neo-liberal economic reforms are staged as the face of that change, pursuing which will ensure that India will also 'realize its destiny' and its due place in the 'comity of nations'. Thus, an external environment is constituted that becomes the validating hinge for what happens internally, which is India's acceptance of market liberalization.

Numerous illustrations where this new world is presented may be found in the speeches. To give some examples,

'The world is a global village [...]'[1]

'In the globalized world of today [...]'[2]

'In a changing global economy where unpredictable forces sometimes operate [...]'[3]

'In a world in transition, nations need an anchor.'[4]

However, the descriptions of this changing world do not just end by indicating how nations become globally more and more interconnected

[1] M. Singh, 'India and the World—A Blueprint for Partnership and Growth', address at the Hindustan Times Leadership Initiative Conference, New Delhi, 5 November 2004.

[2] Singh, 'Towards Promoting Employment led Growth', address at the Shram Awards Function, New Delhi, 4 October 2004.

[3] P.V.N. Rao, 'Indo-Singapore Friendship and Cooperation', address at the banquet hosted in honour of the prime minister of Singapore, New Delhi, 24 January 1994.

[4] Rao, 'Indo-Singapore Friendship and Cooperation'.

and interdependent; the prime ministers link this to India by producing changes as necessitating an open economy. The following excerpts
lucidly point out this argument.

'It is necessary to open up the economy, make it globally competitive,
become an integral part of the global economy.'[5]

'We have to compete with other countries of the world. You cannot be
an island by yourself. [...]'[6]

'Globalization is a historical reality. And nations cannot prosper in
isolation.'[7]

'We will have to modernize [...] to be competitive. We will have to rub
shoulders with others. There is no other way. Let us be very clear about
that.'[8]

'If you have to be competitive, if you have to live in the new world, in
the changed world with the new agenda, the new agenda of integrating
Indian economy into the world economy then there is hardly any choice
for you.'[9]

'We cannot ask the rest of the world to stand still. We cannot freeze
technological conditions. We cannot determine beyond a point what
happens in the outside world. We have to take many of these things as
given and learn to adapt the evolving environment to our advantage.'[10]

'The world has increasingly come to accept that open societies and
open markets are the most natural and stable form of social and economic organization. What is now increasingly clear is that an inclusive

[5] Rao, 'Let us Concentrate on Development', address at a public meeting,
Mangalore, 20 March 1993.

[6] Rao, 'Let us Concentrate on Development'.

[7] A.B. Vajpayee, 'Government Asserts Its Commitment to Economic
Reforms', inaugural address at the 71st Annual Session of FICCI (Federation
of Indian Chambers of Commerce and Industry), New Delhi, 24 October 1998.

[8] Rao, 'The New Industrial Policy', intervention in Lok Sabha during the
debate on the demands of the Industries Ministry, 26 August 1991.

[9] Rao, 'Integrating Indian Economy into World Economy', address at the
Silver Jubilee Celebrations of the Federation of Indian Export Organizations,
New Delhi, 7 October 1991.

[10] Singh, 'Building Competencies for Success', address at the Indian CEOs
Competencies for Success Summit, New Delhi, 22 January 2005.

democracy based on the principles of pluralism and multi-culturalism is the most enduring means of dealing with the challenges posed by open markets and open societies.'[11]

The aforementioned examples highlight how all three prime ministers—Rao, Vajpayee and Singh—justify reforms by embedding them in the transitions of a 'global' world. Here, phrases like 'you cannot be an island by yourself', 'we cannot ask the rest of the world to stand still', and 'there is no other way' are used to produce a sense of urgency. At the same time, the categories of 'open societies' and 'open markets' are intertwined and envisaged as *the only* stable form of social and economic ordering (last illustration). India's adaptation of change in the form of an open economy is thus construed as the only legitimate, feasible, and natural means for the sustenance, even survival, of the nation. Thus, the putative inside is informed of the changed world outside to explain, frame, and validate the embrace of market liberalization. The audiences of these excerpts cited earlier (though clubbed together here within the category of 'internal') are highly varied and scattered—CEOs at a summit in New Delhi, the Federation of Indian Chambers of Commerce and Industry, a public summit in the city of Mangalore, which could be open for all to attend, an awards ceremony (*Shram Awards*) for 'workmen' from public and private sector undertakings, a Lok Sabha debate, and a leadership summit organized by a newspaper. Yet, the same strategy of producing a changing world that requires India to also change can be discerned in these varied addresses clearly addressing different groups.

Producing Security: India's Cautious and Controlled Change

Once change (in the shape of the reforms) has been legitimized under the garb of an external environment, an essential move is to produce an assurance, a guarantee for the audiences that India's embrace of the changes is a cautious, controlled, and measured act. This is done to produce a sense of security, especially for audiences which will directly experience the transitions. This sense of security becomes essential in

[11] Singh, 'India and the World—A Blueprint for Partnership and Growth', address at the Hindustan Times Leadership Initiative Conference, New Delhi, 5 November 2004.

order to take away the fear of the contingency of the future, to establish the reforms as something very Indian and not so new. Thus, changes are hollowed out of the obvious nervousness they induce in a population by the reassurance that what is being done is not an unconscious act instigated through external pressures, but rather a well thought-out plan, the effects of which are under control and predictable. This sense of the reforms being a well-calibrated measure and, therein, the security they promise is produced through two very specific means within the addresses—first, by guaranteeing the audiences that the opening up of the economy will in no way jeopardize India's sovereignty. Second, by stating that even as India adapts to change, its cultural core remains undisturbed. Thus, the safe sanctuary of an unaffected national sovereignty and an unaltered cultural essence provide the space for staging the reforms as undisruptive.

Both of these are spheres where the perceived threat and anxiety of change are the gravest.

Opening Markets to Protect Sovereignty? Preventing Fears of Foreign Investment

The very first strategy of producing a sense of security among internal audiences and making them accept, even embrace economic transitions is done by justifying the cause of Foreign Direct Investments. This has the Janus-faced objective of assuring that India's economic sovereignty will never be jeopardized and, at the same time, pointing to the advantages of foreign investment. Thus, in responding to criticisms levied against the reforms, the prime ministers are seen as making a case for market liberalization. In the following lines, the logic behind foreign investment is legitimized by Rao in the following way:

> Many people are getting nervous about the consequences of Foreign Investment in the country. I want to assert that after all, the plant will be set up in India. There is no possibility that projects built from foreign investment would run away from the country. If roads are built and railway lines are laid, they are bound to remain within the country and there is nothing to be apprehensive about it. Let us welcome all the investment that is available because this capital ultimately will be ours and we will derive benefit out of it. Anyone who makes investment would obviously like to make some profit and there should be no objection to this, as no

one would like to invest if there is no profit in the investment. We should also make it a point to invest the capital that is freed from this investment, in rural programmes.[12]

Here, the audiences are assured of the 'Indian-ness' of the projects that would be undertaken. The inherent logic presented is that the infrastructure built by foreign investment will be an asset for India, which will remain in India. Additionally, the capital saved therein from these inevitably required investments will be used for the advantage of rural populations.[13]

On another occasion, Rao justifies foreign investment in the following way (on similar lines),

We welcome Foreign Investment because it provides the additional resources that we need to achieve a higher rate of industrial growth. It also brings modern technology and management methods which we need to upgrade our industrial sector. I am confident that the competition it brings to the market place will spur greater efficiency among our

[12] Rao, 'Towards a Hopeful Future', address to the nation on Indian Independence Day, New Delhi, 15 August 1992.

[13] Other similar illustrations include: 'There are elements who are attempting to disturb our economic reforms by saying that money is being brought from outside, why is it being brought and on what will it be spent? Whatever may be the source of the money, it will be to set up industry in India. The investor will not take away the industry to his country. He will construct railways, roads. I have already stated whatever infrastructure is created, it will remain with us. Now the foreign investor may remain for whatever time in the country. Later he may like to go away. Structures raised by him will belong to the country. At the most, we have to pay him. They are welcome to join hands with us in the development of India as they are doing in other countries. They are welcome and millions of our people will be benefitted and we are determined to achieve this.' All these external investments are thus presented as if they come with no buts and conditions here (Rao, 'Unity and Stability for Sustained Growth', address to the nation on Indian Independence Day, New Delhi, 15 August 1993);

'Suppose we have to set up a big industry or a plant which needs 5000 crore rupees, then this is the people's money. But if we find some industrialist who is prepared to invest this amount of 5000 crore rupees then the government will be in a position to invest this money elsewhere' (Rao, 'Towards Hopeful Future').

domestic industry. I have no doubt that all of you can face the challenge of competition. Approach your tasks boldly with confidence and you shall achieve success.[14]

These lines, delivered to a very specific audience that comprises of officials, particularly from the public sector enterprises, indicate that foreign investment is presented here as a 'resource', a stairway that provides the possibility to embrace modern technology and management methods which can only benefit the industrial sector. The topic of competition is also evoked because it formulates the crux of the harshest criticism levied against the reforms—stifling competition with 'foreign' actors. Though this is not justified in this excerpt, Rao is seen as turning the argument around on many occasions by claiming that increased competition for public enterprises also implies greater efficiency. Industrial growth is presented as a human necessity for a better 'national' economic future. Both the excerpts highlight how the specific context decides the content of the speech. Before public sector officials, a claim is made for efficiency, whereas before larger audiences who listen to a speech delivered on Independence Day celebrations, promises in the form of investments in rural programmes are used to induce acceptance of foreign investments on Indian turf. This, in fact, echoes of the same strategy which is utilized by the prime ministers to make a case for Indian secularism (see Chapter 5, where I develop the concept of *interface* in the context of Indian secularism), that is, the same term—Foreign Direct Investment—can serve as an interface *par excellence*, a two-sided mirror that allows for the meaning desired in a given context to be reflected back through the prime ministers' words. Thus, whereas before certain audiences the semantic constituents of FDI refer to vocabularies of 'more efficiency', a necessity for the national economy, they refer to something different before a larger national audience where 'the common man' and 'the poor' are the addressed categories. Hence, different contents are emphasized and varying validations in favour of FDI are to be found in the addresses. Two specific arguments/logics—one that emphasizes efficiency, and the other, social benefits and 'rural growth' may be seen at work depending on who the

---

[14] Rao, 'Trading with Care Caution and Expectation', address at the inaugural ceremony of the 65th annual session of the Federation of Indian Chambers of Commerce and Industry, New Delhi, 10 October 1992.

audience is perceived to be. Both are, however, grounded in producing a sense of security and assuring people that the reforms are not a threat, rather that foreign investments are a necessary good.

The logic of explaining increasing privatization is also embedded in a discourse that runs along similar lines. In the following illustration, Rao explains the same, but the reason is extended to a larger context:

> In all areas where the private sector can come, we have to see that it comes in a big way and open up the economy. We have to compete with the other countries of the world. You cannot be an island by yourself. You have to be self-reliant as far as possible but at the same time you must be able to compete with other countries of the world and be in a position to take on the challenges as they present themselves. This cannot happen in a protected economy. This cannot happen in a centralized economy. Therefore, it is necessary to open up the economy, make it globally competitive and become an integral part of the global economy. This is what we have tried to do.[15]

In the given illustration, Rao once again makes a reference to a world outside which necessitates changes within the Indian economy. Hence, the statement 'you cannot be an island by yourself'. Making Indian economy an integral part of the global economy is thus presented as an inevitable reality. Opening up the economy is therein produced as part of a larger plan that will help India be globally competitive. However, this does not imply that India succumbs to change in an unconditional way. The following excerpt unravels a technique of producing security even as the economy faces extreme transitions. Rao's words echo of a sense of caution, whereby privatization is stamped with an Indian flavour. Here, the public sector is given reassurance, but also attacked indirectly in order to normalize the increasing role of the private sector.

> We have never said that we are going to wind up the Public Sector. That was very clear. Whether it is in Davos or in any other place, we said no. We are not for total privatization. Privatization is a sacred word in those countries today. Privatization is not a sacred word here. It is a neutral word, yes. But it doesn't mean we put an Aligarh lock on the gates of all the public sector undertakings and take it as it is. No, they are not for

---

[15] Rao, 'Challenges before the Public Sector Enterprises', address at the inauguration of a conference of the chief executives of public sector enterprises, New Delhi, 30 July 1994.

sale. India is not for sale [...] but at the same time you cannot be sack-
ing. The calf cannot be getting the milk from the cow until the cow dies.
There is a period after which there is a wearing away. When is that period
going to come?[16]

A Janus-faced objective may be traced in operation in these lines. First,
Rao produces a link to the old. The public sector, which not only historically stands symbolic of the Nehruvian era, but also held prominence
in Indira Gandhi's regime, is not completely discarded. The audiences
are informed that no drastic break from a socialist past is at work. The
security produced is that although India has opened up its economy,
privatization shall not be 'total'. Here, total privatization may be indicative of what is perceived as something American. By stating that 'privatization is not a sacred word *here*' (my emphasis), Rao flavours India's
acceptance of market liberalization with a calibrated 'Indian-ness'.
However, the second dimension of the Janus-faced aim is to normalize
that very phenomenon—privatization. This is done by producing a simplistic, easy-to-comprehend, and adaptable referential example. 'The
calf (here standing for the public sector) cannot be getting milk from
the cow (here Indian economy or metonymically India itself) until the
cow dies. There is a period after which there is a wearing away'—that
is, after which the calf should not drink the cow's milk and can sustain
itself (the public sector should not need any state crutches, but rather
sustain itself to support the nation). Thus, the shift from public enterprises towards greater privatization (in the advent of the public sector
not performing well) is produced here as a natural progression, nothing
out of the ordinary, a predictable route to take for the Indian economy.
Most importantly, the dual-faced objectives are enmeshed with a line
that celebrates Indian sovereignty—'India is not for sale'. This may be
viewed as yet another linguistic expression for generating confidence in
India's concrete grip over its own economic trajectory—India will 'open
up', but on its own manageable terms.

India's Cultural Core is Entirely Secure

As stated earlier, the sense of security necessary to ensure that the
reforms are generated not just by guaranteeing the national population

---

[16] Rao, 'Challenges Before the Public Sector Enterprises'.

that there are no external threats to Indian sovereignty, but also by assuring audiences that the shift does not demarcate a breakaway from India's cultural essence. Thus, the prime ministers attempt to render the reforms unquestionable by producing the promise of India's cultural core as unshakeable. In the following lines, the beginning indicates how Rao addresses attacks that have been levied on the reforms and makes a claim for their irreversibility. The second half of the illustration, however, hints at producing security rooted in a self-understanding of being Indian. The nation is produced as a homogenous entity whose fundamental base is unshakeable.

> [...] Sometimes doubts were raised whether this policy would work or not [...] its (the government's) economic and industrial policies will also continue not only for five years but always because we are going to make these irreversible. Let somebody explain to me whether there can be any better policy than this. I am ready to accept. It was asked many times. Many discussions took place but nothing came out. Nobody suggested a better way. Yes, this policy was condemned in speeches: but condemning does not help, it will not fill an empty stomach. Today you cannot shut yourself in a country. Unless you allow fresh air from all sides, you will feel suffocated. Mahatma Gandhi had himself said that he wanted to keep his windows wide open so that fresh air comes from all sides. Yet we should not be blown away by that air. We Indians will not leave our Indianness. For us the interests of the country will be supreme. But we do not want to live in a prison, we do not want our country to be a prison and put a ban on people coming from outside. If people came from outside we are willing to work with them.[17]

Here, when speaking to a homogenized Indian audience, Rao once again utilizes a resource from the past—Gandhi as a national figure—to lend authenticity to what is being presented (positive role of foreign investment). However, more specifically, they highlight that the underlying message is 'We Indians will not leave our Indianness', that is, essentially, the core of India will stay the way it has *always* been (therein a continuity is established even though what is being defended—foreign investments at an unprecedented level—is essentially a new development). However, this core shall be made to 'reshine', but in doing so

[17] Rao, 'The New Economic Policy for the Good of the People', address at Bhumipujan ceremony of Nippon Denro ISPAT Ltd. Kalmeshwar, Maharashtra, 7 March 1992.

India will not be 'blown away'. The project of market liberalization is generated as liberating India from a 'prison' imposed by the former planned economy. India becomes 'open' to the outside. But this is done with extreme caution by asserting that the changes will never jeopardize India's rootedness, its foundational core.

The same claim to this calculated, calibrated move towards an open economy may be traced in Singh's address that follows, which borrows the same statement made by Gandhi as a legitimizing hinge years later. This example occurs in Singh's addresses on three instances.

> Today I want each of you to show the same degree of self-confidence that our freedom fighters showed when they led our country to freedom, in your encounters with new markets and new opportunities. We have been an open society. But in being open to the world, we have not lost our identity as a people. Again I remind you of what Gandhiji taught us. That our nation must be like a house built on firm foundations, whose windows are wide open to let winds blow freely in every direction. 'I want the winds from every corner to blow through my house, but I refuse to be swept off my feet by any of them.' That has been our attitude to the world, culturally and economically for centuries. We must continue to adopt that attitude even as we seek to build a more self-reliant and modern economy.[18]

As evident, Singh evokes the memory of the national struggle for independence and equates it to 'self-confidence' required to engage with 'new markets'. However, a sense of continuity is simultaneously established with the past through the statement 'we have been an open society'. Gandhi emerges as a validating symbol for that past. 'Modern economy' here, standing for an open economy, shares the same semantic space as the term 'self-reliant', echoing once again of the socialist past. A sense of security is produced not just with regards to India's economic future but also vis-à-vis its cultural essence. The two themes of economic liberalization and cultural security are confusingly placed together, the former even suggesting a natural correlation to the latter, with Gandhi being the legitimizing iconic sign that lends credibility to the claim. Thus, the main message indicated in 'we have not lost our identity as a people' shows how a *national* cultural security is produced

---

[18] Singh, 'Building the India of Tomorrow', address to the nation on Indian Independence Day, New Delhi, 15 August 2004.

in guaranteeing people that these economic transitions merely imply that India's exterior is transformed—its quintessence is intact, unbroken, and unchallenged.

Cautious, Calculated, and Controlled Change

In chapter 2, I reflected upon how the projections of India as an emerging economy, 'a powerhouse of the 21st century' with their assumed correlation to market liberalization, become more vigorous and consistently repetitive during Vajpayee and Singh's terms. This does not just reflect that the discourse has acquired a consistency over a period of more than twenty years, but also relates to two core events where external occurrences have helped overemphasize Indian success. These are the Asian economic crisis of 1997 (during Vajpayee's term), and the world financial crisis of 2008 (Singh's term). During both these episodes, the prime minister concerned spoke at length about India remaining largely unaffected by these regional and global crises. A consequence of the same is that the emphasis on India's exceptionally cautious and measured economic trajectory and, therein, its projections as a rising economic power gains momentum. This undertone may be located in the following excerpts from speeches delivered by Vajpayee:

> The world is today paying the price for another dogma. The dogma of the invisible hand of the market forces. We have seen how irrationally volatile the markets have been. We have also seen how market instability in one part of the world quickly travels, like a seismic wave to other parts of the world through the fault lines of the global financial system. [...] We in India have taken a principled stand towards globalization-cautious, calibrated, and steady integration. This approach has served our national interests well. We have remained largely unaffected by the turmoil in the Asian markets.[19]

> We are all aware of the recent crises which have affected the economies of South Asia and Russia. Even Japan is facing difficulties. At the same time, we may note the fact that our country remained by and large unaffected by these economic disturbances. This speaks well of the resilience our economy has developed over the years. Despite being part

[19] Vajpayee, 'India and the US are Natural Allies', address at the Asia Society, New York, 28 September 1998.

of the globalization process, our fundamentals remained strong and helped us to stay on course and prevented any major macro-economic imbalances.[20]

Both excerpts show how Vajpayee utilizes the events of the economic crisis faced by other nations to India's advantage. Indian economy here is profiled as one that has withstood the 'disturbances' because its fundamentals have remained intact in spite of its increasing engagement with the global economy. The words 'calibrated' and 'cautious' very lucidly indicate how a lexicon of careful vigilance is produced to take away the anxiety associated with the reforms and replace it with a poised confidence.

Globalization from Threat to Opportunity: Exceptional India Produces Coevalness with the World

Another perceived threat to a secure stable India is the amorphous term 'globalization'. In the addresses, the prime ministers indicate a cautious approach when speaking on the subject. It emerges that the term is usually semantically associated with economic opportunities, but simultaneous cultural insecurities that stir and agitate the foundational basis of 'India'. In order to induce a sense of self-esteem and cultural durability and undo apprehensions related to the reforms, globalization, which is seen as metonymic of the change that is introduced, is converted into an opportunity rather than being a threat. Vajpayee exemplifies this attempt in the following lines: 'We realize that globalization is both a reality and an opportunity. We are convinced that nations cannot prosper in isolation. [...] India is committed to the continuation of its policy of liberalization coupled with effective social safety nets.'[21]

Here, by speaking of globalization as a reality, Vajpayee embeds it in a narration of inevitability. The generalized term, whose meaning is rarely explained in the addresses, is the face of an unstoppable normative truth with which India must confront itself. However, the contingency,

---

[20] Vajpayee, 'Role of NRIs in National Reconstruction', address at the Global Indian Entrepreneurs' Conference, New Delhi, 11 November 1998.

[21] Vajpayee, 'Medium Term Economic Agenda of the Government', address at the India Economic Summit, New Delhi, 29 November 1998.

the danger, and unease attached to that reality are taken away by simultaneously calling it an opportunity that opens new possibilities for a new India. The following excerpt takes this argumentation a step further when Vajpayee is seen as utilizing a strictly Hindu mythological vocabulary to speak of the threats and possibilities offered by 'globalization'.

> These are difficult times for Indian and global businesses. A massive churning process is taking place in the world economy. The name of this *samudra manthan* in the modern era is globalization. Globalization has brought in unprecedented turbulence but trapped in that turbulence is also the hope of *Amrit* (nectar). It is a moment when the promise of a new phase of long-term prosperity and progress lies in the womb of short-term uncertainty.[22]

Speaking in the aftermath of the Asian economic crisis, Vajpayee lends a Hindu meaning to what globalization connotes. *Samudra manthan* here refers to a Hindu mythological account. A churning (in Hindi, '*manthan*') of the ocean (in Hindi, '*samudra*') was undertaken by the *devtas* (angel-like figures) and the asuras together in the hope of acquiring amrit (nectar) that would enable those who would drink it to become immortal. However, the process of churning also led to the production of *vish* (poison) that was capable of destroying all and had to be drunk by Lord Shiva to prevent the destruction of life. In the aforementioned excerpt, Vajpayee makes a reference to the same account equating the vish, or even the ocean and the process of churning it to the 'short-term uncertainty' induced by globalization, which is termed as the churning of the modern era. Optimism nonetheless echoes in the lines when Vajpayee explains that this turbulence caused by globalization also carries with it the promise of amrit for India. The reforms are thus rendered unavoidable and legitimate before Indian audiences by explaining how 'short-term uncertainties' induced by market liberalization are in reality a preparation phase for 'long-term prosperity'. Once again, in congruence with the tactics of embedding reforms in an inevitable temporal order for internal audiences, the prime minister produces the promise of a successful future.

---

[22] Vajpayee, 'Government Asserts its Commitment to Economic Reforms', inaugural address at the 71st Annual Session of FICCI (Federation of Indian Chambers of Commerce and Industry), New Delhi, 24 October 1998.

Once the laborious task of explaining that India needs to integrate with the world economy if it aims to emerge, in fact, even survive in an increasingly competitive global economic arrangement is done, the contingency attached to this 'adaptation' is taken away by assuring audiences that in fact the cultural core of India will remain the same and intact. However, some necessary adjustments will be made to ensure that India may 'shine'. Thus, a paradoxical reshift towards change may be traced, but that change is first presented as external and then stamped with an 'Indian-ness'. This is attained by claiming that the Indian economy has not been blindly based on either a communist or a capitalist system, but has always followed its 'own way'. Like in Vajpayee's addresses years later, a befitting example of the same strategy may be found in Rao's address delivered in 1994:

> There is a tremendous change in the world. Nobody faced this situation in the past [...] The Communist Party brought a new system for 70 years. That system has been shattered. Nobody is asking about it. Even the persons who hailed from those countries are proudly telling that they left communism and they have come to market economy. But we are not pronouncing it loudly because the great intellectual Jawaharlal Nehru devised mixed economy by giving prominence to both public and private sectors.[23]

Rao strategically attains two simultaneous objectives here. First, establishing that the Communist system has demised (and market economy has therein become the norm). Second, in spite of this 'tremendous change in the world', India stands unshaken and unfettered because it has from very early on embraced a system that is a mixed economy, one that balances economies in communist and capitalist contexts. In saying so, Rao does not just produce a sense of security and controllability towards the economic future, but he also produces the very 'Indianness' of that future. True to its postcolonial flavour, the fabrication of an *Emerging India* first entails the process of constituting 'India' itself and then producing an exceptionalism that makes India unique. The following illustration extends into how this exceptionalism is staged.

> The world of the 1970s has receded into history. The shackling constraints of the Cold War are gone. [...] The decade of the 1990s has

[23] Rao, 'Dunkel Proposals to India's Advantage', address at a public meeting, Nandyal, 6 January 1994.

fallen far short of expectations; nowhere is this more apparent than on the global economic scene. The sense of triumphalism that heralded the wave of global capitalism is now giving way to caution and realism. What was initially seen as an Asian flu is now spreading to other continents [...] does it mean that the world should turn its back to globalization? Our answer is an emphatic 'no'. Rising economic independence is a phenomenon driven by the technological imperative, but we must learn how to manage the change. India has not been as severely affected [...] because we adopted policies that were more prudent [...] we cannot let an unbridled free market system aggravate existing economic and social disparities.[24]

Once again in the aforementioned lines, globalization is first linguistically produced as a threat to economies around the world. However, the immediately following strategy is to emphasize how India has successfully managed to withstand the turbulences of globalization by calibrating change in its favour. Here, economic policies are described as 'prudent' and, in an environment where most nations are affected by the adverse consequences of global capitalism, an Indian exceptionalism is staged. Vajpayee not only indicates that India has withstood the disturbances of change, but also that its cautious approach has enabled it to make that very change 'Indian'. An underlying tone of establishing India as a trendsetter, an emulative ideal, may thus be located here, whereby change is not just presented in a way that it dispels anxieties related to it, but rather converted into an opportunity, a space to profile exceptionality. In chapter 3, I reflected upon Johannes Fabian's canonical

[24] Vajpayee, 'India's Commitment to Global Nuclear Disarmament', address at the UN General Assembly, New York, 24 September 1998. On similar lines, M. Singh delivered the following lines in an address following the global economic crisis in 2008: 'The global economy faces uncertain times. The crisis in the financial markets has cast its shadow on global liquidity. We have also seen sharp rises in petroleum and food prices. It is unfortunate that just as many developing countries were beginning to benefit from the positive potential of globalization, the tide has turned and the economic prospects have deteriorated [...]. The Indian economy has grown at an average rate of 9% in the past four years. It is expected to slow down in 2008–09 reflecting the slowdown in the global economy. Even so, it will grow between 7.5-8%. More importantly our medium term prospects remain strong based on sound fundamentals.' (Singh, 'India-EU: New Synergies for Partnership', address at the India-EU Bussiness Summit, Paris, 30 September, 2008).

work (*Time and the Other: How Anthropology Makes its Object*)²⁵ and the production of an allochronic discourse embedded within the staging of market liberalization in India, whereby a majority of the population is relegated to another genealogical time zone which needs to 'catch up' with the authors and winners of the discourse. The strategy of staging the Indian model as an exceptional one before Indians lends a new angle to that narrative. In the context of a discursively staged 'New World Order', Indian exceptionalism is a means to produce India's coevalness with the 'Western' world. It becomes a gateway to necessitate how reforms will finally lead to India realizing its due place in the world.

For the Putative Outside

'The World Is Changing [...]'

'The world today stands at a new watershed. [...]'²⁶

'The profound changes which have taken place in the world in recent years. [...]'²⁷

'The world has undergone climatic changes. [...]'²⁸

'The pace of change in the last few years has been rapid. [...]'²⁹

'World economic scenario presents a varied picture. [...]'³⁰

'We live in a fast-changing time. [...]'³¹

²⁵ J. Fabian, *Time and the Other: How Anthropology Makes its Object* (New York: Columbia University Press, 1983).

²⁶ Rao, 'Common Indo-China Approach for Asian Resurgence', address at Beijing University, China, 9 September 1993.

²⁷ Rao, 'Indo-German Economic Relations', address at the Indo-German Business Conference, Bonn, Germany, 3 February 1994.

²⁸ Rao, 'Perspectives on Indo-British Relations', address to the Indologists, Nehru Centre, London, 15 March 1994.

²⁹ Rao, 'Strengthening South-South Economic Cooperation', address at the inaugural session of G-15 Summit, 28 March 1994.

³⁰ Rao, 'Challenges before the ESCAP', address at the 50th session of the ESCAP, 5 April 1994.

³¹ Rao, 'G-15 Helps Extend Co-operation among Developing Countries', address at the G-15 Summit, Dakar, Senegal, 21 November 1992.

'The world around us is again in transformation. [...]'[32]

'A changing and rapidly evolving world. [...]'[33]

'During the past few years the processes of history have suddenly accelerated transforming the international landscapes beyond recognition. What is remarkable is first the global scope of the change and second the pace of the change.'[34]

'The end of the Cold War has brought to an end the divided world in the international order marked by intense rivalry between two rival unitary blocks [...] The democratic ideal is almost universally accepted.'[35]

'Major economic changes are taking place in the world around us which have a significant impact on our region. The twin trends of globalization and liberalization have dramatically altered the dynamics of the international economic environment. The increasing globalization of economic processes has been accompanied by the emergence and consolidation of vast new economic groupings. '[36]

'The emergence of a global economy has led to undeniable benefits like faster growth, higher living standards and new opportunities. The rapid spread of Information Technology, riding the crest of a knowledge revolution, has virtually led to the creation of a digital world where the click of a mouse can span vast distances in less than a fraction of a second. A new economy drives the world today.'[37]

[32] Rao, 'Non-Aligned Movement and Global Issues', Address at the 10th Summit of the Non Aligned Countries, Jakarta, Indonesia, 2 September 1992.

[33] Rao, 'India and Japan', address at the Japan Institute of International Affairs on the occasion of the 40th anniversary of the establishment of diplomatic relations between Japan and India Tokyo, 23 June 1992.

[34] Rao, 'Contributing to the New World Vision', address at the French Institute of International Relations on a symposium titled *Challenge and Opportunity in the Post Cold War Era: An Indian Perspective on the Emerging Structure of Inter-State Relations*, Paris, 29 September 1992.

[35] Rao, 'Towards a New World Order', interview to the *Eka International* of Turkey, 16 January 1995.

[36] Vajpayee, 'Shared Vision of the Future', inaugural address at the SAARC Summit, Colombo, Sri Lanka, 29 July 1998.

[37] Vajpayee, 'A Collective Desire to Forge a Bright Future', address at the UN Millenium Summit, New York, 8 September 2000.

All the stated excerpts highlight one prominent idea: also before perceived external audiences as before perceived internal audience, all three prime ministers stage a world in transition. Thus, themes of a post-Cold War world, one symbolic of the move to open economies where globalization and liberalization are necessary, inevitable truths, the spread of information technology, a new economy, etc., abound as illustrations in the speeches before the putative outside as well.

'Destination India': India Has Changed

As shown in the previous sections, collecting support for market liberalization, among audiences that formulate the vote banks on the 'home turf', has been an essential coordinate of the project of staging an economically emerging India. However, equally pressing and important is producing the same for the putative outside. This has entailed a two-dimensional objective. First of 'rectifying' India's image abroad which implied undoing stereotypes regarding bottlenecks, bureaucracy, and an imposing public sector monopoly, coupled with a stifled private sector in the beginning phase of economic liberalization. Thus, the PMs' oratory during the Rao and Vajpayee years reflects a consistent process of reworking that image. The prime ministers as authors and representatives of an essential change, a transformation, are seen as producing a new, 'open' India. The second objective, a more subtle one, is that while redoing the image of India abroad, the PMs inevitably produce India as a homogenous entity and themselves as the legitimate voice of that entity.

Thus, the illustrations cited in this section could be viewed through two lenses: First, reflecting the tedious process of transforming India's image before the world and, therein, presenting it as an attractive 'Investment Destination'. Second, in doing so, wiping the slate clean of all previous images and using the opportunity to constitute a new India by *representing* India before the 'world'. It is in this light that creative oratorical means are utilized to invite the outside world to 'come invest in India' while new identities of Brand India are forged simultaneously. The process of doing the same is visible in several of Rao's addresses. Here the caesura-like moment of change is emphasized through an extensive lexicon of newness and openness. To cite some illustrations:

'New India awaits your enthusiastic participation in the new buoyant environment of open markets and expanding opportunities.'[38]

'For about three years we have introduced a new regime of economic reforms. This, I think, you would be very interested in knowing because this has opened up India, this has depicted India abroad in a new light.'[39]

'I think the so called image problem is a thing of the past. The kind of response I have received during my visits abroad would suggest that India has become a very attractive destination for investment. The Australian government's report titled India: The Midnight Hour also suggests that Indian economy is changing and that India has the potential for emerging as an important economic powerhouse in the future.'[40]

As evident from the second excerpt, the 'outside' lurks subtly in Rao's words even if the address was mainly aimed to address Indians abroad. Similarly, in the two excerpts below, both Rao and Singh (ten years later) show a reflexive awareness of 'the world' outside, which needs to be duly informed of India's new image. The main purpose is to paint this as a historic moment of transition in the economic history of the nation in order to cloak it as an attractive investment destination.

I am confident that with the first-hand knowledge you will acquire, you will be able to promote and project India in its true perspective, that is, as a country which today offers vast opportunities for investment and a large market for consumption...India offers to the world a vast market, availability of skilled manpower including competent professional managers, a diversified industrial base, well-developed capital markets, banking infrastructure and financial services, and above all a stable democratic political environment.[41]

The partnerships we seek and the basis of growth we wish to create should rest on the foundation of our commitment to values of inclusive

---

[38] Rao, 'Growth with Human Face', address while inaugurating a Conference of the International Chamber of Commerce on the theme *Dynamic Asia*, New Delhi, 27 March 1995.

[39] Rao, 'Enormous Scope in India for NRI Investment', address to the Indian Community in Singapore, 7 September 1994.

[40] Rao, 'Reforms and All Round Economic Improvements', interview to the *Asia Today*, 23 September 1994.

[41] Rao, 'Need for Technology Upgradation in Small Industries', address on inauguration of the *India Invesmart*, New Delhi, 18 April 1994.

pluralism and multi-culturalism within the framework of an open society and an open economy. This is the promise our government has made
at home. This is the experience we should happily share with the world.[42]

The given excerpts are not only statements delivered to project
'Destination India', but also a creative playground where 'India' itself
is performed by the speaker. The underpinning aim is to project what
makes the 'New India' so *new*. An obvious, though important, conclusion that follows here is that the discourse of 'India, the emerging economic power' is thoroughly celebrated in the addresses delivered *outside*
of India. This is in sharp contrast to the strategies the prime ministers
employ *in* India. Whereas the transition to an open economy is often
underplayed before internal audiences and is camouflaged in the usage
of a repertoire that relies on a generalized, homogenous past so to not
render the reforms contingent and unsafe, in external spheres all three
prime ministers overplay economic liberalization. Here, the New India
is celebrated without having to disguise it in legitimizing vocabularies
of the past.[43]

---

[42] Singh, 'India and the World—A Blueprint for Partnership and Growth'.

[43] To cite some more examples: 'This country is assured by the grace of God
of the market. There are no shackles anywhere. Therefore I would like to tell
my friends who wish to invest in India that they will never regret coming here.
[…] Yes the policy has served its utility. Today we change policies. We are not
inflexible. We are not wedded to anything' (Rao, 'Financing of Private Sector
Power Projects', address on the inauguration of a conference on *Development
of Financing of Private Sector Power Projects in India*, New Delhi, 23 May 1994);

'Our market liberalization strategy offers enormous scope for investments
[…] in both what could be described as the "Old Economy" and the "New
Economy". In the old economy the scope for investment is clearly pronounced
in the area of infrastructure, particularly construction industries like roads,
ports and civil construction. There is also considerable scope for active participation in […] textiles, cement and steel […] Beyond this, there is of course the
"New Economy" where India offers a particularly attractive destination […]. We
are determined to become a leading power in IT reforms […]You thus have a
wider choice of both the "click" and the "brick" economy' (Vajpayee, 'Growing
Indo-Italian Bilateral Trade', address at Indo-Italian Business Meeting, Rome,
26 June 2000);

'In the last 50 years India has developed certain competitive advantages—a large technical and scientific manpower base, fairly well developed

Modi's Spatializing Oratory

Current Prime Minister Narendra Modi's oratory, since his assumption of the office, reflects interesting continuities and discontinuities with his three predecessors in how an Emerging India is lexically constituted in the speeches as also its link to the reforms of 1991. This rhetorical lexicon is definitely symptomatic of the fact that Modi assumed office twenty-five years after the formal institutionalization of the reforms, a long time span during which his predecessors, Singh and Vajpayee, persistently attempted to naturalize the reforms in a way that they become co-equivalent to the metaphor of motion ascribed to the Indian economy. The aim of this section is to trace the continuities / similarities and the new oratorical moot points through the prism of 155 speeches delivered by Modi (that were analysed for chapters 2, 3, and 4). On the occasion of the 70th anniversary of Indian independence, in his address to the nation, Modi stated from the ramparts of the Red Fort:

> Dear brothers and sisters, today the world is passing through an era of global economy. Every country today is inter-connected and inter-dependent. Economically the whole world is somehow inter-connected in one way or other. However much we may progress in our country, we'll have to keep the global economy, the global arena in view; come up to the global standards, match it also to stay relevant, and contribute, and also lead the global economy when the time comes. Therefore we'll have to be alert all the time. We'll have to comply with the global standards to make ourselves up to date. Recently, you must have seen how the World Bank, IMF, World Economic Forum, credit rating agencies and such other agencies in the world have appreciated the progress

infrastructure, a large network of banks, a well-established capital market, a good education system. India has always had a substantial private sector, active in all areas of the economy [...] we have the advantage of being part of the English speaking world. These factors make India a good destination' (Vajpayee, 'Role of NRIs in National Re-construction');

'A successful exporter is not just promoting the wares of his own company, he is also promoting India and the Indian brand. This brand must be known world-wide as a place for quality products and services [...] any product labelled 'Made in India' should become the first choice of buyers across the world' (Vajpayee, 'Promotion of Exports: A National Priority', Address at the National Export Awards, New Delhi, 21 January 1999).

in India. The world is constantly watching these things due to the decisions taken one after another by India in respect of legal reforms, improvement in system and changes in approach. We have very speedily improved our ranking in 'ease of doing business' ratings. In terms of foreign investment, with regards to foreign direct investment our country happens to be the most favourite destination in the world today. We have left behind even the big economies of the world in matters of growth rate and GDP.[44]

An observation that follows from the excerpt, albeit in light of the speeches delivered by Rao specifically, is how, by the time Modi assumes office, the idea of a transforming global economy is a pervasively repetitive oratorical truth. It persuasively seems to pervade the rhetoric of the current prime minister, who utilizes the repertoire of pre-established words like 'inter-connected' and 'inter-dependent'. A noteworthy difference that emerges nonetheless when one compares these lines to those delivered by Rao is that by this time, there is no urgency to justify and legitimize the overarching validity of international bodies like the IMF, the World Bank, or the World Economic Forum. As we noticed in Chapter 3, Rao required to defend the reforms and rescue them from allegations that they make the Indian economy a 'sell out' for an international economic order. These justifications came in light of aggressive attacks, which viewed Rao as jeopardizing India's economic sovereignty to the IMF and the World Bank. The second half of the given excerpt here, on the contrary, suggests that this necessity to rescue reforms, justify their introduction, and render them irreversible becomes a non-issue for Modi. Instead, it suggests that the IMF and the World Bank become the legitimizing hinges, the measuring grids, for India's economic emergence (as indicated in the lines 'you must have seen how the World Bank, IMF, World Economic Forum, credit rating agencies and such other agencies in the world have appreciated the progress in India'). Thus, much in sync with all three of his predecessors, Modi repeats the vocabulary of a changing world that necessitates that the Indian economy should also transform and not continue in isolation. The noteworthy difference is, however, that the same organizations which were seen as attacking Indian financial sovereignty during the

[44] N.D. Modi, Address to the nation on Indian Independence Day, New Delhi, 15 August 2016.

terms of Rao and Vajpayee become the quantifiers of India's economic prowess.[45]

In Modi's oratory Foreign Direct Investment is essentially a positive, necessary, inevitable, and highly desired truth, a part of a larger global scheme of economic ordering in the world. Whereas we saw how Rao emphatically explained his audiences, especially the perceived internal audiences, that increasing Foreign Direct Investment should not be seen as a threat to be feared but rather as a positive change for India, in Modi's speeches this justification is missing, primarily because there is no necessity for it. The need for FDI thus emerges as an established truth to an extent that it even becomes an iconic marker of, almost a thermometer that indexically reflects, India's growth. The following excerpt illustrates the same lucidly:

> For the last four quarters India has been the fastest growing large economy in the world. In 2014-15, India contributed 7.4% of global GDP in purchasing power terms. But it contributed 12.5% of global growth. Thus its contribution to growth is 68% higher than its share of the global economy. FDI in India has increased by 39% in the last 18 months, at a time when global FDI has fallen.[46]

As evident from the excerpt, Modi statistically attempts to prove India's emergence through its economic growth. An important component of *showing* growth is by claiming that FDI in India has increased by 39 per cent during his term. These lines reflect a paradigmatic shift in how the historicity of market liberalization has been craftily staged on public platforms by the prime ministers in India. From being a

---

[45] Two other revealing examples of the same are: (1) 'India has consistently been ranking as the most attractive destination by several global agencies and institutions. [...] We have jumped twelve ranks in the latest global ranking by the World Bank on ease of doing business. [...] India has jumped sixteen places on the World Economic Forum's global competitive index' (Modi, address at the inauguration of the 'Make in India' week, Mumbai, 13 February 2016); (2) '[...] The World Economic Forum has said that India has reached above 19 ranks as compared to earlier positions and India is moving up and marching ahead rapidly' (Modi, address to the nation on Indian Independence Day).

[46] N.D. Modi, address at the Economic Times Global Business Summit, New Delhi, 29 January 2016.

threatening presence whose existence had to be aggressively justified and defended (in Rao's speeches) to being a silently ignored truth (in Vajpayee and Singh's speeches) to becoming a means to prove, an indicator of India's economic emergence, Foreign Direct Investment has a rather telling discursive trajectory even within the speeches of the prime ministers. This only reproves the point raised by Hilgers that in order to understand these economic shifts in the postcolonial world, one needs to trace the historicity of neo-liberalism and its accompanying vocabulary. The excerpt should not merely be read through the prism of 'how prime ministers exhibit growth' to prove the legitimacy of the reforms, but also as a deeper indication of the paradigmatic shifts that occur in the discursive trajectory of structurally adjusted post-colonies. How (if it is so) do vocabularies explaining and justifying market liberalization creatively transform over time, and what can we understand about economic transitions when we trace these changing vocabularies?

Another moment when Modi seeks this oratorical legitimacy is in the following excerpt, ' India has become the fastest growing economy in the world. We will end this fiscal year with well over seven per cent growth in GDP. IMF, World Bank, OECD, ADB, and other institutions have projected even better growth in the coming days.'[47]

Once again, the very same institutions against the background of which the prime minister needed to defend the reforms after 1991 (Rao) or which were oratorically ignored, meaning that they still bore the lexical weight of being institutions that impinged upon India's economic sovereignty and self-reliance (Vajpayee and Singh), become the very iconic judges of India's growth in Modi's oratory.

In fact, what Modi's repetitive rhetoric elucidates is that India's economic growth, especially when explained to internal audiences, is more emphatically embedded in the logic of an expansive Foreign Direct Investment. Rao's speeches show a potent fear and a cautious, calculated approach when justifying FDI. Vajpayee's addresses also indicate the desperate urge to *justify* increased FDI and his party's support of the reforms when in power, given that the BJP was the strongest opponent of the reforms in 1991. In sharp contrast, Modi's addresses do not justify, but rather *boast* of an increase in FDI. Talking

---

[47] Modi, address at Inauguration of 'Make in India' Week.

of increased FDI thus becomes a resource to stage growth.[48] In the following excerpt, as Modi addresses both a perceived internal as well as an external audience, particularly entrepreneurs and the private sector in an international summit in India, a plan to expand FDI is clearly chalked out, extending to the hitherto 'new' sectors of railways, defence, and insurance.

> We are planning to build smart cities equipped with world class amenities. For this purpose, we have further liberalized the FDI policy in construction sector. I announced that a modern railway system including high-speed rails will be set up. Immediately we opened up railways for 100% Foreign Direct Investment. I announced that defense production in the country would be encouraged. The next step was to open the defense sector for Foreign Direct Investment up to 49%. We have taken similar steps in many other areas. These include bringing 49% FDI in insurance. It also includes liberalization of FDI norms for manufacturing of medical devices.[49]

The excerpt can be read as a prototype for attempts at solidifying the reforms, rendering them affectively irreversible by further liberalizing different sectors. Interesting though is that there is no mention of the reforms per se or of market liberalization. It is exactly in these lines that one may trace the crucial site where the reforms become an *unspoken* fact, a normative truth that does not require any contextualization or justification, and whereby they become synonymous of India's emergence as an economic powerhouse of the world. The power of this oratorical forgetting (in that the reforms are usually not even mentioned) speaks volumes of how, to use Pinney's coinage, the laborious work of allegory has paved the way for 'figure' that produces immediate identifications. By this, I mean that the oratorical work of lexically producing the reforms as the co-equivalent of 'Emerging India' has been done consistently by Modi's predecessors to an extent that when evoking the

---

[48] An illustrative example is: 'Today India is perhaps the most open country for FDI. Most of the FDI sectors have been put on automatic approval route. Our FDI inflows have gone up by 48 per cent since the day my government came into office. In fact, FDI inflow in December 2015 was the highest ever in this country. This is, at a time, when global FDI has fallen substantially' (Modi, address at inauguration of 'Make in India' Week, Mumbai).

[49] Modi, address at the Vibrant Gujarat Summit.

vocabulary of Emerging India, there is no need to mention the reforms per se for Modi.

Beside this noteworthy distinction, however, the spatializing strategy whereby Modi speaks of a world in transition, a changing world where India cannot exist as an 'island', is hauntingly similar to the oratory of all three of his predecessors. An illustrative example of the same are the following lines, 'We must change for both external and internal reasons. [...] Thirty years ago, a country might have been able to look inward and find its own solutions. Today, countries are inter-dependent and inter-connected. No country can afford any longer to develop in isolation. Every country has to benchmark its activities to global standards, or else fall behind.'[50]

In the mentioned excerpt, we find Modi strategically producing the space called 'the global world'. The terms interconnected (also used in the first speech by Modi cited at the beginning of the section) and inter-dependent are used simultaneously, whereas the line 'Thirty years ago a country might have been able to look inward' stand in sharp contrast to Nehruvian import substitution and notions of self-reliance and sufficiency. Just as Vajpayee (see Chapter 3), Modi even uses the same term 'isolation' to define the globally connected world, whereas the last line '[...] or else fall behind' appears to be completely in sync with his predecessors' strategy of producing the need for change as an unavoidable necessity for India.[51] The world with its global markets is thus described as one making change a global reality that requires India to change as well. On the same lines, in the following excerpt Modi states:

> We live in a globally connected world. The actions of one country effect another. Such actions are not only based on trade and investment but also in matters of pollution and environment. A poet had said that no man is an island. Today it can be said that no country can live alone. It is often said that all politics is local. To me, all economics is global. Indeed the distinction between domestic affairs and foreign affairs is increasingly

[50] Modi, address at 'Transforming India' lecture.
[51] Another befitting example of the same: 'My dear countrymen, the world has changed. Now India cannot decide its future by remaining isolated and sitting alone in a corner. The economics of the world have changed and, therefore, we will have to act accordingly' (Modi, address to the nation on Indian Independence Day).

losing relevance. For a country in the modern day, it is not sufficient that its economic policies should only address its domestic priorities. To me, India's policies must be such that they make a positive contribution to the rest of the world.[52]

Once again, we find Modi repeating Rao's vocabulary and the metaphor of the 'island' to describe the condition called globalization. He then reasserts this by saying that 'no country can live alone'. We saw how Rao, Vajpayee, and Singh (to a lesser extent) have attempted to discursively produce globalization with a sense of security, whereby they lexically try to convert the threat perceived from globalization into an advantage. In Modi's speeches, the attempt to convert this uncertainty and insecurity into something positive is done by emphasizing India's role in a global world. Here, rather than being a passive witness of changes in the world, India is projected as an active key player in constituting that world. This is lucidly visible in the last line when he says, 'To me India's politics must be such that it makes a positive contribution to the rest of the world'. The latent unpredictability and insecurity of a changing world is thus converted into a positive asset in these lines by projecting India as a crucial actor contributing to that world. A key conclusion drawn from Modi's speeches delivered to perceived internal audiences is that whereas for his predecessors the task of transforming the amorphous abstraction of globalization from being a threat to being a security is done cautiously and gradually, in Modi's oratory it appears that that discursive transformation has finally been achieved. This confidence is reflected emphatically in the line, 'To me, all economics is global'. Thus, his addresses embrace and celebrate the terms 'global', 'globalization', and 'a globally connected world' rather than showing unease in their usage.

Another consistency that Modi's speeches share with those of his predecessors is that while on the one hand, for perceived internal audiences, the world is projected as being increasingly interconnected, necessitating India to also not live in 'isolation' and engage with it, on the other hand, the world economic situation is frequently produced as being in crisis. This then becomes a context against which Indian emergence is projected. Rao's initial speeches here are the only exception to this pattern. After 1993, however, Rao is also seen as talking about

[52] Modi, address at Economic Times Global Business Summit.

an 'uncertain world' where bipolar cold war politics has given way to a multipolar world in which India becomes a prominent international actor. During his term, Vajpayee produces this global economic crisis in the context of the Asian crisis of 1997, and Singh in the context of the world economic crisis of 2008. Nonetheless, both emphasize how Indian economy has been resilient and sturdy and growing in spite of such crises. Similarly, Modi's oratory is replete with illustrations whereby the global markets are presented as being shrouded in uncertainties in which India *nonetheless* emerges. A graphic illustration of the same is the following excerpt, 'I feel that today our domestic industry and investors are feeling much more confident and optimistic in spite of an uncertain global situation.'[53]

With regard to announcing India as an investment destination, Modi's addresses are completely in tune with the trend started by his three predecessors. During his extensive visits to numerous countries in the two-year term up to 2016, his addresses are replete with instances of claiming that: (1) India has changed and (2) that it is an attractive investment destination.

Some lucid illustrations where different legitimizing techniques are utilized to prove both the given points are, ' India is a land of immense opportunities. Fifty of our cities are ready for setting up Metro Rail Systems. We have to build fifty million houses. The requirement of road, rail and waterways is enormous. There is no time for incremental changes. We want a quantum jump.'[54]

In the excerpt, Modi essentially addresses foreign investors. Two important metaphors of change are attached to India—'a land of immense opportunities' and 'quantum jump'. We find Modi speaking in continuity with his predecessors, only with a newer vigour and a vocabulary induced with greater confidence in an India of the future. In the following lines, all from the same address delivered in Hannover at the Indo-German Business Summit in 2015, Modi furthers the cause of Foreign Direct Investment.

'You will be able to see for yourself the winds of change in India. We are very keen to develop the sectors where you are strong. We need your

---

[53] Modi, address at inauguration of 'Make in India' Week.
[54] Modi, address at inauguration of 'Make in India' Week.

involvement. The scope and potential, the breadth and length of infra-structure and related developments is very huge in India.'[55]

'All this is a historic opportunity for the German companies. You would already be knowing the direction of my Government and the steps we are taking. We have committed ourselves for creating and improving the business environment. I can assure you that once you decide to be in India, we are confident to make you comfortable.'[56]

'I am here to assure the German companies that India is now a changed country. Our regulatory regime is much more transparent, responsive and stable. We are taking a long-term and futuristic view on the issues.'[57]

'At the end it is my advice to you to come and feel the change in India's regulatory environment. Please do not go by old perceptions.'[58]

In the first excerpt cited, the metaphor of the wind is evoked and a plea is made for foreign involvement in India. In the second excerpt, the prime minister even calls this possibility a 'historic opportunity' and promises 'comfort'. The third and fourth excerpts shows us how the thrust on the fact that India has changed is made highly emphatic and a break with the past is introduced 'come and feel the change [...] please do not go by old perceptions'. We thus see how in continuity with the politics of time (as pointed out in chapter 3), whereby a break with 'the past' is introduced, the politics of spatialization is also in operation. Spatially perceived as the 'outside', the audience is convinced that India has changed and it is an evermore welcoming destination for investment.

It is in the same context of producing 'Destination India' that one of Modi's main campaigns called 'Make in India' deserves mention. Launched in September 2014, the campaign is meant to catapult manu-facturing in India both by Indian business persons as well as foreign investors. Within the context of this campaign, which is inevitably mentioned in every speech Modi has delivered to perceived 'external' audiences, India is produced as a rising, safe economy open as a destina-tion for investments. Some illustrations are listed below:

[55] Modi, address at the Indo-German Business Summit, Hannover, 13 April 2015.

[56] Modi, address at the Indo-German Business Summit.

[57] Modi, address at the Indo-German Business Summit.

[58] Modi, address at the Indo-German Business Summit.

[...] 65 percent of the population of India is under the age of 35. This youthful energy is our greatest strength. We launched the Make in India campaign to create employment and self-employment opportunities for our youth. We are working aggressively towards making India a Global Manufacturing Hub. We want the share of manufacturing in our GDP to go upto 25 percent in the near future.[59]

These lines delivered during the 'Make in India Week' in February 2016 (Mumbai), which saw panels with 1,245 speakers and approximately 65,500 participants,[60] show how Modi profiles India as a future 'Global Manufacturing Hub'. This epithet is attached to India in almost all addresses that mention the Make in India campaign since its launch, making it a repetitive descriptive category. The excerpt also indicates how Modi emphasizes the role of youth in realizing the dream of Emerging India. This is also in continuation with the addresses of the former prime ministers, particularly Manmhohan Singh, who repetitively evoked the metaphor of India as a young nation but an old civilization. Another example for the campaign is 'Make in India initiative to encourage the growth of manufacturing in the country. We are working hard to make India a global manufacturing hub. We are promoting, in particular, labour intensive manufacturing.'[61]

In these lines delivered at the Vibrant Gujarat Summit in 2015, an annual event that had already been established as a ritualistic initiative during Modi's chief ministership in the state, we once again see the usage of the description 'global manufacturing hub'. In fact, emphasizing manufacturing (through the 'Make in India' campaign in Modi's case) is not so uniquely new to Modi's government. Singh uses the same grammar of development and growth through manufacturing in his speeches, though the vocabulary used differs. Thus, instead of a consolidated 'Make in India' campaign, we find different titles like 'India as a service brand', 'Made in India', or simply 'Brand India'. This points to yet another important conclusion. Modi's government has only furthered the reforms of 1991 and much of the trajectory resembles

---

[59] Modi, address at inauguration of 'Make in India' Week.

[60] For details, see the official website of the Make in India Week, 13–18 February 2016, http://www.makeinindia.com/mumbai-week, accessed on 17 July 2016.

[61] Address at the vibrant Gujarat Summit in Gandhinagar, 11 January 2015.

that of the previous governments. What often gives Modi's rhetoric a freshness though is the new slogans made popular during his term as prime minister, which have pervaded people's everyday lives through his words, twitters, and other social media channels, hoardings, posters, newspapers, traditional visual media, and a plethora of other means.

Another important lexical category used to project India as a future manufacturing global hub is 'The Ease of Doing Business'.[62] When proving India's growth, Modi mentions the same thrice in the inaugural speech of the Make in India Week:

> 'We have jumped twelve ranks in the latest global ranking by the World Bank on ease of doing business.'[63]

> 'We have laid all round emphasis on Ease of Doing Business.'[64]

> 'We have very speedily improved our ranking in 'ease of doing business' ratings.'[65]

In the following excerpt from an address delivered to an international audience at a business summit in Pretoria, Modi mentions the same again, 'Make in India has become the biggest brand that India has ever had. Both within and outside it has captured the imagination of people, institutions, industries, businesses, media and political leadership. As part of the Make in India exercise, we have given emphasis on Ease of Doing Business.'[66]

An important caveat to add here relates to the question of audiences concerned. In numerous speeches where Modi speaks about the 'Make in India' campaign, the audiences are not necessarily only 'external'. In the light of events such as the Vibrant Gujarat Summit, Make in India Week, Smart Cities Mission, Bloomberg India Economic Forum, and numerous other international summits *organized in India*, one notices how an increasingly large number of foreign investors and business persons are invited to such programmes. This renders the target audiences

---

[62] Interestingly, this category even exists as a drop option on the official website of the Make in India Week, 13–18 February 2016. See http://www.makeinindia.com/mumbai-week.

[63] Modi, address at inauguration of 'Make in India' Week.

[64] Modi, address at inauguration of 'Make in India' Week.

[65] Modi, address at inauguration of 'Make in India' Week.

[66] Modi, India–South Africa Business Meet, Pretoria, 8 July 2016.

increasingly more mixed. This is a relatively newer phenomenon with Modi's addresses unlike those of the previous prime ministers whereby the categories of perceived 'internal' and 'external' were lexically drawn and kept rather exclusive. In the events mentioned earlier, one finds Modi simultaneously addressing Indian business persons and foreign investors within the context of the same addresses. Thus, for example, we find the following three excerpts in the inaugural address of the Make in India Week. It is clear that the first one is directed at Indian industry experts, and the two that follow at foreign investors.

> 'I would like to give our industry some friendly advice. Don't wait. Don't relax. There are immense opportunities in India. You should take advantage of the renewed interest of global players to work in India. Many of them are looking for technological and financial collaborations with Indian partners. This includes high-tech sectors and high-value areas like defence production. I assure you that if you take one step, we will walk two steps for you.'[67]

> 'I have been saying that this century is Asia's century. My advice to you is to Make India your center; if you want this century to be your century. I invite everyone sitting here and also those not here, to be part of India's unfolding story. This is the best time ever to be in India. And it is even better to Make in India.'[68]

> 'I invite and encourage you to make India your work place and also your home.'[69]

As evident, in the first excerpt, Modi addresses Indian industrialists to seize opportunities through partnerships with global players. In the second excerpt, one can sense the spirit of assertion and confidence when Modi brands the century to belong to 'Asia' with India being its epicentre. The temporalizing tactic of inducing optimism is achieved by saying that '*This* is the best time ever to be in India' [author's emphasis]. In the third excerpt, the spatial metaphor of 'home and workplace' suggests how foreign industrialists are invited to 'move' to India. Barring these excerpts, the address blurs any distinctions between external and internal audiences.

---

[67] Modi, address at inauguration of 'Make in India' Week.
[68] Modi, address at inauguration of 'Make in India' Week.
[69] Modi, address at inauguration of 'Make in India' Week.

An increase in the frequency of such events thus bears a direct impact on how a prime minister increasingly attempts to combine the messages for both perceived internal and external audiences. It also reflects an increasing spatial merging of the two categories into the specific category of CEOs, managers, and businessmen, where (or for which) the dichotomy of external and internal becomes irrelevant. This spatial merging of 'internal' and 'external' within the addresses is, however, also symptomatic of the fact that Modi appears to be highly aware and cognizant of the fact that even ritualistic speeches delivered in India and meant for Indians are carefully followed by those deemed to be the 'outside'. This awareness becomes lexically graphic in the following excerpt from the address to the nation on the Independence Day celebrations from the Red Fort.

> I want to appeal to all the people world over, from the ramparts of the Red Fort, 'Come, make in India', 'Come, manufacture in India'. Sell in any country of the world but manufacture here. We have got skill, talent, discipline, and determination to do something. We want to give the world an favourable opportunity that come here, 'Come, Make in India' and we will say to the world, from electrical to electronics, 'Come, Make in India', paper or plastic 'Come, Make in India', satellite or submarine 'Come, Make in India'. Our country is powerful. Come, I am giving you an invitation.[70]

In the earlier lines, a direct plea is made to 'all the people world over' that they should come manufacture in India. In fact, this is the only isolated example whereby a prime minister openly speaks to the perceived outside in a speech as ritualistic as the Independence Day speech. It lucidly points to the confidence one can sense in Modi's oratory with regards to the inevitability, irreversibility, and permanence of the reforms. By Modi's term, the fear attached to FDI appears to not only have vanished, but also drastically converted into something normatively positive, which is why he addresses this issue on a platform where the previous prime ministers have normally shied away from speaking positively about FDI. It is precisely to sharply point to this strategy of spatially merging the two categories of the perceived outside and inside that this section dealing with Modi's speeches does not follow the strict dichotomization sketched in the previous sections of this chapter. Here

---

[70] Modi, address to the nation on Indian Independence Day.

too, like in the case of other prime ministers, the speaker is highly aware of when he speaks to whom. Nonetheless, it is the first time that one sees a repetitive strategy of making such addresses, actually meant for distinct audiences, share the same semantic space of a singular speech. The outside and the inside are lexically sprung into existence, but within the same speech.

In conclusion, an interesting aspect of Modi's oratory, whereby he explains why India is emerging and unstoppable and why it provides the necessary safe environment for FDI to flourish, may be discerned from the following lines, 'India is blessed with three Ds. These are: Democracy, Demography and Demand. To this, we have added the fourth D that is Deregulation. Today's India is this four dimensional India.'[71]

The details of desire are thus merged with the safety of a democracy, the unquenched demand necessitated by Indian demography and the heroic tool to achieve emergence, that is, deregulation, making India truly four-dimensional.

***

This chapter has elucidated how, for the perceived internal audiences, the three prime ministers—Rao, Vajpayee, and Singh—naturalize the reforms by signalling them as a change made necessary by the transitions that the world faces at large. This means that they rhetorically present the outside world as an arena in a state of flux and transitions. These 'global' changes necessitate that India adapts to transformations as well. The changes are presented through keywords such as—'open economy', 'open markets', 'integration with the world economy', 'open society', and 'globalization'. However, this introduction of the necessity to change is accompanied by a simultaneous assurance that India's adaptation to that change is cautious and calculated. This is done to purge the anxiety, fear, and unpredictability attached to change and

---

[71] Modi, address at inauguration of 'Make in India' Week.

On another occasion, Modi states in a similar vein 'Many of you might be interested to know—Why India? India has three things to its credit—Democracy, Demography, and Demand. This is what you are looking for.' (Modi, address at the Vibrant Gujarat Summit).

convert it into something desirable and familiar. The sense of assurance is produced in two distinct ways. Firstly, by giving people the reassurance that the opening up of the economy and invitation to Foreign Direct Investment will not jeopardize India's economic sovereignty and, secondly, by conjuring a sense of confidence in people that, in spite of change, India's cultural core is fundamentally secure.

Finally, the 'threat' of 'globalization' is rhetorically converted into an opportunity, by producing the guarantee that India's embracing of the same threat is a controlled, calibrated move. Thus, that which entails a potent unpredictability 'for the world' is transformed into something which can be utilized to India's benefit. In framing globalization in this particular vocabulary, many nations are projected as being adversely affected by its impact, especially in the context of the financial crises. Staging India's survival of the unfavourable conditions caused by globalization, it becomes a means through which it is profiled as becoming coeval with the 'West'. The analysis has shown how this coevalness is conjured by the prime minister to render change 'Indian' and to stage Indian exceptionalism. Before 'external' audiences, on the other hand, change is overplayed and the aim is to inform the world of a new India which is open to foreign investments.

In the concluding section that analyses the current prime minister Modi's addresses, we come to the conclusion that there are remarkable similarities in his oratory to the spatializing strategies of his predecessors, though not without the flavour of numerous new elements. The content of what is said cannot be separated from the important context that Modi assumed office twenty-five years after the formal institutionalization of the reforms, a long time span during which his predecessors Singh and Vajpayee persistently attempted to naturalize the reforms in a way that they become co-equivalent to the metaphor of motion ascribed to the Indian economy.

In terms of continuities, by the time Modi assumes office, the idea of a transforming global economy is a pervasively repetitive oratorical truth. Thus, similar to his predecessors, Modi repeats the vocabulary of a changing world that necessitates that the Indian economy should also transform and not continue in isolation. The noteworthy difference is, however, that the same organizations which were seen as attacking Indian financial sovereignty during the Rao and Vajpayee terms become the very quantifiers of India's economic prowess during Modi's term.

There is no urgency to justify and legitimize the overarching validity of international bodies like the IMF, the World Bank, or the World Economic Forum.

Similarly, the justifications offered in favour of Foreign Direct Investment by Rao and Vajpayee, that it should not be seen as threat to be feared but rather as a positive change for India, are missing in Modi's addresses, primarily because there is no necessity for it.

Another conclusion that follows is that in Modi's speeches the reforms become an *unspoken* fact, a normative truth that does not require any contextualization or justification, and where they become synonymous with India's emergence as an economic powerhouse of the world. While on the one hand, for perceived internal audiences, the world is projected as being increasingly interconnected by all prime ministers, necessitating India to also not live in 'isolation', on the other hand, the world economic situation is frequently produced as being in crisis (Asian crisis of 1997, world economic crisis of 2008). This then becomes a context against which Indian emergence is projected by all four speakers. In Modi's addresses, the new found vigour, enthusiasm, and confidence with which rather than being a passive witness of changes in the world, India is projected as an active key player in constituting that world.

Whereas for his predecessors, the task of transforming the amorphous abstraction of globalization from being a threat to being a security is done cautiously and gradually, in Modi's oratory, it appears that that discursive transformation has finally been achieved. The aim of producing India as a place to invest is twofold, namely to show that: (1) India has changed and (2) that it is an attractive investment destination.

Modi's speeches do not follow the strict dichotomization sketched in the previous sections of this chapter in terms of the perceived 'outside' and 'inside'. Like in the case of other prime ministers, the speaker is highly aware of when he speaks to whom. Nonetheless, it is the first time that one sees a repetitive strategy of making such addresses, actually meant for distinct audiences, share the same semantic space of a singular speech. The outside and the inside are lexically sprung into existence, but within the same speech. Finally, India's emergence and reliability as an investment destination are projected in the context of four essential coordinates—demography, demand, devaluation, and democracy. Democracy becomes a subtly introduced, yet highly crucial stake in ensuring increased FDI and, therein, India's economic emergence. As we will see in the next chapter, it becomes an even more dynamic combination, a necessary stake, for projecting India as 'safe' when coupled with state secularism.

Speaking the Nation 'Secular'

Elaborately Explicit, Strategically Silent

This chapter unveils how, through their public speeches since 1991, the different prime ministers have profiled India as 'secular'. It will be elucidated how the discursive production of Indian secularity converges with the staging of India's emergence, both for what the prime ministers conceive as the 'outside' world as also for those deemed as 'Indian' (in and outside India).[1]

It investigates how exactly the prime ministers translate the paradigm of *secularism* to the Indian population by showing which vocabulary is adopted to lend credibility to this claim, as well as how the Indian state, through the addresses of the elected head, positions itself vis-à-vis the wider world through the same concept of secularity.

Two concrete events acquire prominence after the introduction of market liberalization. Firstly, the demolition of the Babri Masjid in Ayodhya in 1992 and, secondly, the religious riots in Gujarat in 2002. These two events have made *secularism* an important discursive stake, bringing it to the forefront of active debates. In the face of such conflicts,

---

[1] This is a significantly revised version of the following contribution where initial ideas on the topic were first developed. [A. Bajpai, 'Speaking the Nation Secular: (E)merging Faces of India', in M. Burchardt, M. Middell, and M. Wohlrab-Sahr (eds), *Multiple Secularities: Multiple Secularities beyond the West: Religion and Modernity in the Global Age* (Berlin: De Gruyter, 2015), pp. 39–62.]

which intensified the urgency to reweave the national imagination, the prime ministers' public speeches have tried to rescue the ideal of India's proclaimed 'secular democracy'. This, especially at a time when India's image as socially and culturally unified and safe, particularly for the outside world, was more important than ever before for the materialization of dreams of growth and a prosperous future promised through the reforms (see Chapters 2, 3, and 4).

The sources used for this chapter chiefly incorporate the addresses delivered immediately after the outbreak of violence, when the prime ministers delivered 'Messages to the Nation' on the national television channel (*Doordarshan*) (in 1992–93 after Ayodhya; and in 2002 after Gujarat). In a similar vein, all speeches which were not necessarily delivered in the immediate occurrence of these episodes, but related to the themes of religious pluralism, communal violence, or communal harmony, and offered detailed visions of Indian secularism, as presented by the prime ministers, have been incorporated. Numerous other speeches have also received particular attention—those delivered before audiences at the UN General Assembly, those delivered in the context of the prime ministers' visits abroad, those delivered on the visit of foreign ministers and diplomats to India and other international platforms. Speeches that were delivered by Manmohan Singh (2004–14) to instigate the memory of the events of Ayodhya and on topical issues of national integration and religious/communal harmony have also received special consideration. The current prime minister's (Narendra Modi) speeches also add an important dimension to the analysis. As the residing chief minister of Gujarat at the time of the communal violence of 2002, Modi has borne the maligned image of being associated with/implicated for violence against the Muslim minorities in Gujarat in 2002. Twelve years later, his sweeping electoral victory and appointment as the prime minister of India has implied that the BJP engaged in an electoral campaign, whereby, once again, the classic theme of secularism had to be revisited in an attempt to redesign the party's as well as its candidate's image into one that was acceptable for the Indian population. Chakravarty and Roy aptly sum up that this victory, '[...] underscored that a decisive transformation in extant understandings of Indian secularism and of the oppositional terms of the relationship between religious nationalism and democracy was at hand. To both his supporters and his fiercest critics, the reality of Modi as prime minister spoke of a new India in the making.'[2]

The chapter advances in five distinct parts. The first part portrays how a 'secular' India is produced for Indians (what is referred to as the 'internal' or the 'inside').[3] Here, I reflect upon how numerous definitions, phrases, and terms, which borrow their vocabulary from the Indian context of religious pluralism, are used to make an argument for India's secularism before perceived internal audiences. It will also show how the discursive staging of an 'Emerging India' intertwines with the projections of a secular India. The second shorter part shows how the 'outside' is presented an India which is secular and democratic and in ideological cohesion with the world. A separate third part has been added to the chapter to present an analysis of the current prime minister, Modi's speeches. This section has not been incorporated in the main body of the text as the prime minister has still not finished his complete five-year term, given that new developments in Indian politics continue to inform his oratory. Part four takes cognizance of the conclusions drawn from the detailed analysis of the rhetoric of the four prime ministers and traces the continuities and discontinuities in their oratory on a secular India, which is projected as increasingly emerging. In the final part, the two contexts (internal and external) are brought together and it will be illustrated how the prime ministers conjure temporal and spatial orders to forward the cause of Indian secularity. This implies how, depending on the context (therein the audience), and the references made in the name of a putative past and a putative future, the prime ministers profile India as secular.

---

[2] P. Chakravartty and S. Roy, 'Mr. Modi Goes to Delhi: Mediated Populism and the 2014 Indian Elections', *Television and New Media* 16, no. 4 (2015): 312.

[3] As stated in the Introduction, the terms 'internal' and 'external' (inside and outside) are not products of assumptions made by the author, rather emic categories derived from the analysis of the material, that is, they refer to the distinctions that are drawn within the addresses *by* the Indian prime ministers. Thus, the demarcation exists from the perspective of the speakers and how they draw the categories of the intended audiences within the speeches.

Self-Portrayals for the Inside: Speaking India Secular at Home

In an address to the Upper House of the Indian Legislature in 1993, a few months after the events of Ayodhya, the then prime minister, P.V. Narasimha Rao, stated with regard to the constitution of India,

> The word secular was used in the forty-second amendment (of the Constitution) [...]. The forty-second amendment makes it very clear that the kind of democracy, the brand of democracy in this country is going to be secular democracy. It could be any other democracy, non-secular also, if the nation wants it. But this nation in particular wants secular democracy. And that is what was clarified.[4]

References such as these are obvious instances of profiling India as a secular democracy. The constitution of India, which establishes India's secularity, is evoked repetitively[5] to stress that India is and has to be

---

[4] P.V.N. Rao, 'Agenda Before the Nation', address at the Indian Upper House of Legislature, the Rajya Sabha, 11 March 1993.

[5] To state a few among numerous other examples: 'The first step taken by the people and the leaders of India, after 1947, was to enshrine the Gandhian notion of secularism and tolerance in our constitution, at the same time as we adopted it as a guiding principle of political life in the country. Small wonder, then, that we have been able to build up a humane society, resting upon liberal institutions, in the context of a religious plurality which is without a peer in the world' (Rao, 'Tolerance for a Better World Order', speech delivered at the UNESCO-sponsored symposium on tolerance, New Delhi, 1 May 1995);

'We have given ourselves a secular constitution. Freedom of religion, freedom to manage religious affairs and prohibition of discrimination on grounds of religion have been guaranteed as fundamental rights in the Constitution (Rao, 'Towards a Strong and Vibrant India: Towards a Strong and Vibrant India', speech delivered at the first meeting of the reconstituted National Integration Council, New Delhi, 2 November 1991);

'[...] in the 42nd amendment, this word (secularism) was added. It was made abundantly clear that the kind of democracy we want to have here is a secular democracy and of no other kind' (Rao, 'Agenda Before the Nation', address at the Indian Upper House of Legislature, the Rajya Sabha, 11 March 1993);

'Friends it is matter of common knowledge that the source of India's strength and vitality lies in its immense diversity [...]. We derive our existence as a political community from the Constitution, which we the people gave to

secular. Worthy of observation is that such references often do not explicitly elaborate upon what it is that the term means. They serve, at best, as an opening window to legitimize India's claim to secularism and validate it by emphasizing its constitutional anchorage.

In order to explain the ingredients of the term to perceived internal audiences, however, *all* prime ministers have, at different stages of their respective political careers, resorted to numerous Indian neologisms of the term. Terms and phrases like *tolerance, sarva dharma sambhav* (all religions are true), *dharma-nirpekshta, unity in diversity*, communal non-bias, etc. are employed by all, but not without variances in the meanings implied and the frequency of usage. Each of these phrases has a particular career in Indian politics and is used as a mechanism to authenticate the idea of India as a 'secular' nation.

Secularism as a 'Tolerant' India

One such derivative is *tolerance*. The term is employed repetitively in co-occurrence with *secularism*[6] in addresses that were delivered to Indian audiences in the aftermath of the Ayodhya conflict.[7] During this phase, the objective was to inform the 'inside' that secularism in India ought not to be viewed merely as a constitutional embellishment, but as a lively philosophical idea embedded in India's long tryst with the value of tolerance.[8] It has, however, persisted as a referral point to secularism

---

ourselves and, in the process established the Republic of India. It is because we are a Republic, and not a mere democracy, that we are enjoined to nurture and indeed celebrate, our linguistic, ethnic, cultural and religious diversity' (Singh, 'Towards Safeguarding Needs and Aspirations of Minority Communities', 2 November 2006).

[6] Here, the italicized term connotes the concept itself, not the intended meaning. However, to avoid an over-italicization of the term throughout the body of the text, it has been italicized only on the first instance of its usage.

[7] It may be revealing to note that within the context of thirteen addresses made by Prime Minister P.V.N. Rao, the term is used sixty-three times, while the terms *secular* and *secularism* occur sixty-two times. In most cases, the terms *tolerance* and *secular(ism)* have a co-occurrence in the addresses.

[8] A prominent illustration may be located in the following excerpt from a speech delivered by Rao at the UNESCO-sponsored symposium on tolerance, 'To me, tolerance means the intensely creative interplay between

even in the case of the prime ministers to follow. In the following lines, Manmohan Singh, India's prime minister after 2004, touches upon numerous parallel themes while explaining the term in his address to the National Integration Council,

> For centuries our society has been characterized by a spirit of tolerance. This has been a value which has been at the core of our civilization, at the core of our very concept of a nation. Ours is a society which has rejoiced in its diversity; in its ability to shelter an incredible range of thoughts, ideas and beliefs [...]. It is this wonderful open-mindedness which has enabled all religions of the world to find a place under the Indian sun. As we have grown as a nation, this value which has been enshrined in our constitution has become one of the defining features of our nation.[9]

Here, the *our* and *we* celebrate an Indianness evoked, while simultaneously establishing that the 'spirit of tolerance' is *not new* to India, that it has a distinct history in India's civilizational past ('for centuries'). The notions of tolerance and *diversity* inhabit parallel semantic zones within the excerpt and become the co-equivalents of secularism. The phrase 'at the core of our very concept of a nation' shows clearly that secularism (here, equivalent to tolerance) is a 'defining feature', rather a precondition for the very existence of the Indian nation.

The earlier lines also indicate an attitude generated towards time. Hartog reflects on how memory and heritage have become 'symptoms of our relation to time [...]. Preceding from memory, heritage becomes the memory of history, and as such, a symbol of identity.'[10]

---

different religious and philosophical systems, or between differing secular ideologies and worldviews within a society. Such creative interplay transforms the notion of tolerance from a passive to an active agency, through which an individual or the community enriches the material and spiritual life. Indeed we have in tolerance the pre-history of the liberal notion of dissent, which regards new and challenging ideas as possible basis of novel creativity and enrichment in society. Tolerance as defined within liberal discourse, thus throws open endless vistas of moral and material improvement in the human condition' (Rao, 'Tolerance for a Better World Order', speech delivered at the UNESCO-sponsored symposium on tolerance, New Delhi, 1 May 1995).

[9] M. Singh, 'Sustaining our Diversity and Pluralism: Challenges Ahead', address to the National Integration Council, 31 August 2005.

[10] F. Hartog, 'Time and Heritage', *Museum International* 57, no. 3 (2005): 9.

The remembrance of a staged civilizational heritage is projected as a collective memory which serves to establish a 'national' self, one with a 'wonderful' past embedded in the ideal of secularism. *Tolerance* is presented as a derivative of secularism that provides the common space for both 'traditional' values of Indian past and the ideals of a 'modern' nation-state (as constitutional values) to be projected. In fact, a natural continuity is sketched between the two in order to underline how one has provided room for the other. For example, in the following address, Singh repeats,

> I do sincerely believe that our civilization has made it possible for diversity to thrive and flourish. Every great religion of the world has found a home in this great and blessed land of ours. We Indians are intrinsically a tolerant people. Intolerance is an aberration. Our democracy is built on our civilizational commitment to pluralism. Religious intolerance is alien to both our culture and constitutional values.[11]

The concept of tolerance thus becomes a common meeting ground, a confluence for the past as well as the present. As emerges from these two examples, when explaining the paradigm to internal audiences, there is no hesitation in employing references to religion.

A persistent emphasis laid by *all* prime ministers is that secularism does not imply irreligiousness. On the contrary, the concept is used to celebrate religious diversity. There is an underlying comprehension that in order to appeal to the sensibilities of the listeners, 'religion' cannot be relegated.[12] It is also in this regard that numerous ambivalences arise when it comes to personal religious codes.

Here, a note on the language in which the speeches were delivered also deserves mention. Whereas for those speeches delivered in English, all prime ministers occasionally use the term tolerance, for those delivered in Hindi, the term shifts from *sahisnutā* (forbearance, sufferance), *sabr* (moderation, patience), *sahanaśīlatā* (endurance, passiveness,

---

[11] Singh, Address at the *Indira Gandhi Peace Prize for National Integration*, New Delhi, 31 October 2006.

[12] Another example is 'India is proud of its democratic heritage which is rooted in the country's cultural ethos of tolerance, respect for different viewpoints and a ready embrace of diversity' (Singh, 'UN Democratic Fund: Strengthening the Bulwark of Democracy across the World', address at the launch of the UN Democratic Fund, New York, 14 August 2005).

longanimity), *udāratā* (magnanimity, generosity, charity, liberality, open-ness) to *dhairya* (adherence, patience).[13] Though each of these Hindi terms carries the meaning *tolerance* as one of the synonyms when trans-lated into English, they nonetheless simultaneously connote a plethora of other meanings in Hindi, rendering it vague, open, abstract, and ambiguous in interpretation.

That tolerance as an equivalent of secularism can stand for patience, charity, endurance, and even passiveness, all at the same time, thus opens a new space where the term is creatively left ambivalent in its meaning. A lexical confusion thus prevails, especially when numerous Hindi synonyms are used to substitute tolerance.

This is the most prominent strategy adopted by the prime ministers: that of presenting state secularism as a *fact* while making a claim to a normative understanding of the term as something indigenous and available, known, and also already inscribed in local vocabulary, whereas actually leaving the meaning open.

Sarva Dharma Sambhava

The theme of religious diversity extends further into another promi-nent Indian derivative of secularism, a phrase that has been the bone of contention throughout the history of the secularism debate(s) in India. Often projected as a philosophy that has a specific career in the Indian context, the dictum of *sarva dharma sambhava* is the understanding of secularism which the prime ministers most commonly refer to. The phrase literally translates as 'all religions are true'.

In an address commemorating the socio-religious reformer Swami Vivekananda's participation in the World Parliament of Religions in Chicago in 1893, Prime Minister Rao explains the phrase to his audiences:

> Sarva Dharma Sambhava which we call secularism today, equal respect for all religions, is a unique contribution of our country to the world. It is amazing how people cannot understand secularism. They may be hav-ing different religions in their countries but still, from their point of view it is not an aggregate—one plus one—it is not like that; it is something

---

[13] Satyaprakaśa et al. (eds), *Manaka Angrezī-Hindī-Kośa* (Prayāg: Hindī Sāhitya Sammelana, 1971).

much above the aggregate, and this is what we consider secularism is. Our secularism is neither atheistic, nor irreligious. It is not even indifferent to religion. It accepts religion as a vital element in the life of an individual for so it is in India and among the vast majority of people of the world. It then goes a step further and recognizes the spirit of the long held Indian tradition, that there can be more than one true religion and all of them should be shown due deference.[14]

As evident, the phrase *sarva dharma sambhava* is sometimes even utilized as a direct translation of secularism. In a twist of formulations, the English term secularism is thus appropriated and domesticated or Indianized by adding the Indian flavour of religious plurality to it. It is systematically used to inform Indians and the world that, in fact, secularism as an ideal is not an externally induced paradigm, but indeed a part of India's long-standing heritage. Its roots are to be found in India's *sanskriti*.[15] In the previous lines, remarks such as '[...] is a unique contribution of our country to the world' and 'It is amazing how people cannot understand secularism' quantify that India has not only a long tradition of secularism but is even a trendsetter, a contributor to the paradigm.[16] The same tone of India's syncretic uniqueness and its emulative model of tolerance may be sensed in Prime Minister Vajpayee's oratory, as illustrated by the following excerpt:

> The meeting points of ancient Trade Routes may lie in other parts of the world, but India has always been a meeting point of Faith Routes. Besides all the faiths that originated here, India welcomed the Jews, Syrian Christians, the Catholics, Zoroastrians, Muslims, and people belonging to other religions. We are proud of India's age-old adherence to the ideal of *Sarva Pantha Samabvhava*, which means, respect for all faiths. I suggest that this principle of secularism, which is enshrined in India's Constitution, should be accepted by all countries. Tolerance should become a global ideal. This would go a long way in promoting

[14] Rao, 'Swami Vivekananda—A True Liberal', inaugural address at the centenary celebrations of Swami Vivekananda's participation at the World Parliament of Religions in Chicago, 9 October 1993.

[15] *Sanskriti* may losely be translated as culture. The usage of the word has also become commonplace in colloquial Hindi.

[16] See also, R. Bhargava, 'Indian Secularism: An Alternative Trans-cultural Ideal', in T.N. Srinivasan (ed.), *The Future of Secularism* (New Delhi: Oxford University Press, 2006), pp. 20–53.

understanding, cooperation and peace among peoples belonging to different faiths and cultures.[17]

Thus, two objectives are simultaneously attained in the given excerpts. Firstly, the nation is imagined through a re-projection of India's heritage through shifting references to a homogenized past. This re-projection is embedded in an inherent understanding that secularism in India can neither be atheistic nor irreligious. Secondly, informing Indians *and* the world alike that not only has India always been secular, but that it is even distinct and unique in the world for having a model that is worthy of emulation.

Two observations become noteworthy here. First is the semantic shift in the emphasis not being on drawing the boundaries between the state and the 'religious' sphere(s) in coherence with the theory of the strict 'wall of separation', but rather on propagating an equal respect for all religions. What is asserted is the celebration of Indian pluralism as a basis of its secularism and exceptionalism. Here, the question of what is regarded *private* and *public* acquires importance for defining secularism. However, what my analysis shows is that this very point is not made public by the prime ministers. None of the prime ministers present a nuanced meaning of what is entailed within the *public* and *private* spheres, and how this secularism envisions that 'religion and culture were elevated to an ostensibly apolitical level—above the profanities of the political'.[18]

Second is the absence of irreligiousness/atheism within the purview of the speeches. Excerpts such as the one cited before where Rao states, 'Our secularism is neither atheistic, nor irreligious. It is not even indifferent to religion. It accepts religion as a vital element in the life of an individual [...]' elucidate that in overemphasizing the recognition of religion per se, the prime ministers fail to give due cognizance to the rights of those who identify themselves as irreligious or atheistic as well as to the long-standing history of atheism in India whereby secularism has often sedimented as an important word in people's lexical memories.[19] Of the

[17] Vajpayee, inaugural address at the International Conference on Dialogue among Nations, New Delhi, 9 July 2003.

[18] T.B. Hansen, *The Saffron Wave: Democracy and Hindu Nationalism in Modern India* (Princeton: Princeton University Press, 1999), p. 11.

[19] For a promising ethnography of the Atheist Movement in Andhra Pradesh and Telangana, see S. Binder, *Total Atheism: Making 'Mental Revolution' in South India*, unpublished dissertation, Utrecht University, 2017.

large corpus of 1,202 speeches, not a single reference was found to be the same. Here, a related question to be posed is: In the prime ministers' visions, does secularism protect the rights of religious communities to equal treatment, or does it also envision protecting the rights of individuals who leave a community?[20] Conversion, a commonplace phenomenon, remains absent in the addresses.

Secularism as a Hindu Achievement?

Most references to the term are inflated with a sense of national pride. In the following lines, A.B. Vajpayee, who would later assume the prime ministership in 1999, states:

> Secularism is in the veins of this country. This country never saw a theocracy. It has never seen conflicts between the Church and the state as the West has. Here the king ruled and the priest, at the very most, gave instructions and speeches about discipline. The priests never attempted to amass power from the king and the state. This is a multi-religious country. Even if Christianity and Islam wouldn't have entered, even then this nation would have advanced with the paradigm of Sarva Dharma Sambhava, that is, all religions are true and possible.[21]

Interestingly, Modi, in a similar vein, stated during his electoral campaign: 'Secularism is in the DNA of Indians'. In the earlier excerpt, a clear distinction is established by Vajpayee between India and the 'West'. The perceived Indian audiences are *informed* and *reminded* of how India's secularism has always been a functional dictum, a premise for the definition of its nationhood. A 'we' is thus staged vis-à-vis the 'other', the lose category of 'the West'. Simultaneously, an internal otherization is seen at work here. Christianity and Islam are projected as 'outsiders' who have 'entered' the country.[22] However, what is maintained is that

---

Another important question to be posed is if secularism protects the rights of communities to equal treatment or also of individuals to leave a community.

[20] I am grateful to Margrit Pernau for this insight.

[21] A.B. Vajpayee, Reaction to the No-Confidence Motion of the then prime minister H.D. Devegowda, 12 June 1996.

[22] This is also reflective of a more general rhetoric that may be attached to numerous prompters of *Hindutva*—the claim to a Hindu indigenous population and the entry of the 'outsider'. Many have also emphasized how Muslims

in spite of such heterogeneity, a sense of homogeneity has *historically* prevailed in India owing to the ideal of secularism.[23] Thus, once again, secularism becomes the precondition for the very existence, the imagination of the nation.

It is important here to zoom into the specificity of the aforementioned words delivered by Vajpayee in terms of the internal subtle shifts that may be located in the rhetoric of the first three prime ministers. The only of the three who headed the Bharatiya Janata Party (BJP)-led coalition government,[24] Vajpayee's referential archive to explain the term

---

in India have a Hindu ancestry. Conversion in such contexts has then been dubbed as *Grahwāpsi* or homecoming. One such recent controversial speaker of the same is Dr Subramanian Swamy, president of the *Janata Party* (People's Party) (see the article *How to Wipe Out Islamic Terror* from 16 July 2011, available at http://bharatabharati.wordpress.com/2011/10/04/how-to-wipe-out-islamic-terror-subramanian-swamy/, accessed on 17 March 2012).

[23] This greatness of the Indian tryst with secularism is also celebrated in other speeches by the prime ministers. Some examples, 'India's great contribution to human kind is the idea of Sarva Dharma Sambhava' (Singh, 'Remembering Netaji S.C. Bose—A Great Life Dedicated to Nation Building', address at the birth anniversary celebrations of S.C. Bose, New Delhi, 23 January 2007);

'Secularism in the Indian context can only be explained through Sarva Dharma Sambhava. From the Vedic age until the modern age it is this dictum that has kept us alive' (Vajpayee, speech in honour of the India's first president, Rajendra Prasad, 2–3 December 1992).

[24] The Hindu right-wing comprises, among others, of the BJP as its political faction. BJP politician, Ram Krishna Advani, was highly instrumental in mobilizing the controversial Ram Rath Yatra (1990), a procession undertaken from the state of Gujarat up to Ayodhya, where he was seen as a modern-day *Ram*, the Hindu god whose birth place Ayodhya is claimed to be, on a Toyota car decorated like the deity's mythological chariot with the claim to construct a temple on the spot where the Babri Masjid stood. Most BJP politicians including the prime ministers A.B. Vajpayee and N.D. Modi have held portfolios of the RSS (Rashtriya Swayam Sevak Sangh or the National Patriotic/ Volunteer Organization), which is termed as the cultural guild of the Hindu right wing. Vajpayee's and Modi's personal trajectories as BJP politicians is thus very crucial to the debate on secularism. Together, the BJP and the RSS have historically been ardent in their campaigns for *Hindutva* and a Hindu nation.

secularism, especially to internal audiences, is primarily informed by a *Hindu* and a *Hindi* vocabulary. Here, India always stands for homogenized Hindu traditions, and secularism is primarily a Hindu achievement essentially conceived as tolerance exercised by Hindus (I will show in the final section of this chapter how the rhetoric of Modi and Vajpayee can be situated on the same trajectory). This is a notable difference compared to the rhetoric of Rao and Singh, both of whom are Congress leaders and who, even though not shying away from using Hindu resources to make sense of the term, are seen as emphasizing more on Indian pluralism and democracy as against their BJP counterparts. Though both Singh and Rao also speak of a 'civilizational legacy' and therein attempt to reproject history in producing a present and a future, in Singh's speeches (the two examples stated under the trope tolerance exemplify this), secularism is often slipped as an adjective, an aside, understood as another face of pluralism and Indian democracy. Thus, even though the cosmetic setup of the presentation of the paradigm is the same, the style and the intentionality of use indicate subtle differences.

Post-Ayodhya Chutneyfication

Another factor that emerges from the analysis is that in many references to the paradigm of secularism, particularly before Ayodhya, the term was used as such with no Hindi versions, even in speeches which were delivered in the Hindi language. Here, it was often simply termed as *Secularvād*. As has already been amply documented, there has been no term or co-equivalent to secularism in any Indian language.[25] However, after the events of the demolition of the masjid in Ayodhya, different neologisms were developed, particularly in Hindi. It is in this context that the events of 1992, which formulate a backdrop to this analysis, acquire prime importance. Post a national crisis when the secular fabric of the country and, in turn, its acclaimed unifying ideological common thread came to be questioned, the 'Indian' terminology and lexical archive was developed (or, at least, evoked through a selective reappropriation of history) so as to communicate the term to the Indian audiences. In order to 'save' the idea of secularism and, in turn, to save

[25] P. Chatterjee, 'Secularism and Tolerance', in Bhargava (ed.), *Secularism and its Critics* (New Delhi: Oxford University Press, 1998), p. 345.

the acclaimed founding idea of India itself, the prime ministers were pressurized to attempt and communicate the message in a language that is understood by their audiences. It is against this backdrop that other phrases related to secularism have emerged: a noteworthy term in this context is *dharma-nirpekshta* (literally meaning 'religious non-bias'). 'Dharma' being the Hindi term for religion, though it is widely understood as a *way of life*. The term dharma in dharma-nirpekshta is thus viewed to be more in sync with the idea of religion-as-faith, given that *religion* itself is often not deemed as an appropriate category for understanding the numerous Indian faiths or dharmas.[26]

Vajpayee, in an open address in the north Indian city of Fatehabad, Haryana, stated: 'We are famous for Dharma-nirpekshta. For us Dharma-nirpekshta is not a negative ideology. It is a positive vision. There should be no biases and discrimination on the basis of religion. People are free to practice the religion of their choice. The Constitution provides a guarantee of complete religious freedom [...].'[27]

However, the phrase has often been attacked by the Indian academic world[28] as also by several political actors and parties such that it had to be modified eventually. The term *dharma-nirpekshta* was seen as having a negative approach to religion per se. Once again, the local atmosphere/context contributed to a transformation in the explanation of the term. It led instead to the definition of secularism being modified into the paradigm of *sarva dharma sambhava* (explained earlier) and the category of *sampraday* or *pantha-nirpekshta* (*sampraday* and *pantha* both refer to the term *communal*. Through this transformation, secularism has been developed into a reference to communal non-bias.)[29] Though

[26] For this debate, see A. Nandy, 'The Politics of Secularism and the Recovery of Religious Tolerance', in *Secularism and its Critics*, ed. R. Bhargava, (New Delhi: Oxford University Press, 2005), p. 321.

[27] Vajpayee, open address in Fatehabad, Haryana, 19 August 1999.

[28] For example, G. Spivak, 'The Trajectory of the Subaltern in My Work', keynote lecture at the conference *The Subaltern and the Popular*, University of California, Santa Barbara, available at http://www.youtube.com/watch?v=2ZHH4ALRFHw, accessed on 12 June 2012.

[29] The term communal and communalism have a specific meaning in India, which is embedded in colonial and postcolonial Indian history. This is explained in the forthcoming part, where I elaborate upon yet another understanding of secularism in India.

the earlier lines were delivered by Vajpayee in 1999, the ambivalence in the translation of the secularism concept had already started surfacing in his addresses much earlier. Shortly before the Ayodhya conflict of 6 December 1992, Vajpayee stated as a member of the opposition party BJP (which was a primary actor in the demolition of the Babri Masjid in which Vajpayee was involved as a political figure):

> I feel that from the beginning the term 'secular' should not have been translated as 'Dharma-nirpekshta but as Sampraday-nirpekshta or Pantha-nirpekshta (meaning communal non-bias). That could have deleted many doubts. Even though there could be differing opinions on the meaning of the term but there was one uniting factor in this difference that the face of the state should be non-communal. We are united even today on this question. In the new Hindi edition of the Constitution the term 'secular' has been translated as Pantha-nirpekshta (meaning non-communal or communal non-bias) and thus there has been an attempt to rectify this mistake. It is important that all accept the correct translation of the term.[30]

It becomes lucid that the term secularism, in its historical trajectory in the Indian context, has encountered numerous additions and corrections. The one collectively agreed upon basis is the identification of religious diversity and the acceptance of 'religion(s)' as a primary nation-guiding dictum for Indians. Hence the acknowledgement that secularism in India can never be 'atheistic or irreligious'. However, the 'chutneyfication'[31] of the term with numerous neologisms and derivatives has also produced ambivalences in its concrete understanding. Though clearly stated that the term does not mean that India or Indians are irreligious, it is never really specified by the prime ministers as to how the state and the religious sphere ought to be separated or, in turn, interact with each other.

Communalism

The previous analogies point to yet another decisive conceptual element of the paradigm: *communalism*. In most addresses by all the prime

---

[30] Vajpayee, speech in honour of India's first president, Dr Rajendra Prasad, 2–3 December 1992.

[31] The Hindi term 'chutney' refers to a mixture. It has also been used in the English language with regards to 'Indianization' of the English language.

ministers, continuity is maintained whereby secularism is defined vis-à-vis communalism as its ideological other. This term has a strong 'indigenous' connotation in India. It is generally understood as referring to 'conflict, often accompanied with violence, between religious communities, primarily the Hindus and the Muslims, for political and/or economic gains'.[32] An enormous thrust has been laid upon defining what secularism entails by defining what it ought not to be. In continuity with the attempts to produce a secular India before 'internal' audiences, the profiling of aberrations to this desired ideal-type is also undertaken by the prime ministers often by creating obvious dichotomizations between secularism and communalism.

Rao, for instance, attempts the same in the following address given on the occasion of an award ceremony to honour the citizens who have epitomized communal harmony in their personal lives:

> But of course in a pluralistic society, by definition we have to get over certain tendencies which go against the name of a pluralistic society. And it is here that communalism has to be tackled first because we are secular, because we are pluralistic, because historically there is really no need, no reason at all for any communal feeling in this country. This country has welcomed everyone; this country has absorbed everyone who came from outside, people who came as invaders became permanently part of this country. So this is the kind of attraction which India has held for centuries together and there is no reason why it should not be so hereafter.[33]

Once again, a shifting restaging of history is at work here as a validating hinge for secularism. Secularism is projected as having a life of its own in the country. The phrases 'because historically there is no need for any communal feeling in this country' and 'it should not be so hereafter' indicate that the national imagination is rendered complete by secularism, acting as the conceptual interface between India's rich past and its promising future (see also the third main section of this chapter). Secularism is utilized to explain to Indians that communalism ought to be combated *because* communalism is an attack on India's very survival. In another address, Rao reiterated the statement of India's first prime

[32] R. Vohra, *The Making of India: A Historical Survey* (Armonk-New York-London: ME Sharpe Inc., 1997), p. 2.

[33] Rao, 'Communal Harmony—India's Heritage', address at the Kabir Puraskar presentation ceremony, New Delhi, 13 August 1994.

minister, Jawaharlal Nehru, in stating that, 'We must have it clearly in our minds and in the mind of the country that the alliance of religion and politics in the shape of communalism is the most dangerous alliance and it yields the most abnormal kind of illegitimate breed.'[34]

On another occasion, Rao projects communalism in a metaphor as a 'virus'[35] that plagues the national fabric of the Indian society. India is yet again profiled as a country, '[...] that can never go against religion. But nonetheless needs to protect its identity of those elements that inject its politics with religious fervour or fundamentalism.'[36]

Another distinct mechanism to cause digression from communal violence, which disturbs the continuity of secularism as a cohesive interface between India's past and its future (see the next section), is to locate the 'real' actors that disturb this ideological continuity. Thus, while communalism is the ideological other of secularism for Congress prime ministers and pseudo-secularism for BJP prime ministers, concrete actors that destroy this imagination of a secular India are mentioned to shift the blame. This refers in some cases (as with Rao specifically) to internal actors,[37] and, in Vajpayee's case, to an external actor that instigates national crevices, most prominently Pakistan.[38]

---

[34] Rao, 'Agenda Before the Nation', address at the Indian Upper House of Legislature, the Rajya Sabha, 11 March 1993.

[35] Rao, 'Towards a Strong and Vibrant India', speech delivered at the first meeting of the reconstituted National Integration Council, New Delhi, 2 November 1991.

[36] Rao, 'Communal Harmony—India's Heritage', address at the Kabir Puraskar presentation ceremony, New Delhi, 13 August 1994.

[37] Rao explicitly relates the Ayodhya crisis with the BJP, 'I am sad to state that the BJP–VHP combine has not only failed to respond to my efforts but as a matter of fact have gone about deliberately to not only thwart my efforts but also to mislead the nation [...]. What has happened today in Ayodhya where the Babri Masjid structure has been demolished, is a matter of great shame for all Indians' [Rao, 'Countering Communal Forces', address to the nation in the aftermath of Ayodhya, New Delhi, 6 December 1992].

[38] Given that the Gujarat riots of 2002 occurred when the BJP was in power in the state as also at the Centre, the blame for the existence of religious violence is quite often also deflected implicitly to 'external forces'. During this period, one also finds Vajpayee evoking the memory of the Kargil war of 1999, using Pakistan as a deflection mechanism. The history of the partition, the wars over

Pseudo-Secularism: Ambiguities and Silences in a Multicoloured Story

The aforementioned phrases connected to secularism, which are used by the prime ministers to paint India secular, indeed project a multicoloured, accommodating story. Vajpayee, in an address to the nation in 1996, stated, 'The first mosque in India was established in Kerala under the rule of a Hindu king and his blessings. Similarly after Jesus's sacrifice and crucifixion, India saw the establishment of its first Church. These different places of worship belong to different religions and are a living example of our secular traditions.'[39]

However, some scraping beneath the political rhetoric brings numerous contradictions to light.[40] Whereas, on the surface, the constitution is projected as propagating the idea of non-intervention in religious affairs and a distancing between the state and the religious domain,[41] there exist articles such as those recognizing the rights of religious minorities [Article 30(1)] specifically and, thus, unlike all the articles that are applicable to *all* citizens as individuals, such articles are eventually in recognition of community-based rights. Besides, there are personal laws or religious codes (especially instrumental in the case of marriage and inheritance of property) that govern the lives of people, depending on their religion by birth. Many religious practices have been seen as unjust

the disputed state of Jammu and Kashmir, and even the ungovernable spread of terrorist attacks are all factors that are repeatedly and most blatantly associated with Pakistan, especially in the face of internal threats to religious harmony.

[39] Vajpayee, address to the nation, 19 May 1996.

[40] See A. Bajpai, 'Imagining a "Secular India": Roots, Offshoots and Future Trajectories of the Secularism Debate in India', *South Asia Chronicle*, 2 (2012): 189–218.

[41] For example, Vajpayee comments such as: 'Secular does not mean that we are irreligious or opposed to religion. This is a religious country. But secularism definitely means that religion will not be controlled or run by the state. That the state does not have its own religion. That all religions are equal in the eyes of the state. None shall be discriminated against. Really our secularism is a positive secularism, not negative. And therefore it incorporates the idea of including and engaging with all, walking together. This is not just a wish but a necessity' (Vajpayee, 'Address on the Prevalence of Normalcy in the State of Jammu and Kashmir', 9 January 1999).

and brutal and imply a deprivation of fundamental freedoms guaranteed to the citizens by the constitution. In some instances, the state is thus inevitably pushed to intervene in the 'religious' sphere, thereby technically departing from the principle of a 'strict wall of separation' between religion and state principles.

The state has in the past actively intervened in the personal laws of the Hindu community, for example, abolishing the practices of sati (self-immolation of a Hindu wife on her husband's funeral pyre), the dowry system and untouchability. Regardless of the underlying social necessity of the same for the protection of the fundamental rights of those on the receiving side of these personal customs, it is often alleged (by several BJP politicians like Lal Krishna Advani) that this intervention of the state has been particularly more active in the case of the majority Hindu community. A similar firmness is, however, not shown by the state with regard to several Muslim personal laws, which also come in conflict with the fundamental rights of many belonging to the community. This leniency towards a minority community has led to allegations by the Hindu Right and parties such as the BJP that the Congress governments are only 'pseudo-secular'. Given the context of this ongoing tug-of-war between the BJP and the Congress, one may also state that in the more recent debates on secularism in Indian politics, more than communalism it is the category of 'pseudo secularism' which emerges as being the ideological other of secularism.

One such occasion whereby Prime Minister Vajpayee directly retorts to his Congress opponents touching upon this theme can be seen in the excerpt that follows:

> The shrill propaganda that the BJP is anti-Muslim has indeed had some influence on Muslim voters in the past. But the situation is changing. Muslims in India have seen that the BJP has been growing from strength to strength despite our critics' farrago of lies about us. At the same time, they have also seen that those parties that make monopoly claim over secularism and project themselves as the sole saviors of Muslims have been doing so principally to get en bloc votes of Muslims and nothing else.[42]

Interestingly, Vajpayee made this statement merely six days before the Godhra train episode and the ensuing communal riots in Gujarat.

---

[42] Vajpayee, statement by the prime minister, New Delhi, 21 February 2002.

Another sound example of attacking the Congress as pseudo-secular in a statement made by Vajpayee after the riots is as follows:

> It is indeed strange that I am praised as a 'secular leader' when I condemn, as I recently did, intolerance and other negative features exhibited by certain self-styled champions of Hindutva, but criticized as a 'communal leader' when I point out the negative aspects of militant Islam. Such double standards do no good to a healthy debate on what is true secularism and what is in the interest of our nation and the world.[43]

It is noteworthy that though within political rhetoric the entry of religion into political affairs and vice versa is condemned, the two spheres in reality do entangle in numerous ways. Notions of what comprises the 'political', the 'private', the 'public', and the 'religious' remain floating, constantly negotiated and fuzzy in their boundaries. A prominent example of the same is the excessive usage of religious symbols and icons for the most public and statist affair of electoral campaigns. Here, one finds innumerable examples whereby both the Congress and the BJP have relied on a vocabulary loaded in religious symbolism, appealed to specific religious communities for votes, or given party tickets to television actors who have played lead roles in religious TV serials like *Mahabharat* and *Ramayan*. In a remarkable rhetorical strategy, in addresses to perceived internal audiences, these spaces of ambivalence are left loose and never demarcated. It suffices to state that religion ought not to enter the domain of politics, and communalism or pseudo-secularism (in the BJP's case) are the avoidable others to Indian secularism. But what the intervention of one sphere into another really means is strategically silenced, owing to the ambiguity of the existing distinctions and the permeation of one sphere into the other.

Unity in Diversity Blends with Democracy

In most addresses, the emphasis is diverted on notions of tolerance, communal harmony, pluralism, and what is popularly and repetitively termed as the 'unity in diversity' master code. This phrase, owing its genesis primarily to Nehruvian vocabulary and practices of producing

---

[43] Vajpayee, statement by the prime minister on his speech at a public meeting in Goa, 14 April 2002.

the state's ritualistic calendar (see chapter 1), has acquired a special historical significance in India. Its use is commonplace also in colloquial language. It simultaneously contributes to producing 'India' as well as serving as a justification for its state-directed secularism. For example, as recently as 2005, Prime Minister Singh in an address for a conference on 'Democracy, Development, and Inclusiveness' stated before Indian as well as external audiences, '[…] for us in India, democracy is not just a way of life, it is the way of life. For our nation the defining principle has been and will always be "Unity in Diversity". This is the idea of India.'[44]

Noteworthy again here is how in Singh's addresses derivatives of secularism such as 'Unity in Diversity' become an adjective, an aside whose meaning is explicitly not explained by shifting the emphasis to democracy. Omission is a prominent part of political oratory, used in order to communicate with large audiences. In Singh's addresses, this omission implies an elaborate emphasis on democracy whose coordinates are also never really unpacked, rather assumed. *Secularism* simultaneously is placed next to the concepts of *democracy, unity in diversity,* and *pluralism*, often within the realm of the same sentence. This may be read as a means to understand what colour and flavour the paradigm of secularism is given, sometimes through strategic omission and, on others, through strategic highlighting. The following may be read as another example of the same:

> In a country of the size and diversity like ours, it is only the concern and care for the sensibilities of each other which can ensure a smooth functioning of the institutions we have created. This is the only way to maintain peace and harmony amongst the people of India […]. The delicate fabric of our nation woven around democracy and secularism is the only anchor-sheet for our country's existence.[45]

As evident, the word 'secularism' is often used in co-occurrence with the term democracy.[46] The aforementioned categories of the existing

---

[44] Singh, 'Democracy—The Way of Life in India', address at a conference on Democracy, Development, and Social Inclusion, New Delhi, 8 December 2005.

[45] Rao, 'Countering Communal Forces', address to the nation in the aftermath of Ayodhya, 6 December 1992.

[46] For example, in a random sample of ten speeches of Prime Minister Singh, the term secularism occurs twenty-nine times, whereas the term democracy

Indian tropes to secularism are not mutually exclusive. They find convergence in the thematic content of the prime ministers' addresses. Two such examples where most of these categories are beautifully woven together may be seen in the following lines from Manmohan Singh's addresses (in 2007 in an International Conference of Peace and Non-Violence, and seven years later in 2014 at a conference of the States Minorities Commissions). 'If there is one message India should be remembered for and identified with, it is the message of the Mahatma. The message of tolerance, of pluralism, of the need to "live and let live". Every civilized society must enable the co-existence of all religions [...] the idea of India is the idea of "Unity in Diversity".'[47]

> Pluralism is the keystone of India's civilization and culture. Religious harmony, not mere tolerance, is the bedrock of India's secularism. [...] I think it is of utmost importance to remember that we have age-old traditions of pluralism and tolerance. For India as a country, secularism has been a way of life practiced over centuries. We should be cautious of people who work against India's secular thought by attempting to redefine secularism. Our strength as a country lies in our unity. We should be vigilant against forces that seek to exploit our diversity in religion, language and culture to divide our people.[48]

As evident, 'civilization', 'culture', 'traditions', 'pluralism', 'religious harmony', 'tolerance', 'diversity', and 'unity'—all become the linguistic apparatus that support the cause of secularism envisioned by the state and vocalized by the prime ministers.

---

occurs twenty-four times, mostly co-occurring and clubbed together in the same paragraph in the speech.

[47] Singh, 'Gandhian Philosophy: Transforming Diverse Societies the World Over', address at the International Conference on Peace, Non-Violence, and Empowerment: Gandhian Philosophy in the 21st century, New Delhi, 30 January 2007. In another address, Prime Minister Vajpayee states, 'The essential condition for freedom to exist is national unity. Democracy is essential for national unity. And secularism is an essential component of democracy and national integrity' (Vajpayee, 'Harbinger of Progress', address to the nation on Indian Independence Day, 15 August 1998).

[48] Singh, address at the conference of the State Minorities Commissions, New Delhi, 13 January 2014.

'Since the Dawn of History': Secularism as/and National Heritage

There is yet another mechanism that is used to reinvest the imagination of a 'secular India' with a sense of truth. This is the utilization of what is termed as 'national heritage'. Collective memory is crafted and routinized through words. We have seen how themes of communal harmony (through Hindu–Muslim unity) and cultural pluralism (through the phrase of Unity in Diversity) are produced as a part of popular memory. Jan Assmann categorizes such memory work, which re-evokes those aspects of collective memory that help concretize an identity or 'store it', as *kulturelles gedächtnis* (cultural memory). This memory is socially formative in nature in the sense that it is 'educative, civilizing, humanizing', and normative in that it serves the function of 'providing rules of conduct'.[49] Cultural memory becomes an essential tool for the construal of a national imagination, as it comprises of 'that body of reusable texts, images and rituals specific to each society in each epoch whose cultivation serves to stabilize and convey society's self-image'.[50] This implies 'using the past' and therein also *producing* 'the' past for the cause of India's pluralist secularity. Memory is re-evoked by the prime ministers at varying levels for a dual purpose. Firstly, in order to reproduce the idea of a common past that contributes to the production of being a sum, that is, a unified, national space. Secondly, with a view to recreating or renegotiating the same past by inducing it with new images to fit the agenda at stake in the present. Therefore, to produce India as a secular nation, the prime ministers re-evoke examples from: (i) India's 'civilizational' past, (ii) what is dubbed as 'Indian' mythology and literature, (iii) the first Indian armed struggle for independence in 1857, (iv) the Indian national movement for independence, and (v) Indian national heroes who embraced the paradigm of secularism and are produced as stalwarts in Indian history.

As a starting point, one may state that many of the addresses proceed with sweeping statements that make references to India's civilizational past as an illustration of its secularity. For example, the addresses are replete with phrases like:

[49] J. Assmann and J. Czaplika, 'Collective Memory and Cultural Identity', *New German Critique*, 65 (1995): 127.

[50] Assmann, 'Collective Memory and Cultural Identity'.

'Since the dawn of history [...]'[51]

'The notion of tolerance [...] is powerfully reflected in the history of the civilization of India [...]'[52]

'Our ancient civilization provides a strong base in which to build a model for regulating the interaction of religion and politics [...]'[53]

'[...] [Our] liberal outlook is a distinctive feature of our civilization.'[54]

Such opening and closing phrases that are used before or after discussing the notion of secularism help advance the idea that the paradigm has a clear history in the country.[55] What phrases like 'Indian civilization' or

[51] Rao, 'Towards a Strong and Vibrant India', speech delivered at the first meeting of the reconstituted National Integration Council, New Delhi, 2 November 1991.

[52] Rao, 'Towards a Strong and Vibrant India'.

[53] Rao, 'Religion—A Unifying Force', address at the opening of the International Conference on Religion and Politics, organized by the Rajiv Gandhi Institute for Contemporary Studies, 30 January 1994.

[54] Rao, 'Religion—A Unifying Force'.

[55] In another address, Vajpayee states, 'We have always welcomed winds that came from all four directions. The doors of this country have always been open for one and all. When other nations were witnessing violence, exploitation, fear, persecution owing to religion, even then people came to India. And they found rest and refuge in the lap of Mother India. No one asked them how they came here and why and no one said that they were outsiders. This is the true colour of the soil of this nation and the eternal characteristic of its civilizational culture.' (Vajpayee, address on the 100th anniversary of the Hindu College in New Delhi, 17 February 1999).

On a similar note, glorifying pluralism, Singh states with respect to the state of Kerala, 'The composite and diverse culture of Kerala has been enhanced by the synthesis of a large variety of influences over centuries. From ancient times this blessed land has warmly welcomed travelers and migrants, who have all contributed to the development of its magnificent cultural mosaic. The tradition of religious tolerance and respect for diverse philosophies has greatly aided this process. It is not thus a coincidence that the earliest mosque, church and synagogue in India were all established in this blessed land of Kerala.' (Singh, speech at Kerala Kalamandalam, Thrissur, Kerala, 12 September 2012.)

In another address, he states, 'Indian civilization has a great sense of durability and permanence' (Singh, 'India—The Next Decade', address at the Indira Gandhi Conference, New Delhi, 19 November 2004).

our 'ancient civilization' do is to fabricate vague homogenizations where geographical and temporal specificities are generalized to produce the impression of an all-inclusive national whole. Hidden in these innocent, opening phrases are sweeping oversimplifications that club together experiences of different regions in different temporalities under the common rubric of 'Indian'. This construed totality is then utilized to forward the cause of secularism, which in turn reinforces India's unified heritage.

Five terms, which have their own career in India, and are used to promote the ideal and the imagination of a secular India, find repetitive occurrences in the addresses. These are the categories of *jati* (race), *dharma* (religion), *sanskriti* (culture), *parampara* (tradition), and *itihaas* (history). In the following lines, delivered by Vajpayee on being sworn in as the prime minister, a convergence of most of these categories may be located. However, the same occurs after a reference is once again made to India's 'ancient civilization'.

> Ours is an ancient civilization. It has been built on consensus, on persuasion and not on mere tolerance. It has been built on an active and deep respect for the faiths and practices of all. Our sages say 'Akashaat Patitam Toyam, Yad Gachchati Saagaram, Sarva Devam Namaskaram, Keshavam Pratigachchati.' (Just as drops of rain falling on varied places, all gather and flow to the one sea, so also all worship leads to the same Divinity.) The Tamil Savant Thirumoolar proclaims in his 'Thirumandiram' Ondre Kulam, Oruvane Devan (We are all one clan and there is but one God).
>
> In the Indian perspective, this is the only valid meaning of secularism. My Government is unequivocally committed to this concept of secularism [...]. It is by this tradition that we shall recreate the spirit which was the hallmark of the freedom struggle—persons of all religions, all religions and all professions were working together to create a strong confident and resurgent India.[56]

The categories of civilization, history as memory, religion, tradition, and a 'resurgent India' are interwoven to explain and construe the understanding of secularism. In fact, the term 'tolerance' is given a new expanded meaning, explained as an 'active and deep respect for faith and practices of all'.

In continuation with the same mechanism, the prime ministers evoke illustrations from the amorphous category of 'Indian' mythology

---

[56] Vajpayee, 'Let Us Look Ahead', address to the nation on appointment as the prime minister of India, New Delhi, 22 March 1998.

and literature. It is here that certain literary figures acquire importance. Ancient scriptures, poetry, and epics formulate the reservoir of resources that are drawn to produce the *memory* of India as secular. For example, on one occasion, the Sufi Saint Kabir is quoted in the addresses. Kabir's work reflects a combination of the Hindi language with influences of many local north Indian dialects and bears an immense mass appeal for Indian audiences. As a literary figure, he is claimed to epitomize themes of Hindu–Muslim unity (thus often cited by numerous politicians) and the search for a religion that does not constrain one to a single god or holy book. After stating that the following lines are from poet Kabir, Prime Minister Rao, for instance, invokes Kabir as an example of communal harmony for his audience,

'*Moko kahan dhoonde re bande main to tere paas mein; Na main Mandir, na main Masjid. Na Kabe Kailaas mein; Dhoondhat ho to turut hi milhe, pal bhar ki taalas mein; Kahat Kabir suno bhai Sadhu sab saason ki saas mein.*'[57]

(God says: Where do you go in my search? I am not in a temple, neither in a Mosque; nor am I in the holy site of the Himalayas, the abode of Shiva. If you look deep enough, you will find me in a moment. O Saints! I reside in each breath of all mortal beings.)

A repetitively cited and therein remembered figure in the speeches is the socio-religious reformer Vivekananda, whose words are often quoted by all three prime ministers. His philosophy is staged as exemplifying Indian secularism. Thus, Prime Minister Manmohan Singh makes a reference to the latter, 'Swamiji spoke of our civilizational tradition of accepting the greatness of all religions. He said "We believe not only in universal toleration, but we accept all religions as true."'[58]

---

[57] Poet Kabir, as cited by the Indian prime minister, Rao, 'Tolerance for a Better World Order', speech delivered at the UNESCO-sponsored symposium on tolerance, New Delhi, 1 May 1995.

[58] Singh, 'Religious Harmony—The Bedrock of Indian Civilization', address at the South Asian Interfaith Conclave, New Delhi, 21 April 2007. In another example, Rao quotes Vivekananda, 'I shall go to the mosque of the Mohammedan; I shall enter a Christian Church and kneel before the crucifix; I shall enter the Buddhist temple where I shall take refuge in Buddha and in his law. I shall go to the forest and sit down in meditation with the Hindu—who is trying to see the light which enlightens the heart of everyone.' The underlying idea is to invite the audiences to emulate this ideal invoked by Vivekananda and

On another occasion, the commemoration celebrations of Vivekananda's 150th birth anniversary, Singh stated,

> I have personally been inspired by Swamiji's syncretic views. As he put it so simply, yet profoundly, 'All who have actually attained any real religious experience never wrangle over the form in which the different religions are expressed. They know that the soul of all religions is the same and so they have no quarrel with anybody just because he or she does not speak in the same tongue.'

> This syncretic and pluralistic view of religion is one of the greatest contributions of Hinduism and of the civilisations that took root in this ancient land of ours. The idea that the whole world is one family has inspired millions of people all over the world. But I also believe it is an idea that defines India and the Indian view of the world.[59]

As lucidly clear in the given excerpt, Singh lexically cements the categories of pluralism, syncretism, civilizational ethos ('this ancient land of ours'), and the idea that 'the whole world is one family' and validates them through his reference to a figure of historical weight. In a similar vein, the use of a famous phrase from the Rig Veda on another occasion by Rao, *'Ekam Sad, Vipra Bahudha Vadadti Satya'*[60] ('Truth is one, sages call it by different names'), is meant to revisit the value of religious tolerance embedded in pluralism, India's own historic version of secularism. The earlier illustrations call out for the necessity of another sensitizing lens to comprehend the different scales at work when pluralism is evoked as an explanatory trope for secularism. On numerous occasions in the speeches one reads that secularism is rendered safe by evoking the idea of 'a singular God with multiple names'. (The used template in the speeches usually is, 'A singular God, there is only one Supreme Being, who is worshipped by different names in different religions'.) Influences of old and newer religious worlds, the *bhakti movement* or elements of

---

thus promote the cause of religious tolerance (Rao, 'Swami Vivekananda—A True Liberal', innaugural address at the centenary celebrations of Swami Vivekananda's participation in the World Parliament of Religions in Chicago, 9 October 1993).

[59] Singh, address at the closing ceremony of the commemoration of 150th birth anniversary of Swami Vivekananda, 12 January 2014.

[60] Rao, 'Tolerance for a Better World Order', speech delivered at the UNESCO-sponsored symposium on tolerance, New Delhi, 1 May 1995.

the *Bengal renaissance*, for instance, stand as a different genre of plural-ism in comparison to some polytheistic versions of Hinduism(s), which acknowledge, but sometimes are even indifferent to the existence of multiple gods who are not categorized as one's own. However, both understandings of religious pluralism (that of merging all gods into being one and that of acknowledging 'other gods' by tolerating their presence or being indifferent) are confused in the addresses under the clubbed category of 'ancient Indian religion' or 'Indian mythology' or 'our ancient scriptures', etc.

In pointing out these differences in the underlying trajectories of *pluralism*, I do not intend to challenge that one is more relevant or authentic than the other. I rather wish to question the assumed homo-geneity and givenness of the term *religious pluralism* itself, which is seen as synonymous to *secularism* in the Indian context.[61]

Illustrations do not just draw from resources available in the Hindu epics or mythology. In the following address, Singh refers to the teach-ings of the Sikh sacred text, the *Guru Granth Sahib*, when he states, 'The teachings of the Guru Granth Sahib seek to harmonize the world as we know it. These teachings synthesize the essential wisdom of all reli-gions and earlier mystic saints and the ancient traditional cultural and civilizational ethos of the Indian people.'[62]

The aim is to discursively concoct syncretism as the founda-tional principle of India. A conspicuous strategy to do so is to quote

---

[61] The statement derives its inspiration from Wendy Doniger's article in *The Outlook* titled 'All in the Big Tent: How "Secularism" "Lost" Its Old Stripes in the Service of the New Indian State' (special issue 26 January 2014), which discusses pluralism in Hinduism and numerous renunciant movements in India. The author gives enough evidence in the cause of pluralism and its different forms, but my own contribution here is in deflecting our attention to how pluralism in itself as an Indian trope of secularism cannot be assumed to have a singular meaning. Thus, if the prime ministers use different excerpts from the words of different religious reformers, the same word, pluralism, which is presented as a derivative of secularism, can bear different connotations. These differences are never outlined, and a generalized understanding is used to construe the nation as secular (here, embedded in its pluralism).

[62] Singh, 'Sri Guru Granth Sahib: A Beacon of Light for Eternity', speech on the 400th anniversary of the installation of the Sri Guru Granth Sahib, New Delhi, 30 October 2005.

prominent religious and political personalities. However, these citations appear to be timeless and spaceless references, which are randomly drawn upon without due explanations offered to their historical contexts from an enormous reservoir of cultural resources. Other concrete references incorporate the temporally and spatially stretched examples of the Mauryan Empire ruler Ashoka (3rd century BC), who adopted Buddhism, the literary works of the poet Rabindranath Tagore,[63] the Alwar saints of Tamil Nadu, Jawaharlal Nehru's principle of Panchsheel or The Five Principles of Peaceful Coexistence, etc., to name a few.

In extension of this celebration of the past, on several occasions, the prime ministers revisit one resource from collective 'national' memory that generates the most passionate fervour across the country with references to the Indian National Movement for independence, the first armed rebellion against the British East India Company (1857), and finally national heroes like Gandhi and Nehru. In the following lines, the themes of pluralism and tolerance are re-evoked not just for India, but on a high moralistic ground also projected as an ideal type for the world. Interestingly, the lines were delivered in an external setting (South Africa): 'In an age where people worry about the so called "clash of civilizations," Gandhiji's message would have been that it is indeed possible for us to work for the "confluence of civilizations" Through the institutions of a pluralist democracy we can make our world safer for peace, equality and freedom.'[64]

---

[63] Rao uses Tagore's elucidation of the greatness of Indian culture in that it has historically been a source of spirituality for the outside world and thus home to numerous civilizational interactions 'Come, O ye Aryans, Come, O ye non-Aryans, Come, O Hindus, and Come, O Muslims; And today, Come O, ye Englishmen, and Come, O, ye Christians [...]' [Rao, 'Tolerance for a Better World Order', speech delivered at the UNESCO-sponsored symposium on tolerance, New Delhi, 1 May 1995.]

Tagore's poems, which are replete with descriptions of the scenic beauty of India, as also a nationalistic fervour triggered by the will to free India of colonial rule, are used to generate a spirit of oneness among Indians. This is done in the purview of creating a feeling that all Indians are Indians first, regardless of which religions they practise.

[64] Singh, 'Rediscovering the Relevance of Gandhiji's Message of Peace and Tolerance', speech delivered at the Satyagraha Centenary Commemoration at Kingsmead Stadium Durban, South Africa, 10 October 2006.

The reference to Samuel Huntington's *Clash of Civilizations* becomes rather obvious here. A similar reference was made by Singh's predecessor, Vajpayee, in 2003 at an international conference in New Delhi on 'Dialogue among Civilizations' when he stated,

> Some years ago, a famous writer put forward a thesis about the coming Clash of Civilizations. The thesis was, of course, flawed and baseless. Its main fault was that it failed to recognize that civilizations do not rather, cannot clash. Thus, all civilizations have a civilizing influence on human beings. That is a part of the very definition of a civilization. Nevertheless, we should thank the worthy writer who predicted the coming Clash of Civilizations. [...] The future of mankind is not going to be determined by a Conflict among Civilizations; rather, as some people have beautifully put it, humanity's future will witness a Concert or a Confluence of Civilizations.[65]

We thus find a similar appeal in Vajpayee's address, or rather continuity to his words in Singh's address from 2006, whereby the emphasis is shifted to the dictum of *Vasudhaiva Kutumbakam* or 'the whole world is one family' from the Mahopanishad. Another befitting example of the same may be located in Singh's at the World Sanskrit Conference in 2012 where he reiterated,

> The Sanskrit language has also been the source of values and ideals that have sustained India through the ages. Like the great civilization of India, Sanskrit does not belong to any particular race, sect or religion. It represents a culture that is not narrow and sectarian but open, tolerant and all-embracing. The open-minded seers and thinkers who spelt out their vision and philosophy in the sacred Vedas and the Upanishads were able to balance the opposites in their life and in philosophy. It is this spirit of liberalism and tolerance imbedded in Sanskrit that we must inculcate in our present-day life. The message of the ancient sages of India, who gave us the concept of Vasudhaiva Kutumbakam, the world as one family, continues to be of great significance to the world even today.[66]

The Sanskrit language is thus projected as the source of a much older concept that renders the 'great civilization of India' 'tolerant and all-embracing'. Once again, a resource from an endless repertoire of

---

[65] Vajpayee, Inaugural Address at the International Conference on Dialogue among Civilizations, New Delhi.

[66] Singh, address at the World Sanskrit Conference, 5 January 2012.

phrases and words is utilized to repetitively and almost pervasively introduce tolerance embedded in a homogenized civilizational ethos (derived from ancient Hindu scriptures).

In the following lines delivered by Narasimha Rao in a symposium in 1995 that specifically dealt with the theme of tolerance, it is once again Gandhi who is utilized as an exemplifying illustration and even an ideal. It is maintained through such an example that secularism need not disengage itself with the religious, in fact that it is essential to incorporate when discussing secularism:

> Gandhiji's power and the regard which he enjoyed among the common folk lay in the remarkable fusion in which he married secular with spiritual concerns in his person. Through such means Gandhiji was able to fashion a profoundly original notion of secularism in a country, which enjoys a degree of religious plurality unknown to any other polity in our times. Such secularism was based on an equality of status for different moral and religious systems in the belief that such systems constituted different paths to the same transcendent truth.[67]

The aforementioned three excerpts lead to the conclusion that there has indeed been a continuity in the oratory of the three prime ministers since 1991.

The freedom struggle also becomes a referent in the process of selective memory work to induce a sense of belonging to India and simultaneously to highlight the validity of religious pluralism before Indian audiences in and outside India. Once again, here, religious pluralism gets showcased as the equivalent of secularism. The Independence Day addresses (15th August), which are aired live on television (entirely for hours on the national channel and at least in parts by private news channels), become a site of commemoration in their own right amidst the show of parades of the Indian army battalions and artillery and the Indian Air Force's exhibition of its latest aircraft and the cultural depictions of the lifestyles of the various states of the country through tabloids. It is a day when the prime minister's address to the nation is systematically replete with memories of national heroes and the struggle for independence and cultural and national pride. Not surprisingly, it is also in the same addresses that the stage is set for profiling a *new* India, an *emerging* India, and a *secular* India.

---

[67] Rao, 'Tolerance for a Better World Order', speech delivered at the UNESCO-sponsored symposium on tolerance, New Delhi, 1 May 1995.

Today is an auspicious day for our country. Today we enter the 60th year of our independence. Today we re-dedicate ourselves to the unity and integrity of our country. Today we salute our beloved tricolor. We pay tribute to Mahatma Gandhi and all those freedom fighters because of whose efforts and sacrifices we secured our independence [...]. I give my assurance to every citizen that we will do our utmost to preserve our unity in integrity. Let those who want to hurt us by inflicting a thousand cuts remember—no one can break our will, our unity. No one can make India kneel.[68]

These given lines interweave the topical reference points of Indian independence from colonial rule, the celebration of national figures like Gandhi, the projection of an India which stands confidently in the world, and also the Indian sense of 'Unity in Diversity'. A nationalistic fervour is zealously created in stating that 'no one can break "our" unity. No one can make India kneel'. Also, the first struggle for independence of 1857 is a revisited theme in these specific addresses. On the occasion of the 150th anniversary of the same, Prime Minister Singh stated in his speech on two subsequent days,

The rebels of 1857 fought for freedom from foreign rule. They also fought to protect their *deen* and *dharma*. We must not make the mistake today of interpreting these terms in the narrow sense of the word 'religion.' What the rebels fought to defend was 'a way of life' which they feared the British were destroying [...] What is significant is that despite rallying under the flag of *deen* and *dharma*, the rebellion was united. There was no division between Hindus and Muslims in their resistance to alien domination [...] The events of 1857 stand as a great testimony and tribute to the traditions of Hindu Muslim unity in India [...] Sixty years hence we are a proud, self-confident, an intrinsically secular democratic republic.[69]

'Our freedom struggle is based on unity in diversity and this is also the basis of our national integration today.'[70]

[68] Singh, 'India Marching Steadily towards New Frontiers', address to the nation on Indian Independence Day, 15 August 2006.

[69] '*Deen*' and '*dharma*' broadly refer to the Urdu and Hindi terms respectively for 'religion'. Singh, 'Remembering the Martyrs of 1857 Uprising: A Saga of Heroism and Hindu–Muslim Unity', address at the 150th anniversary of 1857 function in Parliament, New Delhi, 10 May 2007.

[70] Singh, 'First War of Independence: Dazzling Example of India's National Unity', speech on the occasion of the 150th anniversary of 1857 function in Parliament, New Delhi, 11 May 2007.

The aforementioned lines once again remind the people of India of the Hindu–Muslim unity that united the first armed struggle for independence. As I have attempted to show with the examples that were singled out and presented here, there are specific themes which are systematically repeated within the addresses.

Diverting the Gaze: How Prime Ministers Forget

Memory, however, does not merely imply the tactical revisiting of the past[71] in order to conjure certain elements of a common heritage. Remembering is a selective action and thus implies forgetting too. Forgetting happens in three distinct ways in the speeches: firstly, when the prime ministers make a direct plea to the nation to forget the episodes of violence; secondly, when certain elements from the past are tactfully omitted; and thirdly, through diversion mechanisms positively to topics of development and emergence and negatively to questions like terrorism.

An example of the first may be located in Rao's words below, delivered shortly after Ayodhya in 1992,

> There is no need for us to go into history now. The need for us is to make new history and that is why for the first time after many years the secular forces of the country have come together, the secular parties with all their internal differences have come together. And we will forge ahead, we will see that the secular credentials of this country are re-established fully and what our great leaders through the constitution and through their own example told us to do, we will do it to the hilt.[72]

[71] On previous occasions in this chapter, I have specifically referred to the term 'strategic'. However, here, the word 'tactical' is used instead to highlight a crucial difference. De Certeau discusses the difference between tactics and strategy as follows, 'Strategies pin their hopes on the resistance that the establishment of a place offers to the erosion of time; tactics on a clever utilization of time, on the opportunities it presents and also of the play that it introduces into the foundations of power'. Thus, the word strategic is used to highlight a more spatially informed technique of communication used by the prime ministers, whereas tactical on occasions where temporality becomes the analytical axis (see M. De Certeau, *The Practice of Everyday Life* [Berkeley: University of California Press, 1984], pp. 39–40).

[72] Rao, 'Secular Forces Must Come Together', speech during intervention at the no-confidence motion at the Lower House of Indian Legislature, Lok Sabha, 21 December 1992.

Here as well, a clear awareness of time is generated—it is time for India to 'make' new history. Thus, an appeal is made to forget the events that are a national blemish to India's secular image.

The second type of forgetting happens by purposeful silences on previous blemishes on secularism. The history of colonial and postcolonial India is replete with occasions of communal tensions and riots between Hindus and Muslims, such as those following the partition. These tensions have found continuity in independent India as well, but are purposely forgotten within the ambit of the speeches in the prime ministers' rhetorical attempts to profile the nation as secular. It is important to also note that the killing of Sikhs in New Delhi, after the murder of the former prime minister Indira Gandhi by her Sikh bodyguards in 1984, is not mentioned even once by the first three prime ministers when referring to communal violence or making pleas to secularism (only since the Gujarat riots of 2002 was this episode revisited through the prism of communalism when numerous comparisons were drawn between the two). Tactically erasing negative examples of communal riots, though an obvious move, is an important mechanism to craft a secular nation.

The third type of forgetting which is the most prominent and consistent means in the speeches of all four prime ministers: the strategy of diversion.

In a negative sense, this forgetting refers to shifting the topic to external actors like Pakistan or on the theme of terrorism. One befitting example of the same can be seen in Vajpayee's speech delivered approximately a month after the Godhra train burning and the communal riots in Gujarat.

> Today the threat to our nation comes from terrorism. Wherever I went around the world, the heads of state or of elected governments complained to me that militant Islam is sowing thorns along their paths. Islam has two facets. One is that which tolerates others, which teaches its adherents to follow the path of Truth, which preaches compassion and sensitivity. But these days, militancy in the name of Islam leaves no room for tolerance. It has raised the slogan of Jehad. It is dreaming of recasting the entire world in its mold. [...] As far as we are concerned, we have been fighting against terrorism for the past twenty years. Terrorists have tried to grab Jammu and Kashmir through violence, but we have countered them. Jammu and Kashmir is an integral part of India and will forever remain so. No other country's dream will ever come true. Now other nations in the world have started to realize what a great mistake

they did by neglecting terrorism. Now they are waking up, and are orga-
nizing themselves. They are putting together an international consensus
against terrorism.[73]

Numerous themes come to light in this excerpt. First, in a speech delivered in the immediate aftermath of the Gujarat riots, Vajpayee (though
mentioning the riots in the previous part of the same speech) chooses
to divert the topic to international Islamic terrorism in the second part
of his speech. Within the architecture of the speech, thus, the attention
of listeners is diverted from the immediate occurrences in Gujarat to
the topic of Islamic terrorism in the world. Second, though Vajpayee
does mention 'tolerant' Islam, most of the text is dedicated to elements
of Jehad and Islamic terrorism. Third, Vajpayee speaks in the context of
a post 9/11 world, whereby the fight against terrorism became a commonly used phrase, therein gaining its legitimacy from a general international atmosphere. Fourth, the topic is diverted to the unconnected
subject of Jammu and Kashmir from the recently pressing topic of communal violence in Gujarat and the persistent other, that is, the state of
Pakistan (though the name is not mentioned per se, the reference 'No
other country's dream will ever come true' make this association highly
obvious and graphic).

Forgetting in a more positive sense refers to the consistent pattern to
be located in the speeches of all four prime ministers: using the diversion of development, growth, and India's emergence. Here, secularism
is projected as a precondition, a necessity for the materialization of the
promise and dreams of growth (see also Chapters 2, 3, and 4).

This is sometimes done explicitly, especially in the face of communal riots across the country (as in the advent of the Babri Masjid–Ram
Mandir controversy in Ayodhya in 1992 and the Gujarat riots of 2002),
when the internal audiences are directly asked to erase the memory
of such aberrations. After the demolition of the Babri Masjid, Prime
Minister Rao stated in an address to the nation on the occasion of
Independence Day,

> In case for another two or three years, we get bogged down with Hindu-
> Muslim riots, caste disputes and political and religious conflicts, and do
> not pay single-minded attention to economic progress, then our future
> will be bleak. This is the warning, we are receiving from all over the

[73] Vajpayee, address delivered at a public meeting in Goa, 12 April 2002.

world. Our wisdom is also sounding a note of warning. Whether we listen to the voice of sanity or not, it is up to us. I would say we must listen to it. I will give you an example from an Upanishad. There is a dancer. She is dancing while the musical instruments are being played and the songs are being sung. She has a pitcher on her head. She would not allow the pitcher to fall, dance she must, her whole body would sway, but the pitcher would remain on her head. *Maulistha Kumbha Prirakshana Dhiranativa.* This is what our attitude should be. Let There be any calamity; let us be involved in any other activity; but the pitcher of development placed on our head, the pitcher of advancement, the pitcher of economic programmes-that pitcher should never be allowed to topple down. This caution is a must for us. If we are cautious enough to keep moving forward, there will be no problem for us.[74]

In these lines, Rao skilfully uses the means of 'warning the world' and a scriptural reference to the Upanishads to divert the attention to the topic of growth. In fact, secularism (here, implying absence of religious conflicts) becomes a precondition for the larger goal of advancement and development. As in this excerpt, in numerous of Rao's speeches after the Ayodhya episode, the thrust is often rhetorically shifted to India's economic reforms.

Though in Rao's addresses, this implies the usage of terms like 'development', 'growth', 'advancement', and 'progress', by 2002 and the Gujarat riots, Vajpayee's vocabulary comes to be enthused with more optimistic terms like 'emerging', 'rising', and 'shining'. In the speech delivered in Goa after the riots, Vajpayee first diverts the subject to an international consensus against international Islamic terrorism and then continues to add:

We tell them through our own example that a large number of non-Hindus live in our country, but there has never ever been religious persecution here. We have never discriminated between 'our people' and 'aliens'. The modes of worship may differ, but God is one. Only the paths to reach him and realize Him can be different. It is for this reason that India's prestige is growing, India's reputation is rising. [...] We have large foreign reserves. We are progressing in science and technology. Our young men and women are excelling in global competition. Even in the

---

[74] Rao, 'Unity and Stability for Sustained Growth'. Note how in the above lines the element of the outside world is indicated when he states that this is a warning India receives from the world.

midst of an economic recession, India is progressing, India is marching ahead.[75]

The lexical shift in the aforementioned lines from the theme of pluralism to the topic of a 'progressing' and 'marching ahead' India is extremely graphic. Secularism (religious pluralism embedded in the neologisms described in section one) thus comes to share the same semantic space as an excelling and progressing India. This is a remarkable example of how the prime ministers have projected the discourse of a secular India into the domain of the 'India Emerging' story. By the time Singh's addresses are delivered, especially because his term did not see such violent communal tensions (barring the riots in the city of Muzaffarnagar, Uttar Pradesh, which only took place towards the end of Singh's second term as prime minister), the paradigm of secularism comes to occupy the same semantic space as India's emergence more frequently. These statements use metaphors of speed which are rhetorically attached to India. Thus, the terms 'marching', 'rising', 'growing', 'shining', 'turning', 'moving', 'forwarding', and 'changing'—all are used as indicative of a linear trajectory into some space-time compression which is 'ahead' and away from any violent past(s), recent or remote.

This diversion strategy thus stresses an India that is 'emerging', 'transforming', 'on the move', 'on the march to progress', etc., all being occasions that attempt to shift the story and the listeners' attention to a 'new' imagination that is accorded by the prime ministers to the nation. On certain occasions, the themes of secularism and India as an emerging power are beautifully brought together in a way as if the bliss of upcoming economic strength will overrule anything that might question India's secularity. As an example, in the following lines, Prime Minister Singh states that,

> It is not only us but the entire world, which is viewing India as an emerging power of these times. The whole world is eagerly watching the manner in which India is making rapid economic progress. And this economic growth is happening within the framework of a liberal democracy. Our country is a multicultural, multireligious, multilingual and multi-ethnic nation. Nowhere in the world do we have an example of a country of a 100 crore (one billion) people seeking their economic and social destiny

[75] Vajpayee, Address delivered at a public meeting in Goa, 12 April 2002.

within the framework of a secular democracy. It is because of this that the entire world's attention is riveted on us. It is the result of our combined hard work that India today has made its mark on the world stage and we feel proud of our standing in the comity of nations.[76]

Here, India's emergence is presented as taking place within the framework of a liberal 'multireligious' and 'multicultural' secular democracy. India's distinctiveness is embedded not only in that it is an emerging power, but one that is explicitly secular and democratic.

India is on the road to progress. The whole world is watching us with expectation [...]. There comes a time in the history of a nation when it can be said that the time has come to make history. We are today at the threshold of such an era. The world wants us to do well and take our rightful place on the world stage. There are no external constraints on our development. [...] We must have the self-confidence to realize that we are second to none, that Indians are as good as the best. [...] Let us come together, as one nation, strengthened by our plurality, to work shoulder to shoulder and build a new India.[77]

In this excerpt, we once again find that Singh emphasizes India's emergence as 'the best'. But this is done within the framework of its plurality. Here, plurality echoes of one of the multifarious meanings attached to secularism. Noteworthy, however, is that Singh mentions this secularity only as an additional adjective. The core of India is presented as empowered by its plurality that will help realize the dream of a 'new' India.

Another graphic illustration of combining the themes of economic growth, pluralism, and secularism may be located in the following excerpt delivered by Singh in the Lok Sabha in a motion of thanks to the President's address:

Whenever I go abroad, people marvel about the existence of a country of a billion people with all the diversities, with all the poverty of its masses, yet trying to seek its economic and social salvation in the framework of a functioning democracy, in the framework of a democratic polity, in the framework of commitment to rule of law, commitment

---

[76] Vajpayee, 'A Resurgent India: The Roadmap for Lasting Peace and Prosperity', address to the nation on Indian Independence Day, 15 August 2005.

[77] Vajpayee, 'A Resurgent India: The Roadmap for Lasting Peace and Prosperity', address to the nation on Indian Independence Day, 15 August 2005.

to all fundamental human rights. I sincerely hope that whatever we do, we should take pride in these characteristics because we are one-sixth of the human race. If India succeeds in finding its economic and social salvation through democracy, through commitment to rule of law, through respect for all fundamental human freedom, I dare say that we will become the harbingers of a message of change for the better, for the entire countries in the world.

India, therefore, has a message. That message is one of strengthening democracy; that message is strengthening the forces of secularism; that message is the persistent quest of gender equality; that quest is that development must lead to social and economic equity. These are the guiding principles given to us by the Foundering Fathers of our Republic.[78]

Once again, we find that not only are the themes of 'economic and social salvation' combined with the 'forces of secularism', but that the prime minister's words also serve the important role of cementing the nation through the lexicon of national pride, whereby secularism and pluralism become the emulative assets translating into a 'message' that India carries for the world.

Summary

The analysis in this section was undertaken to introduce the lens through which a secular India is profiled for 'internal' audiences. In order to establish India's secularism, *all* three prime ministers draw from a reservoir of internally valid resources. A plethora of Indian neologisms to the term are utilized, and the paradigm is indeed discussed and explained at length. There are several existing tropes to the term and, among others, the notions of tolerance, communal harmony, dharmanirpekshta, the ideal of sarva dharma sambhava (all religions are true), and the master code of unity in diversity are employed to ground India's secularism before its own people. In doing so, the prime ministers speak to their audiences in a language that is understood by them, that is, the paradigm of secularism is lent a domestic understanding. In this regard, secularism is understood in three parallel directions.

Firstly, not as implying irreligiousness or atheism, but as recognizing 'religion' as an intricate part of people's individual and collective

[78] Singh, 'Prime Minister's Reply to the Lok Sabha Debate on the Motion of Thanks on the President's Address', New Delhi, 24 February 2011.

existence. Thus, the language employed to associate the term *secular* with India does not hesitate to use religiously overloaded references. In fact, religious scriptures, mythologies, epics, and philosophies are used to propagate the very cause of secularism.

Secondly, certain elements to the debate are not clarified. Even if it is elucidated that the entry of religion into politics or vice versa is undesirable, a space of ambivalence persists and the boundary between the two spheres is never lucidly sketched. This prevailing ambiguity in the understanding of the ideal produces a lexical confusion where most of the Hindi terminology itself may carry several meanings. The emphasis shifts instead to celebrating Indian pluralism that is seen as the founding basis, even a synonym to secularism.

Thirdly, secularism is explained to audiences in relation to its prominent ideological other, communalism, and pseudo-secularism, depending on the general rhetoric of the party that the prime ministers have belonged to.

It thus emerges that secularism is a theme that is not only staged as being desirable, but also essential for the survival of Indian national integrity. The analysis of the prime ministers' speeches after 1991 has revealed that secularism has becomes an important tool that has helped to concoct a sense of 'nation-ness' or national solidarity. It has also been used as an adequate platform to revisit Indian national heritage, a remembrance of what is loosely and homogenously referred to as 'the Indian' civilizational past, its movement for national independence, its charismatic national heroes, and its rich philosophical literature. It thus contributes to the generation of a 'regime of historicity' (Hartog, see below in the third part of this chapter), whereby collective memory is evoked and simultaneously constructed. The nation is fabricated by a selective restaging of history which often brackets and silences episodes, such as religious riots during Partition, those in the advent of the prime minister Indira Gandhi's assassination that led to atrocities inflicted on Sikhs in 1984, or the ones of Ayodhya and Gujarat.

The Indian variant of secularism, owing to its unique character of being grounded in a genuinely diverse society, is also profiled as a basis of Indian exceptionalism, a trait that makes India distinct in the world. In a remarkable rhetorical strategy to divert the audiences from the theme of communalism, the prime ministers extend the argument of India's uniqueness into the discourse of the new, transformed, emerging

India. Secularism then becomes the basis of Indian uniqueness in that it is repetitively elaborated that India is not only an emerging nation, but that it is *the only* one that seeks emergence within a liberal democratic and secular framework. Here, China and Pakistan are the prominent others against whom the idea of India is materialized.[79]

The section has shown how secularism is presented as a unifying necessity for the sake of the Indian nation. It suffices to end with the statement made by Vajpayee in the immediate aftermath of the Gujarat riots in March 2002, 'If India is not secular, then India is not India at all.'[80]

Responding to the Outside: Secularism as a Shared Ideal

As highlighted in the introduction, this shorter section endeavours to elucidate how the imagination of a secular and an emerging India is projected for the perceived 'outside'. This raises the obvious question of why and whether at all it is imperative for the prime ministers that India be projected as *secular*. The analysis presented below will help answer this crucial question.

Numerous overlapping themes (with those delivered to perceived internal audiences) make an appearance in these addresses. For example the theme of *religious pluralism* or the phrase *unity in diversity* is also celebrated in these speeches. In an address to a joint session of the parliament on the occasion of the then Russian President Vladimir Putin's visit to India in 2000, Prime Minister A.B. Vajpayee noted, 'We are

[79] An illustrative example in this direction: 'India was conceived as a political laboratory in which the boldest social experiment of the 20th century was to be conducted. Among the first of the colonies to ignite the fire of freedom from colonial rule, this land was also the first to commit itself whole-heartedly to development in a democratic framework based on universal adult franchise. The principles that define our Constitution, have come to be accepted as universal principles of civilized existence. Pluralism, secularism, republicanism, social justice and equality of all under the rule of law. We have much to be proud of in this inheritance' (Singh, 'India: The Next Decade', address at the Indira Gandhi Conference, New Delhi, 19 November 2004).

[80] Vajpayee, 'Dialogue Process Should Continue', statement by the prime minister, New Delhi, 10 March 2002.

commemorating this year the fiftieth anniversary of the establishment of our Republic. We have reposed faith in the principles of democracy which are today universal ideals providing for the growth of the human being and society. Our democratic structures are rooted in the cardinal values of pluralism, secularism and tolerance.'[81]

The underlying idea is to paint and celebrate a multireligious, multilinguistic, and multi-ethnic India. This is, however, done carefully and strategically with a more pressing intentionality to present India as not in conflict with a larger comity of nations, that is, in ideological cohesion with the themes of democracy and pluralism (which are depicted as common ideals between the states of India and Russia here). This tendency is a persistent pattern in the speeches. On numerous occasions, the prime ministers rhetorically produce an ideological common ground between India and other countries, especially under the larger umbrella of the United Nations. Vajpayee attempts the same in Washington, 'It is the proud privilege of both India and the United States that our two countries are models–one in the East and the other in the West–of democracy as well as unity in diversity. We both [sic], cherish, preserve and promote universal human rights such as freedom of speech, political choice and religious belief.'[82]

Clearly, the prime minister attempts to achieve multiple ends here. An emphasis is placed on Unity in Diversity, as done also in addresses before internal audiences. Vajpayee also locates India in ideological conformity with the United States, which is projected here as a vibrant diversified democracy. Thirdly, this established image of India is projected as a desired ideal, a 'model' for other nation-states. Another example is the following statement made by Narasimha Rao, much earlier (in 1993), with regard to Indo–UK relations,

> Both our governments share a strong commitment to the UN, its basic purposes and principles as enshrined in the UN Charter. At a time when the UN is increasingly being called up to assume difficult and delicate additional tasks, a particularly onerous responsibility devolves on countries like such as ours in promoting its noble aims. We recognize the

[81] Vajpayee, 'A New Chapter in Indo-Russian Relations', special joint session of the parliament on the occasion of the visit of president of Russia, Vladimir Putin, New Delhi, 4 October 2000.

[82] Vajpayee, 'Gandhiji an Apostle of Peace', speech while unveiling the statue of Mahatma Gandhi, Washington, 16 September 2000.

threat to pluralistic and democratic societies and nation states from religious fundamentalism and narrow ethnic chauvinism. These threats need to be firmly countered through a renewed commitment to democracy and secularism.[83]

Here, the emphasis is placed not just on the paradigms of democracy and secularism, but also on a larger ideological framework of the United Nations. India is thus projected as a *responsible* secular democracy, which embraces ideals that belong to a larger community of nation-states. Such accounts where the prime ministers lexically project conformity with other nation-states and where secularism becomes one of the adjectives or defining characteristics are abundant in the corpus of the addresses analysed. Some illustrative examples of such repetitive utterances made on different international platforms or in India, but where target audiences are also international, by Prime Minister Singh are as follows:

'Singapore and India share values of democracy, pluralism and secularism and this gives both our countries convergent perspectives on many regional and international developments.'[84]

'Relations between India and Australia trace their origins to our colonial period. Even during the Cold War years, Australia remained a visible presence in our popular psyche. A large Indian-origin community of nearly half a million has made Australia its home. Our shared belief in parliamentary democracy, secularism, multiculturalism, and free enterprise provides the basis for our relationship.'[85]

'India and Canada share much in common. We are separated by distance but we are united in our values. We both cherish our freedom, our democratic way of life, our pluralism and our spirit of tolerance.'[86]

'We wish to accelerate the pace of India's transformation in partnership with the international community. A fast growing India can expand

[83] Rao, 'India and the United Kingdom', banquet speech in honour of the British prime minister, Mr John Major, New Delhi, 25 January 1993.

[84] Singh, 'Prime Minister's Statement to the Media on the State Visit of the Prime Minister of Singapore', New Delhi, 11 July 2012.

[85] Singh, 'Prime Minister's Speech at the Banquet Hosted in the Honour of the Prime Minister of Australia', New Delhi, 17 October 2012.

[86] Singh, 'Prime Minister's Speech at the Banquet Hosted by the Prime Minister of Canada, Toronto', 27 June 2010.

the boundaries for the global economy. A democratic, plural and secular India can contribute to tolerance and peaceful co-existence among nations of the world.'[87]

'We share the principles of pluralism, democracy, tolerance and multiculturalism.'[88]

An observation that emerges from all speeches addressed to external audiences is that, though secularism is repetitively evoked, the prime ministers do not elaborate upon its underlying meaning in these addresses. In the external contexts, it seems to suffice to state that *India is secular*.

Thus, the semantic contours of the paradigm are not explained. This seems to be done with an underlying awareness that the Indian context may provide for multiple comprehensions that do not necessarily comply with the idea of a strict separation of the religious and the state spheres, or that oratory in general relies heavily upon religious resources to explain secularism and render it credible. To avoid this clash, the addresses usually entail the term and pause, evoking it yet not explaining it, thus maintaining a teleological idea of a 'modern' secular India.[89]

Another conclusion that follows from the analysis is that in the external settings, the paradigm of secularism is evoked, on most occasions, coterminously with the terms democracy and pluralism, as becomes extremely lucid in all the excerpts cited earlier. Instances of the same may also be located in the addresses meant for perceived internal audiences. However, such co-occurrences of these terms are inevitably to

---

[87] Singh, 'Prime Minister's Address at the 66th Session of the United Nations General Assembly, New York', 24 September 2011.

[88] Singh, 'Prime Minister's Opening Statement at the Plenary Session of the IBSA Summit, Pretoria', 18 October 2011.

[89] It is here again that a regime of historicity may be located. That references to an ancient civilizational past embedded in the soil of secularism, and a 'new', 'modern' emerging India that also embraces secularism are made simultaneously should not be viewed as contradictory stances viewed through the misplaced lens of tradition versus modernity or past versus future. It formulates part of a discursive strategy, whereby both categories of a secular ancient civilization and a modern forward-looking or emerging secular India are allowed to coexist in a present which uses the past and the future for identifying its contours.

be traced in *all* addresses (that deal with one of the themes) delivered to external audiences. In speeches given to Indian audiences, the term democracy, though used repetitively, is not explained in depth, its ingredients are never unpacked as the paradigm of secularism is. This implies that the meaning of the term is not contested as such and has not been open to controversial debates as secularism.

One justification as to why India ought to be secular, especially offered to external audiences (but which also finds continuity with addresses delivered to internal audiences), is with regards to the Jammu and Kashmir conflict. Though in the internal sphere, it is reiterated that there is no other possible environment in which such diversity could thrive,[90] in external settings, the argument is sometimes also presented emphatically before the perceived outside. The paradigm of secularism in such instances serves two simultaneous purposes—first it is used to defend India's ideational basis—that is, to explain that 'India' can survive only if its diversity flourishes under secularism and, second, to project the state of Pakistan as a prominent other. The following lines graphically sketch the same:

> As for Kashmir, it is a part of India. It has always been, right from the word go on 15 August 1947. Before that Kashmir came to India and is a part of India. Pakistan thinks that Kashmir should go to Pakistan because there is a Muslim majority. My answer and India's answer is that what do we do with some states where there is a Christian majority? Where do we send them? This is an absurd situation. We are a secular state. We have Hindus, Sikhs, Muslims, Christians, Parsis, and all the religions of the world are available in India. I can't send people on religious lines to different countries and have only one community or religion in India. That is not my philosophy at all. The basis of the Indian state is secular. If the basis of the Pakistan state is different then I cannot help it. They have every right to have their basis whatever the basis they like. But my basis is I absorb every one. Indian history is witness that for thousands of years we have been absorbing cultures from abroad and also sending our own culture outside. So, there has been so much give and take, so

---

[90] A prominent example of the same is when Vajpayee stated, 'For us Kashmir is not a piece of land; it is a test case of Sarva Dharma Sambhava, secularism. India has always stood the test of a secular nation. Jammu and Kashmir is a living example of this. And this itself is Kashmiriyat.' (Vajpayee, address to the nation on Indian Independence Day, 15 August 2002.)

much of exchange of cultures, it is just not possible for any Indian mind to accept that all people belonging to one religious denomination only should be in one country and no one else should come. That's not the philosophy of India.[91]

As evident, secularism is projected as the paradigm that allows multiple religions to coexist in India, thus formulating the backbone of a unified national space. (As pointed out earlier, Rao categorically stated post Ayodhya, 'The delicate fabric of our nation woven around democracy and secularism is the only anchor sheet for our country's existence.')[92] However, certain other elements also emanate from the address earlier. First, Pakistan is projected as the prominent other in that it lays claims on the state of Jammu and Kashmir which is viewed as an integral part of India. Second, the lines reflect why the Indian state's claim on the controversial territory is ever more emphatic, because to accept Pakistan's accession of the state would be a severe blow to India's secular image. Third, the line 'it is just not possible for any Indian mind to accept that all people belonging to one religious denomination only should be in one country [...]' illustrate how a *pars pro toto* (parts that stand for the whole) synecdoche is employed here so that the 'Indian mind' may be generalized to epitomize acceptance and a secular outlook. Lastly, we return to the theme of temporality in the line, 'Indian history is witness that for thousands of years we have been absorbing cultures from abroad', once again an attitude towards time is generated and a heritage is conjured so as to generate a present and legitimize the inevitability of a secular India.

Secularism in Narendra Modi's Times

As the general elections for 2014 approached, heated debates on the nature of Indian secularism returned to the forefront. This, especially since the BJP's announcement of its next prime ministerial candidate,

[91] Rao, 'Contributing to the New World Vision', address on Challenge and Opportunity in the Post Cold War Era—An Indian Perspective on the Emerging Structure of Inter-State Relations, at the French Institute of International Relations, Paris, 29 September 1992.

[92] Rao, 'Countering Communal Forces', address to the nation in the aftermath of Ayodhya, 6 December 1992.

Narendra Damodar Modi, chief minister of Gujarat, a controversial political figure, who had remained in power in the state since, and in spite of the riots in 2002. At the same time, one finds an internal, relatively recent, shift within the BJP's oratory, especially when it comes to the prime ministerial candidates.[93] This relates to a conscious 'playing down' of the hardliner, right-wing rhetoric that bases itself solely within the ideology of Hindutva and a move to an agenda which relies on themes of development and fighting corruption, profiting from the more recent anti-corruption mass movement(s).

One such illustration of Modi's own attempt at underplaying the Hindutva ideology was the *Sadbhāvanā Mission*,[94] a movement he initiated in his fourth term as chief minister in 2011 and later again in 2012. The aim was to travel across numerous locations in Gujarat, accompanied by one-day fasts (thirty-six in total), for promoting communal harmony and shifting the party agenda completely to developmental issues. In a blog entry dated 16 February 2012 on his own website,[95] Modi made this shift to development lucid by stating,

> [...] On one hand, we have our nation being dominated by the poison of caste, religion based vote-bank politics that has deeply disappointed and broken the trust of every Indian. The 'Divide and Rule' philosophy adopted by the Centre has caused irreparable damage to the image of our great nation.

[93] One could say that this had already begun by 2004 when the BJP launched 'India Shining' as its electoral campaign, making claims for a 'New Emerging' India as its achievement. The agenda, however, reached new heights with Modi's electoral campaign ten years later, whereby the much discussed and debated Gujarat model of development became the showcase example.

[94] For details, see http://www.narendramodi.in/sadbhavana-mission-a-touching-people%E2%80%99s-movement/ (accessed on 8 March 2013).

[95] It is important to note that unlike any of his predecessors, the current prime minister, since his chief ministership phase in Gujarat, has resorted to all forms of new social media for addressing his audiences (as emphasized in Chapter 1). The personal website that continues to be functional even now, in spite of his movements being traced on the PMO's official website, also contains blog entries, which have also formulated an important source for this book. A systematic reading of the same led to the conclusion that these blog entries often combined numerous sentences from Modi's speeches delivered in different scenarios, but, often, also comprised new elements.

On the other hand Gujarat has adopted the path of peace, unity and brotherhood. Gujarat has shunned vote-bank politics and adopted the politics of development. 'Collective Efforts, Inclusive Growth' has replaced the age-old divisive practice of 'Divide and Rule.'

Gujarat's present decade has presented a model of development based on Sadbhavana and progress and our successful experiment in the form of the Sadbhavana Mission has given a new ray of hope to our country-men who are immersed in deep disappointment.[96]

In these lines, the terms *sadbhavana* (literally meaning 'goodwill'), unity, and brotherhood fill the oratorical gap to compensate for the term secularism. Though such excerpts belong to the large corpus of Modi's pre-election speeches, they are an important window to understand three factors from the perspective of this book. First, they explicitly show the intertwining of the two themes of secularism and neo-liberal economic developmentalism—how the Gujarat model became a means to silence the debate(s) on secularism. Second, they may be read as a preparation phase for Modi's entry in national level politics, whereby his tarnished image (as the chief minister of a state where gross human rights violations occurred against the Muslim community) required to be sanitized of communal politics. Third, they highlight another important aspect of Indian politics more generally, especially with regards to the role and image of the prime minister—the need and expectation of having a politician at the level of prime minister who bears the clean image of a leader of national calling, one who can rise, and is seen as being, above the profanities of everyday caste, communal, and regional politics. It is for the same reason that Vajpayee was deemed to be a successful choice as the prime ministerial candidate for not having a hardliner image like Advani.[97] This period of

[96] Modi, 'Sadhbhavana Mission: A Touching People's Movement', Modi's blog entry on his website, 16 February 2012, http://www.narendramodi.in/sadb-havana-mission-a-touching-people's-movement-3054 (accessed on 8 March 2013).

[97] The topic of the prime minister and *other* speeches, whereby politicians like Vajpayee and Modi discard the typical Hindutva-laden vocabulary as the prime ministers, while their important cabinet ministers/party members (Advani during Vajpayee's term and Rajnath Singh/Amit Shah during Modi's term) fill the missing oratorical gap, is certainly a topic that invites further research. For this insightful point on 'Good cop, bad cop' politics, I am thankful to Margrit Pernau.

transformation thus becomes an important intervention to understand the context of Modi's oratory in general.

As possibilities of Modi's prime ministership candidature were prognosed more concretely, the theme of secularism continued being re-evoked, especially by Modi's opponents. A pattern to be ciphered though is that most of Modi's comments on secularism come as a response to allegations. For example, in an interview in 2012, Modi stated, 'My constitution says that the country must be secular, political parties must be secular, leaders must be secular. This is an article of faith, and we believe in justice for all, appeasement of none.'[98]

This retort came as response to Bihar chief minister Nitish Kumar's statement that the nation needed a 'secular leader' as the prime minister. In the earlier excerpt, one finds continuity in Modi's rhetoric to that of the former prime ministers who have repetitively employed the constitution as a legitimizing means to establish Indian secularism. The sentence 'appeasement for none', however, echoes of an indirect attack on political opponents (who, as stated before, have persistently been accused by the BJP for appeasing the Muslim minority for vote banks and therein being 'pseudo-secular'). This, as stated, thus emerges as a consistent strategy employed by Modi when speaking on the subject of secularism—to present it as a normative reality while simultaneously not explaining its ingredients and utilizing it as an oratorical tool to respond to political opponents. In that sense, most of Modi's oratory on secularism revolves around responses to accusations levied on him rather than on laying out its tenets and coordinates.

> The Congress party is now staring at certain defeat. In all likelihood, it won't cross the hundred figure mark. As a last ditch effort out of a sheer desperation, it is trying to hide in the bunker of secularism. The Congress party and some of its allies are trying to resort to fear-mongering among the minority community. However, they do not realize that today's India no longer responds to fear-mongering. Most people can see through such gimmicks.[99]

[98] Modi, interview with *The Economist*, response to Bihar Chief Minister Nitish Kumar's statement 'India Needs a "Secular 'Leader'" for Prime Minister', 28 September 2012.

[99] Modi, interview given to *The Times of India*, 6 May 2014.

Secularism here ('bunker') thus becomes the lexical tool to rhetorically counter political opponents who are projected as 'fearmongering' the Muslim minority to vote against the BJP. In the same interview, Modi repeats the phrase when referring to the Congress party and diverting the political message of the electoral campaign to development. One may locate how Modi tries to establish a common ground with the Muslim minority (while actually never mentioning the same as such and using the term 'the Indian voter'):

> Today it is anachronistic to think that a community won't be interested in development and good governance. In fact, it is an insult to the intellect of the Indian voter by such parties that believe that he can be made to forget about real issues of poverty and development and get him to vote in a particular manner just by making him insecure by fear-mongering. The Indian voter today is more mature than what our political opponent give him credit for. I have heard the statements of several prominent leaders of the minority community asking Congress not to try and make them insecure by fear-mongering. They have started to ask what really has Congress done for the minorities and this is where Congress secures a big zero. It is their mind set that they need not do anything substantive for improving the lives of the people and they can just manipulate them along caste and communal lines [...] now this type of politics has attained its expiry date [...][100]

The strategic importance accorded in his oratory to development acquired a new dimension in 2013, when, in a speech delivered via a conference call[101] addressing the Indian diaspora, Modi stated 'My definition of Secularism is simple: India First. Whatever you do, wherever you work, India should be the top priority for all its citizens. [...] Country is above all religions and ideologies. [...] Nothing less than India's well-being should be our goal. And if this happens, secularism will automatically run in our blood.'[102]

As evident, Modi skilfully shifts the secularism debate to the question of development (usually citing the Gujarat model of development as an

---

[100] Modi, interview with *The Times of India*.

[101] Modi was denied a visa to the US for ineffectively managing the Gujarat riots since 2005, a condition that would change only after his election as the prime minister of India. Since that time, he has visited USA several times.

[102] Modi, speech delivered (conference call) to the Indian diaspora after being denied a visa to visit the US, 10 March 2013.

illustrative example within the context of the same speech), whereby the subjects of religion and secularism were drifted aside for the promise of growth.

Another noteworthy strategy of the current prime minister when dealing with the topic of secularism before perceived internal audiences is the role of wit/humour and, more importantly, sarcasm in inflating the term and its meaning. Three prominent examples will clarify this point. In 2012, in an address at a book launch ceremony, which would normally not qualify as a relevant source for the analysis here, Modi stated,

> 'Lions are the pride of Gujarat [...] the Central Government seems to only be bothered about tigers (refers to 200 Crore grant for tiger conservation). It is unfortunate that despite Gujarat's lion population coming to a rise to 411, it is not coming to the notice of the Centre. Is it because tigers are secular and lions are communal?'[103]

As evident, in a verbal attack on the UPA government's 'Save the Tiger' campaign, Modi utilizes the space for not just making a point for lion conservation in Gujarat, but also as an open statement on the topics of communalism and secularism. It is in examples such as these that one notices how the term secularism is rendered hollow and emptied of meaning for the sake of oratory triumph. On another occasion, Modi refers to the infamous case of the missing buffaloes of a member of parliament (from the Samajwadi Party, which has historically been a BJP opponent in the state of UP).[104] 'People's sons disappear: it doesn't make any news. But a minister's buffalo disappears it became news here in UP. And I was thinking, for sure, the Minister will make a statement that his buffalo's disappearance is a threat to secularism.'[105]

Sarcasm thus becomes a means to achieve two simultaneous purposes: first, to verbally ridicule the state of affairs in the law and order situation in the state (this specifically acquires significance, given that

---

[103] Modi, address at the book release of *My Journey into the Wild* by Sanat Shodhan, Gujarat, 6 June 2012.

[104] The case made headlines in media, whereby it was reported that the MP Azam Khan's buffaloes were stolen (or missing). Approximately 100 local police officers and sniffer dogs were employed to speedily find the buffaloes.

[105] Modi, address at political rally, excerpt in reference to the case of Azam Shah's lost buffaloes in Rampur, Lucknow, 2 March 2014.

Modi made this statement in an election rally which was attended by an estimated 500,000 people). It can also be an attempt made by Modi to overemphasize how much undue importance is given to such episodes under the garb of secularism. And second, to conflate the paradigm of secularism within the cow-buffalo protection / secular-pseudo versus secular debate, and empty the term of its meaning by shifting to the ambit of competitive communalisms.

A final example of resort to sarcastic humour to respond to the numerous allegations made against him by political opponents, and yet a successful presentation of his own viewpoint on the controversial Sanskrit language debate is as follows. In a speech addressed to the Indian community in Dublin, Ireland, where a group of Irish children recited mantras in Sanskrit to welcome the prime minister, Modi stated, 'Now when Irish children are reciting mantras in Sanskrit, singing welcome songs in Sanskrit, it is a matter of happiness. We can do this in Ireland but had there been anything like this in Hindustan, who knows there would be questions raised on the secularism of the country.'[106]

Though sarcastic humour becomes the means to realize oratorical triumph against his political opponents in all three aforementioned examples, it is noteworthy how it simultaneously serves the purpose of maintaining ambiguity, given that none of these elucidate Modi's own vision of secularism, its defining coordinates, and its tenets within the sphere of formal state politics.

The subject of secularism recently returned to the forefront in the wake of the intolerance debate in the Lok Sabha in November 2015. Originally dedicated to a celebration of the Constitution Day (26 November 2015) to commemorate the 125th birth anniversary of B.R. Ambedkar, the session witnessed heated debates on the growing intolerance in the country, as alleged by several politicians from the opposition. Here, incidents of attacks on churches and Christian institutions in New Delhi, the public lynching of Mohammad Akhlaq, an ironsmith from Dadar, UP, who was murdered on suspicion of storing beef in his refrigerator, the *Ghar Waapsi* or 'homecoming' campaign launched by certain Hindu hardliner groups to 'reconvert' Christians and Muslims to Hinduism, the return of national awards by numerous members of the Bollywood film industry and artists across the country, the beef ban

---

[106] Modi, speech to the Indian Community, Dublin, 23 September 2015.

in most states in the country—all become the context that sparked the debate. During the debate, Modi iterated:

> I have said this earlier in this House, but I want to say it again that governments have only one religion—India First. A government has only one holy book—the Constitution of India. The country can only work in accordance with the Constitution. It is through the Constitution that the country is strengthened [...] the foundational principles that have guided the growth of the nation are our strength. They are our spiritual strength.

My Idea of India—Satyamev Jayate

My Idea of India—Ahimsa Parmo Dharma

My Idea of India—Ekam Sad, Vipra Bahudha Vadadti Satya

My Idea of India—Vasudhaiva Kutumbakam

My Idea of India—Sarva Pantha Sambhav.[107]

As the given excerpt shows, the Constitution of India and its foundational principles are equated to a 'spiritual strength', and though Modi shies away from using the term *secularism* itself, each of the phrases used before can be traced among the numerous neologisms utilized to define secularism by the previous prime ministers. Just within the purview of the excerpts cited in this chapter (given that not *all* such utterances were cited to avoid repetition), the phrase *Ekam Sad, Vipra Bahudha Vadadti Satya* (truth is one, sages call it by different names) was used for the first time by Rao in 1995, *Vasudhaiva Kutumbakam* (the whole world is one family) by Singh in 2012, and *Sarva Pantha Sambhav* (all religions are true) used by Rao for the first time in 1992, Vajpayee in 1996 and 2003, and Singh in 2005 and 2007. In these lines, Modi's oratory on secularism thus emerges as being in lexical conformity with those of his predecessors. Thus, to sum up what emerges from an analysis of his speeches for perceived internal audiences—first, the relative absence of the term from the addresses; second, when used, its tenets usually remain undefined (in terms of divisions of state and religious/public and private spheres) and it becomes a lexical means to respond to political opponents; third, often linguistic wit and sarcasm are utilized

---

[107] Modi, Address at the Intolerance Debate in the Lok Sabha, 27 November 2015.

to empty the term of its meaning, though this never occurs within the context of speeches meant to have a ritualistic character (for example, the Independence Day speeches); fourth, in larger state ritualized scenarios like Lok Sabha debates and Independence Day speeches, Modi's oratory relies upon the lexical repertoire built by his predecessors; and fifth and most important is in phrases like 'Secularism to me is India First', one sees how the debate is shifted from an actual discussion of the tenets of the paradigm to the question of development.

Before perceived external audiences, Modi's stance is in complete conformity with that of his precedents. Here, secularism is presented as a normative fact, a statist reality, a non-debatable asset whose coordinates are assumed to be clear and an adjective, which is pushed into the list of terms utilized to define India along with the terms pluralism and democracy. The aim, as for the previous prime ministers, is to produce an oratorical ideological cohesiveness with other nation-states, as also with larger international platforms.

Continuities and Discontinuities in the Oratory of the Prime Ministers

Three important conclusions follow the analysis undertaken for this chapter.

First, the extensive body of material that was analysed for the chapter reflects an internal transition in (the projection of) the 'Emerging India' story and its relation to secularism. The speeches analysed cover a time span ranging from 1991 to the present. As pointed out in the section earlier, in Rao's repertoire, secularism is projected as a precondition for India's growth and for the materialization of the economic reforms. It is thus a strategy to divert public attention from communal disharmony to underline how India *will* or *could* emerge. A new intensity in this projection may, however, be situated in the addresses of the prime ministers to follow Rao. Thus, during Vajpayee's term, the adjectives and metaphors of speed utilized to describe the 'New India' become more frequent. In Manmohan Singh's addresses, secularism almost appears to be an obvious adjective that is slipped beside terms like democracy, sharing the same semantic space as the description of an Emerging India, but where both are not mutually codependent variables, rather coexisting oratorical truths. Narendra Modi's oratory has only rejuvenated the same strategy of rendering development the primary agenda by defining secularism as 'India First'.

The second conclusion that follows is that for perceived external audiences, there are no transitions in the addresses of Rao to Vajpayee through Manmohan Singh and finally to Modi. A consistency is maintained on the paradigm of secularism, and similar rhetorical strategies are employed by the successive prime ministers to profile a secular India, primarily given that the coordinates of the paradigm are never unpacked for audiences and contesting meanings are avoided.

The third conclusion relates to the subtle similarities and dissimilarities in the oratory of the four speakers. One very direct illustration of the same may be noted below. On New Year's eve in 2000, Vajpayee states,

> The Ayodhya issue is another problem from the past that we should not allow to remain unresolved too far into the future [...]. Few can deny that Ram occupies an exalted place in India's culture. He is one of the most exalted symbols of our national ethos. Respect for him transcends sectarian barriers. Many Indian revere him as an avatar of God and some regard him as Maryada Puroshottam. Non-hindus, too, see in him an ideal king. [...] Had it not been so, poet Allama Iqbal would not have penned the following eulogy to Ram,

> The cup of India has always overflowed
> With the heady wine of truth.
> There is something so sublime in her mysticism
> That her star soars high above constellations.
> There have been thousands of rulers in this land
> But none can compare with Rama.
> The discerning ones proclaim him the spiritual leader of India [...]
> His lamp gave light of wisdom
> Which outshone the radiance of the whole of humankind [...][108]

In the aforementioned lines, Vajpayee speaks in defence of his own secular image on being verbally attacked about the same in the parliament when labelled as a 'hardliner'. While Vajpayee attempts to inculcate religious tolerance by citing the example of a Muslim poet writing praise for a Hindu god, he nonetheless evokes the figure of

---

[108] Vajpayee, 'Time to Move on Towards a Better Future', speech delivered on New Year, Karakoram, Kerala, 1 January 2001.

the deity Ram as a 'national' one. Thus, Ram becomes a symbol of Indian 'national ethos', an ideal king whose state in India witnessed an unprecedented era of justice, rather than being a religious deity for its majority population. This is an isolated instance when a prime minister's address evokes the very religious deity's imagery that had been the bone of contention leading to conflict over decades. In no other speech are references made to the deity along similar lines where the imagery of Ram is symbolically projected as representative of a national culture. Similarly, in another controversial speech delivered after the riots in 2002, Vajpayee stated:

> [...] This is our outlook which treats all faiths equally. Yet, accusations are being hurled today that secularism is under threat. Who are these people accusing us? What is the meaning of secularism for these people? India was secular even when Muslims hadn't come here and Christians hadn't set foot on this soil. It is not as if India became secular after they came. They came with their own modes of worship and they too were given a place of honour and respect. They had the freedom to worship God as per their wish and inclination. No one thought of converting them with force, because this is not practiced in our religion; and in our culture, there is no use for it.[109]

In these lines, Vajpayee reiterates the neologisms that were already underlined in the first part of this chapter, that is, all faiths are equal. What is different, however, in comparison to his Congress counter-parts is that he projects India as being secular *before* the arrival of Muslims and Christians. Though these lines appear to be in sync with the rhetoric of a tolerant Hindu India on surface, they also inevitably produce Islam and Christianity as the 'outsiders'. These lines nonetheless made Vajpayee's address controversial, particularly because it was delivered barely a month after the Gujarat violence. The line 'this is not practised in our religion, and in our culture' assumes that 'our' becomes co-equitable to a generalized Hinduism which is tolerant of Islam and Christianity.

In a similar vein, Modi, when asked a question about whether there will be place for Muslims in his vision of India at a leadership Summit (in 2013), stated:

---

[109] Vajpayee, address delivered at a public meeting in Goa, 12 April 2002.

This question is a problem only for those who do not know Hindu and Hinduism. Hindu philosophy says *Ekam Sad, Vipra Bahudha Vadadti Satya*—God is one and there are many ways of knowing and calling him. Hindus are the only ones in the world who say God is one. A Hindu never says 'a Muslim's God', 'a Sikh's God', he says God is one and he says that the God is how the worshipper is [...] a place where such philosophy prevails, the reason why such a question is raised there is because Hinduism has not been understood.[110]

Though the phrase Modi utilizes from the Upanishad has also been used by two of his predecessors, Modi's emphasis here on *Hindu* religious repertoire is comparatively much more emphatic, making secularism essentially a Hindu achievement. This points to the most prominent internal difference among the rhetoric of the four speakers—the resources used to explain secularism to Indian audiences, and the timing of the term secularism and its derivatives within a speech.

In Vajpyaee's rhetoric (as also shown for Modi), one finds a clear generalizing 'Hindu' vocabulary that derives from primarily Hindu and the Hindi language resources. Here also, unlike Singh and Rao, Vajpayee and Modi's religious pluralism emerges as a co-equivalent of Indian secularism, one that is embedded in a generalized polytheistic Hindu tradition, which can *tolerate* or accommodate other world views.

Another notable difference relates to when the word is used in a given address. Given that the events of Ayodhya and Gujarat demanded immediate defence of the paradigm, it is obvious that the term is more frequently explained in the speeches after 1992 and 2002. However, in Singh's addresses, one finds no decrease in the number of times secularism is mentioned. The difference is that here it is not contested as before anymore, but presented as a normative fact which is why it often appears as an adjoining adjective in most speeches. It is repetitively slipped beside other words like democracy, ancient culture, civilizational ethos, liberal, multilinguistic, multi-ethnic, etc., and is therein routinized in the addresses. In the case of Modi's rhetoric, the term becomes a lexical means to counter political opponents, whereas the plea to shift the focus to questions of growth and development become much more aggressive. These differences apart, the prominent similarity in the

[110] Modi, address at the HT Leadership Summit, New Delhi, 5 December 2013

rhetoric of all the four speakers is the unconditionality and inevitability of presenting India as secular. There is an unquestioned finality with which secularism is presented as an assumed necessity.

How Silences Speak and Expressions Silence: 'Secularism' as Interface

Interface

Noun

1. A point where two systems, subjects, organizations, etc. meet and interact: *the interface between accountancy and the law.*
   Chiefly Physics a surface forming a common boundary between two portions of matter or space, for example between two immiscible liquids: *the surface tension of a liquid at its air/liquid interface.*
2. *Computing* a device or programme enabling a user to communicate with a computer: *a graphical user interface.*
3. A device or programme for connecting two items of hardware or software so that they can be operated jointly or communicate with each other: *an application program interface.*

Verb

[no object] (interface with)

1. Interact with (another system, person, etc.): *you will interface with counterparts from sister companies.*
2. *Computing* connect with (another computer or piece of equipment) by an interface: *the hotel's computer system can interface automatically with the booking system [with object]: a device which can be interfaced with a computer.*[111]

From the given analysis, it follows that the paradigmatic notion of secularism formulates an *interface*, 'a common shared boundary', a zone of contact between the *perceived* 'internal' and 'external', as sketched by the prime ministers through their addresses to profile a *secular* India. The prime ministers use the term as a dual-faced mirror, each side of

---

[111] *The Oxford English Dictionary* (Oxford: Oxford University Press, 2012).

this two-way mirror reflects such understandings of the term that are derived from the particular context (internal and external). In internal settings, it acquires different ambivalent understandings that draw their resources from the Indian context of religious pluralism. In the external settings, the term is used as such to concretize the image of India as being in ideological cohesion with the world as an 'emerging' *yet* 'secular' democracy.[112] However, the ambivalences produced by the different understandings to the paradigm are never demarcated clearly in their contours within the addresses. The term secularism thus becomes a terminological common ground on the basis of which the prime ministers produce parallel semantic zones, which allow for multiple comprehensions of the paradigm to coexist simultaneously. Through their speeches, all prime ministers re-evoke and even *creatively reinterpret* it to fit the dual purpose at stake. Given each side finds its own vision duly reflected in the term, cultural misunderstandings are pre-empted and screened out, although different semantics are respectively intended. In this way, the term seems dually convenient, serving both sides of the dual-faced mirror respectively. Secularism, here, is a conceptual interface par excellence.

Besides these spatially located demarcations, secularism is also utilized as a temporal interface between India's projected past and its projected future. It helps construct the image of India's new promising future, while it also bridges with India's past. Thus, it is used to generate a 'regime of historicity', as historian François Hartog summarizes 'methods of relating to time: forms of experiencing time, here and elsewhere, today and yesterday, ways of being in time'.[113] A particular regime of historicity reflects the vantage point of the present, which is 'the focal point of the representation of time; the past and the future are represented, thought of, and felt as departing from and returning to the present'.[114] Regimes of historicity thus indicate how time is produced

---

[112] Here, the *yet* is not used to suggest an opposition between the terms *emerging* and *secular*, but rather to demarcate an opposition which is intended towards the neighbouring state of Pakistan.

[113] F. Hartog, 'Time and Heritage', *Museum International* 57, no. 3 (2005): 7–18.

[114] A. Hannoum, 'What is an Order of Time?', Review of F. Hartog, *Régimes d'Historicité: Présentisme et Expériences du Temps* (Paris: Seuil, 2003), *History and Theory* 47(2008): 458.

from the perspective of the present by instrumentalizing the categories of past and future in order 'to determine what the present is or is not'.[115] India's prime ministers feed into the imagination of an India of the future, to inform the world, as well as 'Indians at home' of an India that is emerging and secular. Simultaneously, the past is utilized as a reservoir for projecting a 'national' heritage. My analysis has shown how the categories of the past and the future are made to converge in the term 'secular'.

When looking at the speeches which were delivered before and after the demolition of Babri Masjid in Ayodhya, and in the face of riots across the country (1991–), the underlying assumption is that after such conflicts, the discursive attempts to 'rescue' the paradigm of *secularism*, as also the idea of national solidarity, are at the pinnacle of their intensity, resonating with the desperation to reweave a national imagery. However, during the same phase, the attempts to paint a 'secular' India also overlap remarkably with the 'emerging' India discourse(s) in that after 1991 and the formal institutionalization of the neo-liberal economic reforms, there was a new vigour with which the narration of a rising India was invested. Speeches delivered to Indian audiences on the commemorational anniversary of Indian independence (15 August 1991–2008) show how the special occasion of 'remembering' independence is used to revisit ideas of India's *secular* national heritage and, as a result, its national unity.

Within the purview of the speeches of the four politicians, subtle differences between the rhetoric of the BJP leaders Vajpayee and Modi and the Congress leaders Rao and Singh highlight not just the ambivalences in translating secularism for Indians, but also that certain categories like *Indian civilization*, *Indian heritage*, *our traditions*, *our past* become shorthand terms, often like secularism itself, presented as undisputed facts. Though cosmetically the same, the visions behind these terms are different (for Vajpayee and Modi, more of a Hindu achievement, and for Rao/Singh, a syncretic mix which also utilizes the lexical archive of other religious resources). More importantly, minus these differences, the paradigm of secularism remains an important stake within the discourse of all the three leaders. All three prime ministers lend their voice to a consistent national master narrative that bases the idea of India itself within the ideal of secularism.

---

[115] Hannoum, 'What is an Order of Time?', 458.

What is new to this discourse is that in the external scenario, the emphasis shifts towards maintaining an ideological cohesiveness with the world. Especially in environments such as the United Nations, where the values of democracy, liberalism, secularism, and pluralism are much celebrated norms, the prime ministers' addresses provide the additional tinge of conformity. These addresses were meant for the 'outside' and do not indulge in elaborate explanations of the secularism paradigm. In most addresses, the prime ministers stop after having stated that India is a secular democracy which now seeks its economic destiny of emergence. No advances follow such statements. Thus, a silence is strategically maintained. Paradoxically, in the 'internal' settings, there appears to be an overemphasized elaboration of the explanations, induced almost with a sense of urgency and desperation. In addition, a vocabulary that employs an overload of 'religious' referents is utilized. However, despite these elaborate explanations, the boundaries between the 'religious' and the state are never explicitly explained. They are rather silenced under the garb of neologisms. Thus, the external reflects spaces of silence, which inevitably *speak* of a strategic quiet maintained in explaining secularism, while the internal reflects an arena of overexpression that nonetheless *silences* the gray zones of controversy looming large over the paradigm in India. The dual-faced mirror of secularism is thus utilized to reflect only what the resources of the given context allow to be reflected.

The externally accorded role and the self-portrayal of India being secular are, however, not mutually exclusive and independent of each other. The rhetorical fabrication of the national 'self' is also a reflex, a response to the portrayal of the 'self' vis-à-vis the 'other'. The Indian prime ministers profile India for the outside to produce its national image, but this image also speaks to the outside's imagination of India. The theme, so aptly summarized in Martin Buber's maxima *Der Mensch wird nur am Du zum Ich*,[116] also reverberates in Homi Bhabha's writings on nationalism, 'The "other" is never outside or beyond us; it emerges forcefully, within cultural discourse, when we think we speak most intimately and indigenously "between ourselves".'[117] This can be gauged in Vajpayee's lines in the aftermath of Gujarat riots,

[116] M. Buber, *Ich und Du* (Stuttgart: Reclam, 2008).

[117] H. Bhabha, ed., *Nation and Narration* (New York: Routledge, 1990), p. 4.

'From Godhra to Ahmedabad, in so many places, there are so many inci-dents of people being burnt alive, including helpless women and chil-dren. This is a blot on the nations's forehead and has grievously harmed India's image in the eyes of the world.'[118]

'I do not know what face I will show them (the world) now after the shameful events in Gujarat.'[119]

Prime Minister Rao is also fully aware of the theme, as the following passage exemplifies:

'I may add here that apart from all these compelling reasons, there is another equally compelling reason, perhaps even more compelling, why India should appear as functioning as a united nation without fissures, without any internal differences on religion, on caste or any other basis. I have had the experience of interacting with several other Prime Ministers and Heads of State during my visits abroad as well as members of the press from abroad. When they do not have anything to say against our policies, the question that is hurled at is what is hap-pening to Ram Janma Bhumi. Now, this has not only remained within the country as one of the most difficult problems but it has travelled abroad and it is figuring in the kind of attitude that other countries, the media of other countries are adopting towards India just as a point of criticism, just to say that whatever the policies, they may be good, but at the same time there is something inherently wrong with India and the Indian society. They cannot remain peaceful. They cannot remain united. This is the kind of innuendo one gets from the questions put to us and from the talks that we have—of course, all done in a very diplomatic, polished language, but nonetheless equally critical if you remove all the embellishments. That is what I think is very important. This problem and problems like this are marring India's image abroad and this is very important from the point of view of what we really want to do with our new policies. We want to integrate the Indian economy with the world economy; we want to become a model for investment, for progress, for peace, for secularism, for tolerance and this is the mission which we have accepted for India. Having accepted

[119] Vajpayee, official statement made by the Prime Minister's Office, New Delhi, 3 March 2002.

[120] Vajpayee, statement made during his visit to Ahmedabad, Gujarat, 4 April 2002.

this, it is necessary to see that whatever is coming in the way of this image being built up abroad is removed at the earliest.[120]

Rao's statement reveals that there is a strong image, a profile or idea of India which is constantly being construed outside of India. More importantly, he points to the importance of Indians' *awareness* of that image abroad. Furthermore, India's future trajectory, its economic rise is presented as inextricably connected with the theme of secularism.

This chapter has attempted to show how secularism is translated by the Indian prime ministers in its most public and official version for audiences within and without. It has elucidated how the Indian prime ministers 'speak' the Indian nation secular, unleashing its (E)merging faces—that is how the external and internal imaginations of India are made to *merge* in the concept of secularism. At the same time, the secular India *merges* with that of an *emerging* India in the same way as India's past and future are lexically made to *merge* in the addresses to conjure a present which is *emerging*.

---

[120] Rao, 'Towards a Strong and Vibrant India', speech delivered at the first meeting oft he reconstituted National Integration Council, New Delhi, 2 November 1991.

Conclusion

Chapter Review

Public speeches of Indian prime ministers, though one of the most popular and pervasive sources of communication with the population, have so far not received adequate and systematic scholarly attention. How have the speaking prime ministers styled and shaped statist visions around the neo-liberal economic reforms and secularism for Indians, and how do they position 'India' through them in the world? In order to answer this larger overarching question posed by the book, Chapter 1 commenced by first tracing the distinct legacy of the prime ministerial office and the tradition of public speech in India. This was especially to emphasize the importance that should be accorded to speeches, particularly those of the prime ministers, as sources in their own right.

The chapter commenced by elucidating how India's first prime minister, Jawaharlal Nehru, negotiated the executive powers of the Prime Minister's Office to make it the most powerful one in the cabinet, hierarchically a higher 'First Among Equals'. Nehru's persona and his overarching presence as a founding father figure in Indian politics became the means to render the authority of the office irrefutable. His visions and his words (right from the hallmark speech on the eve of Indian independence) diffused into a plethora of state rituals. A study of Nehru's legacy is also important for understanding the basis of the project of 'New India' in the decades following independence. This becomes inevitable for tracing the underlying continuities and transitions between Nehru's nation-building project of founding the 'New

India' and the structurally adjusted nation-branding project of 'New India' by the prime ministers after 1991. The chapter has traced how Nehru's visions (for example, the staging of master trope of the 'unity in diversity', or the emphasis on 'Temples of Modern India') and his pervasive public presence textured the office as that of a teacher and caretaker, therein rendering it the face of the nation. His personality has impacted the allure of the office to an extent that he is either overtly praised or criticized as the leader of the nation, but never ignored. As the prime ministers to follow have often been judged through the prism of oratorical styles and the aesthetics of public presence so well established by Nehru, this section also located how the current prime minister, Narendra Modi, attempts to entangle and disentangle himself from the Nehruvian styles of communicating with the Indian population.

The second section of the chapter has traced the gravity of the spoken word in India by embedding it in its long-standing cultural history of orality and aurality. In independent India, Nehru's public presence disseminated numerous inauguration ceremonies, parades, and flag-hoisting events, through which he ritualized the tradition of the speaking prime minister. Not only did he forge the importance of the Prime Minister's Office, but he also institutionalized political speech as one of its defining characteristics. Thus, he not only inscribed the prime minister as the nation's face, but also as the nation's tongue in that he laid the foundations of an oral repertoire of political speech acts which, as has surfaced throughout the chapters, echoes intensely in the speeches of all the four prime ministers. The significance of public speech and orality, which also implies a particular historically shaped context of aurality, becomes all the more understandable if India's long-standing political as also didactic traditions of teaching and learning are taken into account. The concluding section of the chapter has shown how the prime ministers' speeches, even though a more recently ritualized phenomenon since independence, belong to and have been inserted in this enduring cultural context.

Chapters 2 and 3 have engaged with the question of how the prime ministers have marketed the neo-liberal economic reforms as the foundation of India's (achieved and desired) economic success. The analysis has revealed that the reforms have been discursively framed as a normative fact, a preordained trajectory for the Indian economy, and an inevitable means to realize that vision of success. The addresses of the prime ministers are loaded with temporal justifications to cloak economic and ideological shifts in new legitimacy. All speakers have produced multiple temporalizing tactics, whereby the 'reformed' and structurally adjusted present is conceived and conjured in relation to a putative other time, the future and the past, so as to produce its irrefutability.

Chapter 2 has presented the category of 'the future'. It has illustrated that in order to give currency to the reforms, the prime ministers repetitively conjure the vision of an idealized future projected as one of prosperity and success. Growth is presented as a human necessity, and reforms become the inevitable means to realize this dream of growth for all. Other coordinates of the perfect future promised through the reforms are: consistent economic growth within a democratic framework, a vibrant open economy which engages with the world, visions of new urban centres and IT hubs, India's advancement as a future IT superpower, a blossoming knowledge economy, and an educated and employed youth. In this order of time, India's move to the future is understood not so much as an uncalculated measure, but rather a controlled trajectory which does not succumb to 'unlimited capitalism', as Prime Minister Rao has put it. Thus, we learn how the prime ministers establish a difference to the lose category of the 'West' in stating that India does not stand for blind, inhuman capitalism, but that the promise of the future is that growth will be sustainable and, more particularly, equitable. However, as these visions of a future gain momentum along with the projections of an 'Emerging India', one can trace the simultaneous emergence of the category of an 'other' within India emerges behind this rhetoric. This refers to the large sections of Indian population who are no immediate winners of the reforms, but who are tranquilized into the lure of the future, by being relegated to a 'waiting room' condition, to borrow Dipesh Chakrabarty's revealing formulation. The analysis has shown how the PMs attempt to convince the majority of the population at the fringes of the economy of the hope and optimism of the reforms through the claim that they, too, will be incorporated in India's success, but only *eventually*. Trickle-down effect is legitimized by informing people that they ought to wait for the benefits of the transitions to reach them.

The next section of the chapter has shown how, in order to conjure the new neo-liberal present and future, the first three speakers have paradoxically employed a vocabulary of the socialist past. Although what is being introduced is a drastic shift from the economic and ideological frameworks of the Nehru and Indira Gandhi eras, the resources used to present the new (and the future it promises) borrow heavily from the lexicon of Nehruvian developmentalism. Thus, terms like 'self-sufficiency', 'self-reliance', 'sovereign economy', which are reminiscent of Nehru and, to some extent, Indira Gandhi's vocabulary, are used to normalize change. These are slogans and phrases which have spilled over space and time and survived and stuck over in people's lexical memories. Thus, PMs employ the technique of presenting the new by using a vocabulary which is not so new. This is done so as to take away the insecurity, anxiety, and unpredictability of change, and to rather present it as calculated, secure, and familiar. By utilizing resources from India's homogenized past, imbibed with socialist overtones, market liberalization is paradoxically given the cosmetic appearance of being a socialist project. The main objective of the speakers is thus not to inform audiences of a drastic change in operation, but to present that change as continuity, to render it familiar, and therein naturally very 'Indian'. This section has thus elucidated how the project of conjuring the future is never fully devoid of shades of the past. The amorphous category of the future is not just a *looking ahead* into another temporal order, but also *temporally looking back*, using that which is already available as lexical memories to imagine, speak of, and project that order.

In continuity with the overlapping and interwoven nature of the two temporal orders of the projected future and the homogenized and selectively remembered past, Chapter 3 started with the illustration of how another temporal tactic employed is to introduce a brief temporal breach with the immediate economic past. This is done by demonizing the Indian economy before the reforms by using terms like 'sick', 'dark', etc. This should, however, not be read as a complete disconnect with the past which consistently serves as a reservoir of numerous resources utilized to paint the envisioned future and the present. Even though the period before the reforms is given negative attributions, the figure of Nehru persists as an untarnished hero in all descriptions by the first three prime ministers. Aware of the weight of personalities like Mohandas Karamchand Gandhi and Jawaharlal Nehru in the population's lexical memories, the prime ministers resort to these figures as spaceless, timeless signs which are hollowed out of their original meaning. Their words are systematically reiterated, even if their viewpoints and visions of India have stood in contradiction to the aims of neo-liberal economic ordering. The prime ministers thus, de facto, dexterously present 'new wine in old casks'.

This generalizable past is not just celebrated as the long-standing origin of India's 'civilizational ethos', but also as a 'religiously' loaded and mythologically grounded well of long-standing values, which is cunningly tapped by the prime ministers' oratory to present the reforms, as if in cultural continuity with a proud and long-standing heritage.

Another temporalizing tactic of the prime ministers frames the reforms as embedded in a sequence of events, an order of time which is seemingly preordained. In certain speeches the reforms are legitimized by presenting them as part of a larger cosmic scheme whose destiny cannot be questioned nor reversed. Here, the reforms appear as the only way out, the ultimate trajectory which is part of a larger cosmic plan for India.

A separate section deals particularly with the oratory of the current prime minister, Narendra Modi. Here, an analysis of speeches up to 15 August 2016 was undertaken to trace how Modi, who announced his arrival through a revitalized vocabulary of change and 'Good times', has embedded his oratory in temporal legitimizations of a structurally adjusted economy. This is particularly important to see how a prime minister, who is not a founding father of the reforms (like Rao or Singh), and who comes to occupy the office twenty-three years after their introduction, has reified them as the only means towards a prosperous future. In line with the other three prime ministers, Modi's oratory is also heavily embedded in the politics of time. Pasts and futures of the Indian economy are conjured in order to make a case for the present neo-liberalized economic order. Modi speaks of transformation as a catalysing force, though with a vocabulary that carefully projects it as a constant condition of 'work in progress'. Whereas, in one particular regime of historicity employing the present, the Indian economy is produced as having 'arrived', in another simultaneously used one, it is rather projected as one that requires persistent investment by its citizens in order to realize its full potential. Legitimizing references to national heroes (though new ones like Sardar Patel are used more often than Nehru) and a Hindi and Hindu vocabulary of a civilizational ethos abound here, much in consistency with Prime Minister Vajpayee.

A consistency in oratorical content, which follows from the findings of this chapter, is that all four prime ministers cloak transition in the form of market liberalization in the vocabulary of cultural continuity. Even if there are differences of style and repertoires, and the purpose of each government is to show how it will do what the previous governments have failed to achieve, each speaker has attempted to embed the economic order in a longer ethos of cultural security, whereby acceptance of change itself is made into something very Indian. The Chapters 2 and 3 have thus shown how different regimes of historicity, different orders of temporality—embedded in engagements with an envisioned ideal future, an ever looming and selectively remembered past and a pre-ordained messianic temporal scheme—become the necessary instruments in producing India's embrace of neo liberal reforms as inevitable and irrefutable.

Chapter 4 has then flexed the lens to another classificatory category effectively used to profile India's emergence and therein naturalize the reforms. Here, the emphasis shifts from the temporal legitimizations used to ground the reforms as unavoidable to more spatially informed strategies. This means that *what* the prime ministers speak is also a strategic decision determined by *where* they speak. The demarcations between what the prime ministers perceive as 'internal' audiences (Indians in and outside of India) and those deemed 'external' (world audiences) become prominent here.

For specifically Indian audiences, the prime ministers embed the reforms in a changing world scenario where open economies increasingly become the governing norm. This world in transition makes it imperative for India to adapt to change as well. However, it is made clear that even though India changes, this adaptation is a calculated and controlled measure. This is done to once again produce a sense of security. Here a twofold strategy, which will give that security to people, unravels: firstly, Indians are assured that Foreign Direct Investments will not jeopardize India's economic sovereignty and, secondly, that in spite of upcoming changes, India's cultural core is and will remain fundamentally secure. Next, the threat of the amorphous term 'globalization', which both economically and culturally shakes most of the world, is lexically converted into an opportunity which India eagerly grasps. Here, a difference is established to many countries. Unlike many other economies of the world which have been fragile to open markets, India is projected as withstanding external pressures and emerging in spite of them, especially in the aftermath of the economic crises of 1997 and 2008. This is because India's embracement of globalization is a controlled and calibrated move. Thus, what stands as a potent danger and entails anxiety is in turn used to stage exceptionalism, showing how India, unlike many other economies of the world, survives transitions and even benefits from them. This staging of Indian uniqueness, be it in reference to how India's economy has been resilient to the world financial crises, or in reference to its cultural core embedded in its robust 'civilizational past', is thus used to produce India as becoming coeval with the 'West', that is, to state that India has caught up with the world now.

Before external audiences, the message of the first three prime ministers is clear and unidirectional. Embedded in a world which itself is in transition, specifically in a post-cold war context, India too has embraced change and opened its economy to the global economy. Here, the new India is over-celebrated, and the 'outside' is informed of a 'brand India', an India which is the ideal investment destination. These addresses thus highlight vigorous invitations to the outside to come and invest in the economic miracle, which is the new emerging India.

In the concluding section that analyses the current prime minister's addresses up to 15 August 2016, we come to the conclusion that there are remarkable similarities in his oratory to the spatializing strategies of his predecessors, though not without the flavour of numerous new elements. The content of what is said cannot be separated from the context that Modi assumed office twenty-three years after the formal institutionalization of the reforms, a long time span during which his predecessors, Singh and Vajpayee, persistently attempted to naturalize the reforms in a way that they become co-equivalent to the metaphor of motion ascribed to the Indian economy.

Thus, as evident in his speeches, by the time Modi has assumed office, the idea of a transforming global economy has become a pervasively repetitive oratorical truth. Similar to his predecessors, Modi therefore repeats the vocabulary of a changing world that necessitates that Indian economy should continue on the path of transformation and not exist in isolation. The noteworthy difference is, however, that the same organizations which were seen as a threat to Indian financial sovereignty during the terms of Rao and Vajpayee become the quantifiers of India's

increasing economic prowess. There is no urgency to justify and legitimize the validity of international bodies like the IMF, the World Bank,
or the World Economic Forum. Instead of being viewed as organizations that encumber sovereignty they, in fact, become a means to stage
India's economic arrival in the world economy as can be deduced from
the fact that Modi relies on the statistics produced by them to show
India's 'Ease of doing business'.

Similarly, the justifications offered by Rao and Vajpayee in favour of
Foreign Direct Investment, that is, that it should not be seen as threat to
be feared, but rather as a positive change for India, are missing in Modi's
addresses, primarily because there is no necessity for the same.

Another conclusion that follows is that in Modi's speeches, the
reforms become an *unspoken* fact, a normative truth that does not require
any contextualization or justification; they become synonymous with
India's emergence as an economic powerhouse of the world. While on
the one hand, for perceived internal audiences, the world is projected as
being increasingly interconnected by all prime ministers, necessitating
India to also 'open up', on the other hand, the world economic situation is frequently produced as being in crisis (through examples like the
Asian crisis of 1997 or the world economic crisis of 2008). This, then,
becomes a context against which Indian emergence is projected by *all
four speakers*. In Modi's addresses, there is newfound vigour, enthusiasm,
and confidence with which India is projected as an active key player
in constituting the world economic order, rather than being a passive
witness of changes in that order.

Chapter 5 has analysed how the different prime ministers have
profiled India as 'secular'. It elucidated how the production of Indian
secularity converges with the discursive staging of India's emergence,
both for what the prime ministers conceive as the 'outside' world as also
for those seen as 'Indian' (in and outside India).

It follows from the analysis that the paradigmatic notion of secularism constitutes an *interface*, 'a common shared boundary', a zone of
contact between the *perceived* 'internal' and 'external', as sketched by the
prime ministers through their addresses. The prime ministers use the
term as a dual-faced mirror—each side of this two-way mirror reflects
understandings of the term that are derived from the particular context.
In 'internal' settings, it acquires different ambivalent understandings
that draw their resources from the Indian context of religious pluralism.

In 'external' settings, the term is used as such to concretize the image of India as being in ideological cohesion with the world as an 'emerging', *yet* 'secular democracy'.[1] However, the ambivalences produced by the different understandings to the paradigm are never demarcated clearly in their contours within the addresses. The term secularism becomes a terminological common ground on the basis of which the prime ministers produce parallel semantic zones, which allow for multiple comprehensions of the paradigm to coexist. Through their speeches, the first three prime ministers evoke and even *creatively reinterpret* the term to fit the dual purpose at stake. Given that each side finds its own vision duly reflected in the term, cultural misunderstandings are pre-empted and screened out, although different semantics are respectively intended. In this way, the term seems dually convenient, serving both sides of the dual-faced mirror respectively. Secularism, here, is a conceptual interface par excellence.

Besides these spatially located demarcations, secularism is also utilized as a temporal interface between India's projected past and its projected future. It helps construct the image of India's new promising future, while it also bridges with India's past. The three prime ministers feed into the imagination of an India of the future to inform the world as well as 'Indians at home' that India is emerging and secular. Religiously peace guaranteed by state secularism is seen as a necessity for materializing economic emergence. Simultaneously, different elements from a selectively evoked past are utilized as a reservoir for projecting a 'national' heritage. The analysis has shown how the categories of the Indian and non-Indian, and the past and the future are made to converge in the term secular.

When looking at the addresses which were delivered before and after the demolition of the Babri Masjid in Ayodhya, and in the face of riots across the country (after 1992), the underlying assumption is that after such conflicts, the discursive attempts to 'rescue' the paradigm of secularism are at the pinnacle of their intensity, resonating with the desperation to reweave a sense of nation-ness and national solidarity

---

[1] Here, the *yet* is not used to suggest an opposition between the terms *emerging* and *secular*, but rather to demarcate an opposition which is intended towards the neighbouring states of China (projected as undemocratic) and Pakistan (projected as unsecular).

embedded in religious pluralism. The analysis has shown how during this phase the attempts to paint India 'secular' also remarkably overlap with the humble beginnings of the discourse(s) on 'Emerging India'.

In the external scenario, the emphasis, when claiming for state secularism, is towards maintaining an ideological cohesiveness with the world. Especially in environments such as the United Nations, where the values of democracy, liberalism, secularism, and pluralism are much-celebrated norms, the prime ministers' addresses provide the additional tinge of conformity. These addresses are meant for the 'outside' and do not indulge in elaborate explanations of the paradigm. On most occasions, the prime ministers stop after having stated that India is a secular democracy, which now seeks its economic destiny of emergence. No advances follow such statements. Thus, a silence is strategically maintained. Paradoxically, in the 'internal' settings, there appears to be an overemphasized elaboration of the explanations, induced almost with a sense of urgency and desperation. In addition, an oratorical lexicon that employs an overload of 'religious' referents is put to use. However, despite these elaborate explanations, the boundaries between the 'religious' and 'the state' spheres are never explained explicitly. They are rather silenced under the garb of neologisms. Thus, the 'external' reflects spaces of silence, which inevitably *speak* of a strategic quiet maintained in explaining secularism, while the internal reflects an arena of overexpression, which nonetheless *silences* the gray zones of controversy looming large over the paradigm in India. This especially relates to silences maintained on personal religious codes that often come in conflict with constitutional rights and state secularism as well as on how the overemphasis on India not being irreligious (when defining the tenets of state secularism) in effect silences the presence of atheism and non-belief. The dual-faced mirror of secularism is thus utilized to reflect only what the resources of the given context allow to be reflected.

With regards to the oratory of Prime Minister Modi, numerous conclusions are to be drawn on state secularism: first is, the relative absence of the term from Modi's addresses. Second, when used, its tenets and discontents usually remain undefined (in terms of divisions between state and religious/public and private spheres as in the case of Modi's predecessors), and it becomes a lexical means to respond to political opponents. Third, often linguistic wit and sarcasm are utilized to empty the term of its meaning, though this never occurs within the context of speeches that have ritualistic character and weight (for example, the Independence Day speeches). Fourth, in larger state-ritualized scenarios like Lok Sabha debates and Independence Day speeches, Modi's oratory relies upon the lexical repertoire built by his predecessors. Fifth, and most importantly, in phrases like 'Secularism to me is India First', one sees how the debate is shifted from an actual discussion of the tenets of the paradigm to the question of development.

Before perceived external audiences, Modi's stance is in complete conformity with that of his precedents. Here, secularism is presented as a normative fact, a statist reality, a non-debatable asset, whose coordinates are assumed to be clear, and an adjective, which is pushed into the list of terms utilized to define India along with the terms 'pluralism' and 'democracy'. The aim, as for the previous prime ministers, is to produce an oratorical ideological cohesiveness with other nation states, as also other larger international platforms.

Speakers Compared

Consistencies

All four prime ministers have propagated the reforms as irrefutable. In that sense, there are not four different stories but a consistent singular narrative to discover, whereby normalizing reforms has been the objective of each prime minister, regardless of his party affiliation. Here, rather than searching for sanitized and surgically separable differences, what is more revealing is how the discourse conjured by all four prime ministers reflects a process of reifying market liberalization. The anatomy of that discourse reveals a process of utilizing strategies and tactics that establish the reforms as inevitable, as the most promising way towards a collectively aspired prosperous future, rhetorically stabilize them by countering opposition to them, embed them in a longer tradition of an Indian 'civilizational ethos' and finally project them in a way that they become synonymous to the 'India Emerging' narrative. This happens up to a moment of their almost disappearance in the oratory of the current prime minister by whose term they appear to be a pre-established oratorical truth.

Thus, a traceable consistency has been the ongoing appropriation of the reforms by the BJP led governments in spite of their introduction by Congress led governments at the centre. The BJP was one of the severest opponents of the reforms at the time of their institutionalization. Once in power at the centre (1998-2004), however, the Vajpayee led coalition vigorously forwarded the cause of the reforms. This diametric twist in the party's ideological stance vis-à-vis the reforms demanded a thorough justification before audiences. Hence one finds that in his speeches Vajpayee not only supports the reforms, but also attempts to appropriate them as his own. Thus, on numerous occasions in Vajpayee's addresses they are dubbed as a 'de-politicized' issue. Opposition to the Congress led governments on any aspect related to the reforms is only produced through the rhetoric of 'reforming the reform process'. The same may be concluded also for PM Modi, who on no single occasion has questioned or critiqued the reforms, but like Vajpayee criticizes his predecessor's government for not rendering the reforms poor friendly.

The same holds true with regards to the profiling of India as a secular nation. Whether in the addresses of Rao, Singh, or Vajpayee, that India should be secular is never a debated issue. All three governments and their prime ministers have unequivocally and consistently made a case for a secular India. With Modi, who has been in much limelight as a contested figure, secularism becomes a pre-given truth which need not be defended, but whose coordinates are projected as so natural to Indian society that the debate is then shifted to questions of development. It is also here that the two themes of market liberalization and secularism become intensely intertwined.

In Chapter 1, I mentioned two long-standing tropes in Indian politics which have been essential ingredients of Nehruvian nationalism—firstly, the master code of 'unity in diversity', which has helped produce the syncretic image of a pluralist India, and secondly, the staging of Indian exceptionalism, which is utilized to conjure India as different from the wider world. Both these themes have been a consistent element of the addresses of all four prime ministers to constitute an *economically emerging secular India* as well. Both have served the cause of temporal tactics and spatial strategies used by the prime ministers, whether to explain the tenets of state secularism or to embed the reforms in an older civilizational ethos that embraces change. Thus, certain elements of Nehru's rhetorical repertoire have remained consistent and have informed the approach of India's prime ministers, even though the content of the message to be communicated has transformed drastically.

Manmohan Singh (2004–14), who is often celebrated as the architect of the reforms, held the portfolio of finance minister in Rao's Congress government. His addresses echo a familiarity with the Rao's (1991–96) oratory. On numerous occasions, Singh even makes direct references to Rao's speeches. In a similar tradition of inter-referential intertextuality, on several occasions Modi has utilized the repertoire and the, by now iconic, figure of Vajpayee as a legitimizing hinge for his claims.

Inconsistencies

Though the message of reifying the reforms and establishing state secularism as unquestionable is a common agenda for all four prime ministers (barring Modi's relative silence on the topic of secularism, which he breaks when provoked to respond to questions or opposition), their oratory is not devoid of subtle internal differences. These reflect in the repertoire of resources used to lend a cosmetic texture to what is being said.

With regard to market liberalization, we have seen that in order to naturalize change in the shape of the reforms, each of the prime ministers refers to different resources from 'the' past. Congress-affiliated prime ministers, Manmohan Singh and P.V. Narasimha Rao, employ a higher degree of socialist rhetoric reminiscent of the Nehruvian years. This applies especially to Rao. As the initiator of economic transitions, one perceives a greater sense of caution in his addresses. Given the urgency with which the changes were introduced, Rao demonstrates great judiciousness to camouflage the changes in continuity. A.B. Vajpayee's rhetoric is more reminiscent of an amalgamation of Nehruvian developmentalism and a socialist vocabulary borrowing heavily from Indira Gandhi's era (though Indira Gandhi herself is never evoked as a figure). However, this is heavily blended with BJP-laden *Hinduizing* rhetoric. Thus, illustrations, especially from Hindu mythology utilized for the cause of open markets and even foreign direct investment, are replete here.

An important difference informed by the temporal context of the addresses, however, is that unlike Rao, who needed to establish a relation of co-equivalence between a promising future and the reforms, and Vajpayee who needed to justify the shift in the stance of his own political party which was a staunch opponent of the reforms when in opposition,

Modi was required to do none. He neither builds the coequal relation between an open economy and a prosperous future, nor does he justify his government's agenda of favouring and furthering the reforms. Both emerge as a pre-established oratorical truth in his speeches.

Another difference becomes graphic in the politics of using the figure of Jawaharlal Nehru as a referential point for oratorical making claims. Modi, unlike his three predecessors, is seen as disentangling himself from Nehruvian repertoire and vocabulary. However, *the grammar and protocols* of engagement with audiences, the aesthetics of presencing himself, and his spoken word are nonetheless highly similar. This reflects in numerous forms of communication, as well as how his persona diffuses into statist rituals. For example, that Modi now speaks regularly to the nation through the All India Radio has refashioned and reappropriated the Nehru jacket, or that he has an overarching presence in his cabinet, whereby most important announcements and decisions pass through his tongue (some examples being the recent demonetization issue, 'Clean India', and 'Make in India' campaigns, etc., also speaks in the 'I' form when explaining the visions of his government)—all are reminiscent of Nehruvian politics.

Another observation, which is not necessarily a staunch difference, but one reflecting a procedural momentum since 1991 is that with each prime minister, the presentations of 'Emerging India' become more vigorous and emphatic. This can be attributed not only to the transitions in the GDP rates of growth or decreasing inflation rates, which are regularly pompously cited as proof of growth by all the four speakers. It also reflects how the exhibition of India's economic emergence has gained pace in the aftermath of global or transnational economic crises (for example, the Asian crisis of 1997 or the world economic crisis of 2008). In such moments, the prime ministers have brought forth the point that the Indian economy has thrived despite larger economic crises in the world.

With regards to Modi's rhetoric, an observation that emerges is that the challenges facing the project of 'Emerging India' are no longer levied on ideological terrains, that is, questioning the economic order that reifies market liberalization, but rather on how their execution has remained an incomplete process.

Whereas in the rhetoric of the previous prime ministers, even if sustainable and equitable development for the poor and the logic behind evermore open markets to foreign investment existed in different kinds of speeches delivered before varying audiences, in Modi's addresses one sees that the categories of the villager, the poor, the non-elite, the farmer, and the small-scale businessman are merged together under the amorphous entity of 'the common man', who is then defined in terms of unmet dreams and desires. The proverbial epithets like 'Digital India', 'Start-Up India', 'Stand-Up India', 'E-governance', 'M-governance', 'Connected India', 'Design in India', etc., thus address *all citizens at the same time* within the purview of the same speech and are not surgically removed for addresses meant for special entrepreneurial or external audiences only. Modi has thus brought the flashiness of the vocabulary embracing market liberalization, at least at the discursive level, to all strata of Indian audiences, whereby he can speak as comfortably about irrigation and seeds to farmers as about 'Digital India' and 'Make in India'. In other words, there is a vernacularization of the epithets of growth and the vocabulary of emergence that were earlier only made accessible to groups of limited membership in the oratory of his predecessors.

Modi's utilization of epithets that continue to make him highly popular shows that the contents of the discourse(s) used to legitimize the logic of market liberalization and reify it as the only inevitable means for economic prosperity has remained unchanged over the past twenty-five years. What has in fact changed with Modi is the linguistic repertoire used to do the same, whereby a new style and reservoir of idiomatic expressions are used to sell the same contents.

Another difference is that whereas for his predecessors the task of transforming the amorphous abstraction of 'globalization' from being a threat to being an opportunity is done cautiously and gradually, in Modi's oratory it appears that that discursive transformation has finally been achieved. The aim of producing India as a place to invest is two-fold, namely, to show that: (1) India has changed and (2) that it is an attractive investment destination.

Modi's speeches do not follow the strict dichotomization sketched in the main sections of chapters 2, 3, and 4 in terms of the perceived 'out-side' and 'inside'. As in the case of other prime ministers, the speaker is highly aware of when he speaks to whom. Nonetheless, it is the first time that one sees a repetitive strategy of addressing issues actually meant for distinct audiences and share the same semantic space within a singular speech. The putative 'outside' and the 'inside' are still sprung into existence lexically but within the same speech. Finally, India's emergence and reliability as an investment destination are projected in the context of four essential coordinates—demography, demand, devaluation, and democracy. Democracy is a subtly introduced, yet highly crucial stake for the speakers in ensuring increased FDIs in a stable political environment and in therein guaranteeing India's simultaneous economic emergence. It becomes an even more dynamic combination when coupled with state secularism to project India as 'safe' for both its own population, especially its religious minorities, as well as for foreign investors.

With regards to secularism, subtle differences between the rhetoric of the BJP leader Vajpayee and the Congress leaders Rao and Singh highlight not just the ambivalences in translating secularism for Indians, but also that certain categories like 'Indian civilization', 'Indian heritage', 'our traditions', and 'our past' become shorthand terms, often like 'secularism' itself, that are then presented as undisputed facts.

Though cosmetically the same, the visions behind these terms are different. Thus, for Vajpayee, secularism is more of a *Hindu* achievement, whereas for Rao/Singh, it is a syncretic mix which also utilizes the repertoire of other religious resources. Given that the defence of state secularism has mainly emerged in the context of religious strife and communal tensions between Hindus and Muslims, it is striking that none of the speakers resorts to religious resources from Muslim contexts to make a plea for secularism. Within the oratory of all four speakers, secularism then either becomes a syncretic mix of Hindu, Sikh, Bhakti, Sufi, etc., sources proving its long durée in India, or a Hindu tolerance usually expressed in the Hindi language. Given that Rao and Vajpayee's terms bore the marks of religious riots (Ayodhya 1992 and Gujarat 2002), their defensive attempts to rescue the paradigm have been more emphatic as compared to Singh. In his addresses, secularism is usually an additive, an adjective, which is slipped aside with terms like democracy, pluralism, and open society.

*

The following section will engage in a transversal discussion of the findings of the chapters in two ways: (1) discussing how the coordinates of post-reform India are different from the Nehruvian vocabulary of nation building. How can we trace this discursive difference through the oratory of the four prime ministers after 1991? In other words, what are the continuities and discontinuities between Nehru's 'New India' and the newer, post-1991 'New India'? (2) reviewing the results of the chapters in light of what is said and written about 'Emerging India' through sources I have provocatively called 'airport literature'. This is a discursive phenomenon embedded in the wider context of the new market-driven media sphere. Television, but also this literary genre, are part of this new media universe, which is itself a major result of the reforms it celebrates.

'New India': From Nehru to Now

Chapter 1 has shown that the epithet 'New India' is in fact not so new. It seems to be creatively renewed and reproduced by Indian Prime Ministers almost every 2 decades with the latest avatar occurring in Prime Minister Modi's Independence Day speech delivered on August 15, 2017. This epithet is part of Nehruvian repertoire and his lexical legacy. Nehru's vocabulary of a new India included, among others, 'Temples of Modern India', that is, big dams, big industries, and big universities, economic self-sufficiency, non-alignment, development of a 'scientific temper', state secularism, an emphasis on India's unity in diversity, heavy industrialization, control over the private sector, and a mixed economy (see section Chapter 1, *The Legacy of Nehru's Visions*).

Another important legacy of this period was the production of the state as the 'caretaker' of the citizens, an abstraction which was accountable to the population. This conjuring also implied that the citizens themselves were simultaneously produced as the passive receivers of the state's support and pedagogy. Thus, while the state itself was projected as the ultimate benefactor of the people above the profanities of 'politics', the population became what Srirupa Roy terms as the 'infantile citizen',[2] defined through the duality of an intimate relationship with

---

[2] S. Roy, *Beyond Belief: India and the Politics of Postcolonial Nationalism* (Durham, NC: Duke University Press, 2007), p. 20.

and dependence upon state authority. At the same time, however, both the citizens *as well as the state* were consistently construed in terms of a 'darkness' and 'incompleteness' that required perpetual mutual engagement for the progress of the nation. Statist visions continued to project ideas of the ideal citizen, who was willing to learn from state authority and simultaneously contribute to it.[3]

The depiction of the infantile citizen did not end with Nehru's term. After Nehru's death, the term of Congress's syndicate-approved successor, Lal Bahadur Shastri, bore some 'literal' remnants of this idea. Christopher Pinney, in his study of chromolithographs, shows how the image of the *boy* member of the National Cadet Corps (NCC)[4] had pervaded calendars and posters in the context of the Sino-Indian war (1962). Piney writes, 'The picture was captioned, in English, "Land to defend" and depicted an impossibly young member of the National Cadet Corps holding a rifle against a background landscape of Indian troops trudging through the Himalayas [...]'[5]

During his short term as prime minister, Shastri initiated the famous slogan *Jai Jawan, Jai Kisan* (victory to the soldier, victory to the farmer!). Set again against the backdrop of two wars (China in 1962 and Pakistan in 1965), this slogan brought the farmer and the soldier to share the same revered space as national heroes. But, as Pinney rightly observes from a seemingly micro illustration, in popular calendar art, one literally encountered the 'infantile' citizen dressed in a farmer's or a soldier's attire, produced as the prototype of the ideal citizen.

Even later, during Indira Gandhi's era, this theme would continue to pervade public imaginations through multiple means. Pinney records the calendar image titled 'Heroes' (1973), released after another war in 1971, '[...] which developed some of the earlier *Jawan/Kisan* themes [...]. Whereas the early image had simply visualized Shastri's repeated comparison of the two, these later images parachute the perennially young NCC boy, last seen fighting the Chinese a decade ago, into a new alliance with an equally young farmer.'[6]

---

[3] Roy, *Beyond Belief*, p. 20.

[4] C. Pinney, *Photos of the Gods: The Printed Image and Political Struggle in India* (London: Reaktion Books, 2004), p. 169.

[5] Pinney, *Photos of the Gods*, p. 169.

[6] Pinney, *Photos of the Gods*, p. 171.

The toiling farmer, as a figure or a face of the nation's citizenship, the soldier who defends the motherland, the hard labouring factory worker—all these model figures were a fabrication of the socialist era and continued to inspire the imagination of the celebrated contributing postcolonial citizen. This was simultaneously accompanied by the category of the apolitical scientist, who was also a product of the Nehru-initiated centres of higher learning like the Indian Institutes of Technology. The learned scientist who remains outside the ambit of profane politics, the farmer who helps fill national granaries, the soldier who defends the motherland, the factory worker who assists in running the factories meant to make India self-sufficient, and the labourer who helps build the big dams and steel plants—all were categories meant to assist in the perilous work of nation-building, with the nation state being defined in terms of a persistent 'needs discourse'. Whereas the scientist was required to acquire 'scientific expertise', the general category of the Indian citizen was required to acquire 'scientific temper'. Ronald Inden sums up the mood aptly in stating, 'The God that Nehru was trying to embody in the New India was the God of Enlightenment and the progress of "man", the reason of science and technology.'[7]

Later on, Indira Gandhi's vocabulary during the state-led Green Revolution and her famous slogans like *Garibi Hatao* (Remove Poverty) also directed their energies to the figure(s) of the farmer, the construction site worker, and the soldier, usually presented under the umbrella shorthand term of aam admi (common man).[8] But embedded in all

[7] R. Inden, 'Embodying God: From Imperial Progresses to National Progress in India', *Economy and Society* 24, no. 2 (1995): 272–73.

[8] This mood of the era of the 1950s up to the 1980s is also very visibly present in the popular Bollywood films of the times. The most popular themes, especially during the late 1960s up to late 1970s, were patriotism, poverty, and the everyday struggles of the *aam admi*, epitomized most graphically in the films of the Bollywood actor-director Manoj Kumar. For example, in the 1967 film titled *Upkar*, he is seen enacting the Shastri slogan *Jai Jawan, Jai Kisan* by playing both a soldier and a farmer (the film was directed by Kumar on being encouraged by the prime minister himself), the 1970 film titled *Purab aur Paschim* (East and West) juxtaposed lifestyles in the East and the West set within the framework of screen patriotism, whereas the 1974 film titled *Roti Kapda aur Makaan* (Food, Clothing, and Shelter) was based on the slogan popularized by Indira Gandhi before the 1967 general elections, and is a drama dealing with the

these projections was still the figure of the *toiling and tutored* citizen, who needed the state as much as he/she needed the needs created by the state.

Contrast this with the images on the covers of the books that describe the new 'Emerging India' today, and the shift becomes all too apparent. In more contemporary projections of the New India, the farmer, the soldier, and the factory worker have taken a back seat, if not completely withdrawn altogether. The new face of a new India (that is, if any citizens are depicted at all in visual representations instead of maps, laboratories, software industries, or nuclear missiles being launched) is no longer seen as laboring relentlessly, but rather in a call centre attending international calls, in a laboratory experimenting with colourful compounds in test tubes, at an airport boarding flights, flying a Boeing or as an accomplished airhostess/steward, in a hospital performing a complicated surgery, in a software company programming, or, at the very least, in a spaceless, timeless zone, sitting opposite a laptop. A.R. Vasavi aptly summarizes, 'Once the flag bearer of the new nation state and an icon of a newly independent India, the kisan or agriculturist is now placed on the back-burner of the nation's economic, social, and political imaginaries. New economic agendas routinely bypass the agriculturist who is primarily seen as redundant to the new ambitions of a fast globalizing nation.'[9]

This 'absence of reckoning with the agriculturist as an economic agent, a citizen, and social being' has reduced her to being at best a receiver.[10] And this shift in depiction is not a mere visual change. The neo-liberal reforms have often been criticized on grounds of not giving adequate attention to the agricultural sector in a country where the

---

'bare necessities of life'. One of the songs of the film that became very popular, *Mehngai Mar Gayi* (Inflation has defeated me, beaten me down), was seen as emblematic of the relentless struggles of the common man, whose patriotism is nonetheless unfettered, his morality unshaken, and his 'belief' in the state, as a provider and redeemer, unflinching. Each one of the films was an outstanding commercial success.

  [9] A.R. Vasavi, *Citizen Kisan*, India 2012: A Symposium on the Year that was, January 2013, http://www.india-seminar.com/2013/641/641_a_r_vasavi.htm, accessed on 6 March 2013.

  [10] Roy, *Beyond Belief*, p. 200.

economy has primarily been agricultural. The new in the *new* thus India imagines itself by shifting the emphasis away from the 'citizen in need' discourse and has subverted the argument by replacing the citizen kisan with the IT citizen as its legitimate face.

Post-market liberalization stories depict an almost aggressive confidence, an intensity in terms of redoing and repacking the image of the nation, or 'Brand India', as best described by the state-sponsored India Brand Equity Foundation campaign. The primary difference/shift between the Nehruvian vision and the more recent flavours of the nationalist discourse is that the former procured hopes and desires of the future, whereas the latter projects that future as attainable in the here and now. I have explained these various 'details of desire', which the prime ministers present before Indians to inevitablize the reforms in depth in chapter 2. A part of the technique to 'sell' the reforms is to present the future as no longer elusive, but as available to all.

While Nehru's India was seen as one aspiring to become modern (located strictly within his ideas of economic self-reliance, generating a 'scientific temper and expertise', shrugging 'narrow-mindedness', etc.), the *new* 'New India' *is* modern. Roy sums this up in relation to the BJP-led 'India Shining' campaign (2003–04), which projected India's social, economic, and technological progress as never before, making it a power to reckon with on the world stage. 'Unlike the modernizing discourses of nation building, "India Shining" proclaimed modernity as an already achieved goal in India.'[11] This is not to state that these views and projections have not been challenged, even ridiculed from varying spheres. In fact, one of the visible pictures, as the 'India Shining' campaign had been launched, that permeated public imagination was that of an old, scantily dressed and bare-footed beggar or rubbish collector who stands in an ATM vestibule opposite a money withdrawal machine with a confused expression, with the slogan on the picture reading as 'India Shining' adjacent to a sarcastically visible question mark.[12] The campaign has also been projected as one 'gone wrong' with the BJP failing to come back to power at the centre in the ensuing elections. And

[11] Roy, *Beyond Belief*, p. 200.

[12] M.S. Ali, 'India Shining, Bharat Drowning', 28 January 2012. For Image and Article see: http://www.indianmuslimobserver.com/2012/01/28/india-shining-bharat-drowning/, accessed on 10 June 2013.

yet, what makes the narrative of 'India Shining' extremely interesting is that the earlier critical Congress, when in power after 2004, pursued it more rigorously in different versions in the shape of the 'Incredible India' and 'Brand India' campaigns to profile 'global displays of a reformed nation',[13] which is market-friendly and an ideal investment destination.

Thus, while the old vocabulary after independence 'conjured up an "Indian darkness" and defined the nation state as a collection of persistent and unfulfilled problems, failures, and needs',[14] while, at the same time, presenting *the way* to transformation, the new registers differ in that here the moment of the new India is produced as one that has arrived. This does not imply that India has emerged—rather that it has taken off, that is, it is *more prepared* than ever before to emerge. All the bearers of the image of this New India—surgeons, IT professionals, scientists, etc.—are a real, realizable category. The new wave towards a new India is thus not just different in terms of its intensities, aggressiveness, and velocity, but also entails an era of being embedded in that modernity (very specifically, the coordinates of this modernity are seen as those defined by open markets, new consumption habits in spite of a cultural rootedness, and a possibility for an economic-social upward mobility, despite caste and class legacies)—as if the contours of the vision have finally become clear. It is now clear what the envisioned desires are, what the coordinates of that modernity are, but only a question of achieving them that lies at the crux of the matter. In that sense, the new in this new 'Emerging India' is much more celebratory and oozes a language of confidence in expressing its recent triumphs. Thus, a prominent difference in the registers lies in that Nehru's 'New India' was founded on the premise of the *generation of needs*, with a future pointing to the fulfilment of the same. However, the newer vocabulary, as expressed in celebratory literature and campaigns, seems to drift away from that future by inscribing it in the here and now. By this, I do not mean that the current prime ministers do not talk in depth about the promise of the future. What I intend to point out is the constitution of temporal orders, whereby the imagination of the future is not

---

[13] Kaur, 'Nation's Two Bodies: Rethinking the Idea of "New" India and its Other', *Third World Quarterly* 33, no. 4 (2012): 604

[14] Roy, *Beyond Belief*, pp. 105–6.

a distant possibility, but rather a relation to another time, the present, which makes it a real achievable entity in that immediate present.

Another related difference between the older New India and the newer Emerging India stories is that Nehru's 'New India' attempted to chalk a programme that, in its optimistic depictions of the future and needs discourse of the present, produced a homogenized category of *the* Indian citizen. However, the newer stories, in reflecting upon the successes of a few who have 'made it' in a neo-liberal India, inevitably exclude the larger numbers who are ousted by default to the fringes of the economy. In Nehru's India, all were relegated to an eventual time zone of the future, whereas the new 'New India' is often critiqued for its limited beneficiaries. Roy sums up this difference in the following lines:

> [...] the conflation of economic success and nationhood in the glossy advertisements of the India Shining campaign inscribes a rigid division between those who are presently reaping the benefits of the economic miracle, and those who remain outside the circle of light [...] the nation-building imagination had placed all Indians in the waiting room of history and put everyone's future on hold. In contrast, India Shining constitutes the nation as a limited membership club.[15]

Back to the Airport: Tenets of India Emerging India

The multiple imaginations of 'Emerging India', a discursive phenomenon staged in the literary genre that I have called 'airport literature', shows that the Indian nation, including the sign of its very name, has become a marketable commodity, a brand indeed, which promises people money-dynamic perspectives of reliable growth and a visionary future. As can be seen from bookstores and their bestsellers' sections in airports and shopping malls, even in 2017, this wider discourse remains seemingly unmitigated. It presents Emerging India as a tale of irresistible attire, of promising bliss, and miraculous stability, which also the prime ministers are to tell and sell. In this section, I will present the different facets of this literature and discuss its intertextual complementarity to the 'Emerging India' discourse as it is conjured in Prime Ministerial oratory.

[15] Roy, *Beyond Belief*, p. 165.

An important milestone for such prognoses that predicted India's economic emergence was the Goldman Sachs Report of 2003 titled 'Dreaming with the BRICs: The Path to 2050', which stated that India's GDP growth rate between 2015 and 2050 would exceed that of the G6 countries as also that of China, and that its total income would reach up to 80 per cent to that of the United States by 2050. The report did not just attract international audiences, but was also received with much adulation in India by politicians and press alike.[16] In spite of the reports coming from the investment banking firm, whose own credibility came to be challenged after the financial crisis of 2008, the Goldman Sachs Report had a lasting impact, chiefly in triggering the formation of the BRICS[17] collective where a myriad of global financial issues are regularly discussed and debated, especially with regard to the role to be played by its five economies. Thus, a framework meant for future investors triggered the foundation of a group where the 'objects' of analysis became active actors, identifying with a label attached to them.

The Goldman Sachs Report and, more so, the decisions it triggered elucidate how 'external' projections and 'internal' self-portrayals mutually influence each other. As the reader will notice, these themes of 'external' and 'internal', and how the state, more so the prime minister, as the elected representative of the nation, finds himself at the interface between the two, have formed a consistent topic of discussion throughout this book.

The mood of celebration coloured in descriptions of fast-paced change has been a phenomenon reported not just by the perceived 'inside'. Documentaries were also aired on international media along with special shows in which international journalists travelling to Indian cities presented coverage on the Indian Stock exchange, a typical day in the life of an Indian IT worker, or market comparisons between India, USA, and China, snapshots from the rapidly rising shopping complexes in Indian metros, etc.

---

[16] Goldman Sachs, 'Dreaming with the BRICs: The Path to 2050', *Global Economics*, 99 (2003).

[17] BRICs stands for the collective of the emergent economies of Brazil, Russia, India, and China, founded in 2006 which later became BRICS with the inclusion of South Africa in 2010.

For example, the following description of a show called *NOW*, aired by the American Public Broadcasting Service (PBS) in 2008 reads as, 'This week *NOW* reports from Pune, India, where college graduates are getting tech jobs, traditional families are flocking to the new mall, and professionals are hoping their new-found economic might will make their country an even bigger global player. But can America's middle-class—and the rest of the world—afford this unprecedented shift in the global economy?'[18]

Of Covers, Titles, and Tables of Contents

'Don't judge a book by its cover'—this proverb seems out of place in the context of this genre. Its contributors are technocrats, journalists, researchers, travellers, foreign investors, former CEOs who have now become writers. A cursory glance at the covers of the books, magazines, and travelogues conveys the intended message—'India is changing'—lucidly clear. The covers depict what the books are trying to have us read in them. They illustrate the *face* of India's transition, whether projected as already materializing or as a still unaccomplished desire. Airport literature has the exceptional quality of revealing in the iconographic vocabulary of its covers the visions that formulate their subtext, the message of its authors.

Thus, one finds cover jackets that include stereotypical depictions of 'the' Indian woman attired in a saree, but now geared with a laptop,[19] a classical Indian dancer with a call-centre headset,[20] the Hindu deity Ganesha's picture with Mumbai's multiplexes as the mythic background,[21] Ganesha residing on top of a series of such multiplexes,[22]

[18] Programme description, India Rising, special aired at the *Now* show of PBS, June 2008. (See online: http://www.hpbs.org/now/shows/425/index.html, accessed on July 2012.)

[19] See cover of A. Matoo, *The Reluctant Superpower: Understanding India and Its Aspirations* (Carlton, Vic.: Melbourne University Publishing, 2012).

[20] See cover of 'India Inc.', *Time Magazine Cover*, Issue 26 (2006), http://content.time.com/time/covers/0,16641,20060626,00.html, accessed on 25 July 2012.

[21] See cover of D. Lak, *India Express: The Future of the New Superpower* (New York et. al.: Palgrave Macmillan, 2008).

[22] See cover of J. Farndon, *India Booms. The Breathtaking Development and Influence of Modern India* (London: Virgin Books, 2007).

laboratories with scientists manipulating test tubes with chemicals that tellingly reflect the colours of the Indian flag, surgeries being performed in hospitals loaded with equipments, shopping malls with happy family faces after the act of purchasing, the 'common man' with iPhones, or young faces sitting opposite a computer screen in what looks like a spaceless, timeless zone.

These covers may be categorized as what anthropologist Christopher Pinney, in his historical study of the printed image in India, has termed as 'compressed performances'.[23] Volatile, self-reinventing, and yet surprisingly continuous in the messages they wish to communicate, the pictures visually 'compress' the contents of the literature they stand for, thus synthesizing it for the airport audiences, who might be aiming for a quick and light digestion. Much like the tune of a song, which may stubbornly stick back in one's memory even when the lyrics are long forgotten, the combined repertoires of India's past and future are fed in loop so as to remain alive and rooted in public consciousness and be continuously remembered.

What the covers attempt to do through images, effects, and colour combinations also extends to the titles of the books, which experiment innovatively with new metaphors of speed. There have been captions like *India Booms*,[24] *India Arriving*,[25] *India Express*,[26] *Non-Stop India*,[27] *No Full-Stops in India*,[28] *India as an Emerging Power*,[29] *India: The Emerging Giant*,[30] *Emerging Power India*,[31] *India's Emerging Economy*,[32] *Emerging*

---

[23] Pinney, *Photos of the Gods*, p. 8.

[24] Farndon, *India Booms*.

[25] R. Dossani, *India Arriving: How This Economic Powerhouse Is Redefining Global Business* (New York: American Management Association, 2008).

[26] Lak, *India Express*.

[27] M. Tully, *Non-Stop India* (London: Penguin, 2011).

[28] M. Tully, *No Full-Stops in India* (London: Penguin 1991).

[29] S. Ganguly (ed.), *India as an Emerging Power* (London and Portland, Oregon: Frank Cass, 2003).

[30] A. Panagariya, *India: The Emerging Giant* (New York: Oxford University Press, 2008).

[31] S.P. Cohen, *Emerging Power: India* (Brookings Institution Press, 2001).

[32] K. Basu, *India's Emerging Economy*.

India,[33] *India Rising: Tales from a Changing Nation,*[34] etc. The optimism celebrated in these titles reflects not so much the assertion of India's predisposed status as a power, but rather the announcement if its *transition.*

Much of the optimism related to India's emergence is traced back to the institutionalization of neo-liberal economic reforms. A general mood that may be captured in most accounts is a ceremonial pronouncement of the free-trade model. This is also reflected in the 'Table of Contents' of most books on display in the airport bookshops. To give two graphic examples, Gurcharan Das's *India Unbound: From Independence to the Global Information Age*[35] and Arvind Panagariya's *India: The Emerging Giant*[36]. Das is the former director of the corporate firm Proctor and Gamble. He has organized the contents of his book in three sections—*Part One: Our Spring of Hope (1942–65), Part Two: The Lost Generation (1966–91),* and *Part Three: The Rebirth of Dreams (1991–99).* Panagariya, on the other hand, is a professor of economics at Columbia University and ex chief economist at the Asia Development Bank. His book bears a similar periodization in the first section, dealing exclusively with the reforms, which divides modern Indian economic history into four phases, namely: *Phase I (1951–65): Takeoff under a Liberal Regime, Phase II (1965–81): Socialism Strikes with a Vengeance, Phase III (1981–88): Liberalization by Stealth,* and *Phase IV (1988–2006): Triumph of Liberalization.* In both cases, the reforms are hailed as an achievement of the state and seen as the breakthrough moment triggering India's remarkable economic growth.

This is not to state that the reforms have not faced internal criticism in India,[37] a theme I have developed in chapters 2 and 3. It becomes

---

[33] C.U. Bhaskar and N.S. Sisodia (eds), *Emerging India: Security and Foreign Policy Perspectives* (New Delhi: Bibliophile South Asia, 2005), and B. Jalan, *Emerging India: Economics, Politics and Reforms* (New Delhi: Penguin, 2013).

[34] O. Balch, *India Rising: Tales from a Changing Nation* (London: Faber and Faber, 2012).

[35] G. Das, *India Unbound: From Independence to the Global Information Age* (New Delhi: Viking and Penguin Books, 2000).

[36] A. Panagariya, *India: The Emerging Giant* (Oxford University Press, 2008).

[37] Two comprehensive articles, also mentioned in the Introduction, lucidly summarize these oppositions: P. Bardan, 'Nature of Opposition to Economic Reforms in India', *Economic and Political Weekly* (2005): 4995–98; P. Patnaik,

clear, however, that an increasing volume of such literature eulogizes the reforms with a repetitive celebratory vocabulary, usually distinguishing clearly between the 'triumph' of market liberalization and 'the lost generations' of Indian economy before that.

Images in Motion: India as 'Brand'

Such developments at profiling India are not only limited to the sphere of non-state actors. They rather suggest an obvious marriage between the logics of states and those of corporations. Nation branding[38] campaigns are one example in standing. Ravindar Kaur aptly summarizes this relationship between nation and corporation as follows:

> [T]he new relationship between nation and corporation is shaped in an increasingly hyper-competitive environment where nations compete to gain the most favoured 'investment destination' status. The favourite mode of address is to 'dress up' the nation to make it more 'attractive' for potential investors through nation-branding campaigns that show case the effects of structural adjustments, open access to markets, and less government regulation.[39]

The India Brand Equity Foundation also exemplifies such government initiatives after the mid 1990s. The foundation's posters, campaigns, videos, magazines etc. aim at the '(v)isual production of a new India through a range of advertising campaigns that seek to corporatize and commodify the imagined essence of the nation.'[40] Another illustration is provided by the advertisements, billboards, slogans, and posters of the 'Incredible India' campaign launched by the Ministry of Tourism. These more recent endeavours make their presence increasingly felt at international platforms such as World Trade Organization's round-table conferences, the World Economic Forum, the New York Times Square,

---

'International Capital and National Economic Policy: A Critique of India's Economic Reforms', *Economic and Political Weekly* (1994): 683–89.

[38] For a conceptual framework see S. Anholt, *Competitive Identity. The New Brand Management for Nations, Cities and Regions* (New York: Palgrave MacMillan 2007).

[39] Kaur, 'Nation's Two Bodies', p. 605.

[40] Kaur, 'Nation's Two Bodies', p. 604.

and international trade fairs through everyday advertising on taxis and buses or at international airports. A closer probing into the posters, slogans, and videos launched by such campaigns point to the coordinates of the new neo-liberal India, or how the newly emergent nation is imagined through certain defining characteristics. These, once again, include among others, an assertive presentation of India as a global IT hub, emphatic thrust on the rise of the new middle classes, India as a knowledge economy, as a centre for engineering research, with growth in retail, increased medical tourism, and, most importantly, as an attractive investment destination.

However, though both cater to international audiences, an important difference between the 'Incredible India' campaign and the campaigns of the 'India Brand Equity' foundation is that the former aims at portraying cultural elements that make India an attractive tourism destination, while the latter engages more with seductive images, projecting India as an ideal international investment destination. With regards to the new face that campaigns like 'Incredible India' aim to foster, Consolaro points out that, '(h)ere we get an instance of the new Orientalism that has been created in the construction of the New India: it is the exotic, easily marketable "Incredible India" [...] where yoga and mysticism coexist with capitalism and business [...].'[41]

The increasing production of such material continues to cause amusement and awe at the same time. New volumes and travelogues are perhaps being written and added to the bookshelves at airports, even as this book is being read.

Books and Speeches: Intertextual Complementarity

One prominent conclusion that emerges is that in most such accounts, 1991 is celebrated as India's critical moment, even a caesura, and the government associated with the institutionalization of the reforms

[41] A. Consolaro, 'Corporate Democracy: The Times of India "Lead India" Campaign', revised version of the paper presented at the Fourth LUMS Social Sciences Conference on *Media Growth: Global Trends, Social Impacts, Academic Concerns*, Lahore University of Management Sciences (LUMS), 19–21 December 2008, see online: http://www.juragentium.org/topics/rol/india/en/consolar. htm (accessed on 29 August 2013).

is presented as the agent of that change. 1991 is thus inevitablized. Whereas one does encounter sections on the 'challenges ahead' after the reforms and what restricts India's rise, most of this literature, nonetheless, equivocally celebrates the reforms as a positive transition for Indian economy, reifying market liberalization as the only legitimate means towards a confident, economically emerging India. Thus, at large, there is an environment of optimism, and even a confident laudation of the reforms, whereas change itself is overplayed linguistically or aesthetically. A transversal reading of the seductive images produced by the airport literature and the speeches of the Prime Ministers reveals that the addresses by the first two prime ministers have, unlike most such celebratory literature, followed a more cautious approach. Here, change is introduced under the cosmetic camouflage of continuity or embedded in a larger, almost cosmic, order which necessitates the change. The reforms are produced as a calculated and well-calibrated measure. In the case of Singh and Modi, there has been a lesser thrust on establishing co-equivalence between the reforms and India's economic emergence, as they had discursively become inevitable and unquestionable by the time they assumed office. Yet, also for both these prime ministers, the categories of the common man, the farmer, and the poor remain important audiences as the receivers and perceivers of a politics of future. Airport literature usually erases these shadows from both the covers and the titles, usually by showing these categories with new media technologies (IBEF campaigns) or cleaning the background in the images, that show India's majestic natural beauty, of the cluttering human bodies that one inevitably encounters in any given time and place in India (Incredible India campaign). Thus, whereas the prime ministers are cautious to address *all* categories of the population under the amorphous rubric of the 'common man', the literature is celebratory of the caesura of 1991 and the limited club it has benefitted.

This is also related to the question of the perceived audiences. Whereas most of the accounts in the form of books, reports, advertisement campaigns, documentaries, and news coverage cater to a very limited and specific audience confined to international platforms like the World Economic Forum, bookstore chains, or the shops at the waiting lounges at airports or shopping malls, the prime ministers address much larger audiences and, thus, their narrations are more reflexive in responding to the criticisms levied against market liberalization.

However, in spite of these distinctions, the two genres remarkably speak to each other. Both produce spaces of mutual coexistence. Not only do most such accounts and books share the commonality of projecting market liberalization as a means to India's rising future, but also the grammatology of marketing market liberalization is strikingly similar. We have seen in chapters 2, 3, 4, and 5 that in order to 'sell' both the reforms as well as the image of a secular India, that is, to legitimize the basis of the emerging secular nation, all four prime ministers utilize resources from a homogenized, selectively remembered past. This is done to frame the reforms and the secular nation as products of a preordained, temporal order. As shown in chapters 2, 3, and 4, the main objective behind this is to introduce change, but nonetheless with an assurance that India's cultural core is fundamentally secure. Thus, the new is made to blend with the old.

A similar pattern is observable in most of the covers of books, magazines, catalogues, and advertising campaigns, etc., regardless of whether their production was in India or outside. Here also, the new blends with the old to produce the imagery of a rising India. Hence, we have women on the covers dressed in 'traditional' attires (usually a saree) with markers of new technology (headsets, laptops, mobile phones, etc.), or new multiplexes with an image of the Hindu deity Ganesha in the background. The cultural essence of the nation is depicted as firmly rooted in its past and therein secure, but this packaging simultaneously introduces a flavour of change and newness. Ravinder Kaur has succinctly described this as 'the aesthetics of remixing history at the heart of the neoliberal project of India's image makeover as a "land of limitless opportunity" or "Incredible India" for global tourists and investors.'[42] In music, remixing refers to utilizing the tune and elements of an older composition, repeating and rearranging and sonically photoshopping it with new effects to produce something that reminds the listeners of the old tune, but only for a fleeting moment to then introduce new elements that produce a newer and different version. 'Remix is not an altered copy, but original composition in its own right that rearranges the sensory experiences of the audience. In short,

---

[42] Kaur, 'Post-Exotic India: On Remixed Histories and Smart Images', *Identities: Global Studies in Culture and Power* 23, no. 3 (2016): 308–9.

the remix version retains traces of the original even while erasing it to ultimately morph into its own being.'[43] The same aesthetic and lexical remixing of history becomes most graphically visible in the covers, contents, and titles of airport literature, as well as in the speeches of the prime ministers. The new is never devoid of traces of the old, and yet what is sold and told is a new and different composition.

On a wider level, the shared commonality in the semantics of the literature and the addresses, regardless of the nuanced differences in the cosmetic texture, points to another important development in India after 1991. This is the emergent new partnership between the nation and the corporation. A marker of these more recent campaigns is that they denote a shift from nation-building to nation branding. Kaur aptly captures the mood of this partnership in her research on nation branding campaigns after 1991,

> [...] the very idea of development has now become first and foremost a matter of image. In this world of images, one can also witness how a competitive strategy to seek more corporate investments through concerted brand campaigns has redefined the relationship between the nation and corporation. While earlier it was the corporations which sought endorsement and patronage of the sovereign, now it is the sovereign nations seeking to become the most 'favored investment destinations' that purvey the global capital.[44]

One of the most illustrative examples of the same is the 'India Brand Equity' foundation, which was a state-led effort but informed with corporate participation. Given that many of the authors whose books speak of the new India are former or current entrepreneurs, it is no surprise that they employ glossy language and seductive images to profile 'Emerging India'. Interestingly, especially with regards to Manmohan Singh's speeches delivered to international audiences, there is a striking familiarity to the optimistic vocabulary on which such books also rely. In fact, on numerous occasions, Singh is also seen as using the phrase 'Brand India', just as Modi has launched the campaign 'Make in India' to popularize the 'Made in India' brand.

---

[43] Kaur, 'Post-Exotic India'.
[44] Kaur, 'Post-Exotic India', p. 605.

Back to World Orders

In the introduction, I pointed to the wider context informing this study of prime ministerial oratory in India as a means to understand how the nation-state reacts to challenges of spatial reconfigurations of power and legitimacy in the face of perceived threats of 'fragmentation' and 'globalization'. The overarching objective has thus been to invite a closer introspection into how states, as actors confronted by transitions occurring both 'externally' and 'internally', recalibrate themselves to sustain their legitimacy. Moving beyond the polemic debate of whether 'the' nation state has been rendered redundant, irrelevant or not, the chapters in this book have emphasized on asking the question of how precisely the Indian governments have renegotiated their new role and adapted to the state of flux. This has been done by analysing the re-profiling of India from the vantage point of its prime ministers. The analysis of prime ministerial oratory undertaken in this book speaks to this question in two respects:

Firstly, it emerges that debates related to the configuration of new world order(s) have provided the creative, discursive space for staging the 'Emerging India' narrative. This implies that speculations such as the BRICs report, among others, which prognosed the rise of emerging economies like India, or studies based largely within International Relations, which speak of the emergence of 'multiple' power poles, are dexterously used as opportunities by the prime ministers to re-profile the state as an active, important actor in the new world order. The Indian governments, as the official voice of the state, thus wish to project themselves as not just passive witnesses but rather the *enablers* and *overseers* of transformations. In doing so, they thus do not just profit from the discourse(s) on a new world order, but also actively constitute its production.

Secondly, within the Prime Ministers' oratory, 1991 as India's critical moment, is inverted from being one propelling a crisis—for the Indian economy and its religiously pluralist secular image—to one of success. The state, through the words of its elected heads, has linguistically re-profiled itself as the vanguard of a shifting discourse of India, a nation and economy in crisis to India, the stable, secular investment destination and 'Emerging Economic Giant. In short, the analysis has shown how the Indian state has driven on the perceived threats, subverted them and used them to its own benefit by conjuring a sense of nation-ness among Indians, re-presenting India internationally as being coeval with the 'West' and finally re-establishing its own legitimacy as the authoritative vanguard of the nation.

Airports everywhere are like nodal points that connect places which are otherwise territorially disconnected to each other. As we know since Benedict Anderson's *Imagined Communities*,[45] the government, as the 'elected' representative and the voice of the population, is similarly a constant interface between the putative 'insides' and the 'outsides' of places, which are territorially discontinuous and whose inhabitants do not know each other personally. The prime ministers' message(s) are like the nodal points, the connecting bridges among a multiplicity of audiences, including those deemed to be part of the putative inside but also those beyond the state's geographical and institutional boundaries.

Besides these spatially located demarcations, the words of the prime ministers also become a temporal interface between India's homogenized and selectively remembered past and its projected, seductive and desired future. They assist in constructing the image of India's new promising future, while also bridging with its past.

The speeches also become an interface for topically cementing the two evergreen themes of state secularism and market liberalization. Fundamental to this discourse is that secularism is produced as a precondition for India's emergence. It is lexically conjured as the sole means, the fundamental basis for the existence and essence of a pluralist India.

The project of 'India Emerging' is like a 'road in construction'—one of the hundreds of underpasses one sees being built everyday in Indian cities, an ongoing 'men at work', 'work in progress'. The addresses of the prime ministers are an assemblage, whereby the themes of state secularism and market liberalization, the putative external and the internal, the generalized past and the aspirational future are made to *merge* so that India can *(E)merge*.

---

[45] B. Anderson, *Imagined Communities: Reflections on the Origins and Spread of Nationalism*, 2nd ed. (London: Verso, 1991).

Bibliography

Primary Sources

Rao, P.V.N., *Selected Speeches*, vol. 1, June 1991–June 1992, edited by the Publications Division, Ministry of Information and Broadcasting, Government of India, New Delhi, 1993.

Rao, *Selected Speeches*, vol. 2, July 1992–June 1993, edited by the Publications Division, Ministry of Information and Broadcasting, Government of India, New Delhi, 1994.

Rao, *Selected Speeches*, vol. 3, July 1993–June 1994, edited by the Publications Division, Ministry of Information and Broadcasting, Government of India, New Delhi, 1995.

Rao, *Selected Speeches*, vol. 4, July 1994–June 1995, edited by the Publications Division, Ministry of Information and Broadcasting, Government of India, New Delhi, 1996.

Vajpayee, A.B., *Selected Speeches*, vol. 1, March 1998–March 1999, edited by the Publications Division, Ministry of Information and Broadcasting, Government of India, New Delhi, 2000.

Vajpayee, *Selected Speeches*, vol. 2, April 1999–March 2000, edited by the Publications Division, Ministry of Information and Broadcasting, Government of India, New Delhi, 2001.

Vajpayee, *Selected Speeches*, vol. 3, April 2000–March 2001, edited by the Publications Division, Ministry of Information and Broadcasting, Government of India, New Delhi, 2003.

Vajpayee, *Kuch Lekh, Kuch Bhashan*, New Delhi: Kitabkhar Prakashan, 2011.

Vajpayee, *Nayi Chunouti Naya Avasar*, New Delhi: Kitabkhar Prakashan, 2011.

Vajpayee, *Vichar Bindu*, New Delhi: Kitabkhar Prakashan, 2011.

Singh, M., *Selected Speeches*, vol. 1, June 2004–June 2005, edited by S.V. Sharma, Publications Division, Ministry of Information and Broadcasting, Government of India, New Delhi, 2005.

Singh, *Selected Speeches*, vol. 2, July 2005–June 2006, edited by S.V. Sharma, Publications Division, Ministry of Information and Broadcasting, Government of India, New Delhi, 2006.

Singh, *Selected Speeches*, vol. 3, June 2006–May 2007, edited by N. Joshi, Publications Division, Ministry of Information and Broadcasting, Government of India, New Delhi, 2007.

Singh, *Selected Speeches*, vol. 4, June 2007–May 2008, edited by D. Srivastava, Publications Division, Ministry of Information and Broadcasting, Government of India, New Delhi, 2008.

Singh, *Selected Speeches*, vol. 5, June 2008–November 2009, edited by D. Srivastava, Publications Division, Ministry of Information and Broadcasting, Government of India, New Delhi, 2010.

Singh, *Selected Speeches*, vol. 6, December 2009–May 2010, edited by D. Srivastava, Publications Division, Ministry of Information and Broadcasting, Government of India, New Delhi, 2012.

Singh, Speeches 2011–14, available on the official website of the Prime Minister's Office, see http://archivepmo.nic.in/drmanmohansingh/speeches.php.

Modi, N.D., Speeches 2012–14, available on N.D. Modi's personal website before his election as Prime Minister, http://www.narendramodi.in.

Modi, Speeches 2014–16, available on the official website of the Prime Minister's Office, see www.pmindia.nic.in.

Secondary Sources

Adams, J. 'Culture in Rational-Choice Theories of State Formation'. In *State/Culture: State Formation After the Cultural Turn*, edited by Steinmetz, G. Ithaca, NY: Cornell University Press, 1999, pp. 98–122.

Agnew, J. 'Sovereignty Regimes: Territoriality and State Authority in Contemporary World Politics'. *Annals of the Association of American Geographers* 95, no. 2 (2005): 437–61.

Ahluwalia, P. 'Founding Father Presidencies and the Rise of Authoritarianism. Kenya: A Case Study'. *Africa Quarterly* 36, no. 4 (1996): 45–72.

Akbar, M.J., *Nehru: The Making of India*. New York: Viking, 1988.

Anand, A. *One vs. All: Narendra Modi: Pariah to Paragon*. Chennai: Notion Press, 2016.

Anderson, B. *Imagined Communities: Reflections on the Origins and Spread of Nationalism*, 2nd ed. London: Verso, 1991 (1983).

Anholt, S. *Competitive Identity: The New Brand Management for Nations, Cities and Regions*. New York: Palgrave MacMillan, 2007.

Appadurai, A. *Modernity at Large: Cultural Dimensions of Globalization*. Minneapolis: University of Minnesota Press, 1996.

Asad, T. *Formations of the Secular: Christianity, Islam, Modernity*. Stanford: Standford University Press, 2003.

Asad, T., W. Brown, and J. Butler, eds. *Is Crique Secular? Blasphemy, Injury, and Free Speech*. Berkeley: University of California Press, 2009.

Assmann, J. 'Collective Memory and Cultural Identity'. *New German Critique* 65(1995): 125–33.

Austin, J.L. *How to Do Things with Words. The William James Lectures Delivered at Harvard University in 1955*. Oxford: Clarendon Press, 1962.

Ayres, A. and C.R. Mohan. *Power Realignments in Asia: China, India and the United States*. New York: Sage, 2009.

Bajpai, A. 'Speaking the Nation Secular: (E)merging Faces of India'. In *Multiple Secularities: Multiple Secularities Beyond the West: Religion and Modernity in the Global Age*, edited by M. Burchardt, M. Middell, and M. Wohlrab-Sahr. Berlin: De Gruyter, 2015, pp. 39–62.

Bajpai, A. 'Imagining a "Secular" India: Roots, Offshoots and Future Trajectories of the Secularism Debate in India'. *South Asia Chronicle*, 2 (2012): 189–218.

Bajpai, R. *Debating Difference: Group Rights and Liberal Democracy in India*. New Delhi: Oxford University Press, 2011.

Balch, O. *India Rising: Tales from a Changing Nation*. London: Faber and Faber, 2012.

Barber, B.R. *Jihad Versus McWorld*. New York: Random House, 1995.

Bardan, P. 'Nature of Opposition to Economic Reforms in India'. *Economic and Political Weekly*, 40, no. 48 (2005): 4995–8.

Barthes, R. 'Death of the Author' (trans. by R. Howard). In *Image, Music, Text*, edited by R. Barthes. New York: Hill and Wang, 1977, pp. 142–48.

Basrur, R.M. *South Asia's Cold War Nuclear Weapons and Conflict in Comparative Perspective*. New York: Routledge, 2008.

Basu, K., ed. *India's Emerging Economy: Performance and Prospects in the 1990s and Beyond*. Cambridge, Mass.: MIT, 2004.

Bate, B. *Tamil Oratory and the Dravidian Aesthetic: Democratic Practice in South India*. Columbia: Columbia University Press, 2009.

Bate, B. '"To Persuade Them into Speech and Action": Oratory and the Tamil Political, Madras, 1905–19'. *Comparative Studies in Society and History* 55, no. 1 (2013): 142–66.

Bayly, C.A. *Indian Society and the Making of the British Empire*. Cambridge: Cambridge University Press, 2008.

Bhabha, H., ed. *Nation and Narration*. New York: Routledge, 1990.

Bhagwati, J.N. and P. Desai. *India Planning for Industrialization*. Oxford: Oxford University Press, 1970.

Bhargava, R., ed. *Secularism and Its Critics*. New Delhi: Oxford University Press, 2005.

Bhargava, R. 'Indian Secularism: An Alternative Trans-cultural Ideal'. In *The Future of Secularism*, edited by T.N. Srinivasan. New Delhi: Oxford University Press, 2006, pp. 20–53.

Bhaskar, C.U. and N.S. Sisodia, eds. *Emerging India: Security and Foreign Policy Perspectives*. New Delhi: Bibliophile South Asia, 2005.

Bilgrami, A. 'Secularism, Nationalism, and Modernity'. In *Secularism and its Critics*, edited by R. Bhargava. New Delhi: Oxford University Press, 2005, pp. 380–417.

Binder, S. *Total Atheism: Making 'Mental Revolution' in South India*. Utrecht University (2017), unpublished dissertation.

Biswas, S. 'W(h)ither the Nation-State? National and State Identity in the Face of Fragmentation and Globalisation'. *Global Society* 16, no. 2 (2002): 175–98.

Bordo, M.D., A.M. Taylor, and J.G. Williamson, eds. *Globalization in Historical Perspective*. Chicago–London, 2003.

Boron, A.A. *Empire and Imperialism: A Critical Reading of Michael Hardt and Antonio Negri*. London: Zed Books, 2005.

Bose, S. and A. Jalal (eds). *Nationalism, Democracy, Development: State and Politics in India*. New Delhi: Oxford University Press, 1999.

Brass, P. 'The Politics of India since Independence'. In *The New Cambridge History of India*, edited by P. Brass. Cambridge: Cambridge University Press, 1990.

Brennan, T. 'The National Longing for Form'. In *Nation and Narration*, edited by H.K. Bhabha. New York: Routledge, 1990.

Brenner, N. *New State Spaces: Urban Governance and the Rescaling of Statehood*. Oxford: Oxford University Press, 2004.

Broadman, H.G. *Africa's Silk Road. China and India's New Economic Frontier*. Washington DC: World Bank Publications, 2007.

Brosius, C. *Empowering Visions: A Study on Videos and the Politics of Cultural Nationalism in India (1989–1998)*, unpublished dissertation. Frankfurt (Oder): Europa-Universität Viadrina, 1999.

Buber, M. *Ich und Du*. Stuttgart: Reclam, 2008.

Bull, H. *The Anarchical Society*. New York: Columbia University Press, 1977.

Callaghy, T., R. Kassimir, and R. Latham. 'Introduction: Transboundary Formations, Intervention, Order, and Authority'. In *Intervention and Transnationalism in Africa: Global-Local Networks of Power*, edited by T. Callaghy, R. Kassimir, and R. Latham. Cambridge: Cambridge University Press, 2001, pp. 1–20.

Callaghy, T.M. et al., eds. *Intervention and Transnationalism in Africa: Global-Local Networks of Power*. Cambridge: Cambridge University Press, 2001.

Casanova J. *Public Religions in the Modern World*. Chicago: University of Chicago Press, 1994.

Chakrabarty, D. *Provincializing Europe: Post-Colonial Thought and Historical Difference*. Princeton: Princeton University Press, 2000.

Chakravartty, P. and S. Roy. 'Mr. Modi goes to Delhi: Mediated Populism and the 2014 Indian Elections'. *Television and New Media* 16, no. 4 (2015): 311–22.

Chandra, B. and M. Mukherjee. *India after Independence, 1947–2000*. New Delhi: Penguin Books, 1988.

Chandrashekhar, C.P. 'Explaining Post-Reform Industrial Growth'. *Economic and Political Weekly* 31, no. 35 (1996): 2537.

Chandrasekhar, C.P. and J. Ghosh. *The Market that Failed: Neoliberal Economic Reforms in India*. Delhi: Left Word Books/Naya Rasta Publishers, 2002.

Chari, P.R., P.I Cheema, and S.P. Cohen. *Perception, Politics and Security in South Asia*. London–New York: Routledge, 2003.

Charteris-Black, J. *Politicians and Rhetoric: The Persuasive Power of Metaphor*. New York and Hampshire: Palgrave Macmillan, 2005.

Chatterjee, P. *The Nation and its Fragments: Colonial and Postcolonial Histories*. Princeton: Princeton University Press, 1993.

———. 'Secularism and Tolerance'. In *Secularism and its Critics*, edited by R. Bhargava. New Delhi: Oxford University Press, 2005, pp. 345–79.

Chatterjee, N. *The Making of Indian Secularism: Empire, Law and Christianity 1830–1960*. New York: Palgrave Macmillan, 2011.

Clark, I. *Globalization and Fragmentation: International Relations in the 20th Century*. Oxford: Oxford University Press, 1997.

Cohen, S.P. *Emerging Power: India*. Brookings Institution Press, 2001.

Colas, A. *Empire*. Cambridge: Polity, 2006.

Comaroff, J. and J.L. Comaroff. 'Millennial Capitalism: First Thoughts on a Second Coming'. In *Millennial Capitalism and The Culture of Neoliberalism*, edited by J. Comaroff and J.L. Comaroff. Duke: Duke University Press, 2001.

Conrad, S., A. Eckert, and U. Freitag, eds. *Globalgeschichte. Theorien-Ansätze-Themen*. Frankfurt am Main-New York: Campus Verlag, 2008.

Cooper, R. *The Breaking of Nations: Order and Chaos in the Twenty-First Century*. London: Atlantic Books, 2004.

Cox, R.W. 'Towards a Posthegemonic Conceptualization of World Order: Reflections on the Relevancy of Ibn Khaldun'. In *Approaches to World Order*, edited by R.W. Cox and T. Sinclair (reprinted). Cambridge: Cambridge University Press, 1996, pp. 144–73.

Cox, R.W. and T.J. Sinclair. *Approaches to World Order*. Cambridge: Cambridge University Press, 1996.

Das, G. *India Unbound: From Independence to the Global Information Age*. New Delhi: Viking and Penguin Books, 2000.

Dasgupta, S. 'Gods in the Sacred Marketplace: Hindu Nationalism and the Return of the Aura in the Public Sphere'. In *Religion, Media and the Public Sphere*, edited by B. Meyer and A. Moors. Bloomington and Indianapolis: Indiana University Press, 2006, pp. 251–72.

Dasgupta, B. *Structural Adjustment, Global Trade and the New Political Economy of Development*. London: Zed Books, 1998.

De Certeau, M. *The Practice of Everyday Life*. Berkeley: University of California Press, 1984.

De Cillia, R., K. Liebhart, M. Reisigl, and K. Liebhart. *The Discursive Construction of National Identity*. Edinburg: Edinburg University Press, 1999.

De Long, J.B. 'India since Independence: An Analytical Growth Narrative'. In *Search of Prosperity: Analytic Narratives on Economic Growth*, edited by D. Rodrik. Princeton: Princeton University Press, 2003, pp. 184–204.

Delhi Historians Group. *Communalisation of Education: The History Textbooks Controversy*. New Delhi: Jawaharlal Nehru University, 2001.

Doniger, W. 'All in the Big Tent: How Secularism 'Lost' Its Old Stripes in the Service of the New Indian State'. *Outlook India,* Republic Day Issue, January (2014): 18–22.

Dossani, R. *India Arriving: How this Economic Powerhouse is Redefining Global Business*. New York: American Management Association, 2008.

Dunn, J., ed. *The Contemporary Crisis of the Nation State?* Oxford: Blackwell, 1995.

Elkins, D.J. *Beyond Sovereignty: Territory and Political Economy in the Twenty-First Century*. London: University of Toronto Press, 1995.

Engel, U. and A. Mehler. '"Under Construction": Governance in Africa's New Violent Social Spaces'. In *The African Exception*, edited by U. Engel and G.R. Olsen. London: Burlington VT, 2005, pp. 87–102.

Engel, U. and M. Middell. 'Bruchzonen der Globalisierung, globale Krisen und Territorialitätsregimes—Kategorien einer Globalgeschichtsschreibung'. *Comparativ* 15, no. 2 (2005): 5–38.

Engel, U. and M. Middell. 'Introduction: Global Cities, New Regionalisms, Decline and Re-Emergence of the Nation State, Empire, G 20 or Global Governance—Is There a Point of Convergence in the Debate on Changing World Orders?' In *World Orders Revisited*, edited by U. Engel and M. Middell. Leipzig: Leipziger Universitätsverlag, 2010, pp. 7–16.

Engel, U. and G.R. Olsen. *Authority, Sovereignty and Africa's Changing Regimes of Territorialization*. Working Paper Series of the Graduate Centre Humanities and Social Sciences of the Research Academy Leipzig, 7, 2010.

Fabian, J. *Time and the Other: How Anthropology Makes Its Object*. New York: Columbia University Press, 1983.

Fabian, J. 'Of Dogs Alive, Birds Dead and Time to Tell a Story'. In *Chronotypes: The Construction of Time*, edited by J. Bender and D.E. Wellbery. Stanford: Standford University Press, 1991, pp. 185–204.

Fairclough, N. *Language and Power*. London: Longman, 1989.

Farer, T. and T.D. Sisk. 'Enhancing International Cooperation: Between History and Necessity'. *Global Governance* 16, no. 1–2 (2010): 1–12.

Farndon, J. *India Booms: The Breathtaking Development and Influence of Modern India*. London: Virgin Books, 2007.

Ferguson, N. *Empire: The Rise and Demise of the British World Order and the Lessons for Global Power*. New York: Basic Books, 2003.

Ferguson, J. *Global Shadows: Africa in the Neoliberal World Order*. Durham NC: Duke University Press, 2008.

Foucault, M. 'On Other Spaces'. *Diacritics* 16, no. 1 (1986): 22–7.

Friedman, J. and S. Randeria, eds. *Worlds on the Move: Globalization, Migration, and Cultural Security*. London–New York: I.B. Tauris.

Friedman, T.L. *The Lexus and the Olive Tree*. New York: Anchor Books, 1999.

Fukuyama, F. *The End of History and the Last Man*. New York: The Free Press, 1992.

Fuller, C.J. 'Orality, Literacy and Memorization: Priestly Education in Contemporary South India'. *Modern South Asian Studies* 35, no. 1 (2001): 1–31.

Galanter, M. 'Secularism East and West: Review of Smith, D. E.'s India as a Secular State 1965'. *Comparative Studies in Society and History* 7, no. 2 (1965): 133–59.

Gandhi, M.K. 'Ramrajya'. *Young India* (1929): 305.

Ganguly, S., ed. *India as an Emerging Power*. London and Portland, Oregon: Frank Cass, 2003.

Gellner, E. *Nations and Nationalism*. Oxford: Blackwell Publishing Ltd., 1983.

Gerow, E. 'Some Thoughts on Indian Government Policy as it Affects Sanskrit Education'. In *Studies in the Language and Culture of South Asia*, edited by E. Gerow and M.D. Lang. Seattle: University of Washington Press, 1973, pp. 111–24.

Ghosh, A. *Planning in India: The Challenge for the Nineties*. New Delhi: Sage, 1992.

Glaser, B.G. and A.L. Strauss. *The Discovery of Grounded Theory: Strategies for Qualitative Research*. Chicago, IL: Aldine, 1967.

Goldstein, A. et al. *The Rise of China and India: What's in it for Africa*. Paris: OECD Development Centre Studies, 2006.

Goody, J., ed. *Literacy in Traditional Societies*. Cambridge: Cambridge University Press, 1968.

———. *The Logic of Writing and the Organization of Society*. Cambridge: Cambridge University Press, 1986.

———. *The Interface between the Written and the Oral*. Cambridge: Cambridge University Press, 1987.

———. *The Power of the Written Tradition*. Washington: Smithsonian Institution Press, 2007.

Goswami, M. *Producing India: From Colonial Economy to National Space*. Chicago: University of Chicago Press, 2004.

Graham, W.A. *Beyond the Written Word: Oral Aspects of Scripture in the History of Religion*. Cambridge: Cambridge University Press, 1987.

Guehenno, J.M. *The End of the Nation-State*. Minneapolis: University of Minnesota Press, 1995.

Guha, R. 'Transmission'. In *The Indian Public Sphere: Readings in Media History*, edited by A. Rajagopal. New Delhi: Oxford University Press, 2009, pp. 31–48.

Hannoum, A. 'What is an Order of Time? Review of Hartog, F., *Régimes d'Historicité: Présentisme et Expériences du Temps*, Paris: Seuil 2003'. *History and Theory* 47, no. 3(2008): 458–71.

Hansen, T.B. *The Saffron Wave: Democracy and Hindu Nationalism in Modern India*. Princeton: Princeton University Press, 1999.

Hansen, T.B. and F. Stepputat, eds. *Sovereign Bodies: Citizens, Migrants and States in the Postcolonial World*. Princeton: Princeton University Press, 2005.

Hansen, T.B. and F. Stepputat, eds. *States of Imagination: Ethnographic Explorations of the Post-Colonial State*. Durham, NC: Duke University Press, 2001.

Hanson, M. and R. Rajagopalan. 'Nuclear Weapons: Asian Case Studies and Global Ramifications'. In *Security Politics in the Asia-Pacific: A Regional-Global Nexus?*, edited by T. William. Cambridge: Cambridge University Press, pp. 228–46.

Hanson, M. et al. *Internal Conflict and Regional Security in South Asia: Approaches, Perspectives and Policies*. Geneva: United Nations Institute for Disarmament Research (UNIDIR), 2003.

Hardt, M. and A. Negri. *Empire*. Cambridge, MA: Harvard University Press, 2000.

Hartog, F. *Régimes d'Historicité: Présentisme et Expériences du Temps*. Paris: Seuil, 2003.

Hartog, F. 'Time and Heritage'. *Museum International* 57, no. 3 (2005) : 7–18.

Hasan, Z. 'Communal Mobilization and Changing Majority in Uttar Pradesh'. In *Making India Hindu. Religion, Community, and the Politics of Democracy in India*, edited by D. Ludden. New Delhi: Oxford University Press, 2007.

Hilgers, M. 'The Historicity of the Neo-liberal State'. *Social Anthropology* 20, no. 1 (2012): 80–94.

Hirst, P. and G. Thompson. *Globalization in Question: The International Economy and the Possibilities of Governance*. Cambridge: Polity Press, 1996.

Horsman, M. and A. Marshall. *After the Nation-State: Citizen, Tribalism and the New World Disorder*. London: Harper Collins, 1995.

Hudson, A. 'Beyond the Borders: Globalisation, Sovereignty and Extra-Territoriality'. In *Boundaries, Territory and Postmodernity*, edited by D. Newman. London: Frank Cass, 1999, pp. 89–105.

Huntington, S.P. *The Clash of Civilizations and the Remaking of World Order*. New York: Simon and Schuster, 1998.

Inden, R. 'Embodying God: From Imperial Progresses to National Progress in India'. *Economy and Society* 24, no. 2 (1995): 245–78.

Jaffrelot, C. *The Hindu Nationalist Movement and Indian Politics, 1925 to 1990: Strategies in Identity-Building, Implantation and Mobilisation* (with special reference to Central India). New Delhi: Viking, 1993.

Jagannathan, R. 'Who is the Real Narendra Modi: A "Communal Czar" or an "Inclusive Icon"?'. In *Making Sense of Modi's India*. Noida: Harper Collins Publishers India, 2016, pp. 80–8.

Jalal, A. *Democracy and Authoritarianism in South Asia*. Cambridge: Cambridge University Press, 1995.

Jalan, B. *Emerging India: Economics, Politics and Reforms*. New Delhi: Penguin, 2013.

Jeffrey, R. *India's Newspaper Revolution: Capitalism, Politics and the Indian Language Press 1977–99*. London: Hirst & Co., 2008.

Kapila, S. 'Conservatism and the Cult of the Individual in a Populist Age'. In *Making Sense of Modi's India*, edited by Megnad Desai et al. Noida: Harper Collins Publishers, 2016, pp. 40–55.

Kaplan, R.D. *The Coming Anarchy: Shattering the Dreams of the Post Cold War*. New York: Random House, 2000.

Karnad, B. *Nuclear Weapons and Indian Security: The Realist Foundations of Strategy*. Delhi: Macmillan, 2002.

Kaur, R. 'Nation's Two Bodies: Rethinking the Idea of "New" India and Its Other'. *Third World Quarterly* 33, no. 4 (2012): 603–21.

———. 'Good Times brought to You by Modi'. *Television and New Media* 16, no. 4 (2015): 323–30.

———. 'Post-Exotic India: On Remixed Histories and Smart Images'. *Identities: Global Studies in Culture and Power* 23, no. 3 (2016): 307–26.

Kaviraj, S. *The Imaginary Institution of India*. New Delhi: Permanent Black, 2010.

Khanna, P. *The Second World: Empires and Influence in the New Global Order*. New York: Random House, 2008.

Khilnani, S. *The Idea of India*. London: Penguin, 1997.

Kirmani, N. *Gott ist Schön: Das ästhetische Erleben des Koran*. München: Beck, 1999.

Kohli, A., ed. *India's Democracy: An Analysis of Changing State-Society Relations*. Princeton: Princeton University Press, 1988.

———. *State-Directed Development Political Power and Industrialization in the Global Periphery*. Cambridge: Cambridge University Press, 2004.

———. *Democracy and Discontent: India's Growing Crisis of Governability*. Cambridge: Cambridge University Press, 1991.

———. 'Introduction'. In *The Success of India's Democracy*, edited by A. Kohli. Cambridge: Cambridge University Press, 2001.

Kolluri, S. and A. Mir. 'Red-Defining Secularism in Post-Colonial Contexts'. *Cultural Dynamics* 14, no. 7 (2002): 7–20.

Kothari, R. *Politics in India*. New Delhi: Orient Longman: Little Brown, 1970.

Kulke, H. and D. Rothermund. *A History of India* (3rd ed). London: Routledge, 1998.

Kumarasingham, H. *A Political Legacy of the British Empire: Power and the Parliamentary System in Post-Colonial India and Sri Lanka*. London, New York: I.B. Tauris, 2013.

Lak, D. *India Express: The Future of the New Superpower*. New York: Palgrave Macmillan, 2008.

Laxman, R.K. 'Introduction'. In *Brushing up the Years: A Cartoonist's History of India*. New Delhi: Penguin Books, 2008, pp. viii–x.

———. 'In Ink and Line'. In *A Study of Nehru*, edited by R. Zakaria. Bombay: The Times of India Press, 1959, pp. 414–28.

Linke, U. 'Contact Zones: Re-Thinking the Sensual Life of the State'. *Anthropological Theory* 6, no. 2 (2006): 205–25.

Ludden, D. 'Introduction. Ayodhya: A Window on the World'. In *Contesting the Nation: Religion, Community and the Politics of Democracy in India*, edited by D. Ludden. Philadelphia: University of Philadelphia Press, 1996, pp. 3–15.

Lukacs, J. *The End of the Twentieth Century and the End of the Modern Age*. New York: Ticknor and Fields, 1993.

Madan, T.N. 'Secularism in its Place'. In *Secularism and its Critics*, edited by R. Bhargava. New Delhi: Oxford University Press, 2005, pp. 297–320.

Mahurkar, U. *Centre Stage: Inside the Narendra Modi Model of Governance*. Gurgaon: Random House Publishers, 2014.

Maier, C. 'Consigning the Twentieth Century to History: Alternative Narratives for the Modern Era'. *American Historical Review* 105, no. 3 (2000): 807–31.

Malik, P. *India's Nuclear Debate. Exceptionalism and the Bomb*. London, New York, New Delhi: Routledge, 2010.

Mann, M. '1989 in India: Overcoming the Post-Colonial State'. In *1989 in a Global Perspective*, edited by U. Engel, M. Middell, and F. Hadler. Leipzig: Leipziger Universitätsverlag, 2015, pp. 259–96.

Marino, A. *Narendra Modi: A Political Biography*. India: Harper Collins, 2014.

Mathew, G.E. *India's Innovation Blueprint: How The Largest Democracy Is Becoming An Innovation Super Power*. Oxford, Cambridge: Chandos Publishing, 2010.

Matoo, A., ed. *The Reluctant Superpower: Understanding India and Its Aspirations*. Carlton, Vic.: Melbourne University Publishing, 2012.

Mazarella, W. *Shovelling Smoke: Advertising and Globalization in Contemporary India*. Durham, NC: Duke University Press, 2003.

Mbembe, A. 'Provisional Notes on the Postcolony'. *Africa: Journal of the International African Institute* 62, no. 1 (1992): 3–37.

McCartney, M. *India: The Political Economy of Growth and Liberalisation in India, 1991-2008*. London: Routledge, 2010.

Meridyth, R. *The Elephant and the Dragon: The Rise of India and China and What That Means for All of Us.* New York: Norton, 2008.

Meyer, B., ed. *Aesthetic Formations: Media, Religion and the Senses.* New York: Palgrave Macmillan, 2009.

Michaels, A., ed. *The Pandit: Traditional Scholarship in India.* New Delhi: Manohar, 2001.

Middell, M. and K. Naumann. 'Global History and the Spatial Turn: From the Impact of Area Studies to the Study of Critical Junctures of Globalization'. *Journal of Global History* 5, no. 1 (2010): 149–70.

Mir, E. *Our Prime Minister.* Documentary film, produced by Films' Division, Ministry of Information and Broadcasting, 1957.

Mitchell, T. 'Society, Economy and the State Effect'. In *The Anthropology of the State,* edited by A. Sharma and A. Gupta. Oxford et. al.: Blackwell Publishing Ltd., 2006, pp. 169–86.

Mitchell, T. 'The Limits of the State: Beyond Statist Approaches and their Critics'. *The American Political Science Review* 85, no. 1 (1991): 77–96.

Mondal, A. 'The Limits of Secularism and the Construction of Composite National Identity in India'. In *Alternative Indias: Writing, Nation and Communalism,* edited by P. Morey and A. Tickell. Amsterdam: Rodopi, 2005, pp. 1–24.

Morey, P. and A. Tickell, eds. *Alternative Indias: Writing, Nation and Communalism.* Amsterdam: Rodopi, 2005.

Mukhopadhayay, N. *Narendra Modi: The Man, the Times.* Chennai: Tranquebar Press and Westland Books, 2013.

Nandy, A. 'The Politics of Secularism and the Recovery of Religious Tolerance'. In *Secularism and Its Critics,* edited by R. Bhargava. New Delhi: Oxford University Press, 2005, pp. 321–43.

Nath, K. *India's Century: The Age of Entrepreneurship in the World's biggest Democracy.* New York: McGraw-Hill, 2008.

Nayar, R. 'When Did the 'Hindu' Rate of Growth End?'. *Economic and Political Weekly* 41, no. 19 (2006): 1885–90.

Nehru, J.L. 'A Tryst With Destiny', speech delivered on the eve of India's independence, 00:00hrs, 14 August 1947.

———. *The Discovery of India.* New Delhi: Oxford University Press, 1985 (1946).

Nilekani, N. *Imagining India: The Idea of a Renewed Nation.* New York: Penguin, 2009.

Opello, W.C. and S.J. Rosow. *The Nation-State and Global Order. A Historical Introduction to Contemporary Politics,* 2nd ed. Boulder: Lynne Rienner Publishers, 2004.

Pal, B.C. 'Ganges Bath'. *The New Spirit* (1906): 10–11.

Panagariya, A. *India: The Emerging Giant.* Oxford University Press, 2008.

Pantham, T. 'Indian Secularism and its Critics: Some Reflections'. *The Review of Politics* 59, no. 3 (1997): 523–40.

Patnaik, P. 'International Capital and National Economic Policy: A Critique of India's Economic Reforms'. *Economic and Political Weekly* 29, no. 12 (1994): 683–89.

Patnaik, P. 'On the Concept of Efficiency'. *Economic and Political Weekly* 32, no. 43: 2807–13.

Perkovich, G. *India's Nuclear Bomb. The Impact of Global Proliferation.* Berkeley: University of California Press, 1999.

Pieterse, J.N. and B. Parekh, eds. *The Decolonization of Imagination: Culture, Knowledge and Power.* London: Zed Books, 1995.

Pinney, C. *Photos of the Gods: The Printed Image and Political Struggle in India.* London: Reaktion Books, 2004.

Prince, L. *The Modi Effect: Inside Narendra Modi's Campaign to Transform India.* London: Hodder and Stoughton, 2015.

Radhakrishnan, S. *Recovery of Faith.* New York: Harper Brothers, 1955.

Rajagopal, A. *Politics after Television: Hindu Nationalism and the Reshaping of the Public in India.* Cambridge: Cambridge University Press, 2001.

Ramesh, J. *To the Brink and Back: India's 1991 Story.* New Delhi: Rupa Publications, 2015.

Rao, U. *News as Culture: Journalistic Practices and the Remaking of Indian Leadership Traditions.* New York, Oxford: Berghahn Books, 2010.

Reisigl, Martin. 'Rhetorical Tropes in Political Discourse'. In *Elsevier Encyclopedia of Language and Linguistics*, edited by K. Brown, 2nd ed. London: Palgrave MacMillan, 2006.

Reisigl, Martin. 'Analyzing Political Rhetoric'. In *Qualitative Discourse Analysis in the Social Sciences*, edited by Ruth Wodak and Michal Krzyzanowski. New York: Palgrave Macmillan, 2008, pp. 96–120.

Robb, P. *A History of India.* New York: Palgrave Macmillan, 2002.

Rorty, R. *The Linguistic Turn: Essays in Philosophical Method.* Chicago: University of Chicago Press, 1992.

Ross, R.J.S. 'The Relative Decline of Relative Autonomy: Global Capitalism and the Political Economy of State Change'. In *Changes in the State: Causes and Consequences*, edited by E.S. Greenberg and T.F. Mayer. Newbury Park: Sage, 1990, pp. 206–23.

Roy, S. *Beyond Belief: India and the Politics of Postcolonial Nationalism.* Durham, NC: Duke University Press, 2007.

Sääväla, M. 'Entangled in the Imagination: New Middle Class Apprehensions in an Indian Theme Park'. *Ethnos* 71, no. 3 (2006): 390–414.

———. 'Auspicious Hindu Houses: The New Middle Class in India'. *Social Anthropology* 11, no. 2 (2003): 231–47.

Sachs. 'Dreaming with the BRICs: The Path to 2050'. *Global Economics* 99 (2003).

Sahoo, D. 'Economic Growth Efficiency of the Information and Technology Sector of India and Its Relevance to Indian'. *Journal of Infrastructure Development* 4, no. 41 (2012): 41–58.

Sarkar, S. 'Indian Democracy: The Historical Inheritance'. In *The Success of India's Democracy*, edited by A. Kohli. Cambridge: Cambridge University Press, 2001.

———. 'The Anti-Secularist Critique of Hindutva: Problems of a Shared Discursive Space'. *Germinal* 1 (1994).

Sassen, S. *Territory, Authority, Rights. From Medieval to Global Assemblages*. Princeton: Princeton University Press, 2006.

Sastry, S.N.S. *Our Indira*. Documentary film, produced by Films' Division, Ministry of Information and Broadcasting, 1973.

Satyaprakaśa et al., eds. *Manaka Angrezī-Hindī-Kośa*. Prayāg, Hindī Sāhitya Sammelana, 1971.

Sauer, C. 'Echoes from Abroad—Speeches for the Domestic Audience: Queen Beatrix: Address to the Israeli Parliament'. *Current Issues in Language and Society* 3, no. 3 (1996): 233–67.

Schmidt, V. 'The New World Order, Incorporated: The Rise of Business and the Decline of the Nation-state'. *Daedalus* 124, no. 2 (1995): 75–106.

Schwartz, H. 'Sacred Time'. In *Encyclopedia of Religion*, edited by L. Jones, 2nd ed. Detroit et al.: Thompson-Gale, 2005, pp. 7986–97.

Searle, J. *Expression and Meaning: Studies in the Theory of Speech Acts*. Cambridge: Cambridge University Press, 1979.

Sen, A. *The Argumentative Indian: Writings on Indian Culture, History and Identity*. New Delhi: Penguin Books, 2005.

Simon, W.L. and V. Rai. *Think India—The Rise of the World's Next Superpower and What It Means for Every American*. New Delhi: Tantor Media, 2007.

Slaughter, A. *A New World Order*. Princeton: Princeton University Press, 2004.

Smith, A.D. *The Ethnic Origins of Nations*. Oxford and Massachusetts: Blackwell Publishing Ltd., 1986.

Sørensen, G. 'What Kind of World Order? The International System in the New Millennium'. *Cooperation and Conflict* 41, no. 4 (2006): 343–63.

———. *Changes in Statehood: The Transformation of International Relations*. Houndmills: Palgrave Macmillan, 2001.

Strange, S. 'The Westfailure System'. *Review of International Studies*, 25, no. 3 (1999): 345–54.

———. *The Retreat of the State: The Diffusion of Power in the World Economy*. Cambridge: Cambridge University Press, 1996.

Tambiah, S.J. 'The Crisis of Secularism in India'. In *Secularism and its Critics*, edited by R. Bhargava. New Delhi: Oxford University Press, 2005, pp. 418–52.

Tejani, S. *Indian Secularism: A Social and Intellectual History, 1890–1950*. Bloomington: Indiana University Press, 2008.

Tellis, A.J. *India's Emerging Nuclear Posture: Between Recessed Deterrent and Ready Arsenal*. New Delhi: Oxford University Press, 2001.

Tharoor, S. *India: From Midnight to the Millenium and Beyond*, 3rd ed. New Delhi: Penguin Books, 2007.

Tölöyan, K. 'The Nation-State and its Others: In Lieu of a Preface'. *Diaspora: A Journal of Transnational Studies* 1, no. 1 (1991): 3–7.

Tully, M. *Non-Stop India*. London: Penguin, 2011.

———. *No Full-Stops in India*. London: Penguin 1991.

Turner, T. *Globalization, the State, and Social Consciousness in the Late Twentieth Century*, unpublished manuscript.

Udupa, S. 'News Media and Contention over "the Local" in Urban India'. *American Ethnologist* 39, no. 4 (2012): 819–34.

Van der Veer, P. *Religious Nationalism: Hindus and Muslims in India*. Berkeley: University of California Press, 1994.

Van der Veer, P. and C. Jaffrelot. *Patterns of Middle Class Consumption in India and China*. New Delhi: Sage, 2008.

Van Leuwen, T. 'Genre and Field in Critical Discourse Analysis'. *Discourse and Society* 4, no. 2 (1991): 193–223.

Varshney, A. *Democracy, Development, and the Countryside: Urban-Rural Struggles in India*. Cambridge: Cambridge University Press, 1995.

Vohra, R. *The Making of India: A Historical Survey*. Armonk, New York, London: ME Sharpe Inc., 1997.

Wagner, R. and A. Ong. *Ethos, Image, and Social Power among the Usen Barok of New Ireland*. Princeton N.J.: 1986.

Waltz, K.N. 'The Emerging Structure of International Politics'. *International Security* 18, no. 2 (1993): 343–63.

Wedeen, L. *Ambiguities of Domination: Politics, Rhetoric, and Symbols in Contemporary Syria*. Chicago: University of Chicago Press, 1999.

Wilke, A. et al. *Sound and Communication: An Aesthetic Cultural History of Sanskrit Hinduism*. Berlin: De Gruyter, 2011.

Wodak, Ruth. 'Pragmatics and Critical Discourse Analysis A Cross-Disciplinary Inquiry'. *Pragmatics and Cognition* 15, no. 1 (2007): 203–25.

Wodak, R. and M. Meyer, eds. *Methods of Critical Discourse Analysis*. London: Sage, 2001.

Zackariah, L. and U. Iyengar, eds. *Together They Fought: Gandhi—Nehru Correspondence 1921–1948*. New Delhi: Oxford University Press, 2011.

Zakaria, F. *The Post-American World*. New York: Norton, 2008.

Zakaria, R. 'A Many Splenoured Life'. In *A Study of Nehru*, edited by R. Zakaria, Bombay: The Times of India Press, 1959, pp. 3–73.

Zavos, J. *The Emergence of Hindu Nationalism*. Oxford: Oxford University Press, 2000.

Online Sources

Ali, M.S., 'India Shining, Bharat Drowning', 28 January 2012. For image and article, see: http://www.indianmuslimobserver.com/2012/01/28/india-shining-bharat-drowning/ (accessed on 10 June 2013).

Consolaro, A. 'Corporate Democracy: The Times of India 'Lead India' Campaign'. Revised version of the paper presented at the Fourth LUMS Social Sciences Conference on *Media Growth: Global Trends, Social Impacts, Academic Concerns*, Lahore University of Management Sciences (LUMS), 19–21 December 2008. See online: http://www.juragentium.org/topics/rol/india/en/consolar.htm (accessed on 29 August 2013).

Follath, E. 'India at Crossroads on Path to Superpower Status'. *Spiegel Online International*, 6 September 2012. Available at http://www.spiegel.de/international/world/india-caught-between-superpower-dreams-and-harsh-realities-a-851247.html (accessed 15 June 2015).

Gahilote, P. 'Modifying Nehru', *Outlook*. 17 November 2014, http://www.outlookindia.com/magazine/story/modifying-nehru/292518 (accessed on 2 August 2016).

Gupta, S. 'Modi Is Our Most Nehruvian Prime Minister since Nehru', *Business Standard*. http://www.business-standard.com/article/opinion/shekhar-gupta-modi-is-our-most-nehruvian-pm-since-nehru-116052701152_1.html (accessed on 2 August 2016).

India Inc. Time Magazine Cover, Issue: 26 June 2006. http://content.time.com/time/covers/0,16641,20060626,00.html (accessed on 25 July 2012).

Joseph, M. 'Why Do They Say that Modi Hates Nehru?', *Outlook*. 17 November 2014. See: http://www.outlookindia.com/magazine/story/why-do-they-say-that-modi-hates-nehru/292512 (accessed on 14 August 2016).

Malik, S. 'From Narendra Modi's Team, Some Stats: 437 Rallies, 5827 Events, 3 Lakh Kilometres', Election News, *NDTV*. 9 May 2014. http://www.ndtv.com/elections-news/from-narendra-modis-team-some-stats-437-rallies-5827-events-3-lakh-kilometres-560938 (accessed on 26 August 2016).

Spivak, G. 'The Trajectory of the Subaltern in My Work'. Keynote lecture at the conference *The Subaltern and the Popular*. University of California, Santa Barbara. Available at http://www.youtube.com/watch?v=2ZHH4ALRFHw (accessed on 12 June 2012).

'Make in India Week February 13–18', Official website, 2016, http://www. makeinindia.com/mumbai-week (accessed on 17 July 2016).

Modi, N.D. *Mann Ki Baat*, http://www.narendramodi.in/mann-ki-baat (first accessed on 6 January 2015, last accessed on 25 December 2016).

———. 'Sadhbhavana Mission: A Touching People's Movement', Modi's blog entry on his website, 16 February 2012, http://www.narendramodi.in/ sadbhavana-mission-a-touching-people's-movement-3054 (accessed on 8 March 2013).

'Modi rejigs Nehru Panel'. *The Telegraph*. 18 October 2014. http://www.tele graphindia.com/1141019/jsp/frontpage/story_18942143.jsp#.V6tnMh T3BXA (accessed on 15 January 2015).

'Modi govt. and Congress Hold Competing Events to Mark Nehru's 125th Birthday'. *Business Standard*. 15 November 2014, http://www.business-standard.com/article/politics/modi-govt-and-congress-hold-competing-events-to-mark-nehru-s-125th-birthday-114111401265_1.html (accessed on 15 January 2015).

'Narendra Modi to Launch "Chai pe Charcha" Campaign Today', http://www. ndtv.com/cheat-sheet/narendra-modi-to-launch-chai-pe-charcha-cam-paign-today-550542 (accessed on 15 August 2016). For a recorded telecast of the show, see https://www.youtube.com/watch?v=-aZtmizf7CU (accessed on 15 August 2016).

'Nehru in the Times of Modi'. *Outlook*. Republic Day Issue, 26 January 2014.

Swamy, S. 'How to Wipe Out Islamic Terror'. 16 July 2011, available at http:// bharatabharati.wordpress.com/2011/10/04/how-to-wipe-out-islamic-terror-subramanian-swamy/(accessed on 17 March 2012).

'The Nehru Jacket, Now Modi Style', http://timesofindia.indiatimes.com/ india/The-Nehru-jacket-now-Modi-style/articleshow/43043940.cms, 21 September 2014 (accessed on 1 August 2016).

Vasavi, A.R. *Citizen Kisan*, India 2012: A Symposium on the Year That Was. January 2013, http://www.india-seminar.com/2013/641/641_a_r_vasavi. htm (accessed on 6 March 2013).

Index

About the Author

Anandita Bajpai is assistant professor at the Department for South Asian Studies, Institute for Asian and African Studies, Humboldt University, and a research fellow at the Leibniz-Zentrum Moderner Orient, Berlin, Germany. She was awarded her PhD by Leipzig University. Her current project, *Presencing the German Democratic Republic in India*, focuses, among others, on the history of entanglements among university intellectuals and theatre circuits in New Delhi–East Berlin and Kolkata during the Cold War years. Her research interests include digital humanities, political rhetoric, secularism and nationalism in India, and the intellectual history of India–East Germany entanglements.